THE MEAL

PROCEEDINGS OF THE OXFORD SYMPOSIUM
ON FOOD AND COOKERY 2001

François Cautaerts (1810–1881), The Pancake Seller. *(Collection/Photo: Rijksbureau voor Kunsthistorische Documentatie, Den Haag, The Netherlands.) See the paper by Janny de Moor, below.*

THE MEAL

PROCEEDINGS OF THE OXFORD SYMPOSIUM
ON FOOD AND COOKERY 2001

EDITED
BY
HARLAN WALKER

PROSPECT BOOKS
2002

Published in Great Britain in 2002 by Prospect Books, Allaleigh House, Blackawton, Totnes, Devon TQ9 7DL, England

©2002 as a collection Prospect Books (but ©2002 in individual articles rests with the authors)

Typeset by Tom Jaine.
Printed by the Cromwell Press, Trowbridge, Wiltshire.

ISBN 1 903018 24 2

The cover illustration is from Charles Carter, *The Complete Practical Cook*, 1730.

Contents

Folk Mexican Street Food and the Morality of the Meal *Joy Adapon*	9
Hunting for Breakfast in Medieval and Early Modern Europe *Ken Albala*	20
The Funerary Meal in the Cult of the Dead in Classical Roman Religion *Joan P. Alcock*	31
Food in the Passover Seder *Michael Ashkenazi*	42
The German-Texan Meal 1831–2001 *Gwen Barclay*	50
Dining by Design *Peter Brown*	58
The Flattest Meal – Pancakes in the Dutch Lowlands1 *Janny de Moor*	67
The Oyster Supper *Dorothy Duncan*	81
The Filipino Meal: Swift, Slow; Sweet, Sour; Adazzle, Dim *†Doreen G. Fernandez and Pia Lim Castillo*	85
The Middle to Late Sixteenth-Century English Upper-Class Meal *Judy Gerjuoy*	89
Moretum – a Peasant Lunch Revisited *Christopher Grocock and Sally Grainger*	95
A Thousand Years of Japanese Banquets *Richard Hosking*	104
Perpetual Picnics – The Meal in the UAE *Philip Iddison*	113
Structuring the Meal: the Revolution of Service à la Russe *Cathy K. Kaufman*	123
Ring the Doorbell with your Elbow: a Light-hearted Look at the American Potluck Meal *Mary Wallace Kelsey*	134
Meals and Mealtimes, 1600–1800 *Gilly Lehmann*	139
Being American: an Arab American Thanksgiving *William G. Lockwood and Yvonne R. Lockwood*	155

The Fine Art of Eighteenth-Century Table Layouts *Fiona Lucraft*	165
The Medieval Arab Meal, East and West *Charles Perry*	174
African American Meals from Slavery to Soul Food *Tracy N. Poe*	179
A Sumptuous Meal: Navigating the Laws Restricting Wedding Banquets of Fourteenth-century Florence *Eden Rain*	191
Lust, Fear and Loathing on the Village Green *Gillian Riley*	201
Meals and Morality *Barbara Santich*	206
Manners Maketh the Meal: Table Etiquette in England and Iran *Margaret Shaida*	216
A Northern Gourmet: Benjamin Newton on the Move, 1816–1818 *Layinka M Swinburne*	223
From Menu, to Recipe, to Meal: a Renaissance Wedding Banquet *David S. Walddon*	231
Colonel Hawker Tells How to Get a Decent Meal with a Bad Cook and Poor Ingredients *Harlan Walker*	245
Charles Fourier (1772–1837) and the Phalansterian Banquet *Bee Wilson*	255
Drink in the Structure of the Meal: Middle Eastern Patterns *Sami Zubaida*	265
Other Papers Given at the Symposium	271

Introduction

This volume of papers presented at the Oxford Symposium on Food and Cookery follows the pattern of previous collections. The Symposium entitled 'The Meal' was held in September 2001 at Saint Antony's College, under the chairmanship of Dr Theodore Zeldin. Alan Davidson, who was joint-chairman with Dr Zeldin since the first Symposium in 1980, has retired. His enthusiasm, knowledge and wit have both inspired us and given us pleasure through all these years and we miss him very much.

It was very strange to find ourselves worrying about our little meeting in Oxford at the end of the week of the 11 September. Many of us even felt a bit ashamed at the amount of energy we were expending to make the Symposium work under the awful shadow of the events in New York and Washington.

The Organiser was stuck in Toronto for the week preceding the Symposium (arriving in England at midnight on Friday and Oxford on Saturday morning), and she had to rely on several people with whom she could communicate by phone and email to co-ordinate events in the UK before and during the event. Alex Veness, Robin Weir, Emma Roberts and Harlan Walker took over, and without them chaos would certainly have reigned. As it was, in circumstances where more than one-third of our symposiasts were unable to attend, removing half our programme at a stroke, everything ran smoothly and calmly thanks to them and everyone else.

The Afghan dinner was a triumph. Helen and Nasir Saberi not only produced a truly splendid menu, but they moved us all with their beautifully written and touchingly spoken descriptions of the food we were eating and the culture that gave it life. No one could have guessed the accident of timing that would make this dinner so poignant, and we could not have been in better hands. The specialist caterers, led by chef Haji Nabi Qader, gave us the finest banquet possible.

Sunday lunch was again given to us by Sotiris Kitrilikis, sadly without the help of his wife Lidia who died that summer. We thank him from the bottom of our hearts for continuing his generosity in the face of grief.

Of course Saint Antony's must be thanked once again for hosting us, in particular Charles White, in the conference office, and Tony Squirrel, the steward, and his staff. We specially enjoyed working with the chef Mark Walker, who gave so much help to the Afghan team – and much more besides.

Finally we thank Jane Levi for all her work in planning and especially for her skill in getting herself onto an aeroplane from North America on the evening of 14 September – and appearing in Oxford the next morning.

As in previous years, it has not been possible to publish all the papers offered in Oxford. Papers not included in this volume are listed on pages x-y below.

Harlan Walker
July, 2002.

Mexican Street Food and the Morality of the Meal

Joy Adapon

Home-cooking is highly valued in Mexico, and a proper meal prepared at home according to traditional techniques is considered to taste better than anything commercially prepared. There are hundreds of popular local eateries, *fondas* or *cafés*, serving home-cooking, *comida casera*. The proliferation of eateries serving *comida casera* indicates that consumers presumably demand it in preference over other commercial food. As an indicator of its desirability, commercially prepared home-cooking is marketed towards locals who cannot get home to eat. By simulating home-style food, *comida casera* is defined against other food available commercially, like *comida callejera*, street food. Considering how people say that no one cooks better than their mothers, this paper analyses the appeal of eating snacks in the street in contrast to a home-cooked meal.

Findings are based on research I conducted among a close-knit community of people in Milpa Alta, a largely agricultural municipality at the south-eastern edge of Mexico City. Most of the population engage in producing and selling *nopales*, prickly pear cactus, or pork products, or they prepare pit-roast lamb, *barbacoa*, for a living. There are no cinemas, theatres or other public venues of entertainment in Milpa Alta itself; for these it is necessary to go to more central areas of Mexico City. Indeed many residents travel long distances daily to other parts of the city where they sell their produce in open markets. Milpaltenses are both primary producers, as well as consumers who demand the *comida casera* available for sale if they are unable to return home to eat their main meal in the mid-afternoon.

Street food and snack foods (like *tacos*, *quesadillas*, and other *antojitos*) are an important and delicious part of Mexican cuisine. By choice or by force, people eat out in the streets rather than have a meal at home. In Milpa Alta I have been told that eating *tacos* in the market is a major source of fun: '*La mayor diversión es ir a comer tacos en el mercado*'. This appears to contradict the value placed on a home-cooked meal, but as I will try to explain below, understanding marital obligation makes street food seem a clandestine delight. I argue that the attractions of home-cooking and eating in the streets are linked to ideas of morality and illicit pleasure. The logic of this will become clear after understanding notions of greed and generosity, the responsibilities involved in hospitality and marriage, gender complementarity and reciprocity. By describing the meaningfulness of a home-cooked meal, I will try to show why street food is so wrong, before explaining what makes it so right.

Envidia *and* confianza

In Milpa Alta, to call someone *envidioso* was one of the most common accusations that I heard people say about others who somehow displeased them. The words *envidia* and *envidioso* are used to describe a range of characteristics, from envy to greed to being overprotective over family members, and also to not sharing food. When neighbours ask for a sprig of *epazote*[1] or a handful of chiles, they expect to have to pay for it with a peso or two. A person who is *envidioso/a* refuses to share or lend food or other material belongings. He or she is someone who lacks faith and trust, *confianza*.

Confianza characterizes a relationship of intimacy and trust, but also respect and social distance (cf. Lomnitz 1977). This condition exists between friends, family members, and *compadres*, co-parents. Friends with *confianza* need not be formally invited for birthdays, as they should remember these dates and know that there will be a fiesta where they are not only welcome, but expected. It is not uncommon in Milpa Alta for people to take a day off work on their birthdays so that they can be home to host a fiesta where they serve festive dishes such as *mole*, but also *barbacoa, carnitas* or *mixiotes*. If the hosts decide not to serve *mole* to all their guests, they sometimes prepare a small amount of *mole* to give to their *compadres* and other people with whom they have *confianza*. *Confianza* implies trust, openness and sharing, whereas *envidia* implies distrust, being closed, and refusing to share.

Generosity and hospitality

Milpaltenses may have a reputation for being *envidiosos*, but they are also very generous, particularly with food. Whether or not there is a special occasion to celebrate, such as the town fiesta, a wedding, or birthday, if guests show up at someone's house, the hosts are expected to share whatever food or drink they have available. If it is meal-time, a full meal is offered to the guests, even if it means that some members of the household may go without. It is acceptable for a host to take food off her own plate, provided it is as yet untouched, and place it on a new one, just to be able to share it.

Just as giving food is necessary, so is its acceptance. A guest is obliged to eat whatever is offered him or her, and to finish it. Leaving food on one's plate is an insult to the host, because it implies that the guest does not like the food or fails to appreciate it. This kind of coercive hospitality occurs at both informal and formal levels. When visiting friends or relatives, or during private fiestas such as birthdays and weddings, social relations between host family and guest family are ritualized over offering a meal. Likewise, when there are public fiestas, such as the town fiesta celebrating the patron saint's day, town districts, or *barrios*, act as hosts to visiting *barrios*. Couples from the community represent each *barrio* as '*mayordomos*'. The designated *mayordomos* agree to act as hosts by serving a meal when the people of other *barrios* visit to pay their respects.

Public fiestas, therefore, appear to be ritualized versions of already-ritualized social relations. Actions are performed at group level, though they ultimately also benefit and affect individuals. Though men represent the basic social unit, as the head of household, women are crucial to the roles they play as *mayordomos*. Men accept the role of *mayordomo* only with the consent of their wives and families, and as Brandes wrote, 'women's public roles in the fiesta cycle are muted and disguised' (1988: 32), because women take control of the all-important feast. He further argues that 'women exert considerable power' (ibid.), and from this we can infer that it is women's domestic roles as cooks which imbue them with both power and value in the community. Together with their husbands and families, they construct their sociality at domestic and community levels.

In a specific food-related way, public fiesta hospitality is very similar to daily hospitality or family fiesta hospitality. The meal that *mayordomos* serve to visitors is exactly the same meal that they would serve to friends and relatives if they were hosting a family life-cycle occasion – they would offer *mole*, *barbacoa*, or *carnitas* with beans, *tortillas* and/or *tamalates*. The same rules of generosity and acceptance apply, and hosts serve large amounts that guests must consume in entirety. In Milpa Alta this idea is taken so seriously that people often attend parties with a plastic bag or other container in their handbags. This way, if the portions served are too generous, they can surreptitiously stash away any food that they are unable to finish. To pack food away I have also seen people use the plastic cups where drinks are served, or wrap their food in *tortillas* and paper napkins, before hiding it in a bag or leaving the party holding the food behind their backs. Generosity with food is a coercive and necessary community practice, but, at a more intimate level it is also crucial to married couples, as I explain below.

Marital responsibilities
In Mexico, married women are sometimes portrayed as the providers of sex and also, separately, as providers of food. They are capable of great suffering for the sake of husbands, children, and culinary ideals. As access to education has increased, however, many young men and women take on professional jobs,

such as teaching in schools or in accounting. They engage in this work while they are still single and live at home with their parents. Portraying men and women according to occupation or activity thus becomes more complex. As young professional nurses, technicians or clerks, they enjoy some autonomy from the family business and primarily work for a salary. Yet as soon as they marry, many return to the traditional family trades, abandoning their prospective careers. There are two reasons given for this shift in occupation: the family businesses are considered to be 'traditions' and skills that are passed down as 'inheritance'; and secondly, they are often more lucrative than office-based work.

At marriage, when some women quit their extradomestic jobs, their reason is to dedicate themselves to their homes, '*me dedico al hogar*'. In such cases, even if they used to dress seductively when they were still single, they may begin to dress conservatively and stop wearing make-up, out of 'respect' for their husbands. Yet far from being housewives who solely cook, clean and raise their children, they usually help their husbands in their businesses by providing the necessary culinary labour (making *salsas,* etc.), and entering into small commercial ventures on the side. They begin to spend most of their time preparing proper meals, and in return their husbands are required to eat what they serve them. This is especially so when a husband repeatedly comes home very late, and if his wife suspects he is having an extramarital affair. He may be served a large meal on his return, and he is forced to eat it, and even clean his plate, out of corresponding respect for his wife in fulfilling her marital duties.

What this indicates is that notions of love and respect are interwoven in the activities of men and women both in their marital relations and also concerning cooking. When a meal is particularly delicious, the cook's culinary secret, her '*sazón*', is often attributed to her adding a 'touch of love', *sazón de amor*. Since love is also what characterizes the marital bond, it then makes sense that the intimacy of these social relationships would make home-cooking the tastiest, best – somehow construed to be highest in prestige, because such meals are heavily laden with social meanings. Following this logic, eating in the streets, then, lacks the social significance attached to eating in someone's home. It is helpful now to discuss the components that make up a meal in contrast to snacking on the street.

Why eating in the streets is wrong
In Mexico the main meal of the day, *la comida*, is eaten between two and five in the afternoon. The *comida* consists of at least three courses. To start there is a 'watery' or a 'dry' soup, a *sopa aguada* or a *sopa seca*, made with vegetables, noodles or rice. The main course is often meat served in a sauce or with some

other hot *salsa* on the side, and vegetables and *tortillas* as well. Beans are served as the eaters are finishing their main courses, and sometimes there is fruit afterwards. Since the *comida* is a substantial meal, it is not uncommon in Mexico City for banks and offices to allow their employees at least two hours for lunch. This gives them time to go home to eat or otherwise enjoy a full meal elsewhere. Apart from restaurants, little *fondas* offer *comida casera* or *comida corrida*, home-style meals eaten out, 'on the run'. In this manner it is possible to emulate eating at home when it is more convenient to be out.

Sweets are not always included as part of a meal; they are eaten as snacks, bought in the streets or eaten in the evening. The evening meal, or food eaten in the evening, may consist of leftovers from the *comida*, sweet rolls and coffee, *tamales* or snacks, *antojitos*, bought in the market or in a street stall. The *antojitos*, especially, can be as substantial as any meal, and often they contain the same elements all at once (corn/tortilla, beans, vegetable/meat, chile/salsa). However, they are eaten in a different form and are consumed away from home and they are not considered as a proper meal.

So, given the prescriptive nature of the *comida* or meal, it is difficult to say whether a woman makes plans around her obligations to provide and prepare a meal for her family or whether she dedicates any spare moment she has to feeding her loved ones and any guests who may come by. Indeed, it reflects badly on a woman if she fails to prepare a home-cooked meal and instead decides to go to the market and buy ready-made food like *tortas* or *tacos*, for instance. Usually those who are found eating in the market stalls so indiscreetly are people who do not live in Milpa Alta, thus have no family nearby with whom they can eat at home. Those eating in the market are people who work in the government or other offices in Milpa Alta, or they are youths having a snack with their friends after school.

My friend Yadira calls supermarkets where prepared food can be bought '*el paraiso de las fodongas*', 'lazy woman's paradise'. Women ought to prepare food from scratch, she said. She added that the conquest of a man is achieved via his mouth, '*un hombre se conquista por la boca*'. If a man is satisfied with the way a woman cooks, she will always have him in the palm of her hand. A woman must know how to cook and proper women prepare food at home from scratch. Eating in the street indicates that the women of the house are lazy, '*son fodongas*', too lazy to prepare a meal at home.

In Milpa Alta there is even a specific verb for this idea that is only used in the region, *chinaquear*. This concept of shirking one's household, or even womanly, duties is something that few would wish others to label them with. So although there may be times when a woman is too tired, or indeed too lazy, to cook for her family, she tries to be discreet about it. If she decides to buy ready-made food in the market, she most likely would buy it to take away. She could then take it home to eat in privacy so that no one will see her and her family eating in public, to be able later to accuse her of *chinaqueando*.

Mexican street food is one of the broadest-ranging parts of the cuisine, and in Milpa Alta most women know how to make many of the foods that can be bought in the streets, like different kinds of *tacos, quesadillas, sopes, tlacoyos, pambazos, tortas, tamales, gorditas, huaraches, garnachas* and various other snacks. The widow Doña Margarita would only ever suggest to me that we eat in the market when her son and daughter-in-law were away. She would have a mischievous glint in her eye as she said, '*vamos a chinaquear*'. At the stand she would eat with a smile and chat with the food vendors as if they shared a naughty secret. Though she may have been able to prepare the same food equally well, she still enjoyed eating out in this way. Doña Margarita was renowned in her family for making delicious *tamales* during the Days of the Dead, yet it would be difficult to say whether her *tamales* actually tasted better to her than those from the market vendor.

The judgment of flavour or perception of quality is an issue of culinary technical mastery, which is a potentially complex issue (see Adapon 2001). What I wish to convey here is that eating at home has moral value, as does the perception of quality, which is related to the emotional commitment (permanent or temporary) that an eater attaches to the cook. As explained above, the ideal relationship between a man and a woman is that between husband and wife; by extension, the ideal food is a meal cooked by a woman (wife and mother) for her husband and children. Since women's virtue and moral value is also attached to her ability to suffer for her loved ones, both men and her children (Melhuus 1992), the efforts of her labours (her cooking) are also highly valued. Eating a home-cooked meal has equivalent moral connotations, and so eating out in the streets would correspondingly be immoral (or at least naughty). In other words, eating in the streets is technically wrong.

So why is it that street food is considered to taste so good? I am suggesting that the clandestine appeal of street food has a deeper significance than just eating out (i.e., not at home). Because of the meanings attached to home-cooking (food prepared by women, primarily for their husbands) and the importance of love as a secret ingredient (*sazón de amor*), to eat in the street is analogous to having an illicit love affair. It is arguably equally delicious food prepared by others, free from social commitment, hence its sweetness.

Food metaphors, chiles and albur

There is one other dynamic of food and love that is worth describing to gain a more complete picture of how flavour and morality are intertwined. In

Mexico, dishes are defined by the sauce rather than by the meat or vegetable which is in it. In Mexican cuisine, *salsas* are sauces whose primary ingredient is the chile. For food to be palatable, there must be *salsa*/chile, that is, flavour, which materializes from the culinary mastery that a skilful cook possesses. *Salsas* are the most important part of a Mexican meal. There must be a *salsa* or at least some chile on the table for people to enjoy their food (*tortillas*, beans, vegetables, meat). A famous quote is: 'Without chile, Mexicans do not believe that they are eating', and I was spontaneously told the same in Milpa Alta, '*Sin chile no come uno*'.

In Milpa Alta and in other parts of Mexico, I was repeatedly reminded that *salsas* prepared in a *molcajete*[2] were more delicious than those prepared with an electric blender. Food prepared in the traditional manner with traditional utensils were considered to be tastier, healthier and also 'authentic'. Likewise, as just explained above, food prepared at home (i.e. with love) often had connotations of being tastier and better for you than food prepared commercially. Good food means good flavours, and in many ways this depends on women (good cooks) who make good sauces (good chile). When eating a proper meal cooked at home, the social significance stems from the caring involved in cooking food with flavour for specific eaters. If a woman forgets to place *salsa* on the table, she may be teased for being *envidiosa*, keeping all the flavour to herself, effectively failing to fulfil her obligation to feed her family or guests.

More specific to *barbacoa*-makers in Milpa Alta, the primary responsibility of women in that trade is to make the *salsas* that accompany the meat when it is sold in the market. In Milpa Alta people use the words *salsa* and *chile* interchangeably, even if there is only a small proportion of chile in the recipe for the *salsa*. Elsewhere I have gone into greater detail about the importance of chiles in Mexican cuisine (Adapon 2001), as have many other writers before me (see, for example, Long-Solis 1986, Lomelí 1991, Martinez 1992, Muñoz 1996). Chiles are central in Mexican gastronomy, and are arguably the basic unit of the cuisine. They are also central to a variety of jokes where the chile is spoken of metaphorically as a man's penis, most used in *albur*.

Albur is a kind of wordplay, used almost exclusively among men (see Jiménez 1991, Lomelí 1991: 20–6). It is very rare for women to speak using *albur*. If they do, it is amongst other women (not in mixed company) and is of a milder sort. This is because there are overt sexual connotations in the speech games in *albur*. One of the central metaphors used is the chile, which stands for the penis. Since chiles come in so many different shapes and sizes, *albur* and derivative word games can be used in mild to increasingly aggressive ways, and yet also are considered funny. Thus men are able to speak with their friends (*cuates*, those *en confianza*) in terms of sexually penetrating them, without being considered homosexual. As long as a man is the one penetrating, rather than the one penetrated, he still often considers himself to be heterosexual, even *macho* (see Gutmann 1996). A man using *albur* plays upon these sensibilities, as well as on linguistic twists, and depends on speed and wit.

There are other food metaphors that people use in joking conversation to refer to male and female sexual organs. Usually it is obvious why they are chosen, though sometimes the analogy is more obscure. For the vagina there are words such as papaya, *mamey* (a type of fruit), *panocha* (crude sugar), *pescado* (fish), or *mondongo* (a dish made of tripe) (Jiménez 1991: 82, 201). Some other food metaphors for the penis are *longaniza* (a type of sausage), *camote* (sweet potato), *ejote* (young corn on the cob), and *zanahoria* (carrot) (ibid: 202). If these metaphors appear unsystematic, even random, that is because they are not used in an alternate discourse to encode another arbitrary symbolic structure. Rather, as Gow (1989: 575) argues,

> …these metaphors are not structured simply by direct reference to the objects themselves, whether foods or genital organs, but at the level of desire. The use of foods as metaphors for the genitals occurs only in joking, for native people have standard, non-euphemistic, names for the genitalia. The use of food metaphors in joking, I would agree, continuously draws attention to the metaphoric relationship between oral and sexual desire, rather than that between food objects and genitals as objects.

Sexual food metaphors may therefore reveal notions about oral and sexual desire, and not so much about the relations between specific fruits or vegetables. The significance of *albur* is that food, especially the chile, is subject to linguistic and conceptual manipulation by men, explicitly relating it to sex. On the other hand, more generally and among women, the chile is manipulated in another, culinary, way, and is explicitly related to eating and flavour. The relationships among food and cooking and love and sex can be understood through *albur* to have ramifications in the assessment of flavour and morality in terms of *chinaqueando* in the streets or eating a meal cooked at home.

Why eating in the streets is right

To recapitulate, women in Milpa Alta have two kinds of responsibilities: housework (production) and family (reproduction). Equivalently, there are two kinds of human desires: for food and for sex. Recognizing the symbolic value of cooking as a part of women's work, and taking sex into account as part of the socialization of women as members of the community as well as in their relations with men (cf. Paul 1974), it is helpful to make the link between food and sex more explicit. Gow (1989) achieves this in his article on the Piro, arguing that the desires for food are linked to specific food providers, 'systematically related to *certain types of social relations*' (568, italics added). He continues, 'relationships are predicated on the satisfaction of particular desires experienced by the partners in the relationship' (ibid).

When the relationship between cook and eater is very close, like family, the eater is more likely to judge the food as tastier and better because of the social relationship that exists between them, though of course, a cook's talent must also be considered. Hence the importance of a home-cooked meal, prepared by a married woman for her husband. The marital relationship is the crucial social relationship, the centre of the domestic sphere and the source of children. Ideally, food is prepared by women for their husbands and children, and other members of the household. Women's culinary activity is a source of social agency that gives deeper meaning to the home-cooked meal, or the food prepared for family and relations of *confianza*. Daughters rarely take full responsibility of meal provision, but if they do, it is only within the domestic realm. Once they marry, women's culinary agency becomes directed to their husbands and their new households. Failure to feed their husbands can be judged as shirking marital as well as womanly duties, not because of some deep-seated subordination of women to men, but because of the centrality of the marital bond as the source of social (and sexual and gastronomical) fulfilment.

Understanding this, it makes sense that the appeal of home-cooking is based upon its intrinsic meaningfulness, as socially controlled, socially sanctioned sexual desires, instrumentalized for the production of legitimate members of society. Conversely, other cooking, presumably prepared for selfish, economic ends, is meaningful in a different way. Just as food-giving can be seen to be generating positive social meaning (community viability), and eating is correspondingly negative (cf. Munn 1986), the same logic can be applied to cooking. Home-cooking generates positive social ends, whereas commercial cooking generates antisocial (individual) ends. A home-cooked meal should then taste better and should also *be* better than snacks bought in the street. Yet street foods are known to be desirable, marketable, commercially viable, and delicious.

There are two ways of experiencing food as delicious. Home-cooking has the status of the highly moral marital bond, and the value of food sharing, even if under a coercive system. Because of the many rules of greed and generosity surrounding home-cooking, interrelated with the social systems of hospitality at family and community levels, the meal is heavily emotionally laden. In contrast, to snack in the streets is considered a pastime; it is an act of freedom, eating for the sake of pure pleasure without emotional entanglements. Though different vendors produce different qualities of flavours, and there are some things that do taste better when prepared at home, there is no contradiction if it is accepted that we have preferences and opinions about food, just as we have preferences for and opinions about people with whom we socialize.

If eating in the streets is in so many ways wrong, then what is the appeal? In other words, what is it that makes it feel so right? Simply put, if the desires for food and for sex are equivalent, then there is an analogy between a home-cooked meal and socially salient sex between husband and wife, with eating snacks in the street (*chinaqueando*) and having an extramarital affair. Indeed, Vázquez García reports that the ambulatory vendors who sell home-cooked food in the streets are often second wives or unwed mothers (1997: 191). Furthermore, the word in Náhuatl for 'to eat' has the double meaning of eating food and having sex (ibid: 182, Taggart 1992: 81). Street snacks, therefore, are as delicious and clandestine as an illicit love affair, akin to the pleasures of sex without the entanglements of love (amongst social relations).

REFERENCES

Adapon, Joy 2001, *The Art of Mexican Cooking: culinary agency and social dynamics in Milpa Alta, Mexico,* PhD dissertation Social Anthropology, LSE, University of London.

Bayless, Rick and Doreen Groen Bayless 1987, *Authentic Mexican: regional cooking in the heart of Mexico,* New York: William Morrow and Company, Inc.

Bloch, Maurice 1992, 'What goes without saying: the conceptualization of Zafimaniry society', in *Conceptualizing Society,* ed. Adam Kuper, London and New York: Routledge.

Brandes, Stanley 1988, *Power and Persuasion: fiestas and social control in rural Mexico,* Philadelphia: University of Pennsylvania Press.

Foster, George M. 1961, 'The Dyadic Contract: a model for the social structure of a Mexican peasant village', in *American Anthropologist* 63: 1173–1192.

Gell, Alfred 1998, *Art and Agency: an anthropological theory,* Oxford: Clarendon Press.

Gow, Peter 1989, 'The Perverse Child: desire in a native Amazonian subsistence economy', *Man* 24: 567–82.

Gregor, Thomas 1985, *Anxious Pleasures: the sexual lives of an Amazonian people,* University of Chicago Press.

Gutmann, Matthew C. 1996, *The Meanings of Macho: being a man in Mexico City,* University of California Press.

Jiménez, Armando 1991 (1958), *Picardía Mexicana,* Mexico City: Ed. Diana.

Lomelí, Arturo 1991 (1986), *El arte de cocinar con chile,* revised ed., orig. *El Chile y Otros Picantes,* Mexico City: Libros de Contenido.

Lomnitz, Larissa Adler 1977, *Networks and Marginality: life in a Mexican shantytown,* trans. Cinna Lomnitz, New York: Academic Press.

Long-Solís, Janet 1986, *Capsicum y Cultura,* Mexico City: Fondo de Cultura Económica.

Martínez, Zarela 1992, *Food From My Heart: Cuisines of Mexico Remembered and Reimagined,* New York: MacMillan Publishing Company.

Melhuus, Marit 1992, '*Todos tenemos madre. Dios también*': morality, meaning and change in a Mexican context, PhD. thesis Dept. and Museum of Anthropology, Faculty of Social Sciences, University of Oslo.

Munn, Nancy 1986, *The Fame of Gawa: a symbolic study of value transformation in a Massim (Papua New Guinea) society,* Cambridge University Press.

Muñoz Zurita, Ricardo 1996, *Los chiles rellenos en México: antología de recetas,* Mexico City: UNAM.

Paul, Lois 1974, 'The mastery of work and the mystery of sex in a Guatemalan village', in *Woman, Culture and Society,* Michelle Zimbalist Rosaldo and Louise Lamphere eds., Stanford University Press, pp. 281–99.

Taggart, James M. 1992, 'Gender segregation and cultural constructions of sexuality in two Hispanic societies', *American Ethnologist* 19(1): 75–96.

Vázquez García, Verónica 1997, 'Mujeres que 'respetan a su casa': estatus marital de las mujeres y economía doméstica en una comunidad nahua del sur de Veracruz', in S. González Montes and J. Tuñón (comp), *Familias y Mujeres en México: del modelo a la diversidad,* Mexico City: El Colegio de México, PIEM, pp. 163–93.

NOTES

[1] *Epazote* is *Chenopodium ambrosioides*, a herb widely used in Mexican cooking, especially in the central states.

[2] A traditional stone mortar and pestle.

Hunting for Breakfast in Medieval and Early Modern Europe

Ken Albala

There is probably no meal more neglected, maligned and conspicuously skipped than breakfast. Cookbook authors scarcely mention breakfast foods, descriptions of food customs usually fail to discuss breakfast, and many languages do not even have a decent word for it. The Italian *prima colazione* to distinguish it from a proper collation or light snack and French *petit déjeuner* reveal that this whole meal is anomalous. The German *Frühstück* (early morsel) is hardly more convincing. Moreover, in the historical record, evidence of breakfast before the eighteenth century is fleeting. It appears to have been a meal taken on an irregular basis, by invalids or the very young. Sometimes we catch glimpses of labourers and vague concessions to their need for an early morning boost, but for literate Europeans the entire meal seems to have been an embarrassment or nonexistent. Even where we know breakfast was an established custom, there is scant written evidence of anyone actually eating it.

This may have been partly a consequence of current medical opinion which consistently forbad breakfast to normal healthy adults. Taken at face value, we might assume that there was no such meal. The comments of physicians and food writers, however, suggest that breakfast was a regular meal for the majority of labouring people, especially in England and northern Europe. Even in the south, although evidence is less persuasive, breakfast did exist in some form, despite the admonitions of medical orthodoxy.

We do know, as did medieval and early modern Europeans, that the Romans regularly enjoyed breakfast or *ientaculum* which usually consisted of leftovers from the night before: bread and cheese, olives, eggs and honey. Breakfast was also sold by bakers, as Martial tells us. *Surgite: iam vendit pueris ientacula pistor* (Rise: the baker is already selling breakfast to the boys).[1] The meal was probably a natural development of postponing the two larger meals, *prandium* and *coenum*, to later in the day. In fact, the three-meal structure of ancient Rome was roughly similar to the modern American pattern, with an added *merenda* or snack around 5 p.m., and the largest meal of the day some time in the evening.

Breakfast seems to have disappeared among the Germanic tribes who displaced the Romans, probably because they customarily ate two meals and the larger of the two was in the morning. These were the ancestors of 'dinner' and 'supper' as taken throughout the medieval and early modern periods in Europe. The tendency, however, was for these two meals to be consistently pushed later and later in the day. The Normans apparently ate dinner around 9 a.m. and throughout the centuries we find dinner moved, until it rests at 11 a.m. in the Tudor period and 1 p.m. or much later by the eighteenth and nineteenth centuries. Naturally this is when breakfast makes its grand re-entrance, and the image we have of bloated businessmen stuffing their furry cheeks with beefsteaks and oysters first thing in the morning is at least accurate for the wealthiest of Europeans. The 'traditional' British and American breakfast was a natural consequence of moving the other meals to later in the day.

But what of the centuries between the high points of Augustan Rome and nineteenth-century Britain? Did breakfast really exist, or is it lurking somewhere beneath the dazzling contemporary accounts of banquets and grand dining that so preoccupy culinary historians? This paper will attempt to ferret out this elusive meal by seeing what physicians and food writers of the past had to say about it. It may be that their generally negative attitude toward breakfast has helped to obscure the historical record, even if it did not prevent many people from eating it.

The word from which many European languages derive the word for breakfast was the late Latin *disjejunere* or *disjunare* in vulgar Latin (to un-fast). Strangely enough, the word was contracted by the eleventh century to *dîsner* in Old French, and so the word for dinner actually means breakfast. This makes perfect sense, because as the first meal, dinner did break the fast. But existence of this word then tells us nothing about the meal we now call breakfast, eaten first thing in the morning.

The first recorded use of the word breakfast in English, according to the *OED*, was not until 1463 in the household account book of Edward IV that recorded 'Expensys in brekfast'. This is at least direct evidence that some people in the royal household ate breakfast, and that they understood the word. The verb to break a fast existed much earlier, but confusingly, it could also refer to the first meal of the day in which one broke the fast, which was dinner.[2] So there is no indication whether breakfast as we know it was considered a regular meal, or something occasionally indulged in by those who could not make it until dinner.

By the sixteenth century physicians across Europe do refer to breakfast, but only as a meal taken by children, the elderly, sometimes by nurses who need extra nourishment, and consistently by labourers. Healthy adults, however, were told not to eat breakfast. It was generally considered a form of gluttony, along with sitting too long at the table or indulging in 'banquets' late into the night, something fully responsible humans should avoid. The very fact that they would offer warnings is, of course, itself evidence that some people did eat breakfast. But why they should have forbidden this meal is equally interesting.

First, a standard rule of dietary medicine asserted that one should never eat a meal until the previous meal has been thoroughly digested, that is, after the food has been processed and the nutrients have been distributed through the body. This normally took place in the six or so hours after dinner at around 11 a.m. and after supper at night during sleep. With far more than the required six hours of digestion during the night, one might expect physicians to approve breakfast. But they also believed it is necessary to clean out the body's passages before taking another meal. Exercise during the day accomplished this before supper, but in the morning the body was not yet 'purged of superfluities'. This would be done with the usual morning ablutions, and also with morning exercise which burns up the nutrients in a manner of speaking. In other words, one should be up and about a few hours in the morning before eating. Physicians typically recommended that the first meal not commence until four hours after rising. As Christopher Langton explains:

> As concernynge the tyme of eatyng, every man whan he is hungred, if he maye have it, yet one tyme is better than another, and the very best tyme is after excersyce. For then the bodye is clere pourged of all excrementes, and naturall heate is encreased, and made muche stronger.[3]

The natural heat would be the power to digest a meal, which presumably is too weak first thing in the morning without the fortification of some exercise.

Langton recommended meals at 11 a.m. and at 6 p.m. which was fairly typical for the mid-sixteenth century, but he also made an exception for children and the elderly whose digestive powers are weaker and who must eat much smaller meals but more frequently. The great health guru of the sixteenth century, Luigi Cornaro, admitted that he himself in old age became like a child again, eating four smaller meals through the day rather than two large ones.[4] Thus, under ordinary circumstances two meals were considered physiologically sound. Those who did need breakfast were considered exceptions to the rule.

The importance of breakfast could also be determined by the relative size of the two major meals of the day. Where the midday meal was smaller than the evening's we might expect breakfast to be more important, but the opposite is the case. As Lobera de Avila explains, in Venice, Genoa and Spain the custom is *mas cenar que comer*, to eat a larger evening meal because the digestive heat is stronger during sleep. In these places there should be no regular breakfast, presumably because the previous evening's meal had left people sated through the next morning. An exception to this rule would be priests, *qui ocupados de negocios spirituales sin exercicio corporal; hazen una breve colacion por la mañana en lugar de comida*.[5] Only priests who get little exercise eat a meal early in the morning – a 'collation', and as a general rule those who do no labour should eat a larger meal in the morning rather than evening.[6]

The debate over whether the midday meal should be larger or the evening's raged throughout the medieval and early modern periods, and had a significant impact on the breakfast question. Those following Galen, who called themselves Hellenists, all agreed that the evening meal should be larger. This was also the pattern in much of southern Europe. The Arabists (generally following Avicenna as did the school of Salerno) claimed that the morning meal should be larger because a full stomach upsets sleep, and the heat of the sun and movement help digestion.[7] This was the pattern in northern Europe. But why breakfast should be more common where there was a large morning meal is not entirely clear. Perhaps, unlike southern Europeans, northerners woke up hungry because of the smaller supper they ate.

Only the 'Conciliator' Pietro d'Abano (1250–1315) tried to mediate these arguments, insisting that only when the body is clean of superfluous humours should the evening meal be larger, but if the time between meals is small, then it is better to have a bigger midday meal.[8] Interestingly, Nuñez de Oria who describes these arguments only mentions *almuerça* as a meal the ancients ate, so it is possible that there was no established custom of breakfast in Spain, and although the word *desayuno* was in use at this time, it too could refer to a breaking of the fast at dinner time.

There is no doubt that throughout all this discussion people followed their normal custom in the North and South, and dietary writers sometimes expressed their frustration over this. The Jesuit Leonard Lessius claimed that people will generally eat whatever they want despite physicians' counsel, usually eating until they are full, two or three times a day and then go straight to work.[9] This is at least evidence of a third meal in the Spanish Netherlands.

Another objection to eating breakfast was the long-held idea, still current among many people in the West, that one should not exercise immediately after a meal. Theoretically, those who must work in the morning should not eat breakfast for fear that it would burn up or be forced into the veins before being properly 'concocted'. Many physicians tried to explain then how it is that labourers can go straight to work after a meal. Melchior Sebizius claimed that long custom creates a 'second nature', and that the heat of labour helps dissipate the superfluities that in more sedentary people would form scabies or ulcers if they were to try working after a meal.[10] Again, this is an argument against breakfast, but also an admission that workers do take a morning meal. Sebizius explains that among the Germans (in Strasburg) most people take only two meals, but *Famulitio manè etiam jentaculum porrigunt* (Servants often have porridge in the morning for breakfast); and *Operarios quarter cibant, jentaculo, prandio, merenda, et coena* (Workers eat four meals: breakfast, dinner, snacks at sundown, and supper).[11] His emphasis here suggests that only workers could be expected to need a meal first thing in the morning.

The same was the case in France where Gaspard Bachot recommended two meals for his readers but conceded to the fact that *gens de travaille comme laboreurs, pescheurs, vignerons, forgerons* must eat more often. *Faucheurs* (mowers) have a custom of eating four meals a day, even in the heat of summer and autumn.[12] Bachot had also observed *papetiers* in Thiers (Auvergne) rise at 2 a.m. and are usually having supper while others are dining, and have gone to sleep before others have supper. For workers, who seem to defy all rules, he suggests that they at least leave four hours between meals which would mean rising and eating breakfast at about 5 a.m., dining at 9 a.m., having a *merenda* (snack) at 1 p.m. and then supper at 5 p.m..[13]

The English also made a concession to the extra meals labourers must take, but Andrew Boorde limited it to three, 'and he that eate ofter, lyveth a beestly lyfe'.[14] His implication is that fully rational humans can control their physical urges, and workers fall somewhere between the human and the beast. Philip Moore was at least more polite in pointing out that only the idle, presumably his literate readers, must confine themselves to two meals. 'I think it bee moste wholsome for them that leade a quiet and idle life (except thei bee cholericke of complexion) to bee contente with twoo meales in one daie, that is dinner and supper. And let there be seven or eight howers between meales, and lette theim eschue by all meanes possible, drinckyng or banquettyng betwene meales.'[15] Breakfast then, seems only slightly less dangerous than between-meal carousing.

Adding to the argument against breakfast, Humphrey Brooke countered popular wisdom by explaining that lassitude is actually not the result of too little food, but of excess. The 'lumpishness of the limbs and senses' many believe comes from fasting because they feel this way in the morning, and to prevent it they 'carefully provide good Breakfasts'.[16] He insists that this only causes greater weariness and crudities because the body is unable to digest the excess food. It also disposes one to gout. The true remedy for weakness is abstinence. Once again, medical opinion criticizes what was obviously entrenched custom, and 'forasmuch as the generality of People are infirm', he judges it is better to omit breakfast so as to cleanse the stomach and let it be purged of superfluous moisture before eating. For those who do not labour, they eat out of custom, not hunger.[17]

Thomas Cogan, the Manchester schoolmaster, was among the very few authors to openly approve of breakfast. He says although the meal is not mentioned by Galen, 'nor appointed by order of the universities' it is useful for hot English complexions. 'To suffer hunger long filleth the stomack with ill humors' and robust Englishmen need something early to fill their stomachs. He even admits that the English commonly eat three meals a day, and that's fine up until age forty, after which the digestion becomes too weak to handle breakfast.[18] Indirectly he also reveals what was commonly eaten. For the wealthy who eat too much manchet, a fine white bread, which can make them costive (constipated), 'a countrie mans breakefast' of brown bread and butter is a good cure for their 'fine diet'. Although he is obviously discussing the virtues of bran, he also reveals what was common breakfast fare among ordinary people.[19] The 'manner of noble men' especially in cold weather, was to start with a draught of strong wine with toast dipped in for breakfast.[20]

The only other English author to insist on the necessity of breakfast was Thomas Wingfield who pointed out that although 'Galen never ate breakefastes'; he believed them to be necessary 'in thys Realme' especially among youths and the choleric.[21] Not all English authors would admit to the existence of breakfast though. Presumably, Edmund Hollings, a Catholic exile in Bavaria, left the customs of his native country behind. He insisted that all people are used to two meals a day only, and never even mentioned the word breakfast.[22]

We get a glimpse of Scottish customs from Thomas Moffett who describes their meals: 'beginning the morning with a slender breakfast, did in old times fast till supper, feeding then but onely of one dish, using generally so temperate a diet, that not Judges and Kings, but Philosophers and Physitians seemed to have given them precepts.'[23] His comments suggest that the Scots have since changed their customs, but at the very least, there is more evidence of breakfast as a regular meal. For his countrymen he also offered a bit of bizarre advice concerning breakfast. Because the body is dramatically affected by whatever it draws in first, be it food or air, people who live in 'stinking houses or close cities' should eat breakfast regularly to be sure something wholesome enters their body first thing in the morning. Those who live in places with clear and wholesome air can fast until dinner.[24] The only other exceptions would be growing children, and choleric people, the heat of whose stomachs cannot tolerate emptiness. And of course labourers can eat four or five times a day if their work is very toilsome. Once again, breakfast appears to be a regular custom in England, but only under exceptional circumstances. Elsewhere he also suggests that the best breakfasts should be of 'liquid and supping meats' because they are easier to digest as opposed to boiled meats for dinner and roast meat for supper.[25] Whether this reflects actual custom is difficult to tell.

William Vaughan in a dietary designed for colonists to Newfoundland approves of his own Welsh custom of eating oatmeal 'caudels' with butter and raisins. He describes this as 'breakfast to nourish a good complexion'.[26] Apparently the Cromwells often took a breakfast of a caudle with ale and toast, so this appears to have been an established and approved custom among the more puritanical sort, and may account for the practice in the New World as well. Another clue about breakfast in the early seventeenth century is Vaughan's comment that in cold November it is good to eat a hot loaf with butter, cinnamon and sugar in the morning.[27]

The English writer who comes closest to the modern idea of the ideal breakfast is Tobias Venner who recommends a couple of poached eggs with salt, pepper and a drop or two of vinegar with bread and butter followed by a good draught of claret wine.[28] The wine, of course, would eventually be replaced by coffee or tea by the end of the seventeenth century, but here was considered a regular practice. A morning draught of wine 'hath almost with all men so farre prevailed, as that they judge it a principall meanes for the preservation of their health.'[29] Also conspicuous by its absence is any form of meat like bacon or sausages. These were probably considered too heavy to digest first thing in the morning, as most authors insist that breakfast should be the lightest of meals. Venner also suggests that breakfast is not necessary for 25–60-year-olds, nor for students and sedentary people.[30] Although clearly an established practice, physicians were still trying to dissuade some of their readers from taking it in the seventeenth century.

Joseph Duchesne, physician to Henry IV, offers some clues about what the French may have taken for breakfast, though his comments are somewhat more therapeutic than culinary. In describing early morning routine, he stresses the importance of regular bowel movements. To this end he recommends prune juice or a bouillon made with sorrel, borage, purslain, lettuce, cucumbers or similar cold herbs.[31] He also suggests that citrus juice in the morning is good for the stomach and heart, and helps dissolve kidney stones and gravel.[32] Laurent Joubert believed that early morning bouillons and *orge-mondez* (a barley concoction) were used too frequently in the morning, and urged that afterwards one should have a very light dinner to prevent the aperitive and attenuating bouillon from rushing the half-digested food into the veins and arteries.[33] In any case the juice or bouillon for breakfast seems to have been a common practice in France, more than a medical remedy, and may also explain how coffee and tea were so easily fitted into the breakfast slot in the next centuries.

In the south of France also we find only the slightest hints. For example, Symphorien Champier asks whether one ought to eat two or three times in a day, and he tells us that this is a newly disputed topic. In the end though he says that this all depends on how much you can digest, and it is always best to follow custom.[34] This suggests that some people were accustomed to a third meal, and he does specify that the Germans in particular eat a meal in the morning, which he considered unusual.[35]

Evidence of breakfast is harder to find for Italy, though Alessandro Petronio explains that in Rome the food eaten is not very nourishing which is why they need to eat more often and in greater quantity than elsewhere. Two meals a day he considered normal, but admitted that people often eat more.[36]

All this evidence shows that breakfast up through the seventeenth century was only explicitly described and occasionally approved by English authors, and even then usually only under unusual circumstances. In southern Europe it was mentioned less frequently, and hardly ever approved, but many people appear to have eaten it anyway. All across Europe it is clear that labourers did eat breakfast. It is only toward the eighteenth century that the custom spread upward, as it were. This may be due, partly to the replacement of alcohol for breakfast with the new drinks: coffee, tea and chocolate. These added not only a feeling of exotic luxury to the morning meal, but could be touted as medicinal and therefore appropriate for those who had to find an excuse to eat something early. On top of that, the invigorating drinks, especially coffee, were seen as morally sound for industrious Protestants before they took off for work.[37] It took some time for these beverages to make their way from the coffee houses into people's homes, but once they did, it may have also legitimized breakfast.

There were, of course, just as many doctors who condemned coffee and tea as those who praised it. The heat of the arguments itself is evidence that the custom was becoming more and more widespread in the eighteenth century, and a regular feature of breakfast. For example, George Cheyne, who generally approved of these drinks in moderation said 'Green Tea, which when light, and drank neither too Strong nor too Hot, I take to be a proper Diluent, when soften'd with a little Milk, to cleanse the alimentary Passages, and wash off the Scorbutick and Urinous Salts, for a Breakfast, to those who live full and free.'[38] His comments also suggest that serious dieters (who do not live full and free) will want to approach these with caution, but for ordinary people they are fine. For his patients, however, and for those who 'much Use of their intellectual

Faculties, or who would indulge speculative Studies' he recommends thinking in the early morning 'till eleven a Clock, then to take some agreeable Breakfast of vegetable food.' Apart from his bent toward vegetables, this is essentially what physicians of past centuries recommended – nothing at all first thing in the morning.[39]

For most physicians though, breakfast was an approved and firmly established custom by the mid-eighteenth century in England, and again the reason for this was probably pushing dinner into the afternoon. What is unexplainable however is the fact that mealtimes were even later in southern Europe and breakfast never became a regular meal there. Taking chocolate in the morning persisted in Spain and elsewhere as a very small morning nibble, but nothing like the grand breakfasts of northern Europe ever developed. Whether this was the result of a very late evening meal or the lingering medical idea that two meals in a day are sufficient for a healthy adult is impossible to say, but the pattern persists to this day.

NOTES

1. Martial, *Epigrams*, 14,223.
2. Bridget Anne Henisch, *Fast and Feast: Food in Medieval Society*, Pennsylvania State University Press, 1976, pp. 21–23. In discussing meal times William Harrison has some interesting comments: 'of old we had breakfast in the forenoon, beverages or nunchions after dinner, and thereto rear suppers generally when it was time to go to rest...Now, these odd repasts – thanked be God! – are very well left, and each one in manner (except here and there some young, hungry stomach that cannot fast till dinner-time) contenteth himself with dinner and supper only.' William Harrison, 'A Description of England ... for Holinshed's Chronicles', in *Chronicle and Romance*, N.Y.: P.F. Collier and Son, 1910, p. 302.
3. Christopher Langton, *An Introduction to Phisycke with an universal dyet*, n.d. [1550?], facsimile ed. Amsterdam and New York: Theatrum Orbis Terrarum and Da Capo Press, 1970), p. lxxix.
4. Luigi Cornaro, *How to regain Health and Live a Hundred Years*, London: Marshall Bros., 1894, p. 21.
5. Luis Lobera de Avila, *Vergel di sanidad*, Alcala de Henares: Joan de Brocar, 1542, fol. XV.
6. Ibid., fol. XVv. *Si vero paucis debilibus exercitijs et parvis ocupationibus in vita utantur, praecipiendum est ipsis melius prandere quam coenare.* The word collation eventually came to mean a late-night snack of delicacies, but was originally a small meal eaten in monasteries while reading Cassian's *Collations*.
7. Melchior Sebizius, *De alimentorum facultatibus*, Strasbourg: Joannis Philippi et Josiae Stedelii, 1650, p. 1288. See also Gaspard Bachot, *Erreurs populaires touchant la medecine et la regime de santé*, Lyon: Barthelemy Vincent, 1626, pp. 434–7.
8. Francisco Nuñez de Oria, *Regimiento y aviso de sanidad*, Medina del Campo: Francisco del Canto, 1586, p. 59. Adding to this confusion, Avicenna claimed that digestion takes a full 16 hours, and so people should only eat meals every 16 hours, twice on some days and once on others. The most complete discussion of this debate is Oddo degli Oddi, *De coenae et prandii portione libri duo*, Lyons: Jean Barbous for Gennain Rose, 1538, which argues the Hellenist position that supper should be larger. He does mention that servants and workers do eat a larger supper, and wonders how they can remain healthy, but he does not mention breakfast, '*quam, solam servitutem vulgus appellat: praeterea, quae dicta sunt, in die solita quoque munia et aliquando insueta obeant, nocte verò quiescant, ubi maius quidem prandium, minorem autem coenam ingesserint, nescio, qua ratione en incommoda evitare poterint.*'
9. Leonard Lessius, *Hygiasticon*, Cambridge, 1634, p. 12.
10. Sebizius, p. 1369.
11. Ibid., p. 1392.
12. Bachot, p. 388.
13. Ibid., pp. 432–3.
14. Andrew Boorde, *A compendyous Regyment or A Dyetary of Helth*, ed. F.J. Furnivall, London: Early English Text Society, 1870, p. 251.
15. Philip Moore, *The hope of health*, London: John Kingston, 1565, p. 22.
16. Humphrey Brooke, ΥΓΙΕΙΝΗ or *A Conservatory of Health*, London: R.W. for O. Whittington, 1650, pp. 106–7.
17. Ibid., p. 127. Brooke also argues against the current English custom of eating a larger dinner than supper. The evening meal should be larger because the heat draws inward at night fortifying digestion. During the day the ambient heat attracts the body's natural heat and weakens digestion, just as it does in summer, or even sitting in front of a fire. All this would dissuade a careful reader from eating large meals during the day, including breakfast. Brooke, p. 129.
18. Thomas Cogan, *The Haven of Health*, London: Thomas Orwin, 1589, pp. 181–2.
19. Ibid., p. 157.

[20] Ibid., p. 215.
[21] Henry Wingfield, *A compendious or short treatise ...preceptes necessary to the preservation of healthe,* London: Robert Stoughten, 1551, p. Biii^v.
[22] Edmund Hollings, *De salubri studiosorum victu,* Ingolstadt: Typis Ederisnia, per Anrea Angermarium, 1602, pp. 44–5.
[23] Thomas Moffett, *Health's Improvement,* London: Thomas Newcomb, 1655, p. 261.
[24] Ibid., pp. 289–91.
[25] Ibid., p. 296.
[26] William Vaughan, *Naturall and artificial directions for health,* London: Richard Bradocke, 1600, p. 32. Vaughan also recommends 'stale' beer in the morning with sugar to combat melancholy, which he considers even better than wine (p. 34). Like other English authors, he also believes that three meals a day, breakfast, dinner and supper, are fine until age 40. Breakfast should be the smallest meal of the three (p. 291).
[27] Ibid., p. 269.
[28] Tobias Venner, *Via recta ad vitam longam,* London: Edward Griffen for Richard Moore, 1620, p. 87.
[29] Ibid., p. 193.
[30] Ibid., p. 177.
[31] Joseph Duchesne, *Le pourtraict de santé* (Paris: Claude Moral, 1606), p. 360–61.
[32] Ibid., p. 406.
[33]. Laurent Joubert, *Erreurs populaires,* Book II, Rouen: George L'oyselet, 1587, p. 44.
[34] Symphorien Champier, *Rosa gallica,* Paris: Iodoco Badio, 1518, pp. 30v–31.
[35] Ibid., p. 33v. *Vespere igitur et mane reficiendum est non in meridie: vel circa: ut nonulli faciunt: et praesertim Alemanni.*
[36] Alessandro Petronio, *Del viver delli Romani et di conservar la sanità,* Rome: Domenico Basa, 1592, p. 196.
[37] Wolfgang Schivelbusch, *Tastes of Paradise,* tr. David Jacobson, New York: Vintage Books, 1993. The author argues that chocolate was the ideal drink for the indolent Spanish nobility while coffee and then tea were more suited to the industrious Protestant bourgeois North.
[38] George Cheyne, *An Essay on Health and Long Life* (1724), facsimile, N.Y.: Arno Press, 1979, p. 62.
[39] Ibid., p. 86.

The Funerary Meal in the Cult of the Dead in Classical Roman Religion

Joan P. Alcock

That there is a spiritual life after death would still be asserted by theists but few would maintain that the dead had physical needs. Roman funerary customs implied that the dead needed sustenance. In the ancient world the funerary meal was an essential part of the funerary process and for this it took two forms – the funerary meal taken during or after the burial ceremony and the period of mourning, and the meal provided to sustain the dead in the tomb and on their journey to the afterlife. In the Roman world both were important, especially the latter, because of the belief that the dead continued to reside within the tomb. Even when people were cremated the spirit still resided within or close by the burial place, hence the belief that the dead retain all the needs, desires and feelings which they had in life. The funerary cult was based as much on fear as on piety, for the dead were prone to resentment, even vengeance, if they were neglected. To forestall this, the correct rites had to be carried out. In these rites food played an important part.

Funerary rites

When a person died in the Roman empire, the body was washed and anointed. A female corpse was dressed in a long tunic, a male corpse in a toga, sometimes the only time the person wore this awkward garment (Martial *Epigrams*, 9. 57.8). A wreath was placed on the head of a person who had earned one in life (Cicero *De Legibus* 2.24.60) and coins were placed on the eyes or in the mouth to pay Charon for the journey across the Styx (Juvenal 3. 267; Lucian *On Funerals,* 10). For a well-to-do person there could be a lying in state, as revealed by the scene on the relief of the lady on the tomb of the Haterii (Benndorf and Schöne 1867, 221–4, no. 348).

The funeral procession followed. A poor person would be carried swiftly to the grave on a cheap bier. An important person merited an elaborate procession accompanied by family and slaves, hired musicians and professional mourners (Seneca *Apocolocyntosis* 12), a custom which the Romans had inherited from the

Etruscans. According to the Law of the Twelve Tables (Cicero *De Legibus* 2.25.58), all burials or cremations had to take place outside the inhabited part of a town or city so that the dead did not pollute the material world, either physically or spiritually. Until the second century AD, cremation was the normal practice, but gradually inhumation became customary, although in some areas of the Empire, especially Britain, cremation continued alongside inhumation until the fourth century AD.

Once the deceased had been cremated or placed in the tomb, a libation of wine to the *Manes* (spirits of the dead) was poured out. Offerings of food were placed at the tomb to be eaten in a funerary meal (*silicernium*) by members of the family (Cicero *De Legibus* 2.22.55). Sometimes the hungry poor waited close to the tombs to partake of the feast after the mourners had departed (Tibullus *Elegies* 1.5.53), even though this was considered sacrilege.

Household and farm slaves were regarded as part of the family. Slaves, freedmen and soldiers who had no family, usually belonged to a burial club (*collegia funeraticia*) (Waltzing 1898–1910). The members met about once a month to pay contributions towards their funerals. These meetings would be occasions for dining together, convivial friendship and an opportunity for a commemorative meal for their deceased colleagues. The college could purchase a communal *columbaria* for the ashes, where meals were held on specific anniversaries.

Period of mourning

The period of mourning included purification ceremonies and meals eaten by the grave. The first occasion was nine days after the funeral and then on personal anniversaries, such as birthdays, and annual festivals when the dead were commemorated. These had a dual purpose, ensuring that memories of the dead survived in the minds of friends and relations, and reassuring the dead that they were not forgotten by inclusion in the refreshment provided. The dead person would often leave money in a will for the necessary food and drink – bread, cakes, meat, fruit and wine.

The *Parentalia*, held 13 to 21 February, was the feast of parents and kinfolk, when the dead were appeased by food offerings, including a family meal eaten at the grave. Tertullian, who was converted to Christianity in AD 197, writes scornfully of the expense wasted on this means of honouring the dead (*De Anima* 4). The *Parentalia* ended in the public festival of the *Feralia,* when the *Manes* (the spirits of the dead) were honoured. Ovid describers the rites connected with this feast (*Fasti*, 2.533–70). A second festival was the *Lemuria,* held on the 9, 11 and 13 May, when hungry ghosts gathered round the house (Ovid *Fasti*, 5.419–93), the *Lemures* and the more dangerous *Larvae.* Meals had to be prepared for them. At midnight, the head of the family washed his hands in clean spring water, and threw away black beans, while keeping his face averted, saying nine times: 'these I cast, with these I redeem me and mine'. As he made his way out of the house, touching water on his route, the ghosts were believed to pick up and eat the beans.

On anniversaries relations and friends ate commemorative meals at the tomb, and a share was always put out for the dead person. The fact that it was not eaten did not mean that the dead spirit was not partaking of its share; it would be nourished either within its bones or its ashes. To help in the preparation of such meals, kitchens were sometimes provided at mausolea so that the meals prepared might be as elaborate as those eaten by the deceased when alive. The dead might be jealous if they thought they were now held in less regard. Such kitchens can be seen attached to certain tombs at Isola Sacra, the cemetery attached to Ostia, the port of Rome (Calza 1940). These tombs present the appearance of the dwellings of a well-to-do bourgeoisie.

Meals could be eaten in the funerary gardens which were sometimes created round a tomb. Trimalchio, when giving directions for his future tomb, says that he would like to have an orchard with 'every kind of fruit growing round my ashes and plenty of vines' (Petronius *Satyricon*, 71). The Romans had a passion for gardens, which the dead in the tomb were assumed to retain. The Elysium Fields were regarded as an idyllic landscape with abundant flowers and heavenly banquets.

Inscriptions on tombstones mention walled gardens with refreshing water, vines, fruit trees and flowers. There are references to *cenacula* (dining rooms), *tabernae* (taverns), *triclae* (summerhouses), *horrea* (store houses), even *stabula* and *meritoria* (brothels and rooms to let) (Toynbee 1971, 97). An inscription at Langres (CIL XIII 5708) directs that the *pomaria* (orchards) should be tended by three gardeners and their apprentices. At Nîmes, one man made his mausoleum fruitful with vines, trees and roses (CIL XII 3637). Marcus Rufius Catullus, *curator nautarum Rhodianeorum*, who died at Géligneur, had made for himself, his son and his daughter, a tomb with a vineyard and enclosure walls (CIL XIII 2494). Publicius Calistus from Die (CIL XII 1657) left precise details. His tomb was to have a 'vineyard two-thirds of a half an acre in area from whose yield I wish libations of no less than fifteen pints of wine to be poured for me each year'. Presumably they should be poured into the tomb or onto the ground so as to sustain him in the afterlife.

Tombs and tombstones showing food
The tomb of the baker, Marceius Vergilius Eurysaces, *pistor et redemptor* (baker and contractor), and his wife, Atistia, which still stands outside the Porta

Maggiore in Rome, is one of the most elaborate surviving from the late Republican era (Nash 1961–2, II 329–22). A burial chamber was in the upper part of a trapezoidal tomb. At the top of the tomb was a frieze displaying the total process of the baking industry from the sifting and grinding of the corn to the weighing of the finished loaves. The series of vertical cylinders may represent corn measures and the horizontal ones ovens. That the tomb was meant to represent the bakery is shown by a nearby inscription mentioning the tomb as a *panarium*, a bread basket or a bakery. Two figures, carved in relief, found close-by represent Eurysaces and Atistia.

A tomb at Dijon has lost the inscription but not the reliefs. On one side a wine shop is depicted in detail with the customer holding a flask of wine that he has just bought. The adjoining panel has been lost, but it clearly represented a butcher's shop because from the rail along the top hang breasts of lamb and a pig's head. Elsewhere have been found funerary reliefs of apple stalls at Arlon, boats with wine barrels at Trier, a pâtisserie at Metz. The Igels Column in the Moselle valley, which formed the tomb of the Secundinius family, shows several scenes (Dragendorff 1924). One is a kitchen where the meal is being prepared. A servant presses food in a large dish resting on a stool. Another tips food into a dish on the stove, while his colleague stirs it with a long-handled implement. The principal scene represents Secundinius Securus and Secundinius Aventinus reclining on a *lectus*, or dining couch, while their wives sit in basket chairs, one at each end of the table, on which food is placed. Servants take down dishes to serve the meal and wash the dirty plates.

Some tombstones show the *Totenmahl* or funerary banquet (Haverfield 1899), which was adopted by Romans from a motif in Greek art (Dentzer 1982). The deceased lies on a couch, holding out a cup as if to toast the living. A small three-legged table is often placed in front, on which rests food. Such tombstones were popular in the Rhineland and Eastern Gaul (Noelke 1974) and, from there, the idea was probably brought to Britain by the military. Most representations that have survived in Britain are of women. Julia Velva at York (R.C.H.M. 1962, 124, no. 82) and Curatia Din(o)ysia at Chester (Wright and Richmond 1955, 44) rest on couches, holding up goblets of wine, presumably placed in their tombs by their respective families.

One of the finest tombstones is at Cologne, originally created in AD 50 as *Colonia Claudia Ara Agrippinensium* for veterans of the Rhine campaigns (Galsterer and Galsterer 1975). Gaius Julius Maternus, veteran of Legion I Minervia, reclines on a high-backed couch, raising his cup in his right hand and holding a serviette in his left. His pet dog is at his feet. A three-legged table, covered with a fringed cloth is placed in front of him, on which is set a meal of fruit and bread. Servants stand to left and right to wait on him. His wife,

Triclinium in the catacombs at Kom el-Shuqqafa where meals could be eaten before the dead person was eviscerated and mummified (second century AD).

Maria Marcellina, seated in her basket chair, holds a bowl with more fruit. The dead were expected to be nourished by these meals. Even so, none could escape the implacable reality that the pleasures of eating and drinking were ephemeral. Titus Flaminius, soldier of Legion XIV Gemina, on his tombstone at Wroxeter, Shropshire, was uncompromising: 'I did my service and now I am here. Read this and be either more or less fortunate in your life time. The gods prohibit you from the wine-grape and water when you enter Tartarus.'

Meals to feed the dead

'There subsist in the funeral rites of all peoples, in the ceremony of mourning established by religious law or by tradition, customs which derive from archaic conceptions of life beyond the tomb' (Cumont 1922, 44). The Romans believed in a life beyond the tomb, but also held the view that meals shared at the tomb with the dead might not be enough to satisfy them. Food had to be placed within the tomb at the moment of interment or on the funeral pyre. There were two premises. The first was that the tomb was the home for the dead, where they would expect all that they had had in life; the second was that food replenished their energies.

The premise of the tomb as an eternal home was constant in the Roman world. Trimalchio decorates his tomb carefully: 'It is wrong to look after the house in which you live and to neglect the house in which you will stay much longer' (Petronius *Satyricon* 71). Containers for ashes were placed in urns shaped as houses. The elaborate tombs at Ostia (Calza 1940) and those south of Rome, along the Via Latina near to its convergence with the Via Appia Nuova (Ashby 1907) are large square buildings, which take the form of rectangular houses, some having an underground burial chamber surmounted by a two-storey building. Large house tombs were part of the necropolis under the basilica of St. Peter, which once would have stood on ground level outside the walls of the city (Toynbee and Ward-Perkins 1956 37–57). These still show the elaborate external architectural decoration and the internal frescoes, which were devised to provide houses for the dead. The rooms would be for the eating of funerary meals and family reunions.

In the catacombs of Kom el-Shuqqafa at Alexandria, Egypt, dating from the second century AD, the dead were interred in a vast necropolis, reached by a spiral staircase, descending to a depth of 35 metres. A triclinium with three stone benches was provided, where meals could be eaten before the dead persons underwent the ritual of evisceration and mummification, so graphically represented on the wall of the principal tomb. Anubis, the Egyptian god of the dead, but here dressed as a Roman legionary and with a serpent's tail, representative of the Greek divinity, Agathodaeman, and Sobek, the crocodile god, also depicted in Roman military dress, guard the embalmed body, before it is incarcerated within one of the many niches carved out of the rock. When the catacombs were first excavated, wine amphora and tableware were found on a central wooden table in the triclinium.

An elaborately carved sarcophagus found at Simpleveld, Holland, emphasizes the belief of the tomb as home. Round the interior walls are carved all the accompaniments that the deceased lady required in the next world. She herself lies on a couch. By her side is her basket chair, the shelves on which are displayed glass or metal vessels, cupboards, cabinets and chests and a three-legged dining table. Even her bath house is placed there, so that she should feel at home in her tomb, and food and drink were probably placed there. (Espérandieu Vol. 9 1938, 107–9, no. 7795; *Académie des Inscriptions et Belles-Lettres, Comptes Rendus* 1931 351–53.)

The second premise was that the dead are hungry and thirsty and must be nourished by offerings either burnt on the funeral pyre or placed in the grave

(Lucian *De Luctu* 4. 11). Lucian, in his essay *On Funerals* (9), says that the dead 'depend for their nourishment on the libations that are poured in our world and the burnt offerings at the tombs; accordingly a shade who has no surviving friends or relations on earth goes about in the Otherworld as an unfed corpse in a state of famine'. This nourishment could be delivered through pipes. For poorer people this meant the mouth of a flagon protruding above the ground serving both as a grave marker and an entrance for liquid nourishment. These can still be seen in situ at the Isola Sacra cemetery. Three have been found in Britain at Caerleon, Colchester and Chichester (Wheeler 1929; Down and Rule 1971, 720).

Pipe burials may have come from North Africa and passed into Europe along trade routes (Bercui and Wolski 1970). At Caerleon the ashes had been placed in a lead container, which was put into a hole, walled and roofed by stone slabs. From the surface, a lead pipe led into the container so that wine directly reached the ashes, and thereby the spirit of the person. An inhumation in a lead sarcophagus at Colchester received the wine via a lead pipe. Glass and pottery vessels probably contained food offerings. Several examples of this kind of inhumation were found in the necropolis excavated under the foundations of the basilica of St Peter in Rome. In one case, set into a border of a mosaic pavement lid were several holes to allow sustenance to be poured in (Toynbee and Ward-Perkins, 1956, 61, no. 30).

It was not only wine that nourished the dead. The Celts placed joints of meat in the grave to sustain warriors on the way to their Celtic Valhalla, as revealed by burials at Snailwell, Cambridgeshire and Danes Graves, North Yorkshire. The pig was particularly important in Celtic mythology. Pork was characteristic of the feast served to dead warriors. A man carrying a pig on his back often represented the Lord of the Feast (O'Rahilly 1946, 121).

Pigs were also sacrificed to Ceres, goddess of corn and germination. Cicero remarks (*De Legibus* 2.22) that places of burial of uncovered bodies 'do not really become graves until the proper rites are performed and a pig is sacrificed'. Joints of pork have been found in cemeteries in Britain (Sidell and Reilly 1998), while at Ferace, France, both joints and entire piglets were deposited with no evidence that they had been cooked (Ferdière 1993, 41). As in Britain, there is little evidence for beef and mutton but, if the joints had been boned, no evidence would have survived.

At Winchester, a shale trencher, in a cremation burial, had eating implements carefully laid on it, together with half a pig's skull and a leg of pork. Drinking vessels were laid by the side (Biddle 1967). A first-century AD cremation at Gloucester was accompanied by a large wine flagon and eleven plates and dishes in which food remains were found. A grave at Baldock, Hertfordshire, had two lines of pottery set alongside a wooden tray, on which were the remains of animal bones (Stead and Rigby 1986, 63–66). The so-called female gladiator's cremation found in Southwark, London, contained eight pottery vessels into which were placed the charred remains of dates, almonds, a fig, and bones from six chickens and a dove. These had been burned on the funeral pyre with the body.

In the mausoleum at the Lullingstone villa, Kent, into which, about AD 300, two bodies had been placed, an elaborate meal had been arranged – two groups of cutlery, glass drinking vessels, flagons and bowls for holding food. A gaming set had also been provided (Meates 1979, 122–31). Here, in the cold darkness of the tomb, a young couple sustained themselves while playing an endless game of *ludus duodecim scriptorum* in the shades of the Otherworld.

Roman cemeteries, now being excavated outside the walls of London, have revealed both food offerings and eating equipment (Barber and Bowsher 2000). More debris would have survived if environmental conditions had been different or if improved excavation techniques had been developed earlier. For comparison, there is a study of a wide range of food found in tombs in France (Marinval 1993). The finds include the remains of dates, pears, plums, cherries, figs, apples, apricots, nuts, cereals, beans, peas and cabbages. French archaeologists consider that the food selected may have been symbolic. Vegetables, especially beans, symbolized the world of the dead. Beans and lentils had a nutritional value to sustain the dead for their journey but they were also a mark of regeneration, for within them is the embryo giving promise of new life. Fruits represent the principle of immortality. Nuts, such as almonds, symbolize the buried sense of wisdom. Cereals were sacred to Ceres-Demeter, goddess of corn and germination. Apples are symbolic of femininity. Dates, figs and pine nuts, on the other hand, are potent masculine symbols, relating to Attys, consort of Cybele. These products ensure immortality. Attys transformed himself into a pine tree, a god dying each winter and renewing himself.

The *Saturnalia* of Macrobius (7.16) mentioned that eggs were used in the Bacchic mysteries. They have been found in Greek (Cumont 1922, 393) and Roman tombs, for example at York (Wenham 1968, 106–7) and Colchester, and in sarcophagi in Rome. Nilsson (1907) commented that 'the egg, an apparently inanimate and inert substance that carries within it a potent principle of life and that which has a special vital power, must perforce awake or enhance the vital powers of those to whom it is offered'. This theme is also present in Judaism and Christianity. After Jewish funerals, the principal mourners eat hard boiled eggs. Easter eggs are ancient symbols of resurrection of the body. Eggs may therefore have been pre-Christian symbols of life surviving the confines of the tomb.

It was equally valid to burn food on the cremation pyre or even at the side of the tomb, for burning released the life spirit of the object. Lucian, in his essay *Charon* (22), depicts Charon asking Hermes, the messenger who led the dead to the underworld, why corpses are placed in receptacles called tombs: 'Look, there is a splendid banquet laid out and they are burning it all; and pouring wine and mead, I suppose into trenches? What does it mean?' Hermes answers that 'the shades arise and get their dinner as best they may, flitting about in the savoury steam and smoke and drink the wine in the trenches'. Charon replies, 'Eat and drink when their skulls are dried bone? Oh fools and blockheads you little know how we arrange matters and what gulf is set between the living and the dead'. Nevertheless, this was not the common perspective.

With the increasing move towards interment, the belief grew that the tomb was the transitory room before the person began the journey to the afterlife. This journey required clothing as well as food. This may be the reason why so many bodies were buried with their shoes on. Often all that is left for the excavators are the hobnails. Lucian (*Philopseudes* 27) relates that a husband loved his wife so dearly that he ordered all her clothes, jewellery and personal belongings to be buried with her. Seven days after her death, she appeared to him and reproached him for not giving her one of her gilt slippers, still lying behind a chest. He quickly burnt it, so that she might not go barefoot on her journey to the afterlife.

Continuation of the practice

Ritual meals existed not only in Roman, but were present in Greek and Egyptian cultures, and in India and Persia. In China ritual funerary meals continued until the Maoist revolution and they have been noted in modern Taiwan (Ahern 1973; Thompson 1988). In Europe these funerary practices continued into Christian times and the early Fathers of the Church condemned them. Burchard, Bishop of Worms in the eleventh century, preached against eating anything offered to idols, that is offerings made at tombs of the dead (McNeill and Garner 1938, 334). The Catholic Church, however, was always willing to compromise, in that it absorbed pagan rituals and Christianized them, rather than fought against them. In many cultures death was regarded as a release from the sorrows and torments of this world. The good Christian soul, released from the pains of an earthly life, was united with Christ in the next world. The family of the deceased would provide the funerary meal and invite the poor and starving to share in it, thereby achieving merit for their own souls (Litten 1991, 147). This feast was the forerunner of the communal meal to be enjoyed by everyone in the new Jerusalem.

This charitable act was continued in Europe and doles of money and food were handed out on the third, seventh and thirtieth days after death (Litten, 1991, 151). The custom seems to have continued in the case of the funerals of the wealthy, but gradually it was discontinued and ended with the Protestant Reformation. Hamlet's remarks to Horatio regarding the 'funerary baked meats' coldly furnishing the marriage table (*Hamlet* I. 2 180), however, indicated that refreshment was still expected after the funeral and this custom has continued to the present.

Perhaps, the custom of funerary meals by the grave persists in the picnics which Catholic Italian families shared at the deceased member's grave (which the author witnessed in Naples in the 1960s), and in the tradition in some gypsy funerals, where bread and meat is placed on the grave and wine poured over the coffin. The custom of providing mourners at a funeral with, at the least, a cup of tea and a sandwich, may have deeper origins than the demands of common hospitality.

BIBLIOGRAPHY

Ahern, E.M. 1973, *The cult of the dead in a Chinese Village*, Stanford University Press.
Ashby, T. 1907, 'The Classical Topography of the Roman Campagna' Part III, *Papers of the British School at Rome*, 4, 3–157.
Benndorf, O. and Schöne, R. 1867, *Die Antiken Bildwerke des Lateranenischen Museums*, Leipzig: Breitkopt and Härtel.
Berciu, I. and Wolski, W. 1970, 'Un nouveau type de tombe mis à jour à Apulum et le problème de sarcophages à voûte de l'empire romaine', *Latomus* 32. 370–9.
Biddle, M. 1967, 'The Flavian Burials from Grange Road, Winchester', *Antiq. Jnl*. 47. 224–50.
Barber, B. and Bowsher, D. 2000, *The Eastern Cemetery of Roman London, Excavations 1983–1990*, MoLas Monograph 4., Museum of London.
Calza, C. 1940, *La Necropoli del Porto di Roma nell' Isola Sacra*, Rome: Libreria della Stato.
Corpus Inscriptionum Latinarium Vols. XII and XIII, Cerolini Apud Georgium Reimerium.
Cumont, F. 1922, *Afterlife in Roman Paganism*, New Haven.
Dentzer, J.M. 1982, *Le Motif du Banque Couché dans le Proche-Orient et le Monde Grec du VII au IV Siécle J-C*.
Down, A. and Rule, M. 1971, *Chichester Excavations*, Volume I. Civic Society, Chichester.
Dragendorff, H. 1924, *Das Grabmal von Igel*, Trier: J. Lintz.
Espérandieu, E. 1907–1938, *Recueil Général des Bas-Reliefs, Statues et Bustes de la Gaule Romaine*, Paris: Imprimerie Nationale.
Ferdière A. (Ed.) 1993, *Monde des Mortes, Monde des Vivants en Gaule Rurale*, Actes du Colloque Archea/Ager, Orleans, Tours: Féracf/La Simarre.
Galsterer, B. and Galsterer, H. 1975, *Die Römischen Steininschriften aus Köln*.
Haverfield, F. 1899, 'The sepulchral banquet in Roman Britain', *Arch. Jnl*. 56. 326–31.
Litten. J. 1991, *The English Way of Death*, London: Robert Hale.
McNeill, J.T. and Garner, H.M. 1938, *Medieval Handbooks of Penance*, New York: Columbia University Press.
Marinval, P.1993, 'Etude carpologique d'offrandes alimentaires végétales dans les sépultures gallo- romaines: reflexions préliminaires', in Ferdière, *Monde des Mortes, Monde des Vivants en Gaule Rurale*, 45–65.

Meates, G.W. 1979, *The Roman Villa at Lullingstone, Kent*, Volume 1, Kent Archeological Society.
Nash, E. 1961–62, *Pictorial Dictionary of Ancient Rome* 2 Vols., London: A. Zwemmer.
Nilsson, M. 1907, 'Das Ei im Totenkult der Alten', *Archiv für Religionswissenschaft*, 49. 530–46.
Noelke, P. 1974, 'Unveröffentlichte 'Totenmahlreliefs' aus der Provinz der Niedergermanien', *Bonner Jahbücher* 174, 545–60.
O'Rahilly, T. F. 1942, *Early Irish History and Mythology*, Dublin Institute for Advanced Studies.
R.C.H.M. 1962, Royal Commission on Historical Monuments, *Eboracum, Roman York I Roman*, London HMSO.
Stead, I. and Rigby, V. 1986, *Baldock. The Excavation of a Roman and Pre-Roman Settlement*, London: Society for the Promotion of Roman Studies.
Sidell, J. and Rielly, K. 1998, 'New evidence for the ritual use of animals in Roman Britain', in Watson, *Roman London: Recent Discoveries*, 95–9.
Thompson, E.S. 1988, 'Death, Food and Fertility', in Watson, J.L and Rawski, E.S. (Eds) *Death Ritual in Late Imperial and Modern China*.
Toynbee, J.M.C. 1971, *Death and Burial in the Roman World*, London: Thames and Hudson.
Toynbee, J.M.C. and Ward-Perkins, J.B. 1956, *The Shrine of St Peter and the Vatican Excavations*, London: Longmans Green.
Waltzing, J.P. 1895–1910, *Etude Historique sur les Corporations Professionelles chez les Romains*, Louvain: C. Pieter.
Watson, B. 1998, 'Roman London: Recent Archaeological Work', *Journal of Roman Archaeology Suppl. Series* No 24.
Watson, J.L and Rawski, E.S. (Eds), *Death Ritual in Late Imperial and Modern China*, Los Angeles: Berkeley University Press.
Wenham, L.P. 1962, *The Roman British Cemetery at Trentholme Drive, York*, London: HMSO.
Wheeler, R.E.M. 1929, 'A Roman Pipe-Burial from Caerleon, Monmouthshire', *Antiq. Jnl*, 9, 72–73.
Wright, R.P. and Richmond, I.A. 1955, *Catalogue of the Roman Inscribed and Sculptured Stones in the Grosvenor Museum, Chester*, Chester and North Wales Archaeological Society.

Food in the Passover *Seder*

Michael Ashkenazi

For many societies there is an idea of a meal that defines, in some often vague form, the nature of that society, and the way it sees itself. Thus for many North Americans, it is the Thanksgiving meal or its obverse, the hamburger-and-coke which defines or elucidates the concept 'meal', and is strongly associated with important values (pioneering, plenty) in that society. For Japanese the idea of a meal is embodied in the rice, soup, and side-dish combination that structures much of the food aesthetic. In Judaism, and for the cultural matrix the individual Jewish person emerges from, the Passover meal – the *seder* – is the eponymous meal.

There is a great deal of literature surrounding the *seder*. Much of this has centred around the rabbinical and other interpretations of the meaning of the *seder* (e.g. Bokser 1986; Cernea 1995; Meijers 1997; Raphael 1972), and its relationship to Jewish history. My own concern here is with the prescribed foods and their order that are an important, perhaps the most important aspect, of the *seder's* ritual. In order to understand why these specific foods fulfil such an important role I want to look at two things: at the liturgical nature of the *seder* itself (that is, its ritual order), and at the historical bases of the foods embedded in it.

At the outset, even before the ritual meal itself, the festival, insofar as most individuals are concerned, revolves around issues of food. In addition to the normal dietary proscriptions and prescriptions of *kashrut* (the body of Jewish dietary laws), the period of Passover including the *seder* requires an abstention from *hametz*, or leavened foodstuffs. Thus an important element of the ritual, even before the *seder* itself starts, is a ritual search for and disposal of all leavened material, including bread, yeast, beer, and in some communities, even yoghurt and fermented milk products.

The Seder

The Jewish festival of Passover is marked by a week's holiday, of which the first night is the most important. Officially this night, celebrated in Temple times (i.e. before AD 70) in the form of public sacrifices at the Temple in Jerusalem, is the night of the *seder*, a domestic ritual expected to be performed by every

Jewish household. The *seder* (canon, or prescribed procedure) centres around a set of foodstuffs. The nature of these foodstuffs, as well as a procedure for dealing with them, the order of consumption, and so on, are detailed in a written text, the *Haggadah*, which was codified in its final form in the tenth century.[1]

To start with, the *seder* is composed of two significant elements: a canonical liturgy – the *Haggadah* – specifying procedures for what Sered (1988) calls 'domestic ritual' (i.e., as I understand it, without the intervention of a ritual expert), and a celebratory meal. The celebratory meal varies from one Jewish community to another, within certain fixed parameters. What I want to discuss here are the foodstuffs defined and prescribed in detail and encompassed within the ritual of the *Haggadah*, which are virtually identical to all shades and forms of Jewish practice.

The *Haggadah* is a liturgical canonical text (that is, invariable and formally codified by some authority other than the practitioners), read in a ritualistic way by many (by no means all) Jewish households on the fourteenth of *Nissan* (approximately March-April). The textual narrative follows the exodus of the Children of Israel from slavery in Egypt. The text is embellished by prayers, exhortations, stories, songs, and, most importantly, by a fixed order and selection of foods.

The *Haggadah* embodies a series of formal procedures segmented into the following order:

Ur'chatz	Washing hands before the vegetable
Karpas	Eating a piece of vegetable
Yachatz	Breaking the middle *matzah*
Maggid	Telling of the Exodus from Egypt
Rach'tzah	Washing hands before the *matzah*
Motzi	The blessing over *matzah* as food
Matzah	The blessing over *matzah* as a special *mitzvah*
Maror	Eating bitter herbs
Korech	Eating a sandwich of *matzah* and bitter herbs
Shulchan Orech	Eating the festive meal
Tzafun	Eating the *afikoman*

The performance of the *Haggadah* is made up of a number of different modes: recitation, statement and response, songs, riddles, physical manipulation of food objects, and kinesics (bodily postures). This is psychologically and pedagogically sound: nothing more boring than a lengthy lecture. Breaking up a lengthy exposition this way is the traditional equivalent, perhaps, of the 'sound bite': it not only engages the attention of the audience, it engages the attention of all audiences, of whatever age or level of understanding or sophistication. I would argue that this structure is intentional, not an evolutionary accident: it creates a powerful teaching device which, over the centuries, was practised in such a way as to ensure (inasmuch as possible) the popular (as opposed to the literate and educated élite) continuity of Jewish practice.

The different modes are participated in by the diners: songs, formal and informal stories, actions and movement. Significantly, all of these are performed with the ritually important foods placed on the table, and a large number of these 'modes' of text revolve around the food that is central to the ritual and to the meal.

The *Haggadah* specifies how the ritual foodstuffs: three pieces of unleavened *matzah* bread, a piece of roast bone, two kinds of *maror* (bitter herbs), and a *charoset*, a mixture of fruit, honey, and wine, and a hard-boiled egg in salt water for each person, are to be arranged on the table. This, the *seder* plate, is the centrepiece of the table, and the ritual actions make continuous references to, and use of, the ritually prescribed foods that are visual, olfactory, and finally, edible, parts of the ritual.

Central to both the ritual meal and to the ritual that surrounds it is an unleavened bread: *matzah*. It is so central that one of the requirements, made part of the liturgy, is that the *Haggadah* specifies that '…he who has not said the words *pesach* (pass-over), *matzah* and *maror* (bitters) it is as if they had not done their duty [in celebrating Passover].' During the ritual, the *matzah* is manipulated – raised, pointed to, covered and uncovered, eaten alone or with other foodstuffs – throughout the proceedings. Moreover, it is eaten instead of bread for the following seven days after the *seder* ritual: an indication of its liturgical importance.

Of the *matzah* consumed, one particular piece is of cardinal importance to the *seder*: the *afikoman*. I shall discuss the concept in detail below, but in terms of food this is the middle of the three *matzah* placed on the table in the formal arrangement of the *seder* plate. It has a particular role to play: it is sequestered conspicuously (and stolen by younger members of the family to be redeemed for gifts), and it serves to mark the ritual end of the meal.

Wine too, is strongly in evidence. Four full cups are to be consumed ('enough to make your head swim' as one formal legal interpretation has it). But the wine is also manipulated. Wine cups are raised and lowered without being drunk from, and drops of wine are used to mark the ten plagues of Egypt. Each of the four cups to be drunk (abstainers may use grape juice 'provided some wine is mixed in it') must be consumed completely, and a proper blessing must be said over each.

In sum, the process of the ritual revolves heavily around the sensory nature of the foods consumed. The food is not separated from the ritual. To the contrary, it is central to it, punctuating the long and sometimes complex verbal and kinesic performance with food experiences.

Discussion

Analytically, the food elements of the *seder* must be seen in three different contexts: the historical emergence of the ritual, theory about ritual performance, and our understanding of the nature of food in relation to ritual.

The original festival of eating *matzah* is of great antiquity. There is evidence of a domestic communal meal with ancillary 'watch night' for seven days. (Raphael 1972: 41). This may have been associated with another ritual: the public sacrifice at the Temple in Jerusalem that was part of the pilgrimage enjoined on the Children of Israel.

The two centuries before the birth of Christ were a period of religious and intellectual ferment in Judea. One phenomenon during that period was the emergence of communes of like-minded pious Jews – *havurot* – who assembled to preserve and maintain Jewish culinary ritual laws. One can suspect that they emerged as counterpoint to the growing Hellenization of Jewish society in the centuries after the emergence of the Greek kingdoms in the Middle East.[2]

The influence of Greek-Hellenic culture on the Eastern Mediterranean of the time was enormous. Supporting or opposing Hellenization were the prevailing cultural paradigms of that period. Significantly, when the *seder* was taking shape, the original models from which it was borrowed were probably a Greek symposium and a Roman banquet. Roman banquets were themselves highly influenced by the Greek model. Formal symposia consisted of a balanced mix: a subject under discussion (the host might announce the subject with the invitation, or it might be selected *ad hoc*), an appetizer of herbs and eggs, ritual consumption of wine, with a libation, games and questions to involve the entire audience (see Plutarch's *Questiones Conviviales* and Athenaeus, *The Deipnosophists*).

Similarities between symposia and the *seder* abound. For example, the recipe for *charoset* – chopped fruit and nuts moistened with wine – appears in Athenaeus. So does the 'sandwich' of herbs and bread (*matzah* in the *seder*) which is required at the ritual. The key is perhaps in Plutarch, who says that a symposium is a mix of serious and mirthful entertainment, discourse and actions, for the remembrance of pleasures from food is short-lived, whereas the subjects of discussion are remembered forever. I would argue that Plutarch has the wrong end of the stick: olfactory and taste memories are unconscious and extremely long-lived, and they can trigger intellectual memory.

Perhaps the most interesting borrowing from the Hellenic world to the Jewish one, is the *afikoman*. It is remarkable because it illustrates how important the Hellenic world was to Judaism of that period, as a source for both borrowing, and, in this case, opposition. The penultimate act of the *seder*, before declaring the ritual closed, is consumption of the *afikoman*: the central slice of the three *matzah* that are placed, wrapped, in the centre of the table arrangement. This slice of *matzah* plays a central part for children,[3] and is eaten after the main meal. The *Haggadah*, however, provides what might be a startling warning (in the answer to the wise son): Do not end the meal with an *afikoman*. In modern times, where this has been interpreted solely in terms of food consumed, and without context, this is surprising indeed. Moreover, the *seder* must end before midnight (though intellectual discourse is permitted until later). In the historical context, however, this is significant, and a key to understanding much about the *seder*. A Greek symposium often ended with an *epikomion*: revelry after the feast (in other words, the orgy). In the attempt to distance Jewish practice from Hellenic, the codifiers of the *Haggadah* made a couple of remarkable transformations. The revelry after the feast was converted into a dry slice of bread, and this, without a change of name, was made into a doorstop against further revelry. It was not revelry *per se* that was at point, its was a (successful) attempt to wrench disparate Jewish groups from the seductive grip of Hellenistic ways.

The original elements of the *seder* were present in the *Mishnah*[4] (200 CE), a time in which Judaism was struggling to forge a new ideology and practice for itself. The Temple sacrifices were less vivid, since the Temple itself, as well as all vestiges of sovereignty, had been destroyed. In other words, a change from a public-oriented to a family-oriented event took place over a lengthy period. For your average Jewish individual of that period, the sacrifices at the Temple would need to be replaced, and were indeed replaced by a sensory set of activities: the *seder*. The commensal meal, the *seder* had its roots in the need, during the period of Hellenization of the entire Eastern Mediterranean, to craft counterpoints to the seductions of the practices, and foods, of the dominant culture. Greek symposia provided a ready-made template (as well as recipes!) for the creation of an autochthonous practice, which, by 'realigning' the Greek food practices and their implications, make them Jewish.

The *seder* meal was thus an accommodation, culinary as well as ritual, to the dominant culture. The modes of presentation – reclining on couches, a mixture of different modes of text and song, riddles and stories – and the very foods themselves owe much to the Greek originals, preserved to the modern era.

When looking at rituals, I argue, it is extremely important to look at the entire performance and at the details that make it up. Texts such as the

Haggadah – dictated by other than those present, having a set format or liturgical order, involving action and elaboration – become 'serious' events (Rappaport 1979; Skorupski 1976). The seriousness can frame a surprising amount of play, or, to be more precise, the very act of sanctification (a fixed text, a liturgy) combined with the use of a multitude of modes, creates conditions for manipulating the meanings and the actions at a number of levels, often simultaneously: the essence of play.

Moreover, rituals, in general, tend to be 'multi-media events' to use a neologism I usually dislike. We tend to think of 'multi-media' as an alignment of text, sound, and images displayed on a computer screen. This is neither a linguistic nor an empirical limitation. In the case of human actions, notably those that are intended to brand themselves into people's conscious and unconscious memory, multi-media extends much further. Most rituals (consider a mass or any ritual of your experience) will utilize a variety of elements in juxtaposition: action, kinesics, smells, voice, music. The *seder* is a paradigm of multi-media brought, deliberately, into the familial and the immediate. Many Jews of my acquaintance dislike the *seder* and try to avoid it. Yet no one forgets the elements, or does not know how they fit with other elements. This knowledge is not necessarily intellectual: few are able to recall all the *seder*'s nuances, let alone its multiple interpretations. Yet the total effect – orderly ritual actions, kinesics, taste, song – is so subliminally impressive, that it becomes embedded strongly in one's remembered experiences.

The use of smell and taste are cardinal in the *seder*. Olfactory and taste cues linger and are very important in the evocation of mood. It is perhaps reasonable to argue that the eating of *maror* (the bitter herbs), whatever later exegesis was attached to its symbolic significance, was critical in recalling and emphasizing memories of Passover. The taste of bitter foods is as evocative in triggering memory as the taste of more desirable flavours: the bitterness of many medicines is not quite accidental, it ensures you won't want to taste this food again! I would argue that the four standard flavours are being evoked in the *seder*: bitter (*maror*), sweet (*charoset*), salt (egg), and sour (perhaps in the presence of two types of *maror*: the vegetable, and the horseradish). These are more than symbolic elements as they are usually interpreted: they are important mnemonic aides. Given the brilliance with which the *seder* was crafted by its authors, I would hazard a guess that this was not unintentional.

Conclusions

The meta-story of the *seder* (that is, the story around its origins and development) is significant for our understanding of what meals are. A 'meal' is not merely a food event. It is a food event with very complex, elaborate rules of presentation and composition, and significantly, it is consumed within a particular social framework: with or within different groupings of people.

The *seder* is a case in point. It is consumed by a small group (family, extended family, and perhaps individual guests), and it is consumed within a particular group: the Jewish community. It is the nexus, therefore, of two important human contexts. One is the family, the other the cultural community. By structuring a canonical set of actions revolving around food, this particular meal has succeeded in serving as a reinforcement of these two significant groups on the one hand while allowing very broad interpretations and adaptations on the other. For example, the ritual meal, which is prescribed, is followed by a substantive meal that is not. I would think that even in the first and second centuries CE it was becoming clear that the Jewish community was heterogeneous in its daily lives, and that the *Haggadah*'s authors took account of the fact: once the ritual (similar across the entire Jewish cultural community) was performed, and the framework set, each family would enjoy its meal in its own way.

Several important general points arise from examination of the *seder*: there is a process of reinforcement of ideas and practices by using the most elementary reinforcement, food; there is the possibility of play (the *afikoman*); there are formal and informal exegeses; and there are appeals to universal preoccupations with 'things that transcend individual life', to paraphrase Geertz.

The use of canonical liturgies of food is not unique of course to Judaism. Geertz (1977), in one of his earlier works, describes the Javanese *slametan* ritual. In a *slametan*, food is partaken of hurriedly, then taken home to be shared by members of the participant's family. Similar acts are documented in several cultures and religions, including China (Wolf 1978) and Japan (Ashkenazi 1991).

Food is a useful structural device in rituals for a number of reasons. Food is often consumed ritualistically (here defined as in extra-technical manner), and always so in a meal: we use a particular order of dishes and implements; different meals define who will participate; and foods are always manipulated in a non-natural manner. Food is inherently rewarding and thus useful for manipulation of feelings and emotions: one of the cruxes of any ritual. The *seder* illustrates an extreme example: a case where some faced with the need to his (or their) mind to preserve a set of ideological premises, used a meal, rather than some other ritual format, to ensure that these ideas and practices be carried out down the ages. Indeed, this particular format of a meal is paradoxically a bastion, as it were, of Jewish belief and a living remnant of their opponents' – the pagan Greeks and Romans – culinary practices.

REFERENCES

Ashkenazi, Michael 1991, 'From Tachi Soba to Naorai: Cultural implications of the Japanese meal', *Social Science Information* 30(2): 287-304.
Athenaeus, *The Deipnosophists.*
Bokser, Baruch 1986, *The Origins of the Seder: The Passover Rite and Early Rabbinic Judaism*, Berkeley: University of California Press.
Cernea, Ruth Fredman 1995, *Passover Seder: An Anthropological Perspective on Jewish Culture*, New York: University Press of America.
Geertz, Clifford 1977, 'Community ritual in Java', pp. 401-405 in W. Goldschmidt (ed.), *Exploring the ways of mankind*, NY: Holt, Rinehart, and Winston.
Josephus, *Antiquities of the Jews.*
Meijers, Daniel 1997, 'Next year in Jerusalem. A symbolic study of a Jewish ritual', *Ethnologia europaea*, 27:1, pp 59-66.
Plutarch, *Questiones Conviviales.*
Raphael, Chaim 1972, *A feast of History: The drama of Passover through the ages*, Jerusalem: Weidenfeld and Nicholson.
Rappaport, Roy 1979, *Ecology, Meaning, and Religion*, Yale University Press.
Sered, Susan 1988, 'The domestication of religion: the spiritual guardianship of elderly Jewish women', *Man*, 23: 506-21.
Skorupski, John 1976, *Symbol and Theory: A study of Theories of Religion in Social Anthropology*, Cambridge University Press.
Wolf, Arthur 1978, 'Gods, Ghosts and Ancestors', pp.131-182 in Wolf (ed.), *Studies in Chinese society*, Stanford University Press.

NOTES

[1] In practice, as Judaism has evolved in the twentieth century, new variants of the *Haggadah* have emerged: for kibbutzim, for women, for world peace, which have been bowdlerized/ modified to fit particular constituencies.

[2] This issue relates perhaps to Christian themes as well. i.e. the Last Supper: a *havurah* gathering of particularly pious people, such as perhaps the Essenes. The lack of mention of items clearly associated with the *seder* in the Last Supper would tend to indicate that it was a *havurah* meal, perhaps part of the *Pesach* night, and therefore downplayed as a full canonical *seder*: the canon of the *Haggadah* had not been codified, some people did it one way, some another, and *havurah* meals were not necessarily associated with the *seder*.

[3] In some households, this is stolen by the children, who ransom it for gifts, in others, it is hidden by the adults. The children then search for it, and receive gifts for their success.

[4] A multi-volume exegesis on the Laws of Moses which, together with the later Gemara (and exegesis on both *Mishnah* and the Laws of Moses), is known as the *Talmud*: the fundamental basis for Jewish ritual law.

The German-Texan Meal
1831–2001

Gwen Barclay

Iss was gar ist, trink was klar ist, sprich was wahr ist.
(Eat what's cooked, drink what's clear, speak the truth.)

It must have been in the early 1980s when I had my first encounter with German-Texas food in the tiny Central Texas town of Round Top. As I approached the serving counter of the temporary food booth set up to take care of the several thousand people attending the antiques fair, my nose quickly detected something besides the expected aroma of smoked brisket and sausage which was advertised on the hand-made sign behind the volunteer workers. Getting hungrier all the time, I patiently waited in line to place my order and was startled to be asked by a distinctively accented voice, 'which two "sides" do you want: sauerkraut, hot German potatoes, baked beans, German potato salad or creamy coleslaw?' Although it was totally non-traditional to my mind, I quickly decided that I must try the sauerkraut and hot German potatoes with my sliced brisket. Growing up in Texas with smoked brisket being the king of barbecue, I thought that I was fairly well versed in the usual accompaniments but this was a first! But then I remembered Round Top was a haven of German-Texans, dating from before the time of the Texas Republic, 1836–1845.

Needless to say, my plate of barbecue was delicious, if a little different than I was used to. The chunks of potatoes had been peeled and were of a mealy type, such as russets which were locally common. They had been cooked with onion, plenty of butter and chopped parsley. No other adornment was needed. The sauerkraut was mouth-puckering and flavoured with caraway seed. The fat sausage link was of a coarse grind, with just a hint of garlic and it came from one of the nearby sausage markets. The brisket was fork-tender, with the sauce served separately as it should be, since the twelve- to fourteen-hour smoking time would render it inedible if the sweet and sour, tomato-based sauce were put on the meat while cooking. A huge, garlicky dill-pickle wedge was tucked in beside the beef and a thick slice of home-made white bread crowned the three-compartment styrofoam plate.

That mouth-watering memory came back to me when I considered the theme for this symposium. It was such a perfect example of how man moved around the world: for a variety of reasons, taking along knowledge and familiar foods when practical, adapting them to local ingredients, creating new traditions.

Through a number of books written for and by early pioneers, family histories which have been gathered by descendants, and especially during oral interviews with long-time residents of Round Top, I have pieced together the story of how the people lived, ate and enjoyed life here in Central Texas. It was a terribly hard and often cruel existence, but the food traditions which the settlers brought with them played a large part in helping them achieve a successful and rewarding life.

The first German family to establish a home in the Round Top area was that of Friedrich Ernst, who came from Oldenburg in 1831. I never discovered why, but their only cooking utensil was a cast-iron skillet in which the wife Louise cooked cornbread over an open fire. There was plenty of wild game, but Friedrich was not such a good hunter. He did have experience as a gardener in Germany so was soon able to raise a corn crop. A staple of the diet for most settlers, corn remained a primary crop for man as well as animals. The corn was boiled, then grated and baked, in addition to drying for making into a meal for bread. A mortar for grinding was fashioned from a tree log as there was no grist mill nearby.

Though most settlers did bring seeds and cuttings of favourite vegetables, fruit trees and medicinal plants, it was difficult to get gardens established. The growing season is very long and warm in Texas, and plants grew differently from what people were accustomed to in Germany. Still, it wasn't long before the hard-working German housewives had kitchen gardens: potatoes – both white, and sweet which they found out about from their Anglo neighbours – seeds for eggplant and okra were shared by them also; pumpkins, melons, and hard squashes grew well, as did beets, onions and garlic. Several different varieties of cowpeas, especially the black-eyed peas, were always grown alongside the corn and allowed to climb up the stalks; the peas would often reseed naturally. Lettuces, kale, collards and both green and red cabbage were grown in cool weather months. The greens provided much-needed variety to the diet during the winter. Favourite herbs such as dill, coriander, parsley and chamomile were also found to grow best in the cooler months.

Fruit trees were planted and they quickly found success with peaches as well as pears, figs and plums; native grapes were harvested for preserving as well as making into wine. Walnuts and pecans were gathered and much appreciated by German cooks, as were persimmons and mulberries. Apples seldom proved successful around Round Top but were popular further west where the winters are longer and colder. Amazingly, it was only a few years before nurseries were established nearby which supplied fruit and nut trees, as well as flowering shrubs for the landscapes.

What seems to be a strictly American phenomenon was the development of general stores which sprang up at crossroads or often as the first business in a settlement. These wondrous emporiums stocked everything from flour, sugar and coffee to horse bridles, ropes and milk buckets; from gingham, yard goods and penny candy to patent medicines and coffins. In the Ernst family history, wife Louise meticulously listed each purchase: spices (pepper, cinnamon, cloves and nutmeg), cream of tartar, coffee, flour, chicory, baking powder, rice, sardines, mackerel, barley and whiskey. Wheat flour remained an expensive commodity which had to be purchased as experiments in growing wheat, barley and rye were unsuccessful.

The actual town of Round Top was settled first by southern planters who came in the 1840s with their slaves in search of land for cotton. In 1839, a stage stop for mail which had an octagonal-shaped tower on top stood on a hill; the stage drivers would yell out as they approached, 'Round Top!', to give warning to the passengers. The name stuck. A general store was established in the community soon after, and is still in existence, though it now features gifts, antiques and home-made fudge for the many tourists who flock to the charming town. The earliest settlers often came in organized groups from a particular area in Germany. In letters home, they convinced family and friends to join them in this new land, thus creating pockets of German life which remain intact today in Texas.

Direct descendants of these first German immigrants have furnished most of my information about actual meals. Grace Hinze's maternal ancestor came from Saxony through the port of Galveston to Round Top in 1850; he was a wheelwright and helped build the local Lutheran Church as well as one of the most beautiful homes in the area, which is still standing. She keeps to the German traditions of hard work and frugality passed on by her *Oma* or *Grossmutter* (grandmother). Now in her eighties, Grace remembers well the meals. Like many immigrants, they grew almost everything consumed. The German motto of '*make do, use it up or do without*' served them well as they prospered.

The day for German-Texan settlers began with a hearty breakfast, but only after the animals were fed and the cows milked. Another friend tells of her grandfather always starting the fire in the wood stove when he arose to make coffee before going out for the early morning chores. Breakfast (*Frühstück*) was typically bacon or sausage, eggs and home-made bread with jams or jellies. Grace's husband Clarence told me of the mid-morning snack, called *zweites*

Frühstück or second breakfast. It often included a sandwich of home-cured ham or sausage, or *Kochkäse* (cooked cheese) spread on the bread; cookies or sweet rolls and, depending upon the weather, coffee with clotted cream and sugar would also be offered. Clarence and the other workers either came to the kitchen for second breakfast or, during hay-baling time, the food would be taken to them in the fields. At those times, the women of the family took the young children and helped with the work too. Rising bread dough would sometimes be brought to the field so the women's labour was not lost. The dough would be punched down several times during the day until it was convenient to return to the kitchen to bake the bread.

The main meal of the day was at noon, and known as dinner (*Mittagessen*, meaning 'midday eating' or simply *Mittag*). The meal almost always included potatoes, often fried, along with baked or stewed chicken, beef or pork, fish from the pond or small wild game which was still quite plentiful in the area. Stews prepared with tougher cuts of meat were popular one-dish meals. Grace remembers her first smoked brisket in 1934 – very tough she says!

Fried chicken was not common in the early years as young chickens suitable for frying would be killed only for a special occasions. Turkey and dressing, duck and roast beef were favoured for Sunday dinner or meals when either there was a little more help in the kitchen and the cook was not pressed for time. Herring was a traditional Christmas dish for many German-Texan families; they were purchased at the general store, packed in small barrels of brine.

Dumplings or noodles were a popular alternative to potatoes. Several simply cooked seasonal vegetables accompanied the meat: green beans, fresh or dried peas and butter beans, hard squash, cabbage (or sauerkraut), turnips with their green tops, kohlrabi, corn, and lettuces in season, which in Texas is the fall and the very early spring before the weather turns hot. Tomatoes were grown and were used fresh or cooked. Many vegetables were seasoned with a small amount of sugar; raw sliced tomatoes were often served with sprinkled sugar, or cooked and thickened with flour or cornstarch and seasoned with cinnamon and sugar. I am not sure if this custom was brought from Germany or one which the immigrants learned from Anglo neighbours as sugar with many vegetables was popular in the American South until very recently. Sweet rice was also something that all my interviewees spoke about: rice cooked slowly with milk, then sugar and butter added, sometimes egg yolks, and served with cinnamon and more sugar. This was very popular as a side dish at dinner or at breakfast, rather than as a dessert. Pickles of all kinds, piccalilli, chow chow or other relishes often accompanied the meal as did jam or other sweet spreads. Grace remembers eating nothing but pickles and buttered bread when times were hard and food was in short supply.

In late afternoon, another snack was served and this was called 'lunch' (*Abendbrot*, or 'evening bread') by early German farm families It usually consisted of sandwiches (their prevalence was surprising), the ubiquitous *Kochkäse*, small sweet rolls, canned fruit and coffee. *Kaffeeklatsch*, which could be quite elaborate, developed later in the nineteenth century and is associated with more social occasions, much the same as British afternoon tea, but was favoured for afternoon quilting sessions. Supper (*Abendessen* or 'evening eating'), always after sundown, was quite simple: hash browned potatoes, often with leftover meat, a hearty soup of beans with sausage or other smoked meat, or even a dish of clabbered milk with crumbled cornbread or biscuits. Leftover sweet rice often returned as baked rice pudding, with extra milk and eggs, and perhaps raisins. Grace and Clarence, like many families, had only three meals a day, combining the late afternoon and evening events. They always called it lunch.

Let me tell you about *Kochkäse*, (translated as 'cooked cheese') which has come to have quite a reputation in Round Top amongst cooks who entertain. The modern recipe, shared by my German-Texan friend Corine Levien, uses grocery-store cottage cheese, either small or large curd. In the mid-1800s, it would have been made from scratch, using fresh skimmed milk which was allowed to sit at room temperature until it curdled, or clabbered. Baking soda is added to the cottage cheese which helps break down the curds. Flour is added to the cheese which is cooked in a heavy skillet with butter until creamy, then seasoned with salt and caraway. The cheese is served slathered on freshly baked white bread, perhaps with a slice of hard smoked sausage and sometimes toasted under a broiler for a *Kaffeeklatsch*.

A by-product of making butter, buttermilk, was popular with German-Texans. Cottage cheese was served with fruit for morning or afternoon snacks as well as with chopped onions, radishes, peppers and cucumbers for supper. There was milk soup, potato soup, buttermilk soup, buttermilk pie, creamy puddings and pies – and of course butter for all that home-made bread! And don't forget milk punch with brandy and rum!

Desserts as we know them today – cakes, pies, pastries and fruit desserts such as cobbler or *kuchen* (also meaning cake in German) – were mostly reserved for Sunday dinner or special occasions such as holidays and birthdays. Birthdays were a favoured occasion among German-Texan families and neighbours, according to Grace and Clarence Hinze. The celebrations did not have to be announced, people just began to show up since everyone made it a point to remember birthdays. The fare was always sandwiches of various types – most often egg or chicken salad, or *Kochkäse* spread on home-made bread, along with an unending array of sweets. Everyone brought food to share so there was an opportunity for the German-Texan housewives to show off their baking skills.

In the Hinze household, cream pies held reign, along with chocolate cake. The famous Texas Chocolate Sheath (or Sheet) Cake is made with buttermilk and cocoa so it is both delicious as well as thrifty, a point never overlooked by German-Texans. Topped with a fudge-like frosting, it stays very moist and travels well to boot!

There were not a few rather strange recipes which turned up in one of the German-language cookbooks: popcorn pudding; *arme Ritter* or poor knights, which was thick bread dipped in milk and egg, fried and eaten with sugar and cinnamon; and pecan salad with celery and cream was served with cake. I also found a recipe for 'Small Birds Baked in Sweet Potatoes' which sounded like something served in a trendy New York restaurant.

Grace remembers as a child attending a golden wedding anniversary celebration for her mother's aunt at which was served a sweet potato salad. The cooked sweet potatoes were mashed and seasoned with vinegar, raw onion and chopped herring. Grace said this was specially requested by her aunt for the party menu because it had been served at her wedding 50 years before. And we think food of the new millennium with its fusion and cross-culture themes as so unique. We have nothing on these folks.

Another institution was peculiar to rural Texas: the Beef Club. Farm families banded together to make it easier to have fresh meat before the days of refrigeration. Always in the summer, but often year round, a group of families (the Hinzes' club numbered 24) would take turns slaughtering a steer each Friday. One farmer served as butcher and the meat was divided up so each received a share of all the different cuts, the butcher receiving extra for his labours. Saturday dinner with fresh beef was always looked forward to because the remaining meat had to be cooked to preserve it, usually roasted in large pieces or cooked into stews. The rest of the week the family must be content with the leftover cooked beef.

The German-Texans learned to preserve pork after butchering in the fall and winter months by salt curing or brining it before smoking. With our warm weather, it was not usually safe to dry-cure fresh meats or sausage without at least a few days in the smoke house. Blood and liver sausage was steamed, then hung and smoked. The head of the pig was cooked along with the ears and tongue for souse or head cheese, a great German delicacy, always with sweet marjoram. The pig's feet were cooked and pickled to preserve but weren't to everyone's taste. All of these traditional German foods are still enjoyed today in Round Top, but most are purchased at The Mercantile.

Venison was handled in the same way as beef, eating the meat fresh for a day or so, depending upon the weather. Jerky is thin slices of venison or beef which are highly seasoned with spices and quickly cooked in boiling water before drying. Venison sausage was always smoked and remains popular for hunters who shoot a deer in late fall hunting season. It is now possible to buy smoked venison sausage in our area prepared with commercially raised meat.

Along with meats which formed the heart of the meal in early Texas, bread was considered a necessity. Before general stores became established in this area in the early 1850s, finely milled flour of any type was almost unheard of, and even then, the settlers paid dearly. Once railroads came to Texas, commodities such as flour became more widely available. The German-Texans had to make do with corn bread for a number of years, either cooked in the iron skillet, dropped by the spoonful and fried in grease, or mounded on the blade end of a hoe and baked in the fire – giving rise to the name 'hoe-cakes'. Cooks had to make their own yeast, usually with buttermilk, flour and cornmeal. It is interesting to note that despite the tradition of dark, heavy breads in Germany, the German-Texans still cling to the white bread – or 'light bread' as it is known – that they enjoyed once wheat flour was available. Perhaps wholewheat flour and other grains never were widely available since they turn rancid more easily. Today, you rarely find anyone who makes rye or pumpernickel bread at home, but they are popular in bakeries, along with whole-grain breads.

One German tradition which survived the move to Texas very well was the making of beer. Many families made their own home brew, and always brought it out at holiday gatherings and special occasions. At its heyday there were several saloons as well as breweries in Round Top. The local Mercantile reflects the continued popularity of beer with at least ten to twelve German brands offered at any one time.

Gott Hilft Denen, Die Sich Selbst Helfen.
(God helps those who help themselves.)

Another custom which served the German-Texans well was their belief in self-help. The farmers assisted one another with building projects and at harvest time; meat butchering time was always a opportunity for far-flung neighbours to come together for a renewing of friendships and sharing the work. Food always played a huge part in such activities. Housewives helped neighbours with canning or planting a garden if there was illness in a family. Organizations sprang up all over Texas with the idea of taking care of one's own people. Shooting clubs and singing societies with statewide competitions were popular by the mid-1850s; theatrical groups, dance clubs, town bands and literary organizations thrived on the frontier, indicative of the high value placed on the arts and education. Agricultural societies were formed to assist the inexperienced farmers with problems which arose. Many of these groups survive today and serve as a nucleus for the community, and their activities always include the entire family, young and old. The volunteer fire department holds benefit dances and barbecues several times a year and the Fourth of July Independence Day celebration in Round Top is known far and wide for its festivities, especially the parade and the food.

In the 150-plus years since the first German families set foot in the Round Top area, some things have changed very little, yet other traditions have been lost to history. Gardens are rarely planted and the main meal of dinner is often in the evening when all the family returns to eat together. Most people have no time for *Kaffeeklatsch*, some because they are too busy sending e-mail to family and friends who no longer drop by to visit – or they are surfing the Internet looking for records of their ancestors. When family reunion time comes around – and they are very big in Texas – *Grossmutter* still makes her favourite chicken soup, but perhaps with a Mexican twist using tortillas instead of noodles and spiked with *chile serrano* from the supermarket and *cilantro* from the garden. The German clubs still smoke brisket regularly, but chickens are also on the grill. Instead of cooking the pot roast for hours over the fireplace, the German-Texan housewife is more likely to use a crockpot or purchase the beef already cooked. Many families still make sauerkraut but it is now preserved directly into jars rather than the big crock. Today, many people carefully keep the flavour of the German culture while trying to eat more healthily with fewer fats and salt. All the while, they hold on to those thin threads which connect them to their hard-working ancestors, not necessarily practising all the traditions but still very proud and connected to their German-Texan heritage.

Allzuviel ist ungesund.
(Enough is as good as a feast.)

Dining by Design

Peter Brown

Entertaining guests at home around a well-laid-out dining-room table has experienced a sort of renaissance in recent years. A proliferation of cookery programmes, from *Naked Chef* to *The Two Fat Ladies* rekindles our interest in the delights of food and helps focus attention on the pleasures of dining at a table where all the senses are being brought into play.

Large superstores make the realization of this all too easy for us; we obligingly shuffle past a series of well-lit fantasy dining-rooms arranged with matching cutlery, crockery and glass, then stroll painlessly into the warehouse to purchase all the items on display at heavily discounted prices. The economic benefits of mass production and bulk buying are obvious, but it has also meant that patterns of behaviour which were viewed as a prerogative of a privileged middle and upper class, are now being enjoyed by the great majority of the population.

A great deal of attention was paid in earlier years to the question of how to behave in company at table, a situation where people found themselves put closely together, in a position to watch-and-be-watched by others

From medieval times the tables of the wealthy were also structured to maintain the status and importance of the guests. The famous print of the German banquet at Nuremberg (1491)[1] helps us understand this hierarchy when we note how limited were the number of objects for eating being made available on the secondary tables. The lord, however, has a grand standing-salt, a drinking-vessel, a knife and a stack of bread trenchers to which at 'presentoir' is observed adding other slices. Some spoons are shown on adjoining tables, but there is no evidence of forks, an eating implement used in southern European countries at this time. Lorenzo de' Medici, for example, possessed eighteen silver forks and matching spoons in 1491[2] but, as David Mitchell has shown, nearly two centuries were to pass before we see them in common usage in Britain.[3]

The *Book of Nurture*[4] first published in the 1440s provides us with an early written record of a complete table-setting for a lord. In this, the author notes that on spreading the tablecloth, a salt-cellar should be placed at your lord's right hand, to the left of it one or two trenchers, then a knife, then white rolls, then a spoon resting on a folded napkin. The trencher, knife and spoon were then to be protected with an elaborate coverpane.

These coverpanes were not usually available for ordinary guests in the fifteenth century and, given the paucity of knives in early inventories, this gives credence to the Nuremberg print which shows only spoons being provided. All visitors could, of course, bring their own cutlery with them, but records of knives designed for travelling, i.e. housed in their own case, are rare before 1550.

Napery played a far more important role than is generally realized in the arrangement of the sixteenth-century dining-table. Damask napkins and table-cloths were expensive items to be treasured and prized and this reverence may help explain why it is rare to discover references to formal dinners where glasses or cups were being placed or indeed left on the table in the manner that is common today. To reduce the risk of staining the cloth, the vessels for wine or beer were usually filled at the sideboard, away from the table. The base of the glass was then thoroughly dried and brought on a waiter or salver to the person requesting it. The footman waited for the drink to be consumed and afterwards took the glass or beaker back to the sideboard where he would rinse, dry and place it back on display.

Such a system can only function, of course, if there are sufficient servants to attend the dinner guests. In England, the development of a country-house system, where large numbers of dependencies were associated with the estate, meant there was usually a plentiful supply of servants who could fulfil these functions.

By the end of the sixteenth century the most significant development taking place on the dining-room table was the replacement of the bread trencher with ones made of wood or metal.

A 1594 inventory for Sir William Fairfax at Gilling Castle lists amongst the contents:

Pantrye
Item V dozin Trenchers xs
Item one dazin rounde Trenchers ijs

White Plate
Item one dossen of silver plates cont V^{xx} xj ounces
Item ij dossen of silver sponnes cont XLiX ounces
Item one spice box with a sponne cont XV ounces[5]

The Gilling trenchers were made of maple[6] and a clear distinction is noted in the 'pantrye' between the normal rectangular shape and the round examples probably used for the dessert. These 'rroundels', 'trencher plates', or 'posies' as they were often referred to, were charmingly decorated on one side with flowers, animals and improving texts. A fine example in Bill Brown's collection is inscribed with the verse:

The lion snard the mouse entreats for help – the mouse the fetters freates.
Meaning – the men of degree by poorer men released may be.[7]

Sizes varied in diameter from 12cm to 18cm but they are still quite small, being only intended as receptacles for prepared food. The silver plates in the Gilling inventory, however, weigh some 42 ozs each and were probably intended as chargers or servers. Small 'posies' could also be made from sugar and a rare shaped and decorated example is illustrated in a painting by Gaspar van der Hocke, dated 1615.[8] Netherlands paintings are our best source of European table settings for the early part of the seventeenth century. That they depict real objects must be beyond question, the only problem remaining is, has the artist rearranged everything for his or her convenience? One painter who seems more reliable than others is Clara Peeters, working in Flanders from *c.*1615 to *c.*1640.[9] Her settings are extraordinary compilations of food and objects meticulously recorded in marvellous detail. Tables of the wealthy are shown laden with produce from home and abroad, leaving little space for the participant to fit his plate onto the table. Other artists show the table arranged in this way and it is perhaps one reason why the napkin has moved away from the left hand side of the plate and starts to appear on the plate, often folded to enclose a bread roll. It may also be a valiant attempt to keep the bread warm but, whatever the reason, Peeters is utterly convincing and achieves what she set out to do, to appeal to our sensory and culinary appetites.

Other artists made a speciality of these table settings[11] and a study of their works shows the spoon moving away from the side of the plate and taking up its position next to the pie. One such detail is illustrated by van der Hocke[12] where the pie case is used as a form of tureen-like container and the spoons stand guard at the entrance to the 'temple'. There are several toothpicks deployed about the table and these were usually made from rosemary,[13] presumably because the scent would help to freshen the breath.

Personal hygiene was becoming increasingly important at both individual and group level throughout the seventeenth century and had a fundamental effect on the evolution of dining practices. Compared to the Middle Ages, the standards of delicacy required in any given social situation had increased dramatically. 'It is very impolite,' wrote Antoine de Courtin in 1672, 'to touch anything greasy, a sauce or syrup etc., with your fingers, apart from the fact that it obliges you to commit two or three more improper acts. One is to wipe your hand frequently on your serviette and to soil it like a kitchen cloth, so that those who see you wipe your mouth will feel nauseated. Another is to wipe your fingers on your bread, which again is very improper. The third is to lick them, which is the height of impropriety.'[14]

The German philosopher Norbert Elias argues that it was this gradual refinement in manners and civilized behaviour which gave rise to the common usage of the fork.[15] Such a movement would certainly have been a significant factor, but there were other events which must have played their part. The return of Charles II to the throne, for example, bringing with him a long exposure to European dining practices; the dramatic rise in wealth and consumerism; increasing trade with the Far East; and a resurgence in manuals of instruction are just a few of the other contributing factors. What they were all doing, of course, was to help ritualize and refine our so-called 'principles of politeness' and fleshing out new codified behaviour patterns.

In 1682 Giles Rose, one-time master cook in Charles II's kitchen, published his translation of the anonymous 1661 French tome *L'Ecole parfaite des officiers de bouche*.[16] He included the duties of senior members of the household and there are some curious divisions of labour. The butler, for example, was responsible for the carving of fruit into fanciful shapes but, primarily, he carried out the duties we have come to expect of this post.

Rose's description of the presentation of a seventeenth-century dining-room has not been published in recent times and is worthy of repetition:

> The hour of Dinner or Supper being now come [presumably around 3 p.m.], he and his helper or servant, takes the basket into the hall or chambers where they are to eat; not forgetting the pepper-box, and cruet of vinegar both furnished, the one carrying one, the other with them into the room.
>
> And so soon as you are come into the room set down the basket, and so begin to cover the side-table first, with a clean cloth, and then set on your plate; first your bason and ewer; and your flagons ranged against the Tapestry-hanging, mingled one amongst the other; then underneath compose another range of essay (sic) cups, sugarcastars, and glasses with the feet downward, and upon each of them put an Essay Cup, or cover over them.
>
> This done, the Butler begins to cover the table thus, first the table cloth, then the salts, and the riders for plates, or *outer-mese,* then the plates with the coat of arms towards the middle of the table, so many as are necessary, but let them not touch the edge of the table by three or four fingers. At the right hand of each plate place a knife, with the edge towards the plate, then the spoons, the brim or edge of the

spoon downwards, with forks; but be sure not to cross or lay them one on the other, then the Bread upon the plate, and the napkin upon the bread, and so much for covering a table.[17]

The concentration of all cutlery on the right-hand side of the plate (with spoon and fork face down) is a typical French trait.[18] The left hand was used to hold the napkin up to the throat whilst the right hand selects the required item of cutlery to cut or transfer food from plate to mouth. It would be interesting to determine just how much influence Rose's publication had on English presentation at table and whether his manual provided a further impetus for the popularization of forks in England at this time.

Rose also recommends that the number of plates should far exceed the number of persons present and spare plates be formed in piles along the side table with napkins on top folded in *baston rompu* or broken staff, 'and over this another or more, if need so require, unfolded, which serves to wipe the hands when washed.'

Folding napery into fanciful designs was a further innovation for Rose's publication and his instructions were supposed to help the reader create shapes like 'cockleshells, double melons, pheasants and a dog with a choker about its neck.' This section of the book takes its inspiration from an earlier Italian text of 1639 published by Mathias Giegher[19] but Rose did not include the original drawings showing what these creations should look like. The results and instructions are not that easy to follow and it seems doubtful, therefore, that this form of conceit was popular at the table of the late-seventeenth-century English aristocrat.

Rose also alludes to the early use of porcelain. 'After the Butler has thus covered his table,' he notes, 'let him now begin to dish up his fruit either in Plate or Cheyney, or such as he finds in the house ... and to make use of a three pointed fork to present them with.'[20] Finding Chinese plates in country-house stores at this time, in sufficient quantities to serve a large meal, would be rare. Imports to Britain and elsewhere had been sporadic in the last quarter of the seventeenth century and it was not until the safe arrival of the *Dorothy* in 1696 that regular supplies of porcelain plates were made available to the public at large. These brightly coloured imports caused a sensation, stimulating great demand and the Chinese potters were able to include the family crest at only a modest extra charge. Plain unadorned silver plates were relegated to the buffet for display during the first quarter of the eighteenth century, whilst Chinese porcelain dinner plates took pride of place at the rich man's table.

Another significant transformation was the development of flint glass by George Ravenscroft during the 1670s. This heavy 'metal' replaced the imports of rather fragile soda glass with a more robust and inexpensive product and proved the start of English domination of world glass markets which lasted for the next 150 years. There were large quantities of glass produced and purchased for the country-house estate[21] throughout the eighteenth century, but wine and beer glasses still do not seem to have claimed their permanent place on the table at formal dinner parties.

The layout in the centre of the table changed dramatically from the seventeenth century onwards.

Medieval service, with its buffet-like courses of many dishes followed by a void at the close of the meal formed the basis of court dining protocol throughout Europe until the middle of the nineteenth century. More strictly defined rules for this kind of arrangement were imposed at the court of Louis XIV, leading to a modified form of medieval-style service known as *le grand couvert*. The pre-eminence of French food during the seventeenth and eighteenth centuries led to the adoption of this *modus operandi* at every other European court and it became internationally known as *service à la française*. A meal of this kind consisted of two courses served from the kitchen and a third course from the *office* (pantry or confectionery), called *le fruit* or *le dessert*, rather than *la voidée*. Each course usually consisted of the same number of dishes arranged in perfect symmetry, though there was room for variation. A typical first course of an important meal *à la française* might start with a choice of four different soups *(grosses entrées)*, accompanied by four *hors-d'oeuvre*, two fish dishes, four main meat dishes *(relevés* or *grosses pièces)*, twelve side dishes *(entrées)* and four cold dishes *(pièces froides)*. The second course would consist of a variety of roasts *(rôts)* and *entremets* (light dishes, both sweet and savoury). The third course or dessert was frequently laid out on a different table in a separate room and consisted of seasonal fruit, cheese, ices and confectionery.

Although *service à la française* was a visually sumptuous way of dining, it was wasteful and impractical and gradually started to be replaced in France during the early nineteenth century by *service à la russe*. This much simpler approach, in which the dishes arrived at table one after the other, rather than in two large mixed buffet-like courses, ensured that the diners could enjoy the hot dishes at the correct temperature and afforded plenty of room in the middle of the table for decorations. It was apparently introduced into France by Prince Kourakine, the ambassador of Tsar Alexander I, but did not become widespread until the Second Empire, when it was popularized by Urbain Dubois and Emile Bernard, chefs to William and Augusta of Prussia. Their remarkable illustrated book of recipes *La Cuisine Classique* (Paris 1864) was the first work fully to explain *service à la russe*. Dubois was also responsible for its adoption at the English court through his *Artistic Cookery* (London 1870), another lavishly illustrated work with sample dinners *à la russe* for royal occasions and ball suppers of up to 5000 covers. Dubois also discusses *service à l'anglaise,* an English arrangement in which there were two separate courses served on the main table, with removes such as roasts and ham on a side table.[22]

By the second quarter of the eighteenth century, it is recorded that cutlery in England is now being presented on either side of the plate, the fork to the left, with knife and spoon on the right. Fresh cutlery (spoons and forks still presented face down) are brought on at each change of course, but exactly how this arrangement came about is still not entirely clear.

A French visitor to England in 1784, François de la Rochefoucauld, offers a useful contrast between French and English practices:

> I do not like to prick my mouth or my tongue with these little sharp steel tridents which are generally used in England ... I know that this kind of fork is only intended for serving and fixing the pieces of meat while they are cut, and that the English knives being very large and rounded at the point, serve the same purpose to which forks in France are applied, that is, to carry food to the mouth ... The fork seizes, the knife cuts, and the pieces may be carried to the mouth with either. The motion is quick and precise ... In France .. when meat is cut to pieces, the knife is laid down idle on the right side of the plate, while the fork passes from left to right.[23]

Napkins now start the meal on the left-hand side of the setting again, presumably to allow the new-fashioned porcelain plates to be shown off to advantage.

A further innovation at this time was the introduction of specific plates for soup. Lord Fairfax at Gilling paid £88 for '12 Soop Plates' from the great rococo silversmith Fredrick Kandler.[24] John Trusler explains how these would be presented: 'If there is a soup for dinner ... to lay each person a flat plate, and a soup-plate over it, a napkin, knife, fork and spoon.'[25]

Spoons used for soup did not have a round bowl as we know them today (this was an American invention of the 1860s) but normal table spoons were employed for this purpose. Also the presentation of the soup plate in this way was only for show. Each plate would, of course, be taken away to be filled and brought back to the table by the footman.

At the beginning of the nineteenth century the changes in service had dramatic effects on how a table was laid out. Many of the dishes were now being presented on sideboards, leaving more space available on the main table for plateaux or centrepieces and also the concept of self-sufficiency had become a more acceptable mode of behaviour even at formal dinners. This resulted in more and more of the equipage needed to complete the meal being on hand for individual convenience. Thomas Cosnett's *Footman's Directory*, first published in 1823,[26] explains that one wine glass, a glass cooler and decanters can be placed directly on the dinner table and that 'for convenience', he says, 'let the soup plates be all put at the bottom of the table, a little to the left of the person who helps it, and close to the tureen.'

Cosnett was still recommending, however, that cutlery be changed at each course and it was not until the end of the nineteenth century that Mrs Beeton and others[27] were illustrating complete sets of cutlery, ranging outwards on either side of the plate, sufficient for some six or seven courses and with upwards of five or six different types of wine and water glass waiting close-by to be used throughout the meal.

Most of us will recognize elements of this presentation in the 'self-service' dinner parties of today and it will be interesting to observe how we as a society respond to changes in culinary and social behaviour, throughout the twenty-first century and how this will manifest itself in the presentation of the modern British dining-room.

NOTES

[1] Illustrated in Brown, P. (ed.), *British Cutlery, an Illustrated History of Design, Evolution and Use*, London, 2001, p. 68.
[2] Marchese, P., *L'invenzione della Forchetta:* Rome, 1989, pp. 80–1, 84.
[3] Mitchell, D., 'The Clerk's View', in Brown, *British Cutlery*, p. 23–9.
[4] Furnival, F.J., ed. *The Babees Book*, EETS No.32, London, 1868. This includes the John Russell, *Book of Nurture*, pp. 130–1, 197–228.
[5] Peacock, E., 'Inventories made for Sir William and Sir Thomas Fairfax. Knights of Walton and Gilling Castle', *Archaeologia* (1884) pp. 124–31.
[6] Ibid., p. 137, inventory at Walton, 1624.
  'In the little Chamber at the Great Chamber end
  in that p[r]esse 12 dozen of maple trenchers never yet used, 2 dozen of trencher plates.'
[7] Brown, P. (ed.), *British Cutlery*, p. 82.
[8] Brown, P. and Day, I., *Pleasures of the Table,* York, 1997.
[9] Decoteau, P., *Clara Peeters,* Lingen, 1992.
[10] Breusen, P. (ed.), *L'Art Gourmand*, Brussels, 1996, pp. 56–7.
[11] Peter Claesz (1597–1661), Lambert Doomer (1624–1700), Jacob Foppens Van Es (c.1596 1660), Frans Francken the younger (1578–1628), Dirk Hals (1591–1656), Gverrit Willemsz Heda (*fl.*1642–1700), Hieronymous Janssens (c.1624 1693), Roelof Koets (c.1592–1655), Sumon Luttiehuys (c.1610–1667), Jan Olis (c.1610–1672), Abraham de Pape (1620–1666), Peter Gerritsz van Roestraten (1627–1698), Juriaen van Streeck (c.1632–1687), Jan Jansz Treck (c.1606–1652), Jan Jansz den Uyl (1595–1640), Jan Jansz van de Velde (*fl.*1619–1664). I am grateful to Johnny van Haeften for allowing me to consult his extensive archive.
[12] Brown, P., *British Cutlery*, p. 45.

[13] *The Goodman of Paris,* trans, E. Power, New York, 1928, p. 299.
[14] Courtin, A. de, *Nouveau traite de la civilité,* Paris, 1672.
[15] Elias, Norbert, *The Civilising Process,* published posthumously in English in 1996. I am grateful to Richard Wendorf for drawing this to my attention.
[16] Rose, C., *A perfect School of Instructions for the Officers of the Mouth,* London, 1682.
[17] Ibid., pp. 90–1.
[18] Brown, P. & Day, I., *Pleasures of the Table,* York, 1997.
[19] Giegher, M., *Trattato sul modo di piegare, Li tre trattati,* Padova, 1639.
[20] *A perfect School of Instructions,* pp. 86, 93.
[21] Brown, P. & Schwatz, M., *Come Drink the Bowl Dry,* York, 1996, pp. 69–70, 92–102.
[22] I am grateful to Ivan Day for his thoughts in this matter.
[23] Rochefoucauld, F. de la., *A Frenchman in England, 1784,* ed. Marchand, J. (1933).
[24] Northallerton Records Office (Newburgh papers) ZDF,

'HC4 BO.[E] of Fredrick Kandler, Goldsmith against St. James's Church, Jermain Street

	oz		sd	£	s	d
To 12 Soop Plates	244:15 @		7:2	87	14	0
Engra crests & corots				0	12	0

London, Jan 8.1754

[25] Trusler, Rev. J., *The Honours of the Table,* London, 1788.
[26] Cosnett, T., *The Footman's Directory,* London, 1st edn, 1823, revised and enlarged 1825.
[27] Beeton, I. M., *The Book of Household Management,* London, 1881 and revisions to 1901. Also Murray, A., *The Domestic Oracle,* London, c.1850.

The Flattest Meal – Pancakes in the Dutch Lowlands[1]

Janny de Moor

Pancakes are an enormously popular meal in the Netherlands, not only for children, but for all who feel young at heart. The easy-to-make pancake was and is an ideal main dish for parties at home. It is one of the first recipes Dutch children learn to make for themselves.[2] From a culinary point of view, making pancakes may seem all too ordinary to devote a paper to. You can make them with the left hand, so to say. But as the piano concertos for the left hand by Ravel and Prokofiev have demonstrated, outstanding work for the left hand requires a lot of virtuosity.

Perhaps the best testimony to the Dutch addiction to pancakes comes from the far north of the country. A proverb in the province of Groningen runs, 'It's a pity to spoil a pancake for an egg'.[3] Only those who know that the people of Groningen have the same reputation as the Scots in the United Kingdom will understand that this implies an amazing willingness to abandon one's staunchest principles for a good pancake.

Pancakes are not merely a festive meal at home in the Netherlands. At present there are about 110 specialized pancake-restaurants in the country which means that you may find at least one of them in even the smallest town. Most are decorated in a cosy, unpretentious way and offer a wide choice of pancakes at relatively moderate prices. A special guide is issued every two years to enable the true devotees to pick a fine pancake-restaurant wherever they happen to be.[4]

It is not known when the first pancakes were offered for sale outside the Dutch home. Surely much earlier than some seem to think.[5] In any case, when in 1848 the railway station which connected Flemish Duinkerken with Paris was opened, a report about this event states that a 'pannekoukehuys' (pancake-house) was not lacking of course.[6] Probably this was a movable stall. Jan ter Gouw relates that the cheerful woman *Geertje* selling doughnuts at the 'snackssquare' in Amsterdam at the end of the nineteenth century also sold pancakes, as the following lines from the song she used to sing testify: 'I also have pancakes, / with cheese or bacon, whatever you like. / Come my dearest little gourmet, / don't wait until later.'[7]

In a painting by François Cautaerts (1810–1881) an old man invites passers-by from his shop-window to buy a pancake apparently baked by the smiling woman in the background (Frontispiece). Several older Dutch paintings show people baking pancakes in surroundings suggesting an inn or a specialized bakery.[8] A burlesque published in 1633 features a man selling 'flensjes' – a fine type of pancake – in the street.[9] If the flattest meal in the Dutch lowlands has such a rich past and present, it seems worthwhile to retrace its history.

What is a pancake?

Before we can do that, however, we must know what exactly a pancake is. Is the Arab bread called *chutz*, and which others in the Mediterranean call *pitta*, a pancake? I think it is: if baked not in an oven but on a griddle or a kind of upturned metal 'wok', as I have often seen it made in the Arab world. It is just as supple[10] as a pancake, even though it is made of a thinly spread dough and not from a batter. Is an omelette a pancake? It surely is cooked in a frying-pan and can also be folded over, but its substance is made of beaten eggs alone, with no flour added.[11] So I don't think it qualifies as a pancake.

Alan Davidson's unsurpassed *Oxford Companion to Food* has by far the best definition of a pancake, 'a flat cake made from a batter of flour, eggs, and milk, and fried in a shallow pan or cooked on a greased griddle'.[12] Davidson admits that the distinction between pancakes and griddle bread is sometimes not so clear and that thicker pancakes, like the Scottish drop scones, are known. Moreover, it should be noted that not all pancakes do contain milk and eggs, and that very often other ingredients are added, like melted butter, bacon, cheese, various fruits and spices.

I therefore propose a minimalist approach: *a pancake is a supple cake baked on a very hot surface from a poured batter or a thinly spread dough*. All kinds of flour may be used, but flour is an indispensable ingredient in any batter or dough. Leaven, bicarbonate of soda, butter, eggs and a great variety of flavour-enhancing additives are possible, but none of these is essential. The hot surface may be a shallow metal pan, but also a griddle, an upturned 'wok', or some kind of heat-resistant earthenware. The pancake is usually fairly flat and round, but it may well have the shape of a small cushion, like the Dutch 'poffertje', or may be thickish, like the Scots pancake. Its main substance is always supple, however.[13] Only the edges may be crisp or crusty.

Some history

Under this definition pancakes are probably one of the earliest meals eaten in the Netherlands. The more or less flat surface of the pan allowed for maximum exposure to the heat of an open fire and the simplicity of the basic recipe made it an ideal dish to be prepared under all circumstances. The oldest Dutch frying-pans date from the eleventh century.[14] Marine archaeologists have found many earthenware frying-pans in shipwrecks excavated after the 'impoldering' of the Zuiderzee, now the IJsselmeer, the lake in the middle of the Netherlands. These shallow pans had a slightly rising thick earthenware handle and date from the fourteenth to nineteenth centuries. They were apparently used on the hearth in the galley. From 1600 onwards, iron and copper pans are also found in these wrecks, but the earthenware pan remained in use at least until 1900.[15]

The oldest Dutch cookery book, first printed around 1514, contains several recipes for pancakes which are alternately called 'panckoecken' and 'struyven'.[16] Other sixteenth- through eighteenth-century cookery books also testify to the popularity of pancakes.[17] At first the pan is simply called 'panne', but the composite term 'coekenpan' is attested in a record of a partition of an estate in Kampen dating from the year 1635.[18] Baking pancakes in an iron pan is depicted in many pictures and paintings from the sixteenth century onwards.[19] Almost invariably it is a woman who is doing the job.[20] Eduard Trautscholdt has demonstrated that the theme became so popular through a painting Adriaen Brouwer made in Amsterdam between 1625–1627 that it was imitated by none less than Jan van de Velde, Rembrandt van Rhyn, Frans Hals, Jan Steen, Gabriel Metsu.[21] However, the woman with a white headscarf to protect her hair from the smoke is already present in a painting called 'De Pannekoeckebackerij' by Pieter Aertsen (1508–1575) and she is apparently using an earthenware pan similar to the ones found by the archaeologists.[22] In this painting, and many others,[23] children are feasting on the pancakes together with adults. The pancakes usually fill the entire bottom of the pan, but in some cases three or four smaller pancakes are baked at the same time.[24] The Dutch still call such smaller cakes 'drie-in-de-pan' (three-in-the-pan). All these pictures show people eating the pancakes by hand, as cutlery was still unusual.

Occasions

For festive occasions a meal of pancakes was an ideal solution. The amount to be made was flexible, the baking on open fire created a natural centre of companionship in which all generations could participate and ordinary pancakes were inexpensive. As in Britain, Shrove Tuesday is Pancake Day in Holland. Old folksongs testify to this custom, e.g.

> Give me a pancake from the pan,
> Ho man ho!
> Shrove Tuesday is coming,
> so my lord, so![25]

The servants got pancakes and wafers as a special treat,

> It is Shrove Tuesday now,
> he will get something from his master's table.
> The one a warm pancake,
> the other a tasty wafer.[26]

In Tilburg, in the province of Brabant, they sang,

> Darling, it's Shrove Tuesda:y,
> I'm not coming home before midnight.
> Midnight in the moonshine,
> when father and mother have gone to bed ...
> We're going to clank the rumbling pots.
> Here a chair and there a chair,
> a cushion on every seat.
> Between your nose and your chin
> a bacon-pancake will surely fit in.[27]

On Twelfth Day (Epiphany) a joker-king was appointed by lot and the first pancakes were baked. The following period was the high season of 'kermissen' (carnival fairs) at which wafers and pancakes were consumed in great quantities.[28] On Shrove Tuesday the 'king' was the key figure in the festivities which included liberal eating and drinking. A picture in an almanach of 1653 shows him merry-making with friends while a woman on the left is baking pancakes over an open fire.[29] The oldest Dutch cookery book proves that people did not stop eating pancakes after Shrove Tuesday. During Lent it was permitted to continue with them. The batter for these pancakes was sometimes mixed with raisins, apple-cubes or pike's roe.[30]

Of course pancakes were also baked for other occasions, for example at the end of the hop harvest in the province of Gelderland;[31] or at the end of the potatoe and grain harvests in the province of Brabant.[32] On Christmas Eve – in the local dialect of Drente called 'Vretaomke' or 'Dikkevretsaovend' (blowout-eve) – pancakes with sliced sausages were served. The neighbours who had helped out with a childbirth were invited for a special 'wievenmoal' (women's meal) in which pancakes were one of the main dishes.[33] At New Year's Eve, pancakes were baked from Amsterdam[34] to Limburg.[35] On a Sunday night, a boyfriend in Friesland was treated to a pancake with butter and sugar if the girl's family deemed him acceptable. If not, he had to do with a pancake baked in lard and sprinkled with treacle.[36] When it came to a wedding, the Frisian village women

Pancakes on Shrove Tuesday, Comptoir Almanach *1653*.

marched to the bride's home with a very large richly salted pancake, also sprinkled with sugar, the so-called 'solte koek', a symbol of marriage.[37]

Pancakes were also eaten as a first or second breakfast. This custom is attested for the sandy coast of Holland, for Brabant, Gelderland, Drente and Groningen.[38] In the province of Drente, where people rose at five in the morning they ate a slice of home-baked bread as a first breakfast. Then, at eight or nine, they got pancakes, if possible with some rashers,[39] especially during the strenuous haymaking season.[40] In some parts of Drente where they ate pancakes as the first breakfast, the wife had to rise an hour earlier than everybody to bake pancakes of buckwheat, the poor man's wheat. A wry saying from that region runs: 'If you can't bake pancakes, you'll never get a good husband.'[41] One may say therefore that, as in Brittany,[42] the buckwheat pancake was the daily bread of the poorer regions of the Netherlands.

It will always remain a bone of contention, I'm afraid, who brought the pancake breakfast to North America — the English or the Dutch – so I must express myself cautiously. It is sometimes assumed that Dutchmen who between 1609 and 1674 settled in 'New Netherland', the area between New England and Virginia, introduced their traditional buckwheat *pannenkoeken* breakfast to the North American menu.[43]

Pancakes are still a favourite dish at children's parties. I myself vividly recall that on that special occasion, the birthday boy or girl was allowed to stand on the table to write his/her initials on the first pancake with treacle from a spoon held as high as he/she could reach. After this solemn ceremony a frenzy of eating started, mostly in deep silence, with wary glances at the rapidly lowering pile. Every child wanted to stuff as many pancakes as he or she could hold. One of my girlfriends had a 'method' for this: she hopped around the table every now and then, convinced that this would create more room in her tummy.

Accordingly, many old Dutch children's songs praise the makers of pancakes, invariably women – a clear case of careful preservation of a social prejudice throughout the generations.

> Miller mill your mill,
> mill a bag of flour for the little one.
> Mother will bake pancakes then
> which will slip down the little one's throat.
> Treacle, treacle, treacle with flour,
> that slips down the little one's throat so easily.[44]

> Elly Feederelly, put your cloggies by the fire.
> Mother bakes pancakes, but the flour is so dear.
> Ting-a-ling-a-ling-a pancake, flour with raisins,
> Ting-a-ling-a-ling-a pancake, come visit us![45]

The little ladies are deliberately encouraged to follow their mother's example,

> First a little flour,
> then a little milk.
> Are we ten? I'll bake two for all!
> Twenty tasty flapjacks in the pan
> on my little black cooker. Be sure I can do it!
>
> Then lay the table, put the plates ready.
> Sugar in the dish, Oh boy what fun!
> Let me taste first, as mother always does.
> And now I'm going to bake – the batter is good![46]

Another children's song keeps alive the memory of a pancake-baking session that ended in disaster,

> Once upon a time there was a woman
> who wanted to bake pancakes. But the flour refused to rise,
> and the pan toppled over,
> and the cakes were bent,
> and the man's name was Jan van Gijzen.[47]

Nobody knows who 'Jan van Gijzen' was. There is a dark suspicion that he left his unnamed wife simply because she was such a clumsy cook. Is this also the reason why so many women depicted as bakers of pancakes in paintings and etchings are quite old? They at least did not run such a risk and could take a flop philosophically, as an old Dutch proverb states, '"One cannot always be lucky," said granny, and the pancake dropped in the ashes.'[48]

Finally I want to share with you a kind of early Dutch children's 'rap' which was not sung, but said rhythmically by groups on outings by train. Its onomatopoeic nature renders translation hardly possible, but I will give it a try,

> Slowly: *Soup – soup – soup*
> Ever faster: *Potatoes–veggies–meat / Potatoes–veggies–meat / Potatoes–veggies–meat*
> High: *Sheeeeeeeeeeeee!*[49]
> Very fast: *Thick and fatty pancakes / Thick and fatty pancakes / Thick and fatty pancakes*
> Slowing: *Pudding–pud–ding– pud–ding*
> Drawn out: *Ice*[50]

It is a pity that such a typical dream-menu for children – three desserts, with pancakes in the place of honour! – is doomed to sink into oblivion together with their beloved steam locomotive.

Types

Pancakes are often seen as childish food and have a reputation of being dull from a culinary point of view. The nineteenth-century Dutch writer Potgieter sneered at eaters of pancakes who would have no idea of the delicacies he himself was able to afford.[51] A proverb from the province of Groningen states, 'A poor man's pancake and a rich man's illness you can smell from a distance'.[52] But a poet from the province of Limburg counters this with,

> I leave the lord his dainty bits,
> lobster and eel, tench and pike.
> I for my part opt for some wedges
> of a tender buckwheat cake.[53]

Of course everything depends on what kind of pancake you are eating. It does make a difference whether you are served a flaming Crêpe Suzette or a hefty Galette Bretonne. The buckwheat pancake itself is a very simple kind of meal indeed. But, as we have seen already, the Dutch upgraded it from the earliest times by using wheat instead of buckwheat or by adding extra fillings, some of them quite expensive.

There were countless ways to vary the recipe. A cursory reading of pre-nineteenth-century cookbooks yielded an amazing number of possibilities. One could vary with regard to:

The flour: buckwheat groats, buckwheat flour, millet, wheat flour.

The liquids: water, milk, cream, melted butter, wine.[54]

The leavening agents: no leavening at all, or (with wheat flour) yeast, or bicarbonate of soda.

The additives: no additives to the batter; or taste- and consistency-improving additives, such as eggs, bread crumbs; sweet additives, such as cubes or slices of apples and pears, cherries, blueberries; spicy additives, such as cinnamon; herbs (see below); salty additives, such as salt, pike's roe, (smoked) bacon, slices of cheese or sausages.

The grease: no grease at all; or lard, rape oil, butter.

The mode of preparation: the normal technique was to spread out the batter evenly over the entire bottom of the pan. Already the oldest Dutch cookery book contains a detailed description of how to achieve this with the help of a funnel.[55] But since this extra tool is never seen in ancient pancake-baking scenes, it may be assumed that most bakers mastered the art of letting the batter run out evenly in the pan itself. A buckwheat batter with eggs could be handled in a special way to obtain very thin unleavened pancakes called 'flensjes'.[56] Smaller but somewhat thicker pancakes which were baked three or four together ('drie-in-de-pan') required even more dexterity. Finally the Dutch used special pans with shallow round cavities to prepare 'poffertjes', also called 'bollebuisjes': small cushions of leavened batter each baked in a separate hollow or 'eye'.[57]

The filling: no filling; or extra melted butter on the hot surface of the pancake or *poffer*; sweet fillings, such as treacle, sugar, rhubarb, custard, various jams; salty fillings, such as minced meat, cheese, shrimps, fish.

Any combination of these is possible. Small wonder that some present-day Dutch pancake-restaurants boast more than 200 varieties on their menus. One of the most interesting recipes is the Flemish 'Cruydtcoeck', 'Kroetkoek' or '(Tente)groenkoek', a vegetarian pancake in which young leaves of tansy are mixed with the batter. It is supposed to be effective against worms and would stimulate blood circulation in the abdomen, resulting in a very satisfactory love-life. This type of pancake is already mentioned in a work by the Mechlin botanist Rembert Dodoens (1517–1585) and the Flemish still have a confrerie devoted to its promotion.[58] It is this pancake which I have selected to bring along to the Symposium and for which I give a slightly modernized recipe here.

Kroetkoek
For 8 pancakes (diameter 20 cm)
125 g wheat flour • 125 g buckwheat flour
1 sachet dried yeast (7 g) • 500 ml lukewarm milk
1 egg • 1 tablespoon sugar
5 g salt • 3 tbs chopped chervil • 3 tbs chopped chives
2 tbs chopped tansy leaves (if unavailable: chopped sage)
butter for baking and covering

1. Mix flour and yeast. Make a well in which you pour small dashes of milk, stirring, and finally beating the mixture well until it becomes a smooth batter. Whisk the egg through the batter, then also the sugar, salt and herbs. Let rise for an hour under a cover.

2. Heat butter in the pan, stir batter and pour 1 dl from a ladle, turning the pan until the bottom is covered entirely. Bake until the upper side is dry and small holes have formed. Turn and bake the other side a light brown too.

3. Eat with melted salted butter and/or treacle. A vegetarian friend of mine always drinks champagne with this *Kroetkoek,* I suspect in anticipation of what she hopes will follow. But 'Brugse Tripel' (a strong sweetish beer from the city of Bruges) is definitely in better accordance with the place of origin of this recipe.

Epilogue

As we have seen, a flat taste is not what characterizes the flattest meal of the Dutch Lowlands. Yet all the enhancements that have been thought up through the ages are not essential to make a pancake unforgettable. Allow me to illustrate this with a moving story my husband told me. He was nine years old during the winter of starvation which as a result of World War II hit the western part of our country in 1944–45. To alleviate the extreme shortages, the Allied Forces started the first food drops in close proximity to built-up areas on 29 April 1945.

> We all ducked away from the windows when we heard several Allied bombers flying in so low and close. Suddenly we saw sacks instead of bombs raining down in a nearby meadow and when nothing more happened we all ran out to fetch them. I was lucky enough to get hold of a large bale which I protected with my body when immediately after a host of adults came storming on and tried to snatch my prize from me. I could not prevent them from opening the sack which appeared to contain flour. Fortunately an authoritative voice cut in, 'No fellows,

this sack belongs to that boy. Let his family distribute whatever they can spare among the neighbours. They will know where it is needed most.'

Soon after my mother arrived with a (tyreless) bike and the sack was transported home. My parents invited some people to take their share of this gift from heaven. That night we huddled in the twilight around a small emergency stove (*Mayo-kacheltje*). It was fed with splinters of an inside door which we had started sacrificing long ago. Its smoke went up directly into the room. We had no gas, no coals, no logs, no electricity. We had no butter or vegetable oil. No milk or sugar. No yeast or baking powder. Only water. How he managed it is still a mystery to me, but 'Dean' – a young man in hiding with us – baked an enormous, very thick pancake of the flour. It was so delicious! I can still recall its rather dry and smoky taste. It was the best pancake I ever ate. We and our neighbours feasted on such pancakes for more than a week. We called them affectionately 'our bath mats'.

My husband's late mother kept the sack. It was originally meant for Portland Cement. She embroidered part of it to commemorate the Allied food drop which no doubt saved the lives of some of my dearest. I have brought it with me to show you.

NOTES

[1] For their assistance with the research for this paper I want to thank Dr Hans van der Hoeven, Keeper of the Culinary Collection of the Koninklijke Bibliotheek, Den Haag, Drs Lina van der Wolde, researcher with the Atlas van Stolk, Rotterdam; Mrs Ingrid van Beest, J. Koster and F. Meijer, Bibliotheek Rijksbureau Kunsthistorische Documentatie, Den Haag; Christel van Hees, Afdeling Kunstnijverheid and F. de Jong, Afdeling Beelddocumentatie Museum Boijmans van Beumngen, Rotterdam; Drs J.N. Lanting, Groninger Instituut voor Archeologie; Drs J. van Doesburg, Periode Specialist Rijksdienst Oudheidkundig Bodemonderzoek, Amersfoort; Drs H. de Groot, Archaeologist of the town of Utrecht; Drs J. A.G. Veerkamp, Archeologie Amsterdam; Drs K. Vlierman and Dabna van der Poel, Nederlands Instituut voor Scheeps-en Onderwater Archeologie, Lelystad; Mrs Ita Gunnink-Tulp, Kampen.
[2] Unfortunately, as with so many other popular dishes, Dutch supermarkets are taking away this pleasure by offering prebaked pancakes to lazy people.
[3] 'Man mout gain pankouk bedarven om 'n ai.'
[4] *Pannenkoek-Doe-Boek 2000–2001*, 12th edition, Odijk: Vereniging van erkende pannen-koekenrestaurants, 2000.
[5] According to Marianne Moonen & Riek van Rijn, *Neerlands Dis*, Utrecht/Antwerpen: Het Spectrum, 1983, p. 124, the first pancake-restaurants would have been founded in the fifties of the twentieth century.
[6] J. ter Gouw, *De Volksvermaken,* Haarlem: Erven Boon, 1871 p. 244.

7 *Ookheb ik Koekebates / Zoo asje wil met Kaos of Spek; / Kom lieve kleine Lelkerbek / Wagt nou maar niet tot strakjes! (Geertje met de olyloeken,* in Gouw, J. ter, *op. cit.*, p. 659.) The antiquated Dutch 'koekebakjes' is an alternative term for 'pancakes'.

8 E.g. Pieter Aertsen, 'The Pancake Bakery' ('De Pannekoeckebackerij' 1560, Museum Boijmans van Beuningen, Rotterdam). In a painting by Jan Steen, 'de Koekenbakster', a child hands over a coin to a woman baking pancakes in the open air (1625/6–1679, Collection Goudstikker, Memorial Museum, University of Rochester, N.Y.). This too suggests commercial exploitation of the pancake.

9 A. van Mildert, *Boertige Clucht van Sr. Groengeel,* Rotterdam, 1633, p.5.

10 The suppleness is taken into account in the Dutch definition of pancake found in G. Geerts & H. Heestermans (eds), *Van Dale Groot Woordenboek der Nederlandse Taal,* 12de dr, deel J-R, Utrecht/Antwerpen: Van Dale Lexicografie, 1992, p. 2223: 'platte, dunne, ronde oprolbare (meel) koek die in een pan gebakken words' (a flat, thin, circular *rollable* (flour) cake which is baked in a pan). Contrast the definition of 'pancake' in J.A. Simpson & E.S.C. Weiner (eds), *The Oxford English Dictionary,* 2nd ed., vol 11, Oxford: Clarendon Press, 1989, p. 125: 'A thin flat cake, made of batter fried in a pan' which does not reckon with the pancake's malleability, ignores pancakes made of a supple dough and might even include brittle biscuits, like the Jewish *matzos.*

11 Cf. L. Brown (ed.), *The Shorter Oxford English Dictionary on Historical Principles,* Vol. 2, Oxford: Clarendon Press, 1993, p. 1994. Similarly Geerts & Heestermans, *op. cit.*, p. 1991.

12 A. Davidson, *The Oxford Companion to Food,* Oxford/New York: Oxford University Press, 1999, p. 571.

13 This is particularly clear in a painting called 'Pannenkoeken- en wafeleters' (Braunschweig, Herzog Anton Ulrich-Museum, Inv. No 187) by Jan van Bijlert (1603–1671) where one of the participants is about to swallow a flabby pancake held high in his hand.

14 The archaeologists I consulted were unanimous in their statement that the oldest frying-pans (*bakpannen*), excavated in the Netherlands date from the elevent to the thirteenth centuries. Alas! none from the Roman period. At the time the bottom of the earthenware (grey or red) was a bit bulging, which changed in the thirteenth century, when we get red-coloured earthenware around the big cities and frying-pans with a flat bottom and lead glaze.

15 K. Vlierman, 'Koken en kookgerei op (binnenvaart-)schepen 1300–1900', in *Quintessens: Wetenswaardigheden over acht eeuwen kookgerei,* Catalogus Museum Boijmans-van Beuningen, Rotterdam 1992, pp. 50–9. For a beautiful colour photograph of a fifteenth-century earthenware frying-pan excavated from the soil of Utrecht, see J. Witteveen, 'Kookboeken over kookgerei: Het kookgerei van de middeleeuwen tot de twintigste eeuw', *ibidem*, p. 36.

16 Thomas Vander Noot, *Een notabel boecxken van cokeryen,* Brussel *c.*1514, reedited by R. Jansen-Sieben, M. Van der Molen-Willebrands, Amsterdam: De Kans, 1994, pp. 54, 56.

17 Gheraert Vorselman, *Eenen Nyeuwen Coock Boeck,* dat noch noyt in druc geweest is en is vergadert wt vele verscheyden Boecken, als wt het latijne, Fransoys, ende Ytaliaensch, Antwerpen 1560, re-edited by Elly Cockx-Indestege, Wiesbaden: Guido Pressler, 1971, pp. 206, 216, 219, 220; *De verstandige kock, of sorghvuldige huyshoudster,* Amsterdam: Marcus Willemsz. Doornick, 1667, translated and edited by P.G. Rose under the title: *The Sensible Cook: Dutch Foodways in the Old and the New World,* Syracuse: Syracuse University Press, 1989, pp. 22–3, 73, 76, 113, 122; *Koock ende Huyshoudt Boeck* (1686): Receptenboek van de Hemminga State te Beesterzwaag, uit het archief van Harinxma thoe Slooten, getranscriptieerd, becommentarieerd en van illustratie voorzien door drs R.N. Ferro (Academic voor de Streekgebonden Gastronomie, Mededelingsblad en verzamelde opstellen. Periodiek voor de voedingsgeschiedenis, streekgastronomie en toerisme, 12de jaargang nr 3, Studienummer van 1994), p. 13; *Volmoakte Grondbeginzelen der Keuken-kunde,* Amsterdam: Steven van Esveldt, 1758, pp. 8, 10, 16; *De volmaakte Hollandsche Keuken-meid,* 5de cr., Amsterdam: Steven van Esveldt, 1761, repr. Leiden: Sijthoff, 1965, p. 36.

[18] E.F.L.M. van de Werdt, 'Eijne zilveren scale ende oere beste tinnen canne', Materiële Cultuur tot circa 1800, in H.J.J. Lenferink (red), Th. M. van Mierlo (et al.) *Geschiedenis van Kampen,* deel 1, Kampen: IJsselakademie, 1993, p. 77.

[19] Many beautiful examples in C. de Mooij (ed.), *Vastenavond – Carnaval: Feesten van de omgekeerde wereld,* 'sHertogenbosch/Zwolle: Noordbrabants Museum/Waanders, 1992.

[20] In an anonymous satire called *Een tafelspel van Meester Kackadoris, ende een Doofwijf met Ayeren,* Amsterdam [no year, 1595], the main personage wishes, '...that I may get a woman baking pancakes on board, or one who will bake flapjacks on and on, who would slap dozens of them down in the pan unthinkingly' ('cat ic een Panckoekster mach crijghen aen boort Of eender die daer rechte voort struyf wilde backen En diese bij dosijnen onbesiens inde pan wou smacker'). This male ideal was still in full vigour in the nineteenth century when N. Beets (Hildebrand) wrote sarcastically, 'Wet zou Sijmen zeggen as we deer reis met zoo'n hiele bende op de pannekoeken kwammen? Dan mocht het waif den hielen dag wel deurbakken.' *(Camera Obscura,* 49ste druk, Haarlem 1947, p. 222.) Translation: 'What would Sijmen [one of the characters] say when we would surprise him with the whole band coming for pancakes? The wife would have to bake all day long!'. Only in the late twentieth century would Dutch husbands start discovering the joy of baking pancakes for their own families and friends.

[21] E. Trautscholdt, 'De oude Koekebakster: Nachtrag zu Adriaen Brouwer', in *Pantheon,* Internationale Zeitschrift für Kunst 19 (1961), Heft 4, pp. 187–94.

[22] The painting is in the collection of the Museum Boijmans-Van Beuningen in Rotterdam (see n. 8). A black-and-white reproduction may be found in J.M. van Winter, *Van soeter cokene: Recepten uit de Oudheid en Middeleeuwen,* Haarlem: Fibula-Van Dishoeck, 1976, p. 88.

[23] E.g. the painting 'Vastenavond' by Pieter Brueghel II (1564–1638) in the Centraal Museum, Utrecht, Inv. No 2557. Colour reproduction in De Mooij (ed.), *Vastenavond – Carnaval,* p. 121. See also printed etchings in *Comptoir almanach 1664,* Februarius, Sprockel-Maendt (no page numbering); J. Luiken, *Het leerzaam huisraad vertoond in vyftig konstige figuuren,* Amsteldam: Houttuyn, 1771, p. 126.

[24] For example in an etching by Rembrandt (1635), reproduced in Trautscholdt, 'De oude Koekebakster', p. 190, 'De Koekenbakster' by Jan Steen (see n. 8); 'De Pannenkoekbakster' by Gerard Donck (c. 1610–1640).

[25] *Gheeft mij een Panchioek uyt de pan / ho man ho: / De vastelavondt die komt an: / so myn Heer, also!* This text is found in *De werken van G.A. Bredero,* Volledige uitgave, naar de beste oude drukken berzorgd en opgehelderd door J. ten Brink (and others), deel 2, Amsterdam, 1885–1890, p. 69 [1615]. A somewhat different version is given by L. Hiel, *Zing mee,* Dendermonde, 1944, p. 382. A very similar song is attested for the province of Utrecht, cf. T.W.R. de Haan, *Onze Volksrijmen,* Utrecht/Antwerpen: Het Spectrum, 1978, p. 25. Yet another version was recorded by J. van Vloten, *Nederlandsche Baker en Kinderrijmen,* 4[de] druk, ed. M. A. Brandts Buys, Leiden [no year, 1894], p.67. See with regard to the rumbling pot also C.C. van de Graft, *Nederlandse volksgebruiken bij hoogtijdagen,* Utrecht/Antwerpen: Het Spectrum, 1978, p. 44. The incipit of the song is also recorded on a small but still readable note seen in Jan van Bijlert's painting 'Pannenkoeken – en wafeleters', mentioned in note 13.

[26] '...En 'tis nou ooc Vastelavont, hy crijcht licht wet van men Jonckers Tafel, Die iene warme pankoeck, of d'are leckere Wafel.' S. Coster, Werken, Uitg. R.A. Kollewijn, Haarlem: Bohn, 1883, p. 14 [1612].

[27] P. Spapens & M. Willemsen, *Tilburgs Kookbuukske,* Utrecht: Nederlands Centrum voor Volkscultuur en de Sitichting Tilburgse Taol, 2[de] druk, 1997, p.41.

[28] As testified by a rhyme dated 1567 which I found in the Atlas van Stolk (AVS 16A 34, catalogue dl. 1, p. 286).

29 Illustration from the *Comptoir Almanach* 1653, added to his edition of the *Koock ende Huyshoudt Boeck* (see n. 17) by R.N. Ferro, p. 58.
30 Vander Noot, *Een notabel boecxken van cokeryen,* pp. 54, 56.
31 J. ter Gouw, *De Volksvermaken,* Haarlem: Erven Boon, 1871, p. 497.
32 N. Oomen, *Aerpel in 't potje: Oude gerechten uit Brabant,* Maasbree: De Lijster, 1982, p. 86.
33 R. Keuper & H. Harmsen, *Pot-deurmekare: Oude Achterhoekse gerechten en eetgewoonten,* Gaanderen: Uitgeverij Gherre, 1988. p. 55. This custom seems to have very old roots. Thomas Vander Noot's cookery book offers a detailed recipe for very large pancakes with sugar and adds, 'The pancakes described above are usually baked when women are lying in childbed' ('Dese voorscreven struyven pleecht men te backen in kinderbedden dair vrouwen lyggen', Vander Noot, *Een notabel boecxken van cokeryen,* p. 56.)
34 Ter Gouw, *De Volksvermaken,* p. 258.
35 A. van Oirschot, *Plaatselijke en gewestelijke specialiteiten uit Nederland,* Helmond: Uitgeverij Helmond B.V. (no year), p. 135, mentions a 'Jaorskeuk' from the village of Tegelen in which currants and aniseed were special ingredients.
36 Van Oirschot, *op. cit.,* p. 184.
37 Ter Gouw, *De volksvermaken,* p. 546.
38 J. Jobse-van Putten, *Eenvoudig maar voedzaam: Cultuurgeschiedenis van de dagelijkse maaltijd in Nederland,* Nijmegen/Amsterdam: Sun en P.J. Meertens Instituut, 1995, pp. 191, 239, 264, 371; B.A. Koning, 'Oude eetgewoonten uit Groningerland', in *Neerlands Volksleven* 1958–59, pp. 38–39; Spapens & Willemsen, *Tilburgs Kookbuukske,* p. 41.
39 J.C. Wessels-Nijenhuis, *Proemenkreuze: Drents kookboek,* Den Haag: Kruseman, 1974, p. 11.
40 Wessels-Nijenhuis, *op. cit.,* pp. 41, 47–8.
41 J.P. Stam-Dresselhuys & J.C. Wessels-Nijenhuis, *Streekrecepten,* Wageningen: Zomer en Keuning, derde druk, 1974, p. 50. The importance of pancakes as a staple food in Drente, with its sand and high moors one of the poorest regions of the Netherlands, is also apparent in the large number of special terms connected with pancakes. Cf. G.H. Kokcs, *Woordenboek van de Drentse dialecten,* Assen: Van Gorcum, 1997, s.v. Pannekoek, Pankoekskörf, Pankoukjonges (lads offering presents to newly-wed couples), Pankoukspottie (a crude iron pot in which pancakes were taken along to the moors), Pankoekspan, Pannekoekenhussien.
42 Cf. B. Dupaigne, *Le pain,* Milan: Messidor, 1990, p. 465: 'C'est bien que nous appelons en France les crêpes, qui formaient en Bretagne la base de l'alimentation, les crêpes de sarrassin ('blé noir'), de l'eau, mélangée ici du lait et de beurre, cuites sur une plaque de fer…Ces crêpes sont la nourriture par excellence (et non pas un gâteau ou un dessert), le vrai pain des Bretons.'
43 S. Siegelman, S. Conley & B. Kroening, *The Pancake Handbook,* Berkeley: Ten Speed Press, 1994, p. 10. It must be a consolation to those who grudgingly admit this possibility that also the famous Russian *blini* may have Dutch roots. According to Nicolaas Beets (nineteenth century), Tsar Peter the Great would have loved to eat pancakes during his stay at Zaandam (1697).
44 *Molenaartje maal je molen, / maal voor 't kindje een zakje meel, / dan zal moeder pankoek bakken, / die door kindjes keeltje zakken. / Stroop, stroop, stroop met meel, / dat glijdt zacht door kindjes keel.* From J. Van Vloten, *Nederlandsche Baker en Kinderrijmen,* 4de druk, Leiden: Ruitenberg Boek, [no year, 1894], p. 18.
45 *Elsje Fiederelsje zet je klompjes bij 't vuur. / Moeder bakt pannekoek, maar het meel is zo duur. / Tingelingelinge pannekoek, meel met rozijnen / Tingelingelinge pannekoek, komt op bezoek.* From W.J. Stam-Van der Staay, *Een mandjevol amandelen. Een bundel liedjes voor kleuters en jonge kinderen,* 26de druk, Amsterdam: Ploegsma, 1964, pp. 147–8.
46 *Eerst een beetje meel, dan een beetje melk. / Zijn we met z'n tienen?, 'k bak er twee voor elk! / Twintig lekkre flensjes in de koekepan / op mijn zwart fornuisje, Of ik dat ook kan! (bis) // Dan de tafel dekken, bordjes klaar gezet, / suiker op een schaaltje, jongens wat een pret! / Eventjes nog*

proeven, net als moeder doet. / En nu ga ik bakken: het beslag is goed! (bis). From J. Veldkamp & K. de Boer, *Kun je nog zingen, zing dan mee*, Groningen: P.Noordhoff, 4de druk, 1925, p. 12.

47 *Daar was een vrouw, / die koeken bakken zou, / en het meel dat wou niet rijzen; / en de pan viel om, / en de koeken waren krom, / en de man hiette Jan van Gijzen.* From Van Vloten, *Nederlandsche baker- en kinderrijmen*, p. 52.

48 From P. J. Harrebomée, *Spreekwoordenboek der Nederlandsche taal*, deel 3, Utrecht: Kemink, 1870, p. CXI b. Possibly grandma let it fall intentionally. In some Dutch regions the first pancake was thrown into the ashes for the souls of the deceased in purgatory. For this reason it was called 'zielekoek' (soul-cake). Similar customs are attested elsewhere in Europe, cf. J.H. Nannings, *Brood – en gebakvormen en hunne beteekenis in de Folklore*, Scheveningen: Eigen Volk, 1932, p. 28.

49 The train's whistle was imitated by the Dutch word 'sju' = gravy.

50 *Soep – soep – soep / Aardappelen – groente – vlees* (x3) / *Sjuuuu! / Dikke vette pannekoeken* (x3) / *Pudding* (x3) / *IJssssss* Origin unknown to me, checked with my friend Mrs Ita Gunnink-Tulp, Kampen.

51 E. J. Potgieter, *Liedekens van Bontekoe: Blaouw bes, blaauw bes! Potgieter II (Nederlandsche Bibliotheek; 44)*, Amsterdam: Maatschappij voor goede en goedkope lectuur, [no year, 1908], p. 171.

52 'Aarmelu pankouken en riekelu zaikte roeken wied', quoted in K. ter Laan, *Nieuw Groninger Woorden boek*, Groningen/Djakarta: P. Noordhof, 24de druk, 1952, s.v. pankouk. The poor man's pancake stank because it was baked in rape oil.

53 *'k laat de heer zijn lekkere beetjes: / kreeft en paling, louw en snoek, / Ik voor mij verkies de sneetjes / van 'n malse boekweitkoek.* Jan Mattijs Ballings around 1900, quoted in J. Collen & J. Lambin, *Oude gebruiken en gerechten uit Limburg*, Antwerpen/Amsterdam: Helios/ Nederlandsche Boekhandel, [no year, 1977], p. 36. This cake must have been a pancake, because buckwheat does not contain gluten enabling it to form a high risen cake.

54 The latter is attested in the manuscript No 476 of Ghent University, published in R. Jansen-Sieben, J.M. van Winter, *De keuken van de Late Middeleeuwen*, Amsterdam: Bert Bakker 1989, p. 141.

55 Vander Noot, *Een notabel boecxken van cokeryen*, p. 56.

56 The origin of this word is unknown, but I assume it is related to Hungarian *palacsinta* and ultimately to the Latin *placenta*. Fine buckwheat pancakes called 'bokkende' or 'boekende flensjes' are attested in Dutch literature from the seventeenth century onwards. They are invariably seen as a luxury because they needed to be made with eggs, butter and milk. See e.g. H. Poot Kz., *Gedichten: Vervolg of derde en leste deel der gedichten*, deel 2, 2de druk, Delft, 1747, p. 79. Representative recipes are found in *De volmaakte Hollandsche Keuken-meid*, Amsterdam: Steven van Esveldt, 1761, p. 25, where they are called 'Gooise Pannekekoeken'; M. Haezebroek, *De hedendaagsche Kookkunst*, 3de druk bewerkt door J.P. Gros, eerste kok van wijlen Z.M. Willem I, Gouda: B. van Goor, 1852, p. 149.

57 A brass poffer pan is listed in an inventory of the extensive possessions of Margareta van Slichtenhorst Schuyler (c.1630–1711), cf. Rose, *The Sensible Cook*, 22. A poffer pan is also depicted in the etching 'Le goust' (between 1650–1700, Atlas van Stolk 2134/4). A recipe is found in *Aanhangzel van de volmaakte Hollandsche Keuken-meid*, Amsterdam: Steven van Esveldt, 1763, p. 22.

58 B.A. de Winne-De Bodt, 'Confrerie van de Cruydtcoeck en het begijnhof van Diest', in *Academie voor de streekgebonden gastronomie: Mededelingsblad en Verzamelde Opstellen* 16, Nr. 4, Oktober 1998, pp. 62–3. For the modern version see: J. Collen & J. Lambin, *Oude gebruiken en gerechten uit Limburg*, Antwerpen/Amsterdam: Helios/Nederlandsche Boekhandel, [no year, 1977], p. 38.

The Oyster Supper

Dorothy Duncan

Men Serve Oysters... The Oyster Supper sponsored by the men of our congregation last week was a real success. It is a pleasure to watch these men work with such congenial effort; someone was heard to say it was a real pleasure to wash those nice church dishes so many times in one evening. Several one-time residents of our village made a special effort to come back for that supper date.

When local news correspondent, Betty Pegg wrote this report of the Oyster Supper in Greenwood United Church in 1969[1] for *The Stouffville Tribune,* she was describing a tradition that began in that community twenty years earlier, but had its roots in Ontario, Canada, in the nineteenth century. Two years earlier the same newspaper tells us:

In great grandmother's day an oyster meal was popular, but lately oysters have been out of fashion for everyday and only appear on first class hotel menus. Three hundred enjoyed a full oyster supper with all the trimmings. This is the most popular function of the year.[2]

The Oyster Suppers that were organized in many communities in Ontario in the late nineteenth and early twentieth centuries were founded on the traditional love of oysters that the newcomers to the province brought with them. Oyster Suppers were, and continue to be, most popular in the villages settled by English, Scottish and Irish newcomers with encouragement and support particularly from the menfolk in many communities.

It was soon realized that as well as being an occasion for good food and good fellowship, the Oyster Supper had the potential for raising funds for worthy causes that should not be overlooked. The genesis for the annual Oyster Suppers in Greenwood was a meeting in the Greenwood General Store in 1948 attended by the Board of the Greenwood United Church to discuss fund raising. The group of men was unanimous in the decision that an Oyster Supper in the basement of the church was the perfect solution.[3] A nearby community, Mount Zion, had been successfully hosting Oyster Suppers for over a decade, drawing on a large attendance with the descriptive broadsides:

> OYSTER SUPPER
> and
> DRAMA
>
> ---
>
> come to
> MT. ZION
> on
> WEDNESDAY, FEBRUARY 22
> 1939
>
> ---
>
> SUPPER
> In the Basement of the Church, an Oyster Supper will be
> served from 6 o'clock until all have been served.
> (For those who do not like oysters, pork sausage will be served)
> ADMISSION, 40¢ CHILDREN, 25¢
>
> ---
>
> God Save the King!

The original Oyster Suppers offered only oyster soup or stew, crackers (rolled and added to the oysters, and on plates on the tables as well), an assortment of home-made pies, and tea or coffee. As a small child I remember attending an Oyster Supper with my parents at the Pickering Township Hall in Brougham and absolutely refusing, along with all the other children present, to allow the servers to put any oysters in my bowl as I was sure I wouldn't be able to swallow them.[4]

To accommodate this fear or dislike of oysters by patrons who wanted to be part of the community event, other menu choices were offered. Mount Zion chose pork sausages, while Greenwood added baked ham, scalloped potatoes and green peas to the menu. Canadian's love of home-made pies has kept them as the traditional dessert to the present day.

The roles and responsibilities of men and women throughout all of the nineteenth century and a good portion of the twentieth century were clearly defined in rural Ontario. Food selection, preparation and presentation was considered 'women's work'. For men to buy groceries, prepare recipes, set the table, serve meals or wash dishes was virtually unheard of until the advent of the Oyster Supper. Here, roles were completely reversed in many communities, as the men chose the date, booked the location, prepared the advertising (broadsides and notices in local weekly newspapers), ordered the ingredients, often driving many miles to pick up the oysters, set the tables, took tickets, welcomed the guests and served them, cleared the tables and washed and put away the dishes. The one contribution expected of the womenfolk in those communities was the baking and donating of pies for dessert.

One man would often emerge, either by volunteering or selection by their peers, to be the chief cook for this event and would continue to hold the position for years. In Greenwood, for example, the chief cook for over forty years was Bill Brown, a local farmer. About 3 o'clock on the day of the Oyster Supper he would begin to combine and slowly heat the gallons of oysters brought from far-away markets and the donated milk from nearby farms. Home-churned butter, salt, pepper and large quantities of crackers rolled into crumbs, would be slowly added to the cauldrons of soup that were gently simmering over a portable Coleman gas stove in the makeshift kitchen in the church basement. When the edges of the oysters began to curl, the chief cook knew the soup was ready to serve. The challenge was to keep it hot, but not allow it to scorch, until all 300 guests were served![5]

In some communities, Oyster Suppers along with fowl dinners, bake sales, chicken pie suppers and pancake suppers, were organized by women's groups to support their causes. From the diary of Frances Waterman Wood we learn that she sent 'the boys' (her son William and Jack Staples who boarded with the family, both local teachers) to town (Peterborough) for the oysters the morning of the dinner at Bensfort Church in April of 1935, while she baked pies and a cake. The church-women made twenty-two dollars 'above expenses'.[6]

The popularity of the oyster supper in rural Ontario does not appear to be waning as we begin the twenty-first century. Not only have they been a continuing tradition for over a century, but they are still organized for special events or trips down memory lane. In 1993, in honour of the launching of *Origins – The History of Dummer Township* by Jean Murray Cole, the Dummer Township Historical Book Committee sponsored an Oyster Supper in the Dummer Township Hall in Warsaw, Peterborough County.[7] The Committee decided to revive the once popular tradition of Oyster Suppers in Peterborough County after reading descriptions of past suppers in the book they were about to launch.

> Dummer Township Historical Book
> Committee
> presents
> OYSTER SUPPER
> with Live Sketches of Dummer's Past
> Dummer Township Hall
> Saturday February 13, 1993
> 4:00 p.m. & 7:00 p.m.
> Price $12.00   Seniors & Children $10.00
> MENU
> Oyster Chowder/Corn Chowder
> Scones
> Pie Coffee Tea

Oysters can be purchased anytime anywhere – fresh, frozen, canned. No one needs to drive, as they once did by horse and buggy, to distant fish markets to bring back 50-pound pails of oysters in time for the community supper. Local seafood restaurants offer oysters in a multitude of ways. Despite these, and many other changes in everyday life in the last century, the oyster supper never ceases to delight – and to satisfy the original allure of 'exotic, international cuisine' shared with your family and friends once a year.

NOTES

[1] *The Stouffville Tribune,* Stouffville, Ontario, March 27, 1969.
[2] Ibid., April 2, 1967.
[3] Interviews with Egerton Pegg, Donald Goodwin, Kenneth McTaggart, Alfred Pegg, Kenneth Brooks and Douglas Morden, Greenwood, Ontario, July 8, 2001.
[4] Interview with Beula Hamilton Duncan, Courtice, Ontario, June 16, 2001.
[5] Interview with Bill Brown Junior, Greenwood, Ontario, July 15 2001. Bill Junior often helped his father with this task.
[6] *South Monaghan: The Garden of Eden,* Jean Murray Cole, Township of Otonabee-South Monaghan, 1998.
[7] Interview with Jean Murray Cole, Indian River, Ontario, July 12, 2001.

The Filipino Meal: *Swift, Slow; Sweet, Sour; Adazzle, Dim*

†Doreen G. Fernandez and Pia Lim Castillo

As the land, so the meal. The Philippines is an archipelago of 7,100 islands, with the longest discontinuous coastline in the world (twice that of continental United States), and thus a variegated landscape of hills and mountains, fields and forests, and water in various forms and speeds: seas, rivers, estuaries, straits, brooks, flooded rice fields, canals, rivulets, lakes.

All are not only sources of food; they also shape the aesthetics, manner and meaning of the Filipino meal.

The meals and their times

The three principal meals are named according to the time of day when they are consumed: *agahan* (from *umaga*, morning, thus breakfast); *tanghalian* (from *tanghali*, noon, thus lunch); and *hapunan* (from *hapon*, afternoon, thus supper/dinner). In between is a smaller meal that derives its name from Spanish: *merienda* or *minindal*, generally an afternoon snack or tea break, now also used to name morning coffee breaks. There is as well the *merienda-cena*, an early supper that slides between *merienda* and dinner; and the *inuman* or drinking session, where food called *pulutan* (from *pulut*, to pick up with the fingers) goes with the drinks. The difference between meals and *meriendas* is that the latter do not have rice, which marks a full-scale meal; they are called *pantawid gutom*, food to bridge real hungers.

The division into three principal meals would seem to be a Western principle, however, for Filipino meals used to go with the region, the profession, and the day's rhythm. In Barrio Lantad in Negros Occidental, for instance, the fishermen come in from the night's fishing at dawn, and at seven or eight in the morning, after sorting and sending the catch to market, sit around the *sari-sari* store, drinking *tuba* (coconut toddy), beer, or gin; strumming guitars and singing songs about fishes and fishermen (and an occasional English love song); and nibbling at *sumsuman* (Ilonggo for *pulutan*), consisting of fish they had caught which were too small for the market.

After drinking they would go to sleep, and wake up around noon for the real meal. Were the drinks and fish breakfast?

A central-Luzon rice farmer, however, would leave for the fields at about 4 a.m. or earlier, after a hearty meal now known as the classic Filipino breakfast: *sinangag*, fried rice left over from the night before, so as not to start a fresh pot so early in the day; fish already cooked, like *paksiw* (cooked in vinegar, salt and garlic, thus preserved without refrigeration), or fried on the spot; dried, salted *tuyo*, or smoked *tinapa*, or *daing na bangus* (milkfish cut open the day before, and marinated in vinegar, salt and pepper). There might be *tapa* (dried beef or pork slices) or *longganisa* (pork sausages). Everything had to be available and quickly cooked, to start the farmer's early day.

The farmer's next meal could be at noon or earlier, depending on local habit. It could be taken to the fields by wives or daughters (rice, fish, tomatoes), or by the farmer himself. The end of the day brings the last meal: rice, fish, and vegetables generally, meat being expensive.

Industrial and factory workers today generally break the fast at home (*pan de sal*, coffee), take along a lunch pack (rice, fish, vegetables; not usually a sandwich), buy coffee, snacks or drinks at break times, and go home to supper, sometimes picking up some street food – barbecue, *pansit* (noodles) – along the way to take home to the family.

The meal thus went with the flow of the workday, be it urban or rural, on land or on sea. Its contents are generally simple: a lot of rice, fish or meat or even just *bagoong* (fermented shrimp or fish paste, a relish or dip), and vegetables.

The latter constitute an extremely bountiful variety. In this agricultural society, people close to the land know its contours and bounties well, and thus find vegetables in fields (*kulitis*; *Amaranthus viridis*) between other plants; clinging to bamboo supports (gourds, vines); among fruits (green jackfruit is a vegetable; when ripe it is a fruit), flowers (squash, *katuray*, *Sesbania grandiflora*), and roots (sweet potato leaves); in fish ponds (*dampalit* or samphire) and canals (*kangkong* or water spinach); in shade (*pako*, the beautiful edible fern) and sun (*pechay*, eggplants). Most are not supermarket-bound, and found only in provincial markets or the evanescent, day-long ones called *tabu* or *tiangge*.

This rice-heavy, protein-light, low-fat Filipino peasant meal has been called by nutritionists one of the healthiest in the world, especially since it is usually supplemented by noodles, and is generally steamed, roasted, boiled, or sour-stewed, not fried.

The urban meal, with its foreign inputs – fried eggs and bacon, sausages and butter – is heir to the patterns and problems of Western meals.

The fiesta

A feast is by definition not an ordinary meal, but fiestas occur very often in the Philippines, since they celebrate the patron saint's feast – and every city, town and barrio has a patron saint – generally with religious (mass, processions) and community rituals (e.g. folk plays like *comedia* and *zarzuela*), and food as a major element.

The fiesta table speaks for and of ordinary folk and their gratitude for all the days preceding and following the saint's feast. This is their peak statement about food; the meal is celebration, and the best they can afford. Formerly all homes regardless of size were open to all-comers regardless of origin – friends, family, strangers. The tables, humble or élite, were filled end to end, corner to corner, Gerard Manley Hopkins' lines in 'Pied Beauty': '*Landscape plotted and pieced – fold, fallow and plough;*' – platters, plates, trays, little glass dishes, epergnes and more; and also '*Whatever is fickle, freckled (who knows how?) / With swift, slow; sweet, sour; adazzle, dim …*' – the plain brown crispness of *lechon*, the freckled beauty of *lapu-lapu*, sweet desserts and sour soups, the dazzle of décor and the dim humility of little relish plates filling empty spaces.

In the centre are the most special of the fiesta dishes: *lechon* or roast pig; large fishes decorated with mayonnaise and pickles; a roast turkey or capon; noodles like *pancit*, pasta like *canneloni*; meat dishes like *mechado* and *morcon*; *pastel de pollo* and *lengua estofada*. Radiating outwards are rice dishes like *paella*, *arroz a la Valenciana*, *bringhe*; vegetable dishes like cucumbers or *malibalang* papaya (crisp, short or ripe) in vinegar; *achara* pickles or relishes made with green papaya, heart of palm, *dampalit*, mangoes; green mangoes with *bagoong*, tomatoes, onions, and other house specialities.

On a separate table or section is a plethora of sweets: *leche flan* and *natilla*; *macapuno* (sport coconut) balls or strips in syrup; *santol*, pomelo skins, limes in syrup carved in floral patterns; *Brazo de Mercedes* and *Canonigo*; *Gâteau le sans Rival*; *pili* sweets and marzipan; and *pastillas de leche* wrapped in hand-cut *papel de Japon*, their tails hanging down from an epergne and moving gently in the air.

On a less lavish table in a humbler house one might have a roast chicken, or *menudo*, *pansit*, *kare-kare*, steamed shrimps, chicken *adobo*, fish fried or *escabeche*, *lumpia*.

But always, the table must be filled 'with swift, slow; sweet, sour; adazzle, dim' (*horror vacui*, a fear of empty spaces, it has been called) edge to edge, with no margins left. Because there are no empty spaces either in the message this food conveys; it is filled, packed to the brim, and overflowing.

Why? To express joy, to reciprocate the year's bounty, to thank neighbours who helped plough fields, and friends who sponsored baptisms and weddings, as well as the parish priest and the mayor, ancestral spirits, the patron saint and God.

The Pahiyas festival in Lucban, Quezon, has already been mentioned in an earlier symposium. The whole town is decorated with food on the feast of its patron St. Isidore the Worker (a Spanish saint). The fronts of houses are bright with the fuschia, emerald green, lemon yellow, tangerine orange, and cherry red of the *kiping*, leaf-shaped rice wafers made just for the fiesta, and used as decorative element to shape chandeliers, rose windows, fringes and tapestries – then later fried and eaten.

Sausage-makers festoon their house fronts with the famous, oregano-flavoured *longganisang Lucban*; *leche flan*-makers save the year's eggshells for a mural; the baker's fish- and lamb-shaped loaves and the *lechonero*'s roast pig on a spit lie beneath front windows; and everywhere are swagged and draped string beans, little green mangoes, bananas, new-harvest rice (*palay*); palms and vegetables.

A town-wide contest awards a few thousand pesos to the best-decorated houses, whose owners had surely spent much more than that by way of man-, woman- and child-hours and materials.

In sum

The Filipino meal thus has developed from the land, its weather and contours – thus the rice, fish and seafood, vegetables and relishes.

It developed in an agricultural society, where the land supplied the materials, and the life work of farmers and fishermen gave the rhythm and tempo of meals.

It developed alongside the needs of farmers and fishermen, later industrial and city workers – directly focused on their needs, ways, beliefs and evolving lifestyles.

It grew and expanded with inputs from foreign sources: Chinese, Spanish, Indian, Arab, American (indigenized) and more recently Italian, French, Middle Eastern (imported, but moving towards indigenization).

It has become the centrepiece of Philippine life, the focal centre of community and family interaction, showcase of the people's closeness to the land, their flexibility, and feeling for each other.

The Filipino meal speaks so clearly to and of the Filipino, that the food consumed in it is only the merest beginning of a joyous, continuing dialogue from the past, through the present and into the future, on or off the table.

The Middle to Late Sixteenth-Century English Upper-Class Meal

Judy Gerjuoy

When analysing English upper class meals of the mid- to late sixteenth century, there are two types of primary sources that can be used to obtain the necessary information. The first are household accounts, the records kept by great estates of what was bought, sold, and consumed. The second are contemporary cookery books and manuals. Both have their weaknesses. Household accounts often show us a gross picture, but leave out little details. Cookery books and other manuals can give us recipes and tell us how food should be served, but not necessarily how it was. Another source of information, while less reliable, still can help us get a better picture of what was used and how it was used: Art of the period does not always accurately portray what was done, since it was often idealized or symbolic, however, it can be of great utility.

Kinds of food

Tudor Secretary by F.G. Emmison, an account of the life of Sir William Petre, contains, as Appendix E, the provision account book from Ingatestone Hall in Essex 8–14 January, 1548, as Appendix F, the provision account book from December 20, 1551 through January 9, 1552, as well as assorted other information on food. From these records we can get a reasonable picture of what would have been eaten in an upper-class household.

The records show how much and what type of meat, fish, cheese, and butter (sweet and salt) were eaten or used as well as how much bread, and of what type, was baked each week. For the week ending January 2, 1552, they cast 60 loaves of manchet bread, 160 loaves of yeomen's bread, and 12 loaves of carters' bread, as well as 13 dishes of butter, 33 eggs and 2 cheeses. Meat consumed included an ox, a cow, 2 pigs, 4 muttons, a goat, 3 geese, 4 capons, 23 rabbits, a hare, 11 teals, 2 pheasants, 3 ducks, a woodcock, 2 plovers, and a snipe. Fish consumed included 1½ salmons, 2 mudfish, 2 lings, and 2 haberdins.

Fruit and vegetables

Although the records from Petre do not show consumption of fruit or vegetables, they were certainly eaten. *The English Housewife* by Gervase Markham, published in 1615, has an 'Ordering of Great Feasts'. He says, 'she shall first marshal her sallats, delivering the grand sallat first, which is evermore compound; then green sallats, then boiled sallats, then some smaller compound sallats.' He goes on to mention other fish and meat dishes, but the salads are to be served first. The salads in *The Good Housewife's Jewel* by Thomas Dawson, the first part printed in 1596 and the second in 1597, all contain either fruit or vegetables, though some also contain fish. Furthermore, the Petre household accounts show the gardener was supplied with seeds of assorted fruits and vegetables.

Epulario, Or, The Italian Banquet, which was translated from Italian and printed in England in 1598, has 231 recipes for food, not including sauces or drinks. Of those recipes, 45, or 19.5 per cent, contain fruit or vegetables. *A Booke of Cookrye With the Serving in of the Table*, by A.W., published in London in 1591, has many dishes that contain fruit or vegetables, as does *Elinor Fettiplace's Receipt Book* (1604), and *Martha Washington's Booke of Cookery* (late sixteenth/early seventeenth century).

However, the recipe books may not tell the entire story. Giacomo Castelvetro, in 1614, says in *The Fruit, Herbs and Vegetables of Italy*,

> I often reflect upon the variety of good things to eat which have been introduced into this noble country of yours over the past fifty years ... Yet I am amazed that so few of these delicious and health-giving plants are being grown to be eaten. Through ignorance and indifference, it seems to me that they are cultivated less for the table than for show by those who want to boast of their exotic plants and well-stocked gardens.[1]

He is contradicted by evidence from Henry VIII's Privy Purse expenses, which include money spent for apples, cherries, pears, wardens, damsons, oranges, lemons, and pomegranates.[2] A picture of William Brooke, tenth Baron Cobham, with his family, painted by the Master of the Countess of Warwick in 1567, shows the family sitting around a dining-table which is set with assorted fruits and nuts.[3] Based on evidence from household accounts, recipe books and pictures, it is reasonable to assume that the English did eat fruit and vegetables, although perhaps not as much or as many types as in Italy.

Desserts and sweets

While Petre's accounts do not list any desserts and sweets, they are found in cookery books such as we have mentioned. Cakes, sweet biscuits, sugared almonds, dried fruit, candied lemon and orange peel, pies, gingerbread (though not as we eat it today), marzipan and candied ginger were eaten with relish. As C. Anne Wilson says in *Banquetting Stuffe*, 'So important was the banquet course that it was given its own separate venue. In winter the participants might withdraw from the great chamber or the dining parlour to another room; but for summer banquets individual banqueting houses were designed.'[4]

Drinks

A great many different drinks were consumed, both alcoholic and non-alcoholic. These included: beer, ale, perry, cider, milk, buttermilk, caudles, wine, and mead. According to Petre's household accounts, wines remaining in the cellar on 6 December 1551 were: a butt of sack and 12 gallons, 2 puncheons of French wine and 20 gallons, a hogshead of French wine, a hogshead of Gaston wine with a half, a hogshead of red wine with a half, a piece of Rhennish wine, and 4 gallons of malmsey.[5] Most of the cookery books of the time also had recipes for brewing or otherwise making drinks.

Number of people fed

Of the 21 days recorded in 1551–2, only three do not have anyone besides the regular inhabitants of Ingatestone Hall eating either dinner or supper. These extra people, referred to as 'strangers in the hall', include labourers, servants, poor women and men, a curate, working men, and children. Some of these strangers were certainly middle class or better, since some of the strangers were described as servants to other people listed. It is difficult to tell exactly how many people came each time, since there will be a list of names along with comments such as 'and their sons', or 'and their wives'. However, it appears that the high was reached on December 27, when approximately 60 strangers were fed. These were in addition to the family and staff. During the years 1548–52 there were 20 indoor and outdoor servants.[6] It appears that feeding a large number of people was common in the manor houses of the day. For instance, a recipe for a great cake, found in *Elinor Fettiplace's Receipt Book*, would be cut into at least 160 slices, according to the reckoning by the editor, Hilary Spurling.[7]

Order of dishes served

A Proper Newe Booke of Cokerye,[8] gives the order of dishes for supper. It gives as the first service: 'Potage or sewe; A salette; Poudred beyfe sliced; A shoulder of mutton or a Breste; Veale; Lambe; Custarde'. The second course is to be: 'Capons roosted; Connies roosted; Chekins roosted; Pigeons roosted; Larckes roosted; A pye of pigeons of Chekins; Baked venison; Tarte.'

A Booke of Cookrye With the Serving in of the Table,[9] shows a similar, though shorter, listing of dishes. Gervase Markham's *The English Housewife*,[10] published in 1615, shows even more. In the accounts of Ingatestone Hall, the dinners, though not the suppers, appear as elaborate as that listed above. For instance, for dinner on Sunday, December 27, they list: 'Bolyde beiffe 7 peces & a chine; 4 rosting peces; a brest of veal; a legge of motton baked; 11 pasties of beiffe; a loyne of porke & a brest rosted; 2 gesse; a capon; 6 conneis; 2 teles; 2 pasties of venson; 3 pasties of kydd; a woodecoke; a pygge.'

Fast days

These lists and records are for non-fast days, when meat could be eaten. On fast days, which included Lent, all Fridays except if Christmas fell on Friday, the Ember-days at the four seasons, and the three Rogation days, fish would substitute. Fish was not normally eaten in great amounts except on fast days. Some listings of dishes to be served do not list any fish dishes, except on fast days; others, such as Gervase Markham's, list some, but not as many as meat dishes. Friday, January 1, 1552, being a fast day, at Ingatestone Hall they ate: a ling, a haberden, 2 mudfish, 6 plaice, 8 whiting, 1 cod, a salmon, 3 cakes of butter, and 20 eggs.

How much people ate

While it is evident that a great many dishes were served, how much did the average person eat? While I have been unable to find any records of exact amounts eaten per person in a noble house, *The Englishman's Food* quotes amounts given to inmates at a house of correction in Bury, Suffolk in 1588:

> Item, it is order, that every person commited to the said house, shall have for theire diets, theis portions of meate and drinke followinge, and not above (viz). At every dynner and supper on the fleshe daies, bread made of rye, vii ounces troye waight, with a pynte of porredge, a quarter of a pound of flesh, and a pinte of beare, of the rate of iijs. A barrel, every barrel to conteyne xxxvj. Gallands.[11]

To put it in a modern perspective, these prisoners would be getting twice a day as much meat as in a McDonald's quarter-pounder as well as porridge and bread. If this is what was given to a prisoner, then the people in a noble house would be getting a great deal of food, if they wished it.

Why a great number of dishes

Certainly, the evidence in the household accounts and in the cookery books of the period makes it clear that a great many different dishes were served to feed a noble household. This would have been for a variety of reasons. One was simple practicality. In the sixteenth century you did not go to your local grocery store and purchase, for instance, 20 legs of lamb, in order to serve everyone roast leg of lamb. The economics of slaughtering as well as the lack of modern forms of food preservation meant that when you slaughtered an animal, you would use most of it at one time, thereby making it necessary to serve a variety of different dishes. The cook would use a large amount, or most of the animal, in a variety of different ways, thereby reducing waste. But that was not the only, or even necessarily the main reason. Terence Scully in *The Art of Cookery in the Middle Ages* says:

> When faced with the professional obligation to produce a satisfying meal consisting of a number of appetizing dishes, the medieval cook's decisions and choices – ingredients, preparations, cooking methods, garnishes, combinations of dishes, and so forth – frequently involved considerations that went beyond any transient, personal notions of culinary 'art'. Unlike his modern counterpart, he had to weigh another set of data more or less consciously. This data was felt to possess such absolute, objective accuracy that today we would have little hesitation in qualifying it as 'scientific'. It had to do with theories about the fundamental nature of the ingredients the cook was handling, and particularly about the four essential qualities of all foodstuffs. In short, the cook had to know what was good or bad to eat, and how to go about making dangerous foods safer.[12]

While Terence Scully is referring to medieval food, the theory of balancing the four humours was still practised in sixteenth-century England. This theory, which comes from Aristotle and Hippocrates, and then expanded by the Greek philosopher Galen, divided things into four humours. Blood, whose complexion was sanguine and had the qualities of being hot and moist; phlegm, whose complexion was phlegmatic and had the qualities of being cold and moist; yellow or green bile, whose complexion was choleric and had the qualities of hot and dry; and black bile, whose complexion was melancholic and had the qualities of cold and dry. Jane O'Hara-May's *Elizabethan Dyetary of Health* deals with Elizabethan beliefs about health. She quotes extensively from sixteenth- and seventeenth-century manuals and literature which espouse the humoral theory of food. For instance, the introduction to the sixteenth-century book *A Short Discourse on Peppers* references Galen, and how pepper (the spice) can be used to help with humours.

In conclusion, we can state that sixteenth-century meals in English noble houses consisted of a large assortment of dishes containing, if it was not a fast day, meat, fish, milk products, bread, grain products, eggs, fruit and vegetables. While not everyone would have partaken of every dish, there would have been a great variety. Enough would have been prepared to feed between 30 and 100 people a day, both people living in the household and people from outside. The dishes would be chosen not only with concern for taste and texture, but also for balance among the four humours. The dinner would end with a sweet course, often served in another room or place in the manor.

BIBLIOGRAPHY

A Proper Newe Booke of Cokerye [1545], ed. C.F. Frere, London, 1913.
A Short Discourse on Peppers [1588], Amsterdam: Theatrum Orbis Terrarum, 1972.
A.I., *Epulario, Or, The Italian Banquet* [1598], repr. Falconwood, Albany, NY, 1989.
A.W., *A Booke of Cookrye with the Serving in of the Table* [1591], repr. Walter J. Johnson, Amsterdam, 1976.
Brears, Peter, *All the King's Cooks*, London: Souvenir Press, 1999.
Castelvetro, Giacomo, *The Fruit, Herbs and Vegetables of Italy* [1614], ed. and trans. Gillian Riley, Viking, London, 1989.
Dawson, Thomas, *The Good Housewife's Jewel* [1596-97], repr. Southover Press, 1996.
Drummond, J.C. & Anne Wilbraham, *The Englishman's Food*, Jonathan Cape, London, 1959.
Emmison, F. G. *Tudor Secretary*, Phillimore, London, 1961.
Hess, Karen, *Martha Washington's Booke of Cookery*, Columbia, NY., 1981.
Markham, Gervase, *The English Housewife* [1615], ed. Michael R. Best, McGill-Queen's University Press, Kingston, 1986.
O'Hara-May, Jane, *Elizabethan Dyetary of Health*, Oronado, Lawrence, 1977.
Paston-Williams, Sara, *The Art of Dining*, National Trust, London, 1993.
Oxford, Arnold Whitaker, *English Cookery Books to the Year 1850*, Holland Press, 1977.
Scully, Terence, *The Art of Cookery in the Middle Ages*, Boydell, 1995.
Spurling, Hilary, *Elinor Fettiplace's Receipt Book*, Viking, 1986.
Wilson, C. Anne, *Banquetting Stuffe*, Edinburgh University Press, 1986.

NOTES

[1] Castelvetro, p. 49.
[2] Brears, p. 66.
[3] Paston-Williams, p. 135.
[4] Wilson, p. 2.
[5] Emmison, p. 151.
[6] Ibid., p. 133.
[7] Spurling, p. 53.
[8] My copy seems to be unsure about the date, but Oxford gives it the date of 1545.
[9] A.W., pp. 1–3.
[10] Markham, pp. 121–124.
[11] Drummond & Wilbraham, p. 56.
[12] Scully, pp. 41–2.

Moretum – a Peasant Lunch Revisited

Christopher Grocock and Sally Grainger

This poem, included in the *Appendix Vergiliana* but certainly anonymous, has received generous attention from Latin editors in the past half-century.[1] The value of considering *Moretum* at a conference on 'the meal' is fourfold: first, the subject-matter of the poem is the preparation of a meal, albeit a very simple one; second, the level of detail in the poem and the nature of its literary canon makes it possible to have confidence in that detail; third, reconstructing the recipe sheds light on problems in the text and its interpretation; and fourth (and by no means least) the results are delicious!

'The poem is a *literary exercise* which conforms to a specific genre. It contains meticulous description of a *bathetic* event in an epic, grandiose style, for effect: it is a detailed description with technical virtuosity, in the style of the Alexandrian and neoteric poets, of *everyday acts* in epic settings.'[2] Prof. Kenney felicitously styles it an 'Alexandrian Dutch interior'.[3] Its most recent editors say of its author, 'a very observant poet appears before the eyes of his readers, one who seizes upon an individual life for his subject, giving even its tiniest details an accurate examination and an elegant portrayal.'[4] Generically, then, the poem belongs to the mannered miniature epic style known as an *epyllion*; but other traditions also lie behind it and combine to produce its particular flavour.

The first of these is the Roman tradition of exalting the 'sturdy yeomen farmers' who crop up again and again in the founding myths of Rome, and who are praised by Cato in the preface to his *De Agricultura*. Similar attitudes are to be found in Virgil's *Eclogues* and *Georgics*, where the Roman tradition is mingled with a Greek literary one harking back as far as Callimachus in the fourth century BCE and which is found in numerous Latin poems of a similar period to *Moretum* itself, notably in the story of Baucis and Philemon.[5]

A second tradition is that of the depiction of the *locus amoenus*, the 'place of beauty', which is found as far back as Homer. Even Pliny, opening a discussion of allotment-gardens in his *Natural History*, begins with a reference to gardens of the Hesperides.[6] Such a description will be found as a digression at the centre of *Moretum*. Other examples of such depictions include the charming 'old man of Verona' inserted into the fourth book of his *Georgics* by

Virgil.[7] The emphasis on frugality chimed well with the influence of Epicureanism among the literati of Augustan Rome, as other writers such as Horace, dreaming of the quiet life in all modesty on his Sabine farm, show well.[8]

These three strands: the first of a detailed description in high-flown terms; the second of the ideal of the farmer – the 'Good Life'; the third of a rustic garden idyll, come together in what Prof. Kenney calls 'a romanticized view of country life as an image of virtuous and contented frugality'.[9] However, *Moretum* does not lack realism; far from being a quasi-Vergilian paradise, this farmer's lot is one of hardship and toil, depicted by a mingling of high-flown epic phrasing with a gritty subject-matter. As we shall see, if there is nobility in his poverty, it is forced on him by lack of choice, and poverty is a recurring motif in the poem.

Similar views about the reality of the hardships of country life are found elsewhere. Horace, already cited, liked the life of a country gentleman, but could not stomach the country diet (literally!) and was well aware of the dangers of farming.[10] In similar vein, the satirist Persius inveighed against those who trotted out the stock theme of the 'happy farmer'.[11]

Thus the *Moretum* may be regarded as Zola-like in its realistic portrayal of the early winter hours in a poor farmer's day. It pulls no punches in the description of the various activities undertaken by the 'provident hero' Simulus, depicting each one in turn and in precise detail.

Our attempts at reconstructing some of the activities described in the poem have, we hope, shed additional light on, and clarified, some difficult points in it. For example, in l. 46 Kenney understands that many loaves are prepared, interpreting '*grumos*', lit. 'hillocks' or 'heaps', as separate loaves; we think it means the undulations in the dough. Kenney bases his interpretation additionally on his understanding of the amount of grain taken from his 'poor little heap' by Simulus, mentioned in ll. 17–18. Now *grumos* may be a poetic plural for singular – a phenomenon which is commonplace in Latin verse. However, later on we are told that a single round loaf is produced (*orbem*, l. 47). This interpretation is supported by other factors: i) the common practice appears to have been that of grinding only enough flour for immediate use, and not for storage; ii) that unleavened bread is best eaten fresh; iii) the labour involved in grinding flour and the time required to do it – in the dark! – make it unlikely that more than one loaf is intended; iv) a large space is needed to mix dough from 10 to 16 lbs of grain on a flat board (not a dough-trough or bowl); and v) the fact that such a large amount of grain hardly chimes with the consistent theme of poverty, or the size of the grain-heap. Cumulatively these points lead us to seek a different sense for a number of key phrases relating to the bread-baking activity which the Latin will bear but which make practical sense also.

Thus here and elsewhere the reconstruction process assists attempts at understanding what is going on.

The detail in the first half, while not specifically addressing *moretum*, is of equal interest to the food historian as the latter part (ll. 60ff.) – and its detailed illustration indicates the value and accuracy of the portrayal as a whole.

The question that can be asked from the standpoint of an experimental archaeologist and cook looking at the food in *Moretum* is: can a recipe be extracted? Is the poetic material accurate enough to justify following Simulus' detailed *modus operandi* and achieving a successful representation of the 'name and appearance of *moretum*'? One also has to ask what purpose there is in inventing such an activity if the poem is not an accurate representation of a peasant at work in his own home. If, as has been argued, the aim of this genre of poetry is to be precise in detail, then the answer to these questions is 'yes'. Consequently making *moretum* can and should be attempted. Perhaps the poet saw this kind of activity on many occasions and was familiar with the process. Or one can imagine, once he has decided to compose such a poem, even going back to talk to the old farm labourers on a family estate to get all the details as accurately as possible. Displaying remarkably Vergilian talents the poet knows that coriander trembles on its slender stalk; he has seen a labourer at work with a *mortarium* and pestle and he is able to describe garlic in the green in precise detail. The poet's description of the dough and its baking is also very telling. Our poet has watched a hand-turned rotary quern in action – as we have – and he has seen *sub testu* baking, which we can also attempt.

The issue concerning this poem which is most often debated amongst food historians is the type and quantity of garlic used by the peasant. We have tasted some very insipid and bland concoctions under the name *moretum* over the years and from this article it should be clear that we prefer a much stronger product.

Garlic was not a popular foodstuff amongst the wealthy in ancient Rome. The smell and taste was considered common and rustic and this is confirmed by its virtual absence in Apicius. (It appears twice and one of those is an emetic.) Horace was outspoken in his criticism of a dish served to him by his patron Maecenas:

> He whose impious hand has strangled his aged father deserves to eat it. It is more harmful then hemlock. Garlic! Peasants must have iron guts … If ever you are tempted this way again, my humorous Maecenas, I devoutly hope that your girl will push away your face and retreat to the very edge of the bed'[12]

Pliny has much to say about its cultivation in his *Natural History*, but in a discussion of medication rather than for food. Various kinds of garlic were known including wild garlic with a very small undivided head and larger leaves. This is clearly not what was intended in *Moretum*. Pliny makes it clear that garlic with numerous cloves was cultivated. He also says that the more numerous the cloves the stronger the flavour. The bulb in the poem has 'tightly packed innards' and a 'knotty body'; not an easy word to decipher but at the same time not a reflection of a single small bulb similar to a wild variety but of a divided garlic head, likely to be similar to varieties known today. An average-sized head is about 2–2½ inches (say 5–6.5 cm) across. Such a head generally contains 8–10 cloves. We know that the mixture was pretty strong, as the fumes cause Simulus some distress.

What is clear is that the garlic was freshly picked and therefore very little of the flesh was wasted. The bulb is 'kept back with its fresh green leaf' and this is a good description of green garlic; the outer skin is removed but the entire central portion of the vegetable is usable: the upper leaf and the whole body. The internal layers have not had time to dry yet and are still juicy. It seemed strange at first that the poet did not use the term *spica* or *nucleus* which are the terms for a single clove of garlic but there was no need as, in effect, the clove had not yet been separated by dry layers. Fresh garlic is different from the normal dry variety we see every day. It is by no means mild – there is considerable pungency to the vegetable – but it is fresher and sharper then the stored variety. It is also very much more juicy and this is the key to the finished *moretum*. The consistency must be relatively firm: the mixture is rolled into a ball, and so the quantity and quality of cheese must be such that the juice from the garlic as well as the oil and vinegar are absorbed and the finished product is not sticky.

Simulus picks four fresh garlic bulbs. He peels all four, and despite the singular *bulbum* in l. 94, which might at first reading imply that he appears to put only one in the mortar, we believe that all four bulbs are used, both for practical and philological reasons. First, it is very unlikely that a miser like Simulus would waste either time or effort – or garlic – in peeling but not using it. Moreover, the action being described here refers to the successive peeling, washing and dropping in the mortar of each bulb one at at time (l. 92 *singula*), which is why the singular is found to describe each bulb; the plural is picked up again, referring to all four, with his in l. 96.

There are few cheeses that can compete with such a quantity of garlic in terms of texture and flavour. The cheese must have been made from either sheep's or goats' milk. (Cows' milk cheese in ancient Italy was very rarely made.) It should be salt-hardened and has been smoked somewhat as it hangs from the rafters. It is also shaped like a wheel and has a hole from which it is strung up. A colleague who tends to make a mild *moretum* uses a smoked ricotta cheese. It satisfies two of the requirements, as it is similarly shaped in order for it to be smoked but it is relatively mild in flavour and certainly can not compete with four garlic bulbs. Pecorino Romano, which is hard, sharp, Parmesan-like in texture, is a worthy adversary for the garlic. It is both very absorbent and strongly flavoured which is far more crucial to the recipe.

The herbs are easily dealt with. Coriander and rue are very common in Apicius. Rue is a very bitter sharp herb, rarely used today, and in the past its medicinal properties were valued before its culinary use. In quantity it is an abortefaciant and so should always be used with care. It can also cause serious skin allergies for those sensitive to it. Its sharp bitter taste is a perfect counter-balance for the garlic and salt cheese. The celery leaf has been rejected by Kenney as unsuitable; he replaces it with parsley on the grounds that other kinds of *moretaria* contain it (see below). This is an unnecessary emendation. Celery leaf occurs frequently in Roman recipes.

A basic recipe

8oz Pecorino Romano – grated
4 smallish green garlic bulbs or *c.* 20 small dry cloves
1 tbs olive oil
1 tsp white wine vinegar
1 large handful fresh coriander
the green leaf from one celery head
1 tsp fresh chopped rue

Put all in food processor and push button *or* obtain a *mortarium* and follow Simulus' method!

The other *moretaria* are interesting largely because they contain no garlic.[13] The origin of the name may shed light on the similarities. Lewis & Short suggest that *moretum* derives from *mordeo* – a bite or snack. *Moretaria* stems from 'a mixture ground in a *mortaria*' – the receptacle used by Simulus to make his *moretum*. The recipes found in Columella are given no name but clearly represent a similar mixture. Cheese is included in the basic recipe but walnuts, sesame seeds, pine nuts and hazelnuts are also suggested as ingredients with the basic herb mixture. It may be said that the peasant *moretum* containing garlic was rejected by those of higher status who added nuts and seeds as an alternative.

Translation

The translation which follows is from Professor Kenney's revised text (1984). It tends towards a literal approach; the tenses of the original are preserved, as is the use of names of gods and goddesses to stand for processes (e.g. 'Vulcan and Vesta' for 'fire and hearth'; 'Ceres' for 'grain', 'flour'). It has not always been possible to render the Latin in exactly this way (e.g. *liquores, fontes, unda* – all meaning 'water').

Phrases marked thus + + indicate a doubtful text in the original Latin. The bracketed numbers in the text mark the line number in the Kenney edition.

Moretum

Already night had passed ten of its winter hours and the bird that wakes us with its song had foretold the day, when Simulus,[14] the rustic tenderer of a tiny plot, fearing the hunger-pangs of the approaching dawn, lifts his limbs laid softly on his lowly pallet and groping carefully through the darkness probes the hearth, which he finally felt through pain, for the smallest of embers was still left in a burned-out log, and ashes were hiding the glow of the hidden embers. He brings his lamp close by to these with his head bowed low, he pulls out with a needle the wick's threads which are not moist with oil, and stirs up the flagging fire, blowing hard on it. While it is barely alight he moves away, and with cupped hand shields the light from the draughts, and opens up the +closed cupboard door, peering inside.+ A humble heap of grain was poured out on the ground; from this he drew for himself as much as his measure allowed, which exceeded eight pounds in weight[15] twice over. (19) He goes from there, and standing by his quern he places his trusty light on a small shelf which the wall held firm for that very purpose; then he freed both arms, and clad in the skin of a shaggy goat he gives a thorough wipe with its tail to the surfaces and the lap of the millstones.[16] Next he summons his hands to the work, sharing it out to both: his left concentrates on supply, while the right provides the effort. This one turns round the familiar disc and urges it on (Ceres, crushed, flows down from the swift pounding of the hard stones). From time to time the left hand takes over from her exhausted sister, changing places. Now he sings some countrymen's songs and eases his toil with his rustic voice, and occasionally shouts out 'Scybale'. She was his only helpmate, African by birth[17] – her whole face testified to her native land, with frizzy hair, swollen lips and dusky colouring, broad-chested, with drooping breasts and a flattened stomach, slender thighs and wondrously extensive feet. He calls her and commands her to put wood on the fire to burn and to heat the cold fluids with flame. Once the whirling work had reached the appropriate point, he transfers the flowing flour to a sieve in his hand and shakes it; and the unwanted siftings are left on the very top, while the pure Ceres drops through the holes, and is sifted clean. Straightaway he piles it on a smooth board, pours warm ripples over it, pulls together the mixture of both springwater and flour, kneading and turning it as by hand and water it is made firm, from time to time sprinkling the mounds with salt. Now that it is thoroughly kneaded he lifts his work and squashes it into a round disc in his palms, and marks it with intended divisions,[18] equally spaced. Then he carries it to the hearth (Scybale had cleaned the place fittingly beforehand) and covers it with a *testum* and heaps the fires over it. (51) While Vulcan and Vesta each play their part, Simulus does not stop work in the empty hour that intervenes, but searches out another resource for himself. Lest Ceres unaccompanied is unpleasing to the palate, he gets ready some accompanying foodstuffs. No +sides of bacon, butchered+ and hardened with salt, weighed down his meat racks by the hearth; but a cheese, pierced through the middle of its orb with a string made of broom, and an old bunch of dill, were hanging there: therefore the resourceful hero toils at another resource for himself. (60) There was a garden adjoining his little house, over which a few hurdles and recycled rushes with their thin stems stood guard; it was tiny in extent, but productive with its different plants. He lacked nothing that a poor man needs; sometimes a wealthy man used to look for more from this poor one. His little plot cost him nothing save his attention: if ever rainy weather or a festival day kept him idle in his little home, if perhaps his work at the plough was done, that time was devoted to the garden. He knew how to set out different plants, how to sow seeds in the broken[19] earth, and how to divert nearby streams round his plot in a skilful way. (71) Here grew cabbages, here beets which spread wide their leaves, prodigious sorrel, mallow and elecampane, here skirret and leeks which owe their name to their heads, and lettuce, a pleasant relief to noble foods, and many a radish forces its pointed root into the earth, and the heavy marrow which grows into a broad belly. But this harvest was not for its master (for who was more stinting than he?) but for the populace, and on market days he would carry his bundles on his shoulder into the city to sell them, and would return home from there with an unburdened neck and a heavy purse, scarcely ever with a purchase from the city market in his train: (82) red onions and a patch of welsh onions tamed his hunger, and cress that screws up your face with its bitter taste, and endives, and rocket that revives flagging Venus. Now he was planning something along these lines as he entered the garden; and first with his fingers he gently loosens four garlic bulbs from the earth and lifts them along with their tightly-packed innards, then he plucks the delicate fronds of celery, and rue that grows up straight, and coriander that trembles on its slender stalk. When he has gathered these, he sits beside the cheerful fire and with a loud voice asks his maid for the mortar. Then one at a time he lays bare each bulb in its knotty body and strips off its outer layer, and scatters the waste product all over the floor as he throws it aside; (94) the bulb, kept back with its fresh green leaf,[20] he bathes with water and places it in the hollow circle of stone. On them he sprinkles grains of salt, the cheese, hardened by the shrivelling salt, is added, he heaps on top the aforementioned herbs, and with his left hand he gathers his tunic[21] under his hairy thigh, while his right hand first softens the pungent garlic with the pestle, and then grinds all together equally in a mingled paste. His hand goes round and round; gradually each ingredient loses its own characteristics, and there is one colour out of many, not all green, because the hard lumps of cheese resist, and not all pale from the milk product,[22] because it is so often changed by the herbs. Often a keen waft is launched at the man's open nostrils, and he damns his breakfast[23] with his face turned away, he often wipes his tearful eyes with the back of his hand and in his wrath utters curses to the undeserving fumes. (95) The work was making progress; the pestle no longer jerking but moving in slow circles with greater pressure. Therefore he drizzles on drops of Pallas' olive oil, pours over it a dash of strong vinegar, and again stirs it up and examines the mixture. Then at last he scrapes round the whole mortar with two fingers and pulls the contents into a single ball, so that there stands together the name and appearance of a *moretum*. Meanwhile Scybale, herself busy, rooted out the bread, which he took in his hands with joy, and with fear of hunger now driven away Simulus walks confidently to meet this day; clad below the knee in matching leggings and in a cap, he forced his obedient oxen under the yoke bound with thongs and drove them to the cornfield, where he plunged the plough into the earth.

BIBLIOGRAPHY

Kenney 1966: *Moretum*, in *Appendix Vergiliana*, ed. W. V. Clausen, Oxford Classical Texts, 1966.
Kenney 1984: *Moretum: The Ploughman's Lunch,* Bristol Classical Press, 1984.
Petruelli 1983: *Moretum*, ed. A. Petruelli, Pisa, 1983.
Salvatore et. al. 1997: *Appendix Vergiliana*, Scriptores Graeci et Latini Consilio Academiae Lynceorum Editi, ed. A. Salvatore, A. De Vivio, L. Nicastri, G. Polara, Rome, 1997.

NOTES

[1] Prof. E.J Kenney has added a detailed commentary and translation to a revision of his original text in the Oxford Classical Texts series (Kenney 1984; Kenney 1966); almost simultaneously, Alessandro Petruelli produced an equally detailed commentary to a text with facing translation in Italian (Petruelli 1983); and more recently, a new edition of the *Appendix Vergiliana* has appeared under the auspices of the Academia Lynceorum at Rome (Salvatore et al. 1997).

[2] D. O. Ross, 'The *Culex* and *Moretum* as post-Augustan literary parodies', *HSCP* 79 (1975) 235–63, at p. 261, quoted in Kenney 1984, p. xxvi; our italics.

[3] Kenney 1984, p. xxx.

[4] Salvatore et al. 1997, p. 295, our translation of *acutissimus denique ante legentium oculos poeta exstat, qui rebus uitam quandam inicit easque uel minimas accurate perscrutatur eleganterque depingit.*

[5] Ovid, *Metamorphoses*, viii. 618–724

[6] Pliny, *H. N.* xix. 49.

[7] Virgil, *G.* iv. 116–48; Petronius, *Sat.* 135.7–18

[8] See for example Horace *C.* 1.17; *Epp.* 1.16; *Epod.* 2.

[9] Courtney 1984, p. xxvi

[10] Horace, *Ep.* 3., *Epp.* I. vii. 82–95.

[11] Persius, I. 69–75.

[12] Horace, *Ep.* 3.

[13] Apicius, vi.4.2 'condimenta moretaria'; 1.21.1 *moretaria* – herbs with no cheese or garlic; Ovid, *Fasti* iv. 367ff 'a dish of *moretum*' – white cheese and herbs; Columella 12.59.1,2,3,4 with various nuts and cheese; Don ad Ter., *Phormio* 2,2,4 where a rustic consumes a garlic mixture from his mortaria.

[14] The name means something like 'snub-nosed', or perhaps 'snooty': cf. Greek *simos*.

[15] Literally 'twice eight pounds' which is the way in which all translators have rendered this. However one smallish loaf can scarcely require more than 16 oz. of grain, which reduces to rather less flour.

[16] i.e. the inner, grinding, surfaces, and (presumably) the central hole; or else the area it sits on.

[17] Again, the name is suggestive: Greek *skubale*, 'dusky'. The reference to *custos*, 'keeper', is a clear imitation of the story of Baucis and Philemon in Ovid's *Metamorphoses* and is a means of dating the poem.

[18] Latin *quadra*, but no specific number is indicated, despite the similarity to 'quarter'. The word simply means 'divisions', and refers to the spaces between the lines, not the lines themselves.

[19] reading *occatae*.

[20] translating, and rather expanding, the single word *gramine*; the garlic is relatively fresh, with a green top.

[21] MSS *uestem* – which makes some oblique sense if he has gathered his tunic up to support the mortar. *Sub crure* doesn't mean totally beneath, but just one side wedged down.

[22] *lacte*, lit. 'from the milk'.

[23] translating *prandium*, which seems to stand equally for lunch – see the end of the poem.

A Thousand Years of Japanese Banquets

Richard Hosking

From the earliest detailed historical evidence to the present day, the Japanese have had three principal styles of banquet. The earliest, at its height of glory at the end of the Heian Period (AD 794–1185), was *Taikyo Ryori*,[1] seen primarily at the imperial court or staged by high-ranking aristocrats, 'seen' being the operative word, since the greatest emphasis, as is the norm in Japanese culture, was on appearances.

Next came *Hon Zen Ryori*, which had superseded *Taikyo Ryori* by the sixteenth century; it continued as the norm until the Second World War and is still occasionally encountered. The emphasis continued to be on appearances, often with impressive tables of food for display only. In both these styles of banquet all the food was on display from the beginning, and was therefore eaten cold, apart from the soups.

In recent times a third style has come to the fore, based on the meal served at a full tea ceremony, with the emphasis on seasonality and with the food brought on in successive courses so that everything is freshly prepared and hot dishes can be eaten while still hot. This is known as *Kaiseki Ryori*, and is currently available even in London, if ordered well in advance.

The Taikyo *banquet*

Food figures in the earliest Japanese written records, and what the Japanese ate from the earliest times has been well established. By the eleventh century AD illustrated documents were devoted to describing in detail court banquets hosted both by the emperor and by senior aristocrats, with all the food depicted and labelled and all the banqueting arrangements described and recorded in detail.

The most important document of this kind is a scroll painting entitled *Ruiju zoyosho* ('A miscellany of essential related topics'). This scroll, now in the Tokyo National Museum, not only shows all the food on the tables carefully labelled, but also illustrates the buildings that were erected for the banquet and the layout of the seating. Several dated banquets are depicted. The style of food at such banquets was known as *taikyo ryori*, 'large banquet cuisine', of which there were various grades depending on the status of the host and of the guests.

The menu consisted mostly of seafood, wild fowl, confectionery and fruit, vegetables apparently being held in low esteem. At the house-warming banquet given by Yorinaga Fujiwara in Kyoto (the seat of the court) in 1136, there were several dishes of *ayu*,[2] a delicious fluvial fish scarcely known outside Japan, sea bass, sea bream, trout, octopus, carp, pheasant, spiny lobster, various dried fish shaped like flat tiles, steamed abalone, grilled octopus and plovers. There was also *namasu*[3] of turbot,[4] crab, sea squirt, and jelly fish. The condiments for all these were *hishio* (the forerunner of soy sauce), sake, vinegar and salt, to be mixed according to the diner's taste.

For dessert, there were chestnuts, dried persimmons, three types of citrus fruit (mandarins), rice cakes and several kinds of Chinese-style confectionery (*togashi*). Rice completed the menu, which was eaten with silver chopsticks and spoon.

Eating with chopsticks, which came from China, was established in Japan by the eighth century. In addition, the court adopted the Chinese spoon and used Chinese-style tables and chairs, a custom which the emperors continue to this day. The common people never took to the Chinese spoon, since the Japanese lift soup bowls to the mouth and drink straight from the bowl. After the waning of Chinese influence at court from AD 894 onwards, the court gradually abandoned the use of spoons, though even today spoons of the ancient kind are still made.

At such a banquet, the guest of honour was served at a private 'high' table about a metre square and the other guests sat together facing him in groups around tables two metres square or larger. These tables were placed on mats, and most of the guests sat on the floor, so naturally the tables were quite low. High-status guests, however, sat on stools with higher tables. The food, which was served in individual portions and consisted mostly of luxuries, the equivalent of *foie gras* and caviar, was all placed on the tables before the meal started, and over the years there were developments in presentation. In a New Year's banquet of AD 1116, all the food was prepared beyond recognition and piled high on plates in a style of presentation known as *takamori*. Twenty years later at the banquet described above, the individual items, though still piled high in *takamori* style, are recognizable for what they are, so that a lobster looks like a lobster and a trout, a trout.

Very little alcohol (sake) would have been drunk at this rather formal party, for afterwards there was a second party for drinking, naturally less formal. Eight to ten foods were served, including hot soups, and there was entertainment of singing and dancing. The rigid formality of the long first party was relaxed and differences of social status were ignored. This custom for a second, less formal, party for getting drunk after the main party continues to the present, so that it can be said that the basic form of the Japanese banquet was established in the

Heian period. It is bad form not to attend the second party, since inebriation is very important to the Japanese psyche and performs a significant function in an otherwise rather rigid and formal society.

By the late twelfth century, the warrior class was wresting power from the aristocracy, and the first shogun (military leader) Yoritomo Minamoto punished samurai for showy display and luxurious living. As time went by, however, the economic base of the warrior class (samurai and their *daimyo* [lords]) improved and so did their meals, so that by the Muromachi period (AD 1392–1568) the samurai class began to have great influence on culinary practice, an influence which established *hon zen ryori* as the official banquet style.

The Hon Zen *banquet*

Zen is the name of the short-legged individual table, which is associated with formal and upper-class dining. *Hon* means 'main', since at this style of banquet each person would have three tables, the second to his left and the third to his right.

Hon zen ryori had its beginnings in the thirteenth century and was founded on the basic meal of Buddhist monasteries, a bowl of rice, a bowl of soup and a side dish of vegetables, usually pickled. This was referred to as *ichiju issai* (a soup and a vegetable dish, the rice being taken for granted). This was just too frugal, especially for active warriors like the samurai, so *ichiju san sai* (a soup and three side dishes) became the norm, and this was the basis of the *hon zen* banquet by simple extension: one soup, five dishes; or two soups, five dishes; or two soups, seven dishes; up to three soups, eleven dishes. These would be arranged on three or more small tables, the main table right in front of the diner being a little larger than the others. The banquet was intended primarily for display and was not necessarily very tasty. Appearances were everything. This was remarked on very astutely by a visiting Portuguese Jesuit missionary, who was in Japan in the late sixteenth and early seventeenth centuries, João Rodrigues:

> In general, the banquets which were held in Japan up to the time of Nobunaga [late sixteenth century]… had a certain number of tables and dishes which were fixed as regards the number and quality of things offered. In these banquets many of the dishes were served on plates in the form of pyramids neatly arranged;… but they served only for decoration and were there to be looked at and not eaten. Special people prepared these banquets and we ourselves had experience of them for some years after our arrival in Japan…. They were wont to hold these banquets more as a rite to show honour and regard towards the person

of the guest than to enjoy eating tasty dishes.... The food was cold and insipid as it was cut up in portions and brought in on tables, and the only thing that was hot was the shiru or broth, which one was able to enjoy. These were the principal dishes of the banquets and the rest was merely additional, for they were made of things highly prized by them... The more solemn the banquet among the Japanese,... the greater the number of broths and shiru provided for each guest. Each of these is made from different things; some are made from high-quality fish; others from the meat of birds which they prize, such as the crane, which ranks in the first place, the swan in the second and wild duck in the third. This is still true even today, for on no account will they use anything but wild game and never the domestic animals and birds which they rear...on no account whatsoever will they eat ass, horse, cow, much less pig (except boars), duck, or hens, and they are naturally averse to lard. They eat only wild game at banquets and their ordinary meals, for they regard a householder who slaughters an animal reared in his house as cruel and unclean; on the other hand, they do not show this compassion towards human beings because they kill them with greater ease and enjoyment than they would an animal.... Although these *shiru* are called broth, ...they are actually fish or meat dishes with their sauce, seasoned together with different spices, and not broth just by itself.[5]

A typical example of a *hon zen* banquet provided for an early nineteenth-century diplomatic mission to Japan has been recorded in the greatest of detail, both in words and pictures. The story is as follows.

The Korean diplomatic missions: Chosen Tsushin-shi[6]

During the seventeenth and eighteenth centuries, whenever a new shogun came into power, a large diplomatic and cultural mission of between 400 and 500 envoys, scholars, poets, philosophers, calligraphers and painters sailed from Korea to Japan and were lavishly entertained at various stops on their progress through the Inland Sea, on their way to Osaka and thence by land to Edo (Tokyo), the shogun's place of residence.

There were altogether twelve such missions and very detailed records, including drawings and paintings were kept of them. There is, for example, a scroll painting of the banquet served to the three highest officials of the last mission, in 1811. This was a *hon zen* banquet of the most impressive kind, mainly intended to create a grand visual display. The food was largely to look at and be impressed by, rather than to be eaten, however records show that in the mornings and evenings the three top envoys were served meals of seven–

five–three, that is to say seven dishes on each diner's main table (*hon zen*), five on his second table (*ni no zen*) and three on the third (*san no zen*), without counting soup or rice. For lunch, it was a meal of five–five–three. There was also an alternative menu of three soups and fifteen dishes.

On the Inland Sea island of Shimo-kamagari, not far from Hiroshima, in the *Gochiso Ichiban-Kan* museum, realistic full-scale models of all the dishes are on display.

> On the main table (*hon zen*) in front of each diner there was: dried dolphin fish; dried octopus; *kamaboko* (steamed fish paste); dried fan shell, pickled melon; sea bream dried, steamed and shredded, all served with salt and *hishio* (the forerunner of soy sauce) as condiments, and rice as display only.
>
> On the second table (*ni no zen*) there was dried salt shark; cuttlefish rolled and sliced; cubes of abalone served in the shell; sliced *karasumi* (*botarga*, a great delicacy in Japan); dried salt fillets of *ayu* (sweet fish – see note 2); also two soups, one of dried sea slug, taro, hollowed-out burdock, *daikon* (white radish) and grilled tofu; and another of salt chicken, shiitake mushrooms and *udo*[7] tips.
>
> On the third table (*san no zen*) there was salt grilled breast of quail; cubed turbo on a bed of *wakame* seaweed, served in the shell; boiled rock lobster; also two soups, a thick soup of carp and a clear soup of sea bream.
>
> There were also two other tables of three dishes, one with *sashimi* of carp, sea bass and *mirukui* (a kind of clam);[8] *sake* flavoured with salt-pickled apricot, ginger and cured bonito and a mixed bowl of sea bream, salt *matsutake* mushroom, salt duck and shark; the other with slices of abalone paste rolled in *kombu*; a cedar box filled with sea bream, blood clam and abalone in sauce and a mixed dish of grilled whiting, horse mackerel, eel and 'small bird'.
>
> In addition, there was a large array of dishes and artificial flowers for display only.

The alternative menu of three soups and fifteen dishes was as follows: *Miso* soup with sea bass, arrowhead[9] and *kuzu*[10] dumplings; clear soup with quenelles of sea bream, shiitake mushroom and water dropwort;[11] another clear soup with cod, turnip and welsh onion.

The dishes were, 1: grilled sea bream, gilded with egg yolk; 2: tofu grilled to resemble Castella cake;[12] 3: white radish pickled in *miso*; 4: salmon *teriyaki*;[13] 5: pheasant *teriyaki*; 6: *namasu* of wild duck; 7:

wild duck grilled on a cedar board, 8: deep-fried tofu balls; 9: rolls of salt-dried squid; 10: thick slices of abalone simmered in soy sauce; 11: *furofuki*[14] topped with *miso* and mustard; 12: braised cod; 13: *sashimi* of turbot; 14: citron-flavoured *miso* served in a shell of citron peel; 15: pieces of chicken grilled on skewers (*yakitori*). This was accompanied with rice.

How much of this food the high officials were expected to eat is not entirely clear, probably not very much. Although *hon zen ryori* still exists, it mainly survives in a debased form as the style of food at wedding banquets, where all the food is on the table from the start, and only the soup is hot.

Already there was a much more satisfactory type of banquet in existence, which had its origins in the meal served at the tea ceremony, and which had become independent of the cult of tea.[15] Naomichi Ishige, the distinguished Japanese food anthropologist, comments: 'This *kaiseki ryori*, which had begun in opposition to *hon zen ryori*, ultimately influenced its form and made the meals of the formal banquet style more substantial.'[16]

The Kaiseki *banquet*

Rodrigues early in the seventeenth century writes:

> They also abolished, or do not now hold, banquets of five or seven tables, but ordinarily use three. They likewise did away with the earthenware vessels of ancient tradition.... But they now use lacquered ware instead;... these are not harmed by water, nor can damp or grease penetrate them because they are almost like glass, and nothing sticks to them when they are washed. Or else they use delicate ware from China or other glazed ware made in Japan itself.
>
> As regards the actual food, they did away with the dishes placed there merely for ornament and to be looked at, and also the cold dishes; in their place they substituted well-seasoned hot food which is brought to the table at the proper time, and is substantial and of high quality. This was done after the fashion of their *cha-no-yu* [tea ceremony] which they greatly imitate in this matter. They also omitted the multitude of broths or *shiru*, and now give only two or perhaps three. These will include on the first table a light one of herbs and tasty vegetables along with the rice and they start with this; another will be of some prized bird and this is the principal dish of the banquet; the third will be of another substantial and esteemed thing, and they drink often and intermittently while they are eating. The wine is produced... almost at

the end. So food at banquets nowadays and at ordinary meals gives pleasure and enjoyment, all apart from the wine, and it is not only for the sake of ceremony and courtesy and merely to look at, as in former times.[17]

Rodrigues dates this 'new' style of banquet from the time of Oda Nobunaga (1534–1582) and *Taiko* (Toyotomi Hideyoshi: 1537–1598).

The underlying basis of both the tea ceremony and banquet styles of *kaiseki* is the serving of fresh foods in season. The other two styles relied heavily on dried, salted or pickled foods. Where the banquet style differs from the tea ceremony is that in the banquet style menu, all the principal methods of cooking should be represented. Thus following the hors d'oeuvre there will be clear soup followed by *sashimi* (raw fish), grilled food, deep-fried food, simmered food, food in a light vinegar dressing, a composite rice dish with *miso* soup and pickled vegetables (*ichiju issai* as mentioned above) and dessert, usually fresh fruit. Under influence from the tea ceremony meal, there might be a course of *hassun*, a selection of delicacies such as *botarga*, sea urchin and other rareties from land and sea. The menu is very flexible and gives great scope to imaginative chefs.

Here is the menu of a *kaiseki* banquet for twenty-eight people, each course served in succession, recently enjoyed in London:

> **Hors d'oeuvre**: 'Ice-house'[18] yam tofu with *nameko*[19] fungi, Japanese citron and a topping of salmon roe with fresh *wasabi*. **Soup**: Chilled soup with wax gourd[20] dumplings, watershield[21] and prickly ash[22] leaves. **Sashimi**: Slices of fresh raw turbot and squid with *wasabi* and soy sauce. **Grilled food**: Sea bass coated with a purée of fresh soya beans and grilled, with a garnish of *mioga* ginger. **Deep-fried food**: Deep-fried prawns coiled with *udon* noodles; deep-fried asparagus; with *tempura* dip, grated white radish and welsh onion. **Simmered food**: Eel with burdock and other vegetables simmered in a thick beige-coloured sauce with Japanese pepper (*sansho* – prickly ash seeds). **Vinegared food**: Slices of cold cooked beef with a variety of vegetables in a slightly sweet vinegar dressing, with sesame sauce and soy-citrus dip. **The main course** (rice): Rice steamed with chicken and vegetables with *miso* soup and vegetable pickles. **Fruit**: Macedoine of fresh fruit and agar jelly in light syrup.

This menu keeps strictly to traditional ingredients. For the present, innovation and development are not in the structure of the meal, but rather in the gradual introduction of non-traditional ingredients, such as unusual imported vegetables, meats or fish. Atlantic lobster is now farmed in Hokkaido. Unimaginably good beef is produced in Matsuzaka and other places. Caviar is also often used, and sometimes even cheese.

Ingredients are also used in non-traditional ways, such as salmon as sashimi. Until recently salmon was always grilled or pickled to avoid the danger of parasites; now it even appears on sushi, at least when prepared by non-Japanese. Almost any food can be incorporated into a *kaiseki* meal, though tomato would be very rare and avant garde, almost outrageous, despite the fact that some of the best tomatoes in the world are grown in Japan.

Japanese food habit is not static, but is always on the lookout for new and interesting ways of using all manner of foodstuffs. The imagination of top Japanese chefs knows no bounds. When it comes to the structure of a banquet, however, apart from wedding receptions and their *hon zen* style cold food service, there is no real challenge to the *kaiseki* form.

Acknowledgement

I owe an enormous debt of gratitude to my friend Naomichi Ishige, Director of the Japanese National Museum of Ethnology, especially for giving me a copy of the draft of his forthcoming *History of Japanese Food*.

BIBLIOGRAPHY

Cooper, M. (ed. and tr.), *This Island of Japon. João Rodrigues' Account of 16th-century Japan*, Kodansha International, Tokyo and New York 1973.

Hosking, Richard, *A Dictionary of Japanese Food. Ingredients & Culture*, Tuttle Publishing, Rutland Vermont and Tokyo 1996.

——, *At the Japanese Table*, Oxford University Press (China) 2000.

In Japanese:

Aki kamagari gochiso ichiban, Shimokamagari cho 1989.

Chori yogo jiten, Zen koku chorishi yosei shisetsu kyokai, Tokyo 1998.

Gochiso ichibankan, Shimokamagari cho 1994.

Heibonsha dai hyakka jiten, Heibonsha, Tokyo 1984-1995, 20 vols.

Matsushita, Sachiko, *Iwai no shokubunka*, Tokyo Bijutsu, Tokyo 1991.

Sekai no tabemono. Nihon hen, N. Ishige, S. Tsuji and S. Nakao eds., Asahi shimbunsha, Tokyo 1982-83.

NOTES

[1] *ryori* means 'cuisine, style of cooking, as well as the act of cooking'.

[2] *Plecoglossus altivelis*.

[3] *namasu* consists of thin strips of fish or meat in a light vinegar dressing.

[4] *Batillus cornutus*.

[5] *This Island of Japon. Joao Rodrigues' Account of 16-century Japan*, p. 237.

[6] *Gochiso Ichibankan*, Illustrated Catalogue no.1, Shimokamagari cho, 1994.

[7] *Aralia cordata*.

[8] *Tresus keenae*.

[9] *Sagittaria trifolia* var. *edulis*.

[10] *Pueraria lobata*.

[11] *Oenanthe javanica*.

[12] A steam-baked sponge cake, browned on top and bottom, introduced in the 16th century from Iberia by the Portuguese.

[13] A glaze of soy sauce and sugar makes the grilled food glisten.

[14] Boiled white radish topped with flavoured *miso*.

[15] For the distinction between the two types of *kaiseki* meal, see Hosking, *At the Japanese Table*, pp. 57, 58.

[16] Unpublished MS of 'The History of Japanese Food'

[17] *This Island of Japon*, p. 240.

[18] The Imperial ice-house in Kyoto was opened for summer use at the end of June, giving rise to this epithet for chilled food served soon after that.

[19] *Pholiota nameko*.

[20] *Benincasa hispida*.

[21] *Brasenia schreberi*.

[22] *Zanthoxylum piperitum*.

Perpetual Picnics – the Meal in the UAE

Philip Iddison

'We ate coffee and dates for breakfast, dates and fish at midday, and coffee and dates in the evening. We didn't eat bread, we sometimes had a little rice.'[1]

In the past there was a limited choice of food for the population of the Emirates and as a result meals were also simple. The availability of some foods was very seasonal and there was undoubtedly monotony in the diet. Most people had an intimate association with the sources, production and preparation of food as well as its consumption. Food was relatively plentiful and the social structure ensured that no one lacked food for sustenance. The quotation emphasizes the simplicity and repetition, which were some of the characteristics of meals before economic development made the world's diverse food resources available to the Emiratis.

Many of the basic attributes which identify a meal in Western culture are absent in a traditional meal in the UAE. There is no specific room dedicated to the eating of meals and there is no furniture associated with meals. Similarly there is no cutlery and crockery for individuals and no glassware. The guest list is liable to change. The precise timing of the meal may be indeterminate. There will be no sequence of courses and at a large banquet there may be several 'sittings' to accommodate all the diners. There are no alcoholic beverages. Only within the family will adult men and women eat together at the same meal. There is no lingering over the food, eating is a brisk activity and as soon as you have eaten your fill you rise and leave the food. The duration of a meal will often depend on the arrival time of the principal guest and his continuing presence; when he goes the meal will end. No food is wasted; any excess is gifted to someone.

Most daily routines were carried out in the open air due to the climate[2] and this applied to meals as well. Thus the meal would have had the semblance of a picnic to a Western observer. However, the general lack of structure which is typical of a picnic meal should not be inferred from an Emirati meal. Meals were as structured and formal as they are in many other societies.

Two principal formalities are the passing of incense and the drinking of coffee. Both often precede and conclude a meal. The metallic ring of pestle against mortar during the pounding of fresh-roasted coffee beans would act as a signal, effective over a long distance, that coffee was about to be prepared with the probability of further hospitality to follow. Similarly the smell of frankincense, myrrh or a mixed preparation called *bokhur* acted as an olfactory hint of an imminent meal. The incense offered at the end of a meal marked its completion and guests were expected to leave promptly once it had circulated.

The differences from formats in other societies are worthy of study and understanding as part of an assessment of the social role of food in UAE society. One very basic division must be established. This is the difference between private and public meals. This fundamental division also roughly coincides with the social rules on the mixing of genders at meals.

The private meal was and still is eaten within the company of the immediate family. This is the routine day-to-day meal format. The family will eat together, men, women and children. It is only in this context that adult men and women will eat together. The key qualification is kinship.

The public meal was a relatively rare event in the past. The principal event that occasioned a public meal was a wedding.[3] More infrequently a circumcision ceremony[4] would be cause for a communal celebration. The rules of bedouin hospitality required that a meal be provided for a complete stranger or group of strangers who had entered the sphere of influence of a nomadic family, however the sexes would not be mixed at such an event. Hospitality in the form of a meal was rarely offered for business purposes in the past but this is becoming a more popular modern occurrence.

Emirati society greatly admires an individual's ability to organize events and achieve results on the verge of the deadline. A simple example in the past has already been mentioned, the arrival of unexpected visitors at a desert encampment. An animal would have been slaughtered and a meal prepared in quick order to honour the guests who would in the interim have been entertained with coffee and an exchange of news. The modern equivalent is a father visiting the management of a five-star hotel on Tuesday with an announcement that the hotel will be catering for 250 guests at his son's wedding on the following Thursday evening.

Family meals during the day are: *futour*, the breaking of the overnight fast or early-morning breakfast;[5] *re-uque*, the slightly later and more substantial morning meal which may be served as late as noon; *khuda* or *ghuda*, the lunchtime meal which is now eaten after offices close at 2.30 p.m.; and *aa-sha*, the evening meal. A more informal meal for visitors during the day is *fou-alla*, a meal that can occur any time and which consists of snack food served with tea or coffee. *Ikhghawa* is literally 'with the coffee' and again would consist of light food.

The privacy of a family meal ensures that it has rarely been recorded. Anecdotal accounts of the current situation with family meals show that the changes in meal structure and function observed in Western society are also occurring in Emirati families. The reduction of extended family groups, the pace of modern life and the number of alternative distractions available, such as supermarket convenience foods and fast-food franchises, is eroding the function of the meal as a regular social gathering for family members.

Accounts of a number of meals in the United Arab Emirates illustrate these points. Simplicity combined with hospitality is a good starting point.

Fresh bread at the hospital

Gertrude Dyck arrived in Al Ain in early 1963 to work as a nurse at the Oasis Hospital. Many of the patients were accompanied by their families who would camp outside the hospital grounds whilst the patient received their treatment. It was natural for the locals to extend hospitality to the hospital staff, and offering coffee was traditional. On this occasion what amounted to a full, albeit very simple, meal was provided:

> I remember one particular time when the man of the household was the chef,[6] and he baked some bread for us. He had no oven, no bread pans, no big mixing bowl. He didn't need them. He mixed the flour, salt and water in a small bowl with his fingers, and kneaded it a bit. Then he pushed the coals of a desert bush fire to one side, made a flat cake of his dough and placed it on the hot sand, where the fire had been, and then put some of the coals on top of the dough. He left it to bake for a few minutes and then took it and brushed the sand from it and broke it into pieces in the bowl. He poured a bit of water over it to wash off some sand (for our sake, I presume) and then poured some liquid butter on it from a small kettle, and then some local honey from a small bottle. He offered it to us with pride. We admired what he had accomplished too and of course, ate with him. It was quite tasty with the butter and honey, and rather 'crunchy' with the sand. We appreciated his hospitality. Custom demands their best, and the local Arabs were masters of this attribute.[7]

The simplicity of this meal is a hallmark of traditional bedouin hospitality.

Meals in a sheikh's hareem

Patricia Holton wrote an account of her intermittent contacts with a sheikh's family starting in the mid-nineteen-seventies. She had looked after the sheikh's son whilst he was at school in London. Her hospitality was returned with an invitation to join the family in Abu Dhabi and Al Ain. Arriving on her first visit she joined the family at their winter retreat on the coast near Abu Dhabi in a tented camp. Awaking on the first morning she recalls her breakfast:

> Beside my palliasse was a round tin tray about two feet in diameter. On it were two pyrex cups, one with a saucer, one filled with sugar. There were two metal spoons, a piece of silver baco-foil holding some tea bags, a tin of 'Rainbow' condensed milk and a plate with two hard-boiled eggs. There was a rustling and the pad of sandals on sand. The tent flaps opened and one of the serving girls came in, followed by a manservant carrying a shovel of burning coals for the brazier. The maid squatted beside me and began to make tea from a tall blue thermos which she had brought with her and peeled the eggs. The sons had already breakfasted and I must hurry.[8]

The simplicity of this breakfast was the same for all the members of the sheikh's retinue staying at the camp. The tea bags, condensed milk and Thermos are markers of the adaptability of Gulf customs to modern products and utensils.

A few days later she was taken to visit a local sheikh's camp where she ate a mid-morning meal for the first time, bedouin-style, with no utensils:

> That morning however I was on my own. The girl beside me realized my confusion and began carefully to explain what was in each dish. Harees - a kind of glutinous porridge of lamb and cracked wheat; bilaleet – a sweet vermicelli with an omelette on top; and kabees – a strange combination of flour, oil and sugar which looked and tasted something like a sweet couscous. It too was served with an omelette on top. The girl showed me how to dip into the bowl with the thumb and first and second fingers, how to make a kind of ball and push it off the fingers into the mouth with the thumb.
> 'Try the harees. It is the easiest.' She said.
> So began my first meal 'bedu' style. The harees proved to be delicious and I stuck to that in spite of the urging by the others to try each dish.[9]

These are typical and traditional dishes for many types of Emirati meal. There are no strong associations between particular dishes and specific meals apart from what is dictated by the practicalities of food preparation and preservation. For instance it would be unlikely that boiled goat and rice would be served at an early-morning breakfast.

During the cooler months of winter, early-morning meals were eaten indoors or in a tent. At other times of the day and during the hotter months, meals were traditionally eaten outside, under shade when necessary. Elderly Emiratis still feel uncomfortable about living and eating in air-conditioned buildings.

Breakfast with the Undersecretary

A trip last year to view engineering projects at Al Quo'a village, 140 kilometres south of Al Ain, with the Undersecretary of the Al Ain Municipality ended with a breakfast invitation for the whole group from one of the local village residents. The meal was described as breakfast but was eaten at noon. It was an opportunity for the local resident to present his case for some favour or action on the part of the Undersecretary and could thus be viewed as a modern business breakfast. In offering the hospitality to the whole entourage of some twenty people, additional merit would accrue.

The meal was preceded by a reception in one of the two main rooms of the *majlis*.[10] In modern Emirati houses the *majlis* is usually constructed as a freestanding building at the edge of the compound with a separate entrance. This enables male visitors to avoid the possibility of seeing the women of the house, an important condition of hospitality. We assembled in the *majlis* reception room and sat on chairs around its perimeter. The host and his sons passed around cold water and soft drinks. Hosts are attentive to their guests and usually abstain from eating or drinking in front of their guests. This was followed by coffee, a thin brew strongly flavoured with cardamom, served from vacuum flasks into small porcelain cups. The proceedings were brisk and very informal as more men arrived, greetings were exchanged and conversations started. An incense burner, *madkhan*, with frankincense on burning charcoal was passed around for the men to cense their beards and clothes.

After twenty minutes or so we were ushered into the other major room of the *majlis* building. There was no furniture in this room. A cloth was spread on the floor in the middle of the room and on it were several large circular mats woven from date palm fronds. Upon the mats all the food had been placed in a variety of dishes made of glass, metal and plastic. The only utensils were some serving spoons and there were no plates. The main dish was a boiled lamb; served on multiple layers of flat bread, *khubz*. It was accompanied by dishes of *harees*, *balaleeth*,[11] *aseeda*,[12] *wagafi*[13] and honey.

The group ate lightly, understanding that we were probably being offered the family's lunch by our host. After twenty minutes or so the Undersecretary rose and that was the signal for everyone to leave in turn and take coffee and incense again in the *majlis* reception room.

The hospitality of meal giving is still very much rooted in the home base. Traditional food dishes are still first choice for offering to guests. The skills of the family cook are viewed with pride and best exemplified in traditional food rather than modern introductions.

Wedding feasts

Patricia Holton details the meals during the wedding of a sheikh's son,[14] which took place towards the end of the 'seventies or early 'eighties in Al Ain. The celebrations lasted about a week and drew guests from Saudi Arabia, Qatar and the Oman. For the three nights and four days of the main celebrations in advance of the wedding, involving traditional dance and music provided by the guests, copious food was provided for the male guests at a specially prepared celebration ground. The cooking was on a grand scale with fifty cooks tending copper cauldrons, each big enough to hold two butchered camel calves.[15] The invitation was general and any one could attend, providing they were male.

In comparison, the women's celebrations were very private affairs in the confines of the respective family homes. They culminated in the *maksar* feast at which the bride's dowry was on display on the day before the wedding. Only the married women were invited, the bride did not attend being in strict purdah until the wedding day. Even the bridegroom's unmarried sister did not attend. The food was the traditional selection of *harees, thareed*,[16] fruit and coffee, boiled lamb, goat and camel served on mounds of rice and finally more coffee and dates.

Gertrude Dyck describes a very simple wedding celebration in the desert from a similar era. The women gathered in the tent with the bride in seclusion behind a blanket draped across one corner. The men held a *majlis* under an acacia tree nearby and ate a meal of rice and boiled goat. The remains of this meal were later offered to the women. The festivities extended over two days and once again it was literally 'open house'.

These wedding feasts and celebrations were a very public display of a family's hospitality, social and political position in the local as well as the surrounding tribal communities. It also established the family's wealth, although at that time this was a relatively understated objective of the whole event. Ostentation was still to arrive on the scene.

Some twenty years later, driving through one of the suburbs of Al Ain late on a Thursday afternoon, I noticed some outdoor cooking activity by the roadside. Making a U-turn to go back and investigate, I passed two large tents and also noticed the UAE flags, both heralding an imminent wedding party. It was on the edge of a *shabiya*, an old housing area for national families.

Cooking activities were well advanced. Nine or ten huge aluminium pots were bubbling on fires in an area protected with makeshift screens of eight-by-four sheets of plywood nailed to stakes driven into the ground. Each pot rested on three concrete building blocks and was fired directly by tree trunks of acacia wood, which were fed into the fire progressively. The pots varied in size but most were about five feet in diameter and thirty inches deep. The largest pot probably contained a thousand litres of water and would weigh one ton. A water tanker, parked nearby, had provided the liquid to fill them up.

Across the road in neat piles lay the viscera and hooves of eight young camels, almost certainly young bulls, the cows being too valuable for the pot. They had been slaughtered and butchered on the spot, there was no sign of the skins and all the edible delicacies such as heads, hearts, livers etc. had probably gone in the pot. The fatty humps would certainly have been put in, they are considered a delicacy, despite a rather unappetizing gelatinous consistency to a western palate.

Several Pathan or Pakistani cooks tended the pots. One was using a garden shovel to turn over the contents and extract a sample of the cooking liquor to taste it. Bones protruded from the cooking liquid and dried limes, *loomi*, bobbed around on top. The pots had been liberally dosed with saffron or more likely turmeric as they had an insipid yellow colour. Carrot and onion peelings around the pot indicated some of the other ingredients. I saw the cooks adding half-kilogram packets of cumin and several kilo packs of salt per pot.

Large aluminium buckets were being knocked into shape ready to receive the meat and bones when they were cooked and it was time to cook the rice in the cauldrons. The cooked rice would be heaped on large oval aluminium serving trays and the meat would be piled on top to serve to the wedding guests. I had seen similar preparations in a back lane in Khadimiyah in Baghdad in 1984. There the pots were *qidr*, the traditional copper pots with conical sides.

Passing by the site next day, the tents were being dismantled and all that remained of the kitchen area was a selection of fire blackened concrete blocks, some fine ash and, across the road, eight circles of bloodstained sand.

In the interim the male and female guests had assembled in separate tents to eat the wedding feast. But at least this wedding feast had resembled the sheikh's wedding celebrations, despite its brevity. Wedding celebrations, held at the local five-star hotels, have become a reflection of the pace of modern life. Guests will assemble in the hotel lobby to see and be seen, to chat and renew old acquaintances. The meal that follows is typically as brief as eighteen minutes from the first guest being ushered to the buffet table to the last guest leaving the food. This is taking 'not lingering over your food' to the extreme but is the modern practice.

A state banquet

Jan Morris records in literary style an outsider's view of a major ceremonial meal that was held at Buraimi in early 1956. Such meals were probably rare events. The Sultan of Muscat and Oman, Said bin Taimur, had completed his first overland trip within his sultanate from Salala to Buraimi and a state meeting was arranged with Sheikh Shakbut bin Sultan, the ruler of Abu Dhabi Emirate. After the business discussions, a formal meal was taken the next morning:

> A tent had been erected for the occasion, of considerable size, but the banquet was much too big for it, and the food stretched away on its runners far beyond the confines of the marquee. I cannot begin to describe the profusion of it all. There were huge camel haunches, of course, stuffed with spices and other meats; platters of obscure and sickly sweet things; great slabs of mutton; unfamiliar savouries of all descriptions, and a plethora of the more usual Oriental stalwarts: mountains of rice; and two plates, strategically disposed, of succulent bustard. The guests ranged themselves on the ground about this splendid buffet, the Sultan and the Sheikh at the head, the rest of us packed tightly around the sides. The qadi blessed our food in his beguiling, quavering voice; and the banquet began.
>
> I would not say that it was a comfortable meal, for the decrees of Arabic etiquette were so rigid, the company so exalted, the occasion so memorable, and the desire of everybody present to do the right thing so intense, that very few of us got anything to eat at all. In the first place, you might only eat at such events with your right hand, and this rather limited your field of action in an arena as wide as this; in the second place everybody thought it wise to keep an eye on the two rulers, to follow their unimpeachable example; and in the third place the two rulers were no less inhibited than anyone else; so that we sat there hamstrung, hardly daring to speak. Sometimes somebody grabbed a handful of rice and squeezed it between his fingers, to remove the grease, with a slight but perceptible squelching noise. Sometimes some rash spirit made an attack on a camel haunch, only to find that the particular piece he coveted was so firmly affixed to the rest of the meat that he had

to embark upon an appallingly embarrassing struggle with sinews, bones and stuffing before he could detach any of it. The bustard, *pièce de resistance* of the feast, had been planted so firmly in the middle of the table that it was virtually impossible to reach it, and it remained there in a condition of complacent virginity.

So we toyed with that marvellous spread for an hour or so, making no appreciable dents on it, until the two rulers, smiling at each other sententiously, led the rest of us out of the tent. A huge crowd of onlookers – camel men, soldiers, villagers, slaves – had gathered on the ridge above the marquee and stood there poised, like a wave at the turn of its crest, as we walked slowly towards the camp. As soon as the Sultan and Sheikh were out of sight, and were shaking hands ceremonially, that vast tattered army leapt off the sand dunes and fell on the food like ants, not desisting until every scrap of it had gone, camels and sweetmeats and rice and all; somebody even trod across the table cloth to rape the bustard.[17]

This account encapsulates many of the characteristics of a formal meal in the past in the United Arab Emirates. Although not explicitly stated there would have been no women at this meal. All the food was presented in one service. There were two sittings, the first formal, and the second very informal.

Conclusion

These brief examples highlight some the characteristics of traditional meals in the UAE. The lack of accoutrements ensures that the emphasis is on the food and the guests. Eating is viewed as an essential part of life and one to which no undue social ostentation should be attributed. It is an attribute of the bedouin that 'generosity consists before anything else in providing food'[18] and in this respect UAE society is still close to its bedouin roots.

Simplicity was a strong attribute and still holds centre stage as a limited number of traditional dishes are still very popular, particularly at wedding feasts.

The gender division is very noticeable and although signs of erosion of this strict social rule may be observed in other areas of Emirati activity, it is still mandatory at public meals.

The association between food and hospitality is strongly marked. It effectively precludes a restaurant culture amongst Emiratis. If you have food you give it to people, you would never sell prepared dishes of food. Any food prepared in your own home is valued more highly than commercially-prepared food. For a wedding, food prepared under your own direction and control is an acceptable substitute for home-cooking, taking into account the requirements for mass catering at such an event.

BIBLIOGRAPHY

Brock-Al Ansari, Celia, *The Complete United Arab Emirates Cookbook*, Emirates, Dubai, 1994.
Dyck, Gertrude, *The Oasis – Al Ain Memoirs of 'Doctor Latifa'*, Motivate, Dubai, 1995.
Holton, Patricia, *Mother Without a Mask*, Motivate, Dubai, 1991.
Lancaster, William and Fidelity, *Draft Commentary and Archive compiled for the National Museum of Ras Al Khaimah*, unpublished manuscript held in the RAK National Museum, Ras Al Khaimah, UAE, compiled 1997–2000.
Ministry of Communications, *UAE Climate*, Cultural Foundation, Abu Dhabi, 1996.
Morris, Jan, *Sultan in Oman*, Sickle Moon Books, London, 2000.
Thesiger, Wilfred, *Arabian Sands*, Penguin, Harmondsworth, 1964.
van Gelder, Geert Jan, *God's Banquet – Food in Classical Arabic Literature*, Columbia University Press, New York, 2000.
Wilson, R Trevor, *Camels*, Macmillan, London, 1998.

NOTES

[1] Statement by an elderly resident of Sha'am, a fishing village in the northern emirate of Ras al Khaimah, to William and Fidelity Lancaster.
[2] Overall mean temperatures through the year vary from 18 to 35 degrees Centigrade.
[3] A burgeoning youth population and general increase in the population of nationals is ensuring that wedding celebrations are a growth service industry.
[4] Gertrude Dyck gives an account of a circumcision ceremony that took place in Al Ain in September 1963 for 40 young boys, including a son of Sheikh Zayed who sponsored the event by paying for the food and the celebration.
[5] The special meals associated with the main religious festivals, Eid al Adha and Eid al Fitr and the holy month of fasting, Ramadan, are not considered in this paper as they constitute a separate study in their own right.
[6] Food preparation was women's work hence the comment about the cook. Men prepared coffee and would cook on hunting trips or when travelling, effectively the situation on this occasion. Bread baked in the sand was classic traveller's fare.
[7] Gertrude Dyck.
[8] Patricia Holton.
[9] Patricia Holton.
[10] The *majlis* is both the location and the event, a reception for guests or visitors.
[11] Holton's *bilaleet*, fine dried wheat noodles cooked and then steamed with cardamom, sugar, rosewater and saffron, topped with an omelette to serve.
[12] A sweet dish made from flour that has been parched in a dry pan subsequently cooked with water, clarified butter, sugar, cardamom, saffron and rosewater.
[13] *Wagafi* is thin flat bread, thinner than *khubz* but thicker than *regag* bread.
[14] This was the same boy who had been her ward in London. He was marrying the girl who had been her guide four years previously when she had eaten her first breakfast bedouin-style. That had not been a chance encounter!
[15] Young calves in the age-range 3 to 9 months appear to be the most favoured, weighing in at 50 to 100 kilograms.
[16] A thin stew of meat or chicken soaked into paper thin *regag* bread in the serving bowls.
[17] Jan Morris.
[18] Geert Jan van Gelder.

Structuring the Meal: the Revolution of *service à la russe*

Cathy K. Kaufman

Anthropologists tell us that our choices in structuring meals contain a language that reveals other aspects of our social and cultural identity. An abundance of food may be a code for political power, whereas food taboos may express long-forgotten economic policies or notions of purity and danger. While profound cultural currents subtly mark our prandial choices, what about the deliberate attempts by those who prepare food for a living to alter the way we eat? I refer to the nineteenth-century evolution from serving *à la française* to serving *à la russe*. How has this shift in the way a meal is served changed (i) the dynamics among the guests at table; (ii) the relationship between the cook and the diner; and (iii) our concept of a satisfying meal?

Compared to our usual mealtime formula of a single starter, followed by a single garnished 'main' course and capped with a sweet, menus for well-to-do folk at any time from the late Middle Ages until the early twentieth century seem staggering. Modern cookbook authors cite health concerns for our more paltry feasts,[1] yet it was precisely medieval and Renaissance dietary theories that encouraged a table of many diverse dishes. The gracious medieval host required variety to ensure that each health-conscious diner would find something appropriate for his individual humoral temperament. In effect the diner composed his own menu from the many offerings. The cook worked hard to accommodate: in one fifteenth-century recipe, a large pike is divided into thirds, with each section cooked by a different technique and accompanied by a different sauce. The result was a single fish with different humoral properties depending on the section selected.[2] Even as dietetic theories began to change in the early modern era, with parallel changes in the kitchen's products,[3] seventeenth-century authors took for granted that guests with different humoral temperaments, and thus different needs, would be at table.[4]

This deeply-ingrained presumption that a diversity of dishes on the table could promote good health is only part of the reason why *service à la française* could evolve in the seventeenth century. Unlike the comparatively simple processions of foods of earlier generations, *service à la française* was a self-consciously elegant display with its rule-bound choreography of dishes. It reflected a society in which having 'good taste' was paramount.⁵ Usually comprised of three, although occasionally more, courses of dishes, *service à la française* was designed to dazzle the eye as much as feed the stomach. The number of dishes tantalizing the guests at courtly meals might approach one for one in each course,⁶ although no diner was expected to sample them all. Many of the dishes were small and never were intended to serve everyone at table. The cornucopia of delicacies expressed the host's good taste. Specific rules governed the contents, size and placement of dishes, communicating to the diner the importance of the dish and of the meal itself. Symmetry was the key to laying the platters and tureens; the only permitted exception was for the so-called *volants*, 'flying' dishes (such as a hot, fragile soufflé) sent from the kitchen that servers offered to the guests but never placed on the table.⁷

It was the relatively rare amphitryon who relied upon his cook to devise menus. At least in the wealthier households, the *maître-d'hôtel*, the chief operating officer in charge of dining, would consult with the master on the menu and then communicate the decisions to the kitchen. A good *maître-d'hôtel* knew something about cookery, as he was charged with supervising both the acquisition of foodstuffs and the overall workings of the kitchen, in addition to his many front-of-the-house responsibilities.⁸ The cook was a subordinate; rather than being judged by the managerial skills needed to superintend a banquet, one of the cook's most important attributes was his sense of *propreté*, meaning cleanliness.⁹ With some obvious exceptions, such as Vincent La Chapelle and Marie-Antoine Carême, who played the dual roles of *maîtres-d'hôtel* and *maîtres cuisiniers*, cooks were domestic servants in the back-of-the-house. While cooks busied themselves with inventing new recipes, the *maître-d'hôtel* masterminded the meal, setting the menu, selecting the serving dishes and planning the arrangement of dishes on the table. He could be assisted by any one of the many written guides available that formed part of cookery books or manuals for household management. The guides typically provided sample menus and table diagrams and were widely disseminated, so that an experienced diner, while perhaps not predicting the exact novel concoction coming from the kitchen, could anticipate the *maître-d'hôtel*'s assemblage of game birds, butcher's meats, ragoûts and roasts among the many choices served *à la française*.

Service à la française was dramatic. No guest entered the dining room until the first course of dishes had been laid; once in the dining room, the 'luxuriousness and sumptuousness,' to borrow Carême's phrase, could not fail to seduce:

> Is there nothing that is more impressive than a great dinner as currently served in the French style? One must be persuaded by our plan.

> The rich and elegant platters in vermeil, ornamented with figures perfectly carved; the antique vases, elegant chalices, beautiful golden candelabra, the beautiful crystal to drink our excellent French wines, the beautiful desserts composed of our exquisite fruits, the flowers and the bonbons; then this service of the food, that, being uncovered at the moment when the *seigneurs* are seated at table, diffuses throughout the dining room a sweet fragrance perfumed by good cookery.[10]

One can hear the collective gasp at this denouement

Yet for all of its rigorous rules and pomp, the actual mechanics of dining *à la française* in all but the most formal diplomatic and courtly meals encouraged an intimacy among the diners.[11] While servants were present until the dessert course to lend assistance and perform various tasks, including the orchestrated removal of the first course and replacement of each dish with its second course counterpart, they rarely performed all of the serving functions. A critical part of the *maître-d'hôtel*'s job was to make sure that the dishes were properly placed on the table, with similar foodstuffs being strategically separated, so that the servers would need to intrude upon the guests as little as possible.[12] The hosts would serve soup, portion fish and often carve and serve roasts; the diners themselves might assist in the ritual of carving and would add nearby side dishes to individual plates, or pass such smaller dishes as convenient, always returning them to their appointed spot to maintain the visual harmony.[13] The array of dishes made a written menu impractical, and part of the dinner etiquette included questioning one's tablemates about their preferences and assisting them to those delicacies. Thus the diners actively shared dishes and participated in creating not only their own meal, but that of their companions. *Service à la française* encouraged a sense of communion among the diners.

From a culinary perspective *service à la française* was deemed flawed, for the food suffered from the difficulties inherent in simultaneously serving many different, hot dishes and from the inevitable wait, once the table was laid, while the diners assembled:

> This objection, it must be admitted, is very serious; it merits the attentions of amphitryons as well as cooks. Isn't it regrettable, in effect, that on a table splendidly served, where no expense is spared to flatter the taste and the desires of the guests one eats dishes that have cooled down or lost something of their essential qualities?[14]

To combat this deterioration François Urbain Dubois urged the widespread adoption of *service à la russe*.¹⁵ This style of service, now virtually universal in our contemporary restaurants, generally involves the expedited preparation of complete, individual plates for each diner by the kitchen or service staff. Rather than feasting on multiple dishes within several courses, the meal was divided into a larger number of single-dish courses, the number of which could vary, but might easily run to ten or more.¹⁶ No hot food appeared in the dining room until after the guests were seated and service proceeded briskly therefrom.

I do not mean to paint too starkly the shift from *service à la française* to *service à la russe*, as it was a process that evolved over decades and with all sorts of variants and hybridized approaches to service. Urbain Dubois, anticipating objections to an 'empty table devoid of luxury' because lacking hot food at the start of the meal, encouraged spectacular displays of cold foods that could symmetrically dress the table in the best *à la française* style. He also was reluctant to eliminate completely the luxuries of choice and variety, so fundamental to *service à la française*. He thus permitted the kitchen in an important meal to offer two choices within each course of the meal and proposed lengthy course menus. Ultimately the diner might feast on as many, or even more, dishes than he actually sampled in a meal served *à la française*. Urbain Dubois' main point, however, was the palate:

> If the method of presenting dishes to the guests, instead of systematically arranging them on the table, flatters the eyes less that the senses, it obviously has resulted in savouring dishes served at the best temperature and perfect goodness, since they are cut as soon as they are cooked, and eaten as soon as served.¹⁷

Flavour takes precedence over style.

The very generalized distinctions sketched between the two types of service are less interesting than what these distinctions imply about the relationships among the diners and between the diner and the cook. It is perhaps no accident that *service à la russe* emerged as the dominant public meal structure at the time when vocational cooking was struggling, with limited success, to become a profession in which its more able practitioners could reap the economic rewards and social status attendant to members of professions.¹⁸ To be professionals, cooks must be thought to have specialized knowledge, which entitles their culinary judgments to be relied upon by the non-specialist public. While cooks always needed expert technical skills to execute a complicated service, and good cooks were appreciated as talented craftsmen, or perhaps even as artists, the structure of serving *à la française* tended to keep cooks in a secondary role. They were, for the most part, following the designs of the *maître-*

d'hôtel, the front-of-the-house face with the power to guide the menu selection. Until cooks could exercise this power in menu planning, thereby structuring the meal and controlling all the workings of the kitchen, cooks would have difficulty reaching professional status.

The shift from serving a meal *à la française* to *à la russe* changed everyone's experience of the meal. Looking first at the dinner plate, *service à la russe* treats all diners equally. The dinner plate is no longer the unique and personally-tailored product resulting from the diner's selections at table and the solicitous assistance of his companions.[19] There is a whiff of the standardizing assembly line in even the most gracious meals catered *à la russe*. This uniformity, ironically, eliminates part of the meal's sense of communion, for while diners share the same savours, they do not physically share the food. The diners do not need to interact with their companions to get their meal and the phrase 'please pass…' falls into desuetude. Gone also is the dialogue over preferences among the delicacies and the opportunity for active exchange about how best to construct one's dinner from the offerings. The diners are, increasingly, an audience for a predesigned plate, rather than participants in structuring their own plate.

The need to plate away from the table also puts new responsibility on the kitchen for the elegant presentation of the food. Grimod de la Reynière quipped that '[a] man who knows how to carve and serve well, no matter how little presentable he may be in other ways, is not only universally admitted, but in many houses is valued above all other guests.'[20] Skill in carving and serving traditionally had been class markers, as Grimod, of all people, slyly knew. Urbain Dubois warned that cooks need to practice and acquire skill in portioning foods neatly,[21] undoubtedly aware that most cooks came from a class where less emphasis was placed on such ceremonial skills. In carving and portioning the food, the kitchen usurped the domain of the host or guest, always the kitchen's social superiors. The anonymous hands of cooks were unseen guests at table, performing functions formerly performed by the dining peers at table; it was the cooks who acted as the generous host once had, and both cook and diner needed to adjust.

The pace of the meal also accelerates, or at least appears to accelerate, because of the constant bustle of the servers removing and replacing a larger number of courses. Charles Ranhofer, the chef at New York's Delmonico's, offered the following horrifying timetable in *The Epicurean*:

> American service, like the Russian, must be served quickly and hot. As easily understood by the following card, a dinner of ten minute intervals can be served with fourteen courses in two hours and twenty minutes

and if at eight minute intervals, in one hour and fifty-two minutes, the same as an eight course dinner of ten minute intervals will take one hour and twenty minutes, so at eight minute intervals it will take one hour and four minutes.[22]

Eight courses in sixty-four minutes could be accomplished only if, '[a]s soon as one course is being passed around, the following one should be brought from the kitchen so that the dinner can be served uninterruptedly and eaten while hot and palatable.'[23] Ranhofer's schedule shifted the decision as to how to pace the meal from the dining room to the kitchen, another telling adjustment in the relationship between the cook and the diner. The cook's goal was service of the perfect work of culinary art, at least insofar as perfection was judged by the palate.[24] The diner's role again was as audience member whose job it was to appreciate the art in its peak condition.

Not all of Ranhofer's contemporaries approved of his frenetic pace in the service of culinary art. Auguste Escoffier sensibly urged tailoring the number of courses to the time allotted for the meal:

> [O]ne can sometimes succeed in organizing an ultra-fast service [of long menus]. But what happens thus is perfectly inconvenient and ridiculous: the guests don't have the time to touch the dishes that are served to them. The effort is in one server placing a garnished plate in front of a guest while another surges from behind the first and removes it from him... . It is one hundred times better to serve a very short menu, but well balanced and perfectly executed, so that the guests will be able to savour without haste, rather than to parade food in front of them and to repeat the torture of Tantalus, a long stream of dishes which they never have the time to touch.[25]

Escoffier's advice is quite radical and underscores the revolutionary shift from serving *à la française* to *à la russe*. For centuries a fine meal had been judged by copious offerings, if not copious quantities. The fourteen-course menus advocated by Ranhofer and many others show cooks trying to reconcile the opulent offerings of *service à la française* with the relentlessly ticking clock of *service à la russe*. Escoffier butchered the sacred cow of bountiful variety, offering diners only a few choice cuts, rather than the whole critter, in the streamlined menu.

Written menus became an absolute necessity for dining *à la russe* because, per Urbain Dubois, guests no longer 'see the dishes on the table; here, in effect, social conventions require that the guests be given information about the composition of the dinner, so that they can settle their choice and gauge their appetite.'[26] Responsibility for creating the menu now lies with the *chef de cuisine*. Significantly Urbain Dubois uses the term *chef* in describing the person who formulates the menu, rather than the term *cuisinier*, which had been the conventional way of referring even to important cooks for centuries and was still used by Urbain Dubois elsewhere.[27] The *chef*, while still a culinary practitioner, has assumed the planning role of the *maître-d'hôtel*, formerly the liaison with the host. The *chef* now structures the meal.

Menu planning became increasingly important as the number of dishes served declined. This is a twentieth-century phenomenon, rather than an immediate consequence of the emergence of restaurants, as one might suppose. Menus in the Parisian restaurants of the early nineteenth century read like the table of recipes in cookery books, continuing, theoretically, to offer the diner vast choice, such as 22 different veal preparations.[28] Urbain Dubois complained that 'men of our craft know perfectly well that a dinner of eight *entrées* pretty much absorbs in its mix all the distinguished elements that we use in cooking, and that to multiply the number in an exaggerated standard finds us forced to use elements worthy at the most of an ordinary dinner.'[29] If one of the *raisons d'être* for *service à la française* was the opportunity to display 'good taste' in the judicious selection of dishes from a table befitting the Land of Cockaigne, that exercise in good taste now devolved to the chef:

> Drawing up the menu — which is all at once a summary of the work and a plan for dining — is a more serious thing than normally supposed, for it is not only a question of setting up a list of a certain number of dishes according to known tastes or set prices; but to choose these dishes with discernment, grouping them harmoniously and to achieve, with these scattered notes, a flavourful orchestration.
>
> A well-composed menu immediately gives the impression of a confident plan, a lofty talent, and a poised spirit knowing all of the resources available to the culinary arts.[30]

Ninety years later, a carefully drawn-up plan for dining, flavourfully orchestrated, is still the hallmark of fine restaurant dining.

A current passion among chefs and gourmets alike is the tasting menu, patterned after the early meals catered *à la russe,* in which the diner surrenders all choice to the chef and sups on a varying number of petite plates in an order dictated from the kitchen. According to the 2001 Zagat Survey, no fewer than 84 restaurants in New York offer tasting menus, and certain very élite spots, such as Berkeley's Chez Panisse or Chicago's Charlie Trotter's, offer nothing else. That diners are willing to surrender all choice, in generations past their marker of good taste among themselves, suggests a further development in the relationship between the chef and eater, a perception of the chef as professional taste-maker, an *arbiter elegantiae*. The chef is presumed to possess a specialized insight into structuring a meal that makes acceptance of his or her 'flavourful orchestrations' the mark of a sophisticated palate.

All of the hoopla over Ferran Adrià's El Bulli, a Michelin three-star restaurant in Spain, illustrates the point. Revered as serving some of the world's most creative food, Adrià's twenty-odd-course tasting menus resurrect the frenzied first generations of *service à la russe*: a diner who briefly excuses himself from the table risks destroying Adrià's keen tempo syncopating the meal. Dishes often come with the waiter bearing instructions from the kitchen as to the precise number of bites that a diner should take to eat the particular dish: 'This is trout-egg tempura. Two bites, quickly.'[31] Thus not only is the diner told what to eat and when to eat it, but is even told how to eat it.

I thought that Adrià's ability 'to climb inside my mouth,' as one happy patron put it, signalled the nadir in the diner's relationship to the chef. I have since learned of even more extreme examples, the so-called international Makwa dinners, 'prepared by over-the-top inventive chefs … [for] foodies who like to think they're brave enough to try anything in the name of culinary sensation and experimentation.'[32] Eighteen courses over four hours demanded a bizarre submission to the chefs' whims, as diners were instructed to rub sandpaper between the fingers of one hand while eating langoustine tartare with the other, bob for sea-urchin-smeared *foie gras* in an icy fish brine with their hands firmly bound, or wear a cheap, scented fibreglass face-mask over their nose and eyes while nursing rose-water milk from a baby bottle. The New Yorkers who partook of this feast had it easy, as dinner was served at 8 p.m.; two European Makwa chefs served the identical menus simultaneously, starting at 2 a.m. local time, presumably to bond the palates globally. Eating this meal must have been an inner-directed, intellectual exercise, burdened with more artificial sensory constraints than the most overly-styled table design of a meal *à la française*.

A new Manhattan restaurant, The Tasting Room, has piqued my interest because it runs counter to the *à la russe* pattern. Abandoning traditional menu divisions between appetizers and main courses and offering no predetermined tasting menu, the restaurant simply lists its dishes with two separate prices, one for a 'taste' and one for a 'share.' In a spectre of *service à la française*, diners are encouraged to compose a menu from as many of the different dishes as desired; it is presumed that the dishes, even in 'tasting' portions, will be shared. As portions tend to be small, diners tend to order more plates than our normal meal structure suggests. The dishes are presented in two courses (save for dessert), in whatever order the diners select. There is even the occasional (completely unintentional) 'remove' and replacement of a dish within a course, required by the restaurant's tiny tables. Of course, there is none of the spatial choreography of dishes that distinguished a true *à la française* meal; such service is impossible within cramped East Village quarters. Diners' reactions to The Tasting Room have been mixed, from 'welcoming the ability to sample and … feeling sated but not stuffed,' to critiques showing some unease with this meal structure: 'restaurants are for eating; socializing … [is] the province of bars.'[33]

Brillat-Savarin said, '[t]he truth is that at the end of a well-savoured meal, both soul and body enjoy an especial well-being.'[34] This may be part of the reason why *service à la française* endured for over two hundred years, despite the recognized difficulties of serving food in its peak condition. Once we move past the table artefacts, the jumble of dietary theories and 'taste' displays that mandated a variety of dishes, and the need for a *maître-d'hôtel* to organize the whole event, we are left with the fact that *service à la française* was a convivial way to eat. It was, in a certain sense, the very quotidian family-style meal writ large, where camaraderie and communion were woven into the fabric of the meal.

As described by the late nineteenth- and early twentieth-century chefs, *service à la russe* emphasized pleasing the palate more than the eye. The unfortunate by-product was the elimination of the shared dishes and sense of communion in meals served *à la française*: we break bread with our companions metaphorically, rather than literally, as we no longer share a common loaf. This pre-eminence of the palate, in its most extreme examples, has created a chef's reign of terror. To quote Adrià, 'when the food starts coming, concentrate on the dish, then speak about the dish.'[35] His acolytes obey and confess to 'having discussed nothing but food' over the progress of the meal.[36] My thesis, that the pre-eminence of the palate underlying *service à la russe* empowered chefs as never before and contributed to the increased stature chefs now enjoy, undoubtedly gives us much eating pleasure. Yet even Adrià's fans say that this omnipresence of the chef is 'disorienting.'[37] How dear the price of this pleasure is has yet to be determined, but if some of the anonymous naysayers to The Tasting Room's palimpsest of *service à la française* are any indication, we have paid too much for good restaurant eating. We have structured our meals at our temples of gastronomy into occasions for fêting food, rather than opportunities for communion.

NOTES

[1] Henri Paul Pellaprat, *Modern French Culinary Art* (Avanelle Day & David White, trans.), Cleveland, Ohio: World Publishing, 1966.

[2] Amiczo Chiquart, *Du fait de cuisine* (Terence Scully, ed. and trans.), New York: Peter Lang Publishing, Inc., 1986, pp. 31–32.

[3] Rachel Laudan, 'A Kind of Chemistry,' *Petit Propos Culinaires* 62, p.8 (1999).

[4] L.S.R., *L'Art de bien traiter* [1674], reprinted in *L'Art de la cuisine française au XVIIème siècle*, (Gilles et Laurence Laurendon, eds.) Paris: Éditions Payot & Rivages 1995, p. 21. ('I well know that in matters of novelty, it is not easy to please everyone and that, like the humors, tastes differ.')

[5] See generally Jean-Louis Flandrin, 'Distinction Through Taste' in *A History of Private Life: Passions of the Renaissance* (Philippe Ariès and Georges Duby, eds., Arthur Goldhammer, trans.), Belknap Press of Harvard University, 1989.

[6] See e.g. Marie-Antoine Carême, *Le Maître-d'hôtel français*, Paris, Firmin Didot, 1822. Carême's menu dated January 17, 1813 for 40–45 covers, served 42 dishes in the first course and 40 in the second course, including *volants* in both, t.1, p. 100.

[7] François Urbain Dubois, and Émile Bernard, *La Cuisine classique*, (18th ed.), Paris: Flammarion, 1898, p. xv.

[8] See e.g. Giles Rose, *The Perfect School of Instructions For the Officers of the Mouth...*, London: R. Bentley and M. Magnes, 1682, pp. 1–11.

[9] Audiger, *La Maison réglée* [1692], reprinted in *L'Art de la cuisine française*, n. 4 supra, pp. 464; 479.

[10] Carême, t.2, p. 151.

[11] See e.g. François Massialot, *The Court and Country Cook*, (J.K., trans.) London: W. Onley, 1702, p. 46; Carême, t.2, p. 85. The cookery books and service manuals, including Carême's, suggest ways of adapting menus for 'less sumptuous' meals and the needs of the bourgeoisie.

[12] Vincent La Chapelle, *The Modern Cook* (3rd ed.), London: Thomas Osborne, 1744, p. iv.

[13] For more detailed descriptions of *service à la française*, see Claudine Marenco, *Manières de table, modèles de moeurs: 17ème–20ème siècle*, Cachan: Éditions de l'E.N.S.-Cachan, 1992; Peter Brears, 'A la Française: The Waning of a Long Dining Tradition', in *Luncheon, Nuncheon and Other Meals* (C. Anne Wilson, ed.), Stroud: Alan Sutton, 1994; Jean-Paul Aron, *The Art of Eating in France: Manners and Menus in the Nineteenth Century* (Nina Rootes, trans.), New York: Harper & Row, 1975.

[14] Urbain Dubois, p. xv.

[15] *Service à la russe* or various mixed forms of service had been used in certain European settings throughout the eighteenth and first half of the nineteenth centuries, even by Carême, although Carême thought it inappropriate for the most elegant meals. By about 1880, *service à la russe* had become the dominant style.

[16] See e.g. Charles Ranhofer, *The Epicurean* [1893], New York: Dover Publications, 1971; Oscar Tschirky, *Serving a Course Dinner by Oscar of the Waldorf-Astoria*, New York: Higgins & Seiter, 1902; Auguste Escoffier, *Le Livre des menus*, Paris: Flammarion, 1912.

[17] Urbain Dubois, p. xv.

[18] See generally Amy Trubek, *Haute Cuisine: How the French Invented the Culinary Profession*, Philadelphia: University of Pennsylvania, 2000.

[19] This stands one of the underlying planks of *service à la française* on its head: an invitation to dine was enough to communicate at least a rough social equality among the diners, while their dinner selections acted as distinctive markers.

[20] Alexandre-Balthazar-Laurent Grimod de la Reynière, quoted in Giles MacDonogh, *A Palate in Revolution*, London & New York: Robin Clark, 1987.

[21] Urbain Dubois, p. xvii.

[22] Ranhofer, p. 4.

[23] Ranhofer, p. 11.
[24] It is unfair to suggest that *service à la française* was not also concerned with serving food in its peak condition; in my example from Carême, the *volants* were all transient soufflés, which obviously could not wait for diners to enter the dining room but had to be brought and served immediately. The issue is one of emphasis.
[25] Escoffier, p. 8.
[26] Urbain Dubois, p. xix. Peter Brears makes the interesting point that, under *service à la française* as practiced in late eighteenth-century England, a hostess would announce to her guests that 'either they 'saw their dinner', meaning that no further dishes would be appearing, or that there would be 'removes' and what they would be.' See n. 13, p. 94.
[27] Although the term 'chef' meaning leader had been used in France since the Middle Ages, it does not seem to have been applied to the head cook until the middle of the eighteenth century. *Dictionnaire historique de la langue française*, Paris: Dictionnaires Le Robert, 1998; *Trésor de la langue française*, Paris: Éditions du centre national de la recherche scientifique, 1977. Cookbook titles of the seventeenth through nineteenth centuries tend to use the terms *cuisinier* or *maître-d'hôtel*, but not *chef*, reinforcing the cook's status as artisan.
[28] Rebecca L. Spang, *The Invention of the Restaurant*, Harvard University Press, 2000; see especially Chapter 7.
[29] Urbain Dubois, p. xx.
[30] Escoffier, pp. 5–6.
[31] Michael Paterniti, 'Ferran Adrià,' *Esquire*, July 2001, p. 118.
[32] Florence Fabricant, 'The Night They Bobbed for Foie Gras,' *The New York Times*, December 5, 2001, F3.
[33] Anonymous, 'The Tasting Room.' Online postings, July 2001, http://www.newyork.citysearch.com'
[34] Jean-Anthelme Brillat-Savarin, *The Physiology of Taste*, (M.F.K. Fisher, trans.) Washington DC: Counterpoint, 1994, Meditation XIV, p. 148.
[35] Paterniti, p. 138.
[36] Paterniti, p. 139.
[37] Paterniti, p. 139.

Ring the Doorbell with your Elbow: a Light-hearted Look at the American Potluck Meal

Mary Wallace Kelsey

A meal for which participants share the responsibility of providing the food and taking it to the meal-site has been popular in parts of the United States for years. It has become even more common recently, partly because more women are working outside the home. Also, because families participate in many activities, they are too busy to do traditional entertaining – preparing the entire meal for guests – often.

I grew up in the north-eastern part of the United States where the 'shared' meals were called Covered Dish Suppers (or Lunches) and were held mostly in churches, or at club meetings. I don't remember people entertaining at home this way, but a colleague says that in her Midwestern home town, special-interest groups or committees from the family's church had covered dish meals in individuals' homes.

When I moved west I learned that the term 'potluck' was used to describe such meals. My family had used the term potluck in a different way; we might be with a friend shortly before meal-time, and invite the friend to come home with us for potluck, sharing whatever was to be served for the family. My unabridged dictionary from 1967 gives a similar definition. The 1987 edition of the same dictionary gives that definition first then, as the second definition, the meal to which guests all take some food is described.

A friend who had grown up in my home town and spent much of her life on the east coast of the US moved west a few years ago to work in a programme for the elderly. For the first social function she planned for her group, she sent invitations to a Covered Dish Supper. No one came. Later, that easterner learned that her clients didn't know what a Covered Dish Supper was.

The 1967 edition of Emily Post's etiquette book has no mention of the type of meal where everyone shares the preparation. The sixteenth edition, published in 1997 and now authored by the wife of one of Mrs Post's descendants, has a few paragraphs on hosting a BYOF (bring your own food) dinner, or a 'bring-a-dish' party. She also calls it a 'chip-in' dinner. The author emphasizes that the invitation, either oral or written, must say at the outset that the guests are being asked to provide some of the food or beverages. She calls this 'organizing' a party, rather than 'giving' it, as far as the hosts are concerned. (6)

Other terms for potluck include 'shared' meals, or 'basket' meal. Members of a Midwestern church describe meals to which families brought baskets of food, then set the dishes on a serving table as a buffet for all to share.(2, 9) In the pioneer days, probably around the middle of the nineteenth century, these basket meals may have been supplements to a barbecued buffalo or pig. (9)

On a trip to New England in the 1980s, I was caught by the title of a cookbook, *Ring the Doorbell With Your Elbow*, and had to purchase it. The author explained that this is a family expression she grew up with. It meant that when you went to an event at someone's home you'd have to ring the doorbell with your elbow because your hands would be full with the food you were taking to share at the party. (5) The book contains recipes recommended for taking to potlucks.

Several people have suggested that the term 'potluck' comes from 'potlatch', feasts that were celebrated by Indians on the north-west coast, territory that became Canada and the United States. (Indians are now known as First Nations in Canada, and Native Americans in the US.) The potlatch was a given by one tribe – usually the chief was the host – for another. This was a lavish celebration, lasting several days, with much food, entertainment and gift-giving. The guests did not take food to a potlatch, but they were expected to reciprocate in due time by inviting their hosts to a similar event. (8) This is not the same as a potluck.

Potluck meals may be structured or not. Frequently, the notice for an organization's potluck will ask that members whose last names begin with A–H take main dishes, I–Q take salads, and R–Z take desserts. Occasionally the notice will ask each family to take a main dish and a salad or a dessert. There's always more than enough food at the latter meal.

The meal may be more structured by assigning guests specific foods to take, or by the hosts indicating what they'll provide and suggesting what others might take. We've been invited to a dinner with a Hawaiian theme where the hosts roasted a pig and asked the guests to take side dishes or desserts to accompany the pork. Another form of potluck suggests that each family take meat, fish or poultry to grill for themselves on the host's outdoor barbecue grill, and a side dish or dessert to share.

Letitia Baldridge, who says that a potluck is 'an American way of entertaining and a good one at that', suggests that the host supply cocktails, the main course, and coffee. While asking guests what they'd like to bring, she says, the hostess should help to make a workable menu. For example, if there's to be a fruit cup starter, then a fruit salad would be repetitious. Ask the guest if a salad of greens would be acceptable to bring. Baldridge also says that guests 'should bring the course in a nice-looking container that can go from refrigerator or stove straight onto the buffet table'. She continues, 'In the best of all situations, the hosts should insist on washing the containers and delivering them back within a week to their owners, rather than making the guests troop out to the kitchen to wash their own containers and carry them home'.(1) This has not been my experience with potlucks at someone's home!

A fairly recent book on American foods mentions that potluck meals were given in the US in the early 1940s, during World War II. Reasons for this type of entertaining were to have some social contact for women whose husbands were in military service and who found traditional entertaining difficult because they were working outside their homes, and because food rationing made getting enough ingredients difficult. (3) [I want to comment that wartime food rationing was minimal in the US compared with rationing in the UK.]

A particularly structured meal is the type done by groups wishing to learn more about the cuisine or food history of a particular part of the world. A committee is formed to do the research and a menu is planned. Recipes are made available to volunteers who prepare the dishes as authentically as possible and at the meal someone speaks about the foods, the culture being studied and/or the history involved. A group which has been noted for this is the Culinary Historians of Boston.

As I spoke with colleagues about this topic, I learned that most of us share the concern of food safety when we sample offerings brought to a potluck meal. I take tiny servings of possible 'food-illness-causing' dishes and if the chicken, potato or pasta salad isn't cold, I don't eat it. My husband takes a large serving of whatever I've brought, whether or not he likes it, because he knows it's been safely handled. A group we belong to has an annual day-long picnic, at which we gather about three hours before the meal. Picnic notices for this group always remind us to take the food on ice in insulated containers, with the note that if a dish needs to be served hot it should be transported cold and heated in a microwave oven which will be available in someone's recreational vehicle at serving time.

I'll confess that I always wonder about offerings at our Symposium Saturday lunch. Did that interesting-looking home-made item sit in someone's B&B room overnight? When my husband and I used to hire a cottage in the Cotswolds during Symposium week, I'd prepare something in our cottage kitchen and take it, still cold, to St Antony's where those in charge of the lunch would put it in the cooler until serving time. Now that we stay at a B&B, I take something prepackaged or non-perishable at room temperature.

Other comments about potluck food had to do with quality. One person said that most of the casserole dishes were mushy. Another complained that donors used to take their best offerings, speciality items, but now many don't do much food preparation. Selections appearing at the potluck might include a bucket of fried chicken from the local fast-food take-out (takeaway in the UK), a container of salad from the delicatessen section of the supermarket, or a foil pan of lasagna from the market's freezer case, baked at home just before the event. The commercially-prepared products, if handled carefully by the purchaser, may be safer than a home-made item, and so preferable for those concerned about food safety.

For those who miss the high-quality home-made foods, there's some nostalgia to be found in reading the comments written by cooks about recipes in the *Farm Journal's Best-ever Recipes* cookbook. 'I wouldn't dare show up at a potluck without a batch of these rolls.' 'This is the most popular cake at our monthly community potluck suppers.' 'Men head for this cake whenever I take it to a potluck.' 'My reputation as a good cook began when I appeared at a church supper with several batches of lemon squares.' 'I brought squash medley as my contribution to a school potluck. Everyone tried it and then returned for more.'(4)

In fiction, there's some attention paid to high-quality offerings at potluck meals. For example, in *The Baked Bean Supper Murders*, the suppers are annual fund-raising events in a small Maine coastal village. Members of the group giving the suppers make the food in their homes. Baked beans, using two different recipes, are featured, and there's steamed brown bread (a cornmeal-rye-molasses bread leavened with baking powder) and cabbage salad. Then there are assorted casserole dishes to be enjoyed before the pies are served. (7) Because of space limitations, there are two seatings at the suppers. The first seating gets 'the best of the baked beans and brown bread, the crispest cole slaw [cabbage salad], the hottest and most savvy casseroles' as well as the 'flakiest pies…the airiest lemon meringues, the richest and butteriest apples, the darkest and spiciest mincemeats'. The author explains that the 'contributions of the newest, or least gifted cooks' would be saved for the second seating because the committee members feel that the people who showed their appreciation by arriving early should have the best of the offerings. (7)

In spite of the demise of top-quality home-made foods, potluck meals are not losing their popularity in many communities in the US. The exceptions may be with groups of older people who no longer want to do much, if any, food preparation, and would prefer to pay for catered meals at their social events.

REFERENCES

1. Baldridge, Letitia, *Letitia Baldridge's Complete Guide to the New Manners for the '90s.* New York, Rawson Assoc., 1990.
2. Linn County Historical Society, *From Pioneering to the Present,* Volume III. Pleasantville, Kansas. *The Linn County News,* 1982.
3. Lovegren, Sylvia, *Fashionable Food. Seven Decades of Food Fads.* New York, Macmillan Publishers, 1995.
4. Manning, Elise W., editor, *Farm Journal's Best-ever Recipes.* Philadelphia, Countryside Press, 1977.
5. McCartney, Wilma M., *Ring the Doorbell With Your Elbow.* Revised Edition. Shelbourne, Vermont, The New England Press, Inc., 1981.
6. Post, Peggy, *Emily Post's Etiquette.* 16th Edition. New York, HarperCollins Publications, Inc., 1997.
7. Rich, Virginia, *The Baked Bean Supper Murders.* New York, Ballantine Books, 1983.
8. The Reader's Digest Assoc., Inc., *Through Indian Eyes.* Pleasantville, New York, 1995.
9. Stratton, Joanna, *Pioneer Women. Voices From the Kansas Frontier.* New York, Simon and Schuster, 1981.

Meals and Mealtimes, 1600–1800

Gilly Lehmann

It is something of a cliché to say that the tendency of mealtimes to become ever later is universal, found in all civilizations. But why the pressure towards later meals can increase dramatically at some periods has been less examined. When J.P.V.D. Balsdon commented on the shifting meals and mealtimes in ancient Rome, he ascribed the change simply to the 'development' of society:

> As a society develops, the main meal of the day is eaten later and later. At first the main Roman meal, *cena*, like English dinner in the seventeenth century, was at midday. In both cases as this meal moved forward, at one end of the day it dispossessed the evening meal (*vesperna* in Rome, supper in England), for which there was no longer any need, and at the other end it created a gap which required to be filled by a new meal, *prandium* in Rome, lunch in England.[1]

Balsdon's account does not emphasize how long the process of forward movement leading to displacement actually took: lunch did not arrive until the late eighteenth century, and even then was by no means considered as a 'proper' meal; this development was not complete until the nineteenth century. And it is not true to say that supper became superfluous. Although some historians of mealtimes have taken satirical comment on supper becoming confused with breakfast rather too literally, supper never disappeared entirely. The process was less neatly simple than Balsdon suggests, and in England there is still considerable confusion over what meals were eaten when. The starting-point of this investigation must therefore be a description of how meals and mealtimes changed, and although I shall focus on the period 1600 to 1800 it is instructive to take a longer view in order to see how the narrower period stands out as one of important shifts.

The number and names of daily meals

The basic model of a 'traditional' day divided by three main meals, breakfast, lunch (or dinner, depending on social class and geography) and dinner (or supper or high tea, again depending on the same variables), provides a reassuringly structured timetable against which to measure a perceived decline in standards, whether these are seen as nutritional or social or moral. The demise of the 'traditional' English breakfast is often seen as a sign of the influence of modern, rushed lifestyles, with the cup of coffee on the hoof for the office worker, or the briefly-fashionable 'power breakfast' for the executive, proving that time is the key factor in eliminating one of the markers of the daily rhythm. The hasty sandwich at the desk instead of lunch is another sign in the same direction. The accusing finger tends to point here at the physiological consequences of what is considered as nutritionally inadequate. The decline of the evening meal taken by the family together (now that each family member can take what he pleases from the freezer and put it into the microwave) is seen as a disturbing sign of the breakdown of family life and of the socialization of children through the formalized meal. The older, formal 'grammar' of three meals a day is giving way to a destructured and even anarchic tendency to ingest food on impulse rather than according to a ritualized, socialized timetable, and it is easy to see the moral connotations that are ascribed to this development.[2] But all this presupposes that the pattern of three meals a day is an immutable part of daily life in a civilized society, whereas in fact this is simply not true.

The only constant throughout the past in England has been the permanence of dinner as the main meal of the day, although the hour has changed very considerably. Less permanent is supper, sometimes considered as a 'real' meal (and this usually meant that it included either meat or hot food, or both) and sometimes seen as a mere snack, often depending on the nature of the occasion, festive or everyday. The least permanent of the three meals is breakfast, which was a 'real' meal for only a brief period, roughly from the early eighteenth century until the middle of the twentieth century. Within that period, breakfast amongst the wealthier classes changed its nature completely: while the eighteenth-century breakfast was based on tea, coffee and chocolate, with light breads and cakes for solids, the 'traditional English breakfast' of bacon and eggs and other such substantial items was a nineteenth-century phenomenon which persisted (albeit in less splendid form) into the twentieth century but was already in decline by the 1960s. By 1988, 17 per cent of adults ate no breakfast at all, while 25 per cent had only bread in some form.[3] Thus breakfast as the first meal of the day is little more than a brief interlude in a long tradition of informal snacks.

Because breakfast was not considered as a 'real' meal before the eighteenth century, it is not easy to determine when it was taken or what was eaten by whom. In his study of French meals and mealtimes, Jean-Louis Flandrin showed that while the medieval and Renaissance élite usually took only two meals a day (dinner and supper), workers took anything up to five, with breakfast as the first meal, taken at 9, some time after starting the day's work, the hour for this varying according to the season.[4] The situation was much the same in England, but the disapproval of breakfast for the upper classes seems to have been weaker. Although some English writers did not entirely approve of breakfast (Andrew Boorde said in 1542 that 'a labourer maye eate thre tymes a day' but that two meals a day, presumably dinner and supper, were quite enough for 'a rest man', and 'he that doth eate ofter, lyveth a beestly life'[5]), others considered that it was necessary in England for healthy people: Sir Thomas Elyot recommended breakfast four hours before dinner, and then supper six hours after dinner; Thomas Cogan gave similar advice.[6] With dinner at 11, this meant breakfast at 7 and supper at 5. Household accounts and ordinances confirm that the élite did consume breakfast, although it was apparently reserved for the family and their guests.[7]

Thus in the late medieval period and throughout the sixteenth century, breakfast was being consumed even by the élite. But it was not a 'real' meal in the sense that it was served in private (the Berkeley regulations state that guests were to be served breakfast in their chambers), without any of the elaborate ceremonial which accompanied dinner and supper. Breakfast was hardly more of a formal meal than the 'drinking' which came between dinner and supper, and replaced supper on Fridays.[8] At the other end of the day came the 'all night', bread and wine which was prepared for the upper echelons to sustain them until the next morning: allowances for this are set out in Edward IV's Black Book (*c.* 1471–2) and in the 1478 ordinance. The latter text stipulates that the food should be ready in daylight from Candlemas to Michaelmas, and by 8 in the winter.[9] The late medieval and Tudor pattern was two main meals and three snacks, although the breakfast snack could be a fairly substantial meal.

The uncertain status of breakfast persisted into the seventeenth century until well after the Restoration. Pepys's diary does mention breakfast (17 times), but much more frequently Pepys refers to his 'morning draught' (88 times, 49 of these with food in some form), the difference apparently being that at 'breakfast' the solids were the main item, while the 'morning draught' was essentially liquid. There does not appear to be any difference in the time of taking these two snacks, which belong to the sphere of sociability: Pepys never records taking either when alone at home, and this represents a change from earlier habits, suggesting that breakfast was on the way to becoming a 'real' meal, something to be shared with others. They probably represent the first moment of consumption in the day: Pepys might also have a quick mid-morning snack around 10, and he often had an afternoon snack, usually sweet, whereas the morning food was always savoury. Only once does Pepys record a sweet breakfast, on 3 August 1662, with 'a fine breakfast of bread and butter and sweetmeats and other things, with great choice, and strong drinks'. Elsewhere, the 'morning draught' was of coffee (once) and chocolate (three times), but the sweet breakfast which was to revolutionize eating habits had not yet come in.[10] This is in fact a very similar pattern of consumption to that of the earlier period amongst the élite, with dinner as the main meal, supper being less important though still more of a 'real' meal, and snacks in between.

Soon, however, breakfast was to change from being based on beer and wine with savoury foods to what is now seen as 'French' with breads and cakes accompanied by the new drinks, chocolate, coffee and tea. The transition can be seen in the diary of Claver Morris, a doctor in Wells at the end of the seventeenth century: he records eating both types of breakfast.[11] Amongst the élite the new style had taken over by the early years of the eighteenth century, and at the same time the hour seems to have moved forward, so that the most frequently recorded breakfast hour in the eighteenth century is 9 or 10, with marginally more references to the later hour. As we shall see, this goes with an important phase during which the dinner hour rapidly became later and later, pushing supper forward too as it went. Taken later and composed of different foods, breakfast was more sociable and thus it gained in status. Meanwhile, supper, pushed ever later, was becoming more of a snack than a 'real' meal, except when company was present and everyone stayed up later than usual. Eighteenth-century diaries and letters confirm the difference between a family snack (close to the 'all night' of the medieval period) and a festive supper including hot dishes.[12]

The advancing dinner hour meant that by the middle of the eighteenth century there was an uncomfortable gap between breakfast (especially if it was taken at 9 rather than 10) and dinner, now eaten amongst the gentry at 4. It was 'morning' until one dined, and increasingly, the period after dinner was seen as devoted purely to leisure. The advantage of this timetable was that there was time for some activity before breakfast, and then a period of about five hours to complete any tasks before dressing for dinner. The problem of the gap between breakfast and dinner was solved not by making breakfast a more substantial meal, but by inserting a new meal, lunch, at first an informal snack of cold meat, which was to develop into the midday meal in the nineteenth century. But partaking of some form of refreshment between meals was nothing new: 'drinking' had taken place between dinner and supper at an earlier period, as we have seen. The focus here is not to re-examine the development of the terminology of the new meal, which hesitated between 'nuncheon', 'luncheon', and 'lunch'. These questions have been dealt with by Anne Wilson.[13] What is more interesting in relation to the number of meals is that in the first half of the nineteenth century the midday lunch tended to displace supper as the 'second' meal of the day: supper became more of a snack, while lunch gradually took over its functions as the next most important meal after dinner. The residual linguistic confusion today over 'dinner' and 'lunch' (is dinner the main meal of the day, or is it the evening meal? is lunch a secondary meal, or is it always the midday meal, even when it is the main meal of the day, as in 'Sunday lunch', a dying institution? and is Christmas dinner the same thing as Christmas lunch?) originates partly in the shifts which began in the late eighteenth century.

And yet even at the end of the eighteenth century the basic number of meals had not really changed: one main meal, another secondary meal, and three lesser meals or snacks in the course of the day were still the norm, just as in medieval times, for the élite. In the fifteenth century, dinner and supper had been the two main meals, with breakfast, 'drinking' or bever, and 'all-night' as the snacks. By the very end of the eighteenth century, dinner was the main meal, with lunch and supper vying for position as the second meal, depending on the circumstances: a ball could make supper more important, a day's sport, which could push dinner as late as 5 or 6, might make the midday collation the second meal. Breakfast, which had become a more sociable meal with the advent of the new beverages and their accompaniments, remained a light, sweet meal throughout the eighteenth century. Indeed, the English found the French breakfast of hot soup and meat disgusting: in 1791 Maria Holroyd, visiting the Duc de Bouillon en route to Switzerland, commented that 'though we poor English were allowed Tea, the smell of the hot victuals was intolerable.'[14] Only when breakfast began to move backwards as lunch became more substantial did it revert to being an essentially savoury meal, and it is this which finally led to the nineteenth- and twentieth-century distribution of meals with three main meals (including meat and hot dishes) and elevenses and afternoon tea (or less elegantly, tea-breaks) between.

Much has been made of the 'invention' of afternoon tea, variously ascribed to the Duchesses of Bedford and Rutland in the 1840s,[15] but there is no real need to go duchess-hunting. Almost as soon as it was introduced in England, tea-drinking after dinner became associated with the ladies, who met to drink the new beverage and to talk scandal, according to contemporary observers.[16] In the eighteenth century, tea and coffee were served in the drawing-room after dinner, following a suitable interval to allow the gentlemen to imbibe at the dining-table. Although both tea and coffee were available, contemporaries always called this 'tea', and although the usual interval between dinner and tea was only two hours or even less (tea appeared about two or three hours after the start of dinner), bread and butter and cakes were served. In other words, a form of 'afternoon tea' was already a standard feature of the eighteenth-century day. In 1786 Sophie von La Roche was offered bread and butter during her 'tea-visits',[17] and in 1792 Louisa Holroyd, who was living in Bath, described these after-dinner tea-parties to her sister:

> You would call these parties rather sober, but for a poor creeping Christian like me, they do very well; go at a little after 6 or 7 and return at 9, have in the mean time abundance of tea, wine, bread and butter, milk punch, cake buttered and plum cake, etc. etc.[18]

This is not yet afternoon tea, but it is far closer to it than to a mere refreshment after dinner, and the hour, combined with the nature of the foods, marks it off from supper. Tea and supper were not interchangeable in the eighteenth century; tea was a sober affair, in contrast to suppers which were more festive, and less feminine in the foods which appeared on the table, with meat as an essential component. The nineteenth-century version of afternoon tea was indeed a particularly feminine affair, with appropriately dainty foods; also different was the way it fitted into the day: in the eighteenth century tea was taken after dinner, in the nineteenth century before dinner. But tea as a snack continued to be sandwiched between the two main meals, the difference being that these were dinner and supper in the eighteenth century, lunch and dinner in the nineteenth.

This account of the changing pattern of distribution of meals through the day shows that for most of the period under consideration, the norm was two meals a day rather than three, with supper as the second meal at least until the end of the eighteenth century, when its position began to be challenged by lunch. The usual explanation for this is that the displacement was the result of dinner moving from being a late-morning meal to an afternoon and finally an evening meal, but this begs the question of what prompted this movement in the first place. To try to understand how it happened, we need to look at when exactly the main periods of movement occurred.

Changing mealtimes and daily rhythms

Throughout the medieval and Tudor periods, the hour of the main meal, dinner, remained virtually constant, although the medieval distinction between flesh days and fasting days also influenced the timetable. The medieval household ordinances cited above frequently state either that the first (flesh) dinner was to be at 10 or that preparations for serving dinner should begin at 10. There were two sittings in hall in order to feed the large households, and the aim was to finish these two sittings 'within the compass of the lord's meal', which of course took much longer, given the elaborate ceremonial which accompanied it; one of the royal household ordinances, however, states that half the officers who were to serve the king and queen should eat at the first sitting, half at the second, so that the sovereigns could be served at any time.[19] Where preparations for serving began at 10, dinner for the lord would be served at 10.30 at the earliest, since a fifteenth-century courtesy book states that the marshal of the hall was to order the officers to get ready to serve the meal half an hour in advance.[20] This does not take into account the elaborate ceremonial which preceded the actual meal, so eating may not have begun until even later. A complication for the medieval period is that the dinner-hour varied according to the season and to the religious calendar: dinner on fast days was later than on flesh days, usually at 11 rather than 10.[21] There is no evidence here that dining later was a sign of status: the royal ordinance just mentioned suggests that the privilege of the lord was to be able to choose when to dine, just as he could make his choice at table from amongst the numerous dishes presented to him.

Under the Tudors, the royal and aristocratic dinner hour was still at around 11, and Viscount Montagu's household regulations from the end of the sixteenth century tell the gentleman usher to start preparations for serving dinner at 10.[22] It was those rather lower down the social scale who dined and supped later: William Harrison gives 11 and 5, or between 5 and 6, as the dinner and supper hours of the nobility and gentry, 12 and 6 as the hours for London merchants and 12 and 7 or even 8 for farmers.[23] The élite kept earlier hours than those who had to work. By the early seventeenth century, the hours had moved on only slightly: the regulations for the household of Prince Henry in 1610 state that the officers were to be ready to receive orders for service in the presence chamber by 11 and 6.[24] Charles I maintained a more conservative timetable: his household ordinances command the household officers to be in attendance by 10 and 5 to receive directions about the service.[25] The medieval organization of the day persisted amongst the élite at least until the Civil War.

The first signs of change come in the middle of the seventeenth century. Pepys's diary shows that dinner in London had moved on to 12 or 1; although Pepys frequently mentions going home to dinner 'at noon', it is clear that dinner was often later, especially when guests were invited: on 13 January 1662 Pepys was put out when some of his guests arrived before 12 and he had to keep them entertained until they finally sat down to dinner at 1, before the remaining guests had arrived. This and other references suggest that the 1660s were a period of instability in the dinner hour, which could be at any time between 12 and 2 in the normal course of things, although Pepys occasionally dined as late as 4 when pressure of work kept him at the office. What is also striking is that dinner was available at all hours, whether from cookshops or from taverns, again pointing to a period of shifting mealtimes. By the end of the century, the dinner hour had moved forward, even in the provinces: Claver Morris dined between 12 and 1.[26] On grand occasions, dinner was even later: when William III dined at Belton with Sir John Brownlow, the meal was served at 3.[27] This seems to mark the start of the fashion for ever-later dining: to dine late was a mark of status by the early eighteenth century, whereas this had certainly not been the case in the late sixteenth century.

Contemporaries were aware of the sudden change in tempo: in 1710 Richard Steele wrote a humorous piece in the *Tatler* complaining about the new fashion for late dining which meant that supper was now so late that it was in danger of being confused with breakfast. One should not take this complaint too literally, but Steele did point out that within his memory (he was born in 1672), dinner had 'crept by Degrees from Twelve a Clock to Three, and where it will fix no Body knows.'[28] After the rapid forward movement of the last quarter of the seventeenth century and the early decades of the eighteenth, the pace of change slowed. Steele's 3 o'clock was the aristocratic hour in London; amongst the gentry and in the provinces, 2 remained the most frequently-mentioned hour until at least the 1750s. What is striking is that the dinner-hour was becoming an instrument of social differentiation. At first foreign tourists were confused by the variable dinner hours of the English: in 1727 César de Saussure wrote that in London one dined at 2 or 3, although many people ate even later; by the second half of the century some of them realized that the differences were due to social class. In 1782 Moritz noted that in fashionable Westminster people dined at 4 or 5, while in more middle-class areas 3 was the usual time; a few years later Archenholz confirmed Moritz's observation, and added that working people dined at 1.[29] This was not lost on the natives either. In 1775 James Boswell, en route to London, fell into conversation with a mercer from Durham:

> The mercer told me that […] he drank tea twice a day, and had sometimes a friend to dine with him, or eat cold meat at night. […] He said, to a man accustomed to dine between two and three, it seemed strange to dine at one, as they do in this country. Everything is comparative. He looked big, as one who dined between two and three. How *little* and how *poor* would he seem to a fashionable man in London who dines between four and five![30]

Boswell's observation shows that both he and the mercer were thoroughly aware of the social connotations of the different dinner-hours. This explains why it is impossible to indicate any 'standard' hour for dinner in the eighteenth century: there is the forward movement, which itself was by no means constant, but there are also the social and geographical variables to be taken into account; also, given the prestige of later hours, a family dinner was taken earlier than one to which company had been invited.

After a slight pause in the middle of the century, the dinner-hour began to move on faster again. In the 1750s, the most fashionable circles were dining at 4, and by the 1770s this had become the standard time for the aristocracy and gentry in the provinces. Between about 1780 and 1810 there was another period of acceleration, during which the fashionable dinner hour moved on to 5 in the 1780s and 6 in the 1790s, with the gentry and the provinces catching up and eating at 5 in the early years of the nineteenth century. Thereafter, once lunch was established as the midday meal, it was invariably served at about 1, while dinner moved to a slightly earlier hour at first, 4 or 5 until about 1820, before moving forward again to reach 7 or 7.30 in fashionable circles by 1850, while the middle classes dined at 6. By 1900 7.30 was the average dinner hour.[31] In the 1930s the usual breakfast hour was 8, the midday meal was still at 1; the evening meal was between 5 and 6 for those who took 'high tea', while those who took dinner ate at between 7 and 8.[32] These hours have hardly varied since, although breakfast is no longer at a fixed time, given its transformation into a casual snack rather than a meal.

It will be seen from this account of mealtimes that the main period of change was from the middle of the seventeenth century to the beginning of the nineteenth, with a brief pause in between. But this change concerned first of all the urban élite, with the provincial gentry and the urban middle classes following the trend more slowly. And the working classes' mealtimes remained much the same, even though the names of their meals changed, since the rhythm of the working day was imposed for much of the period by the hours of daylight. Eighteenth-century working people dined at 1, only one hour later than in the Elizabethan period. Why did the dinner hour become so much later amongst the élite?

Some possible interpretations

The major periods of change were roughly from the 1670s to the 1720s, with another rapid acceleration from about 1780. The first of these periods corresponds to changes in culinary styles, as the French culinary revolution began to take hold in élite circles. The later dinner may be part of the adoption of French fashions, although Flandrin identifies the main periods of change in French dinner times as 1580–1610, when dinner moved forward by two hours, followed by a further three hours' delay between 1704 and 1782, and another three hours from 1782 to 1807. But Flandrin also points out that it was the reign of

Louis XIV that made the 'deviant' hours of the court the norm for fashionable society.[33] Since the influence of Versailles was the dominant factor in culinary fashion, this may be one element. But another is that the changing dinner hour in England arrived at the same time as the new beverages, coffee, tea and chocolate, were becoming more widely used amongst the élite. And simultaneously, breakfast tended to be taken later as it changed from a savoury to a sweet meal. Consumption of the new style of breakfast carried prestige, since the beverages were still expensive, and this is probably why breakfast became a meal to invite people to; a more leisurely breakfast meant a later dinner.

However, the main factor behind the periods of change is probably changing social structures. The first period coincides with the one during which a middle class (at least in London) was beginning to prosper and make its presence felt, and this created pressure for the élite to re-invent the signs of distinction. At an earlier period, there does not seem to have been this pressure for change: the movement of the dinner hour was extremely slow from the fifteenth century until about 1650, and although Harrison differentiated between the meal times of the élite and those of the merchants and farmers, the gap between them was not very great. Once the movement had begun, pressure from below kept the dinner hour moving, the mid-eighteenth-century pause marking a brief hiatus. By the time the provincial middle classes had adopted 3 as their usual dinner hour, in the 1770s, this pressure was renewed and hours in élite circles moved on more rapidly again. Given the evidence for the importance of the dinner hour as a social marker in the eighteenth century, social pressure seems a more convincing explanation than the mechanical one that dinner took place after 3 because that was when the Stock Exchange closed, advanced by some commentators such as Moritz.

Today, the fears that changing meals and mealtimes are signs of imminent breakdown of social structures echo the complaints of the past about the perverse nature of élite behaviour, transforming day into night with their late meals. Then as now, these complaints are vastly exaggerated, but they do express our inherently conservative attitudes to food, with a tendency to look back to a 'golden' past of a more orderly society. There were periods of flux in the past, and what is perceived as the 'traditional' model of meals was not a permanent fixture.

NOTES

[1] J.P.V.D. Balsdon, *Life and Leisure in Ancient Rome* (London, 1969), p. 25.
[2] For a discussion of the implications of these shifts, see Claude Fischler, *L'Homnivore*, Paris, 1990, pp. 203–207. I take the term 'grammar' from Fischler.
[3] See Christina Hardyment, *Slice of Life: The British Way of Eating Since 1945*, London, 1995, pp.200–201.
[4] See Jean-Louis Flandrin, 'Les heures des repas en France avant le XIXeme siècle', in *Le temps de manger: alimentation, emploi du temps et rythmes sociaux*, dir. by Maurice Aymard, Claude Grignon, Françoise Sabban, Paris, 1993, pp. 201–204.
[5] Andrew Boorde, *A Compendyous Regyment*, ed. F.J. Furnivall, London, 1870, p. 251.
[6] Elyot, *The Castel of Helth*, London, 1539, ff. 42v–44; Cogan, *The Haven of Health*, London, 1584, pp. 184–93.
[7] See for instance C.D. Ross, ed. 'The Household Accounts of Elizabeth Berkeley, Countess of Warwick, 1420–1', *Transactions of the Bristol and Gloucestershire Archæological Society* 70 (1951), pp. 81–105, passim; the royal ordinance for 1478, in A.R. Myers, ed. *The Household of Edward IV: the Black Book and the Ordinance of 1478*, Manchester, 1959, p. 213, and the rules for the Earl of Northumberland's household in 1512, in [Henry Percy] ed., *The Regulations and Establishment of the Household [sic] of Henry Algernon Percy*, London, 1770, pp. 73–98; Viscount Montague's household book for 1595, in Sir William H. St John Hope, *Cowdray and Easebourne Priory*, London, 1919, pp. 125–6; the Berkeley rules for 1601 in John Smyth, *The Lives of the Berkeleys* (1618), ed. Sir John Maclean, Gloucester, 1883, vol. 2, p. 420.
[8] For examples of this, see F.G. Emmison, *Tudor Secretary: Sir William Petre at Court and Home*, London, 1961, p. 143 (for the 1540s and '50s); D.G. Stuart, ed. *Manchets and Bakemeats: extracts from the household accounts of Thomas 3rd Baron Paget*, University of Keele, 1974, p. 24 (the accounts date from 1580; Paget was a Catholic).
[9] See Myers (1959), pp. 90–7, 218.
[10] The comments on Pepys' eating habits are based on a computer analysis of the diary, ed. Robert Latham & William Matthews, London, 1970–83. For further details, see Gilly Lehmann & Mercedes Perez Siscar, 'Food and Drink at the Restoration', *PPC* 59 (1998), pp. 15–25.
[11] See Edmund Hobhouse, ed. *The Diary of a West Country Physician, A.D. 1684–1726*, London, 1934, p. 21.
[12] For examples of the distinction, see John Beresford, ed. *The Diary of a Country Parson: the Reverend James Woodforde, 1758–1781*, London, 1924–31, 5 vols., passim. For a full table of eighteenth-century mealtimes, see my forthcoming book, *The British Housewife*.
[13] See C. Anne Wilson, 'Luncheon, Nuncheon and Related Meals', in Wilson, ed. *Luncheon, Nuncheon and Other Meals*, Stroud, 1994, pp. 33–50.
[14] J.H. Adeane, ed. *The Girlhood of Maria Josepha Holroyd*, London, 1896, p. 40.
[15] See, for instance, Arnold Palmer, *Movable Feasts*, London, 1952, p. 100, who attributes it to the duchess of Bedford; according to Mark Girouard, it was the duchess of Rutland who started the fashion for afternoon tea in 1842; see Girouard, *Life in the English Country House*, Harmondsworth, 1980, p. 293.
[16] See Congreve, *The Double Dealer*, Act I, i & vii.
[17] «Man nimmt um 7 Uhr Thee, mit Butterbrod, und die Theebesuche dauern oft bis 11 Uhr, von welchen man dann leicht schlafen geht». La Roche, *Tagebuch einer Reise durch Holland und England*, Offenbach am Main, 1791, p. 391.
[18] Adeane (1896), p. 127.
[19] For the two sittings, see C.M. Woolgar, *The Great Household in Late Medieval England*, London, 1999, p. 88. Woolgar also supplies a useful table of the daily routine of the aristocratic household, p. 85. The ordinance which divides the 24 officers into two groups so that one would always be ready is that of 1478, in Myers (1959), p. 216.

20 See R.W. Chambers, ed. *A Fifteenth-Century Courtesy Book*, London, 1914, p. 11. This is a transcription of B.L. Additional MS 37969, 'A Generall Rule to teche every man to serve a lorde or mayster.'

21 The regulations for the household of Princess Cecily, mother of Edward IV, state that dinner on 'eating days' was at 11, on fasting days at 12. See *A Collection of Ordinances and Regulations for the Government of the Royal Household*, London, 1790, p. 38. The regulations for the household of the infant Prince Edward (the son of Edward IV) in 1473 (wrongly dated as 1474 in 1790), in the same volume, confirm this: dinner was at 10 on flesh days, 11 on fasting days (p. 29). The royal ordinance of 1478 places the first dinner on flesh days at 9, but on fasting days at 11; see Myers (1959), p. 214.

22 For the Tudors, see the Eltham Ordinances of 1526, in *A Collection of Ordinances* (1790), p. 151; for Viscount Montague, see Hope (1919), p. 126.

23 See Harrison, *The Description of England*, ed. Georges Edelen, New York, 1994, p. 144.

24 See *A Collection of Ordinances* (1790), p. 338.

25 PRO LC 5/180, f. 9.

26 See Hobhouse (1934), p. 18.

27 See Elizabeth Cust, ed. *Records of the Cust Family, Series 2: The Brownlows of Belton* (London, 1909), p. 149.

28 *The Tatler*, n° 263, 14 Dec. 1710.

29 See Saussure, *Lettres et Voyages*, ed. B. van Muyden, Lausanne, 1903, p. 229; Carl Philip Moritz, *Reisen eines Deutschen in England im Jahr 1782*, Berlin, 1783, p. 85; Johann Wilhelm von Archenholz, *England und Italien*, Carlsruhe, 1791, vol. 3, p. 7.

30 Ryskamp & Pottle, eds *Boswell: The Ominous Years*, London, 1963, p. 79.

31 See Palmer (1952), p. 37; John Burnett, *Plenty and Want*, London, 1979, p. 79; Gerard Brett, *Dinner is Served*, London, 1968, pp. 101–2.

32 See Burnett (1979), pp. 309–13.

33 See Flandrin (1993), pp. 210, 218.

APPENDIX: Mealtimes – sources

Breakfast

1512: at 8 or 9 (aristocracy). T. Percy, ed. *The Regulations and Establishment of the Household of Henry Algernon Percy, the fifth Earl of Northumberland* (London, 1770).

1600: at 7 (provinces, travellers). G.W. Groos (ed. & trans.), *The Diary of Baron Waldstein: A Traveller in Elizabethan England* (London, 1981), 137.

1705: at 9 (Edinburgh, aristocracy/gentry). R. Scott-Moncrieff, ed. *The Household Book of Lady Grisell Baillie* (Edinburgh, 1911), xlvii.

1711: at 10 (London, gentry). H. Williams, ed. *The Correspondence of Jonathan Swift* (Oxford, 1963–65), vol. 1, 269.

1715: after 9 (London, gentry). W. Matthews, ed. *The Diary of Dudley Ryder* (London, 1939), 81.

1723: soon after 9 (provinces, aristocracy). C.G. Lennox, ed. *A Duke and his Friends* (London, 1911), vol. 1, 74.

1739: at 9 (Bath, gentry): G. Sherburn, ed. *The Correspondence of Alexander Pope* (Oxford, 1956), vol. 4, 200.

1743: at 9 (Scotland, aristocracy/gentry). Scott-Moncrieff, ed. *The Household Book of Lady Grisell Baillie* (1911), 273.

1753: at 10 (provinces, aristocracy/gentry). E. Cust, ed. *Records of the Cust Family*, series 2 (London, 1909), 219.

1756: at 9 (provinces, aristocracy/gentry). Cust, ed. *Records of the Cust Family*, series 2 (1909), 281.

1756: after 9, and at 11 after a late night (provinces, gentry). B. Grant, ed. *The Receipt Book of Elizabeth Raper* (Soho, 1924), 11, 12.

1766: at 9, and at 10 for a 'public breakfast' (Bath, clergy). B. Mitchell & H. Penrose, eds *Letters from Bath* (Gloucester, 1983), 70, 75, 96.

1770s: at 9 (Scotland, aristocracy). J. Godber, 'The Marchioness Grey of Wrest Park' (*Bedfordshire Historical Record Society* 47, 1968), 90–91.

1770: at 9.30 or 10 (provinces, gentry). Abdy, 'Journal', in A.A. Houblon, *The Houblon Family* (London, 1907), vol. 2, 119, 129.

1782: at 10 (London, aristocracy/gentry/middle-class). C.P. Moritz, *Reisen eines Deutschen* (Berlin, 1783), 85.

1784: at 10 or 11 (London, aristocracy/gentry). N. Scarfe (ed. & trans.), 'A Frenchman's Year in Suffolk' (*Suffolk Records Society* 30, 1988), 14.

1784: at 9 (provinces, aristocracy/gentry). Scarfe (ed. & trans.), 'A Frenchman's Year in Suffolk', 21.

1786: at 10 (provinces, aristocracy). J.H. Adeane, ed. *The Girlhood of Maria Josepha Holroyd* (London, 1896), 14.

1790s: at 10 (Scotland, aristocracy and gentry). B. Faujas de St Fond, *Voyages en Angleterre, en Ecosse, et aux Iles Hébrides* (Paris, 1797), vol. 1, p. 289, vol. 2, 80.

Dinner

1468: at 10 in summer, 9 in winter (princely household). Regulations for household of George, Duke of Clarence, in *A Collection of Ordinances and Regulations for the Government of the Royal Household* (London, 1790), 89.

1470s: at 11, or 12 on fasting days (princely household). Regulations for the household of Princess Cecily, in *HO* (1790), 38.

1473: at 10, or 11 on fasting days (princely household). Regulations for household of Prince Edward, in *HO* (1790), 29.

1478: at 9, or 11 on fasting days (royal household). Ordinance of 1478, in A.R. Myers, ed. *The Household of Edward IV: the Black Book and the Ordinance of 1478* (Manchester, 1959), 214.

1512: at 10 or 11 on fasting days in summer (aristocracy). Percy, ed. *The Regulations and Establishment[...]* (1770), passim.

1550s: at 11 (London, gentry). Source D.N. Durant, *Bess of Hardwick* (London, 1999), 21.

1570s–80s: at 11 (?, aristocracy and gentry), or 12 (merchants and farmers). W. Harrison, *The Description of England* (ed. G. Edelen, Washington & New York, 1994), 144.

1595: after 10, probably around 10.30 (aristocracy). Viscount Montagu's household book, in W.H. St John Hope, *Cowdray and Easebourne Priory* (London, 1919), 125.

1599: at or before 12, since dinner finished before 1 (provinces, gentry). D.M. Meads, ed. *The Diary of Lady Margaret Hoby, 1599–1605* (London, 1930), 67.

1610: after 11, probably at 11.30 (princely household). Regulations for household of Prince Henry, in *HO* (1790), 338.

1660s: at 12 or 1 (London, gentry/middle-class). Pepys, *Diary*, ed. R. Latham & W. Matthews (London, 1970–83), passim.

1702–28: around 2 (provinces, gentry). M. Blundell, ed. *Blundell's Diary and Letter Book* (Liverpool, 1952), 51.

1705: at 12 (Edinburgh, aristocracy gentry). Scott-Moncrieff, ed. *The Household Book of Lady Grisell Baillie* (1911), xlvii.

1708: at 2 (London, gentry). Williams, ed. *The Correspondence of Jonathan Swift* (1963–65), vol. 1, 74.

1710: at or after 2 (London, gentry and middle-class). Z.C. von Uffenbach, *Merkwürdige Reisen*, vol. 2 (Frankfurt, Leipzig, 1753), 440, 452, 595.

1711: at 3 (London, aristocracy). Williams, ed. *The Correspondence of Jonathan Swift* (1963–65), vol. 1, 205.

1715: at 2 (provinces, gentry). Matthews, ed. *The Diary of Dudley Ryder* (1939), 112.

1723: at 2 (provinces, aristocracy). Lennox, ed. *A Duke and his Friends* (1911), vol. 1, 74.

1727: at 2 or 3 (London, ?gentry,). C. de Saussure, *Lettres et Voyages* (intro. B. van Muyden, Lausanne, 1903), 229.

1739: at 2 (Bath, gentry). Sherburn, ed. *The Correspondence of Alexander Pope* (1956), vol. 4, 200.

1742: at 3 (London, gentry). Sherburn, ed. *The Correspondence of Alexander Pope* (1956), vol. 4, 385.

1743: at 2 (Scotland, aristocracy/gentry). Scott-Moncrieff, ed. *The Household Book of Lady Grisell Baillie* (1911), 273.

1745: at 1 (provinces, gentry). G. Eland, ed. *Purefoy Letters* (London, 1931), vol. 2, 382.

1749: at 2 (provinces, gentry). Eland, ed. *Purefoy Letters* (1931), vol. 2, 387.

1750: at 4 (London, aristocracy/gentry). M.-A. F. du Bocage, *Recueil des Œuvres de Madame du Bocage* (Lyon, 1762), vol. 3, 45.

1756–7: at 6 after a late night, but normally at 3 (provinces, gentry). Grant, ed. *The Receipt Book of Elizabeth Raper* (1924), 11, 14.

1760s: at 3 (Edinburgh, gentry). E. Mure, 'Some remarks on the change of manners in my own time' in W. Mure, ed. *Selections from the Family Papers preserved at Caldwell* (Glasgow, 1854), vol. 1, 271.

1763: at 2 (Edinburgh, gentry). J. Lettice, *Letters on a Tour through various parts of Scotland, in the Year 1792* (London, 1794), 527.

1765: at 4 (London, middle-class). P.J. Grosley, *Londres* (Lausanne, 1770), vol. 3, 191.

1766: at 2 (Bath, clergy). Mitchell & Penrose, eds *Letters from Bath* (1983), 75.

1770s: at 3 (Scotland, aristocracy). Godber, 'The Marchioness Grey of Wrest Park' (1968), 90–91.

1770s: at 3 or 4 (provinces, middle-class). Mrs. E. Gray, *Papers and Diaries of a York Family, 1764–1839* (London, 1927), 43.

1770: at 4 but noted as late (provinces, clergy). J. Beresford, ed. *The Diary of a Country Parson* (London, 1924–31), vol. 1, 102.

1770: at or after 3 (provinces, gentry). Abdy, 'Journal', in Houblon, *The Houblon Family* (1907), vol. 2, 120, 130–131.

1771: after 4 or at 5 (provinces, upper gentry). E.J. Climenson, ed. *Passages from the Diaries of Mrs. Philip Lybbe Powys* (London, 1899), 137.

1772: at 5 (London, royalty) or at 6 (London, French ambassador). J.A. Home, ed. *The Letters and Journals of Lady Mary Coke* (Edinburgh, 1889–96), vol. 4, 102, 115.

1775: at 1 (provinces, tradesmen), at 2 or 3 (London, tradesmen), between 4 and 5 (London, gentry). C. Ryskamp & F.J. Pottle, eds *Boswell: The Ominous Years, 1774–1776* (London: 1963), 79.

1777–8: at 2, noted as abnormally early; usually at 4 (provinces, aristocracy). M. Elwin, ed. *The Noels and the Milbankes: their Letters for Twenty-Five Years, 1767–1792* (London, 1967), 63, 98.

1778: at 4, noted as fashionable (provinces, lesser gentry). A. Vickery, *The Gentleman's Daughter* (New Haven & London, 1998), 334 n. 32.

1779: at 3 (provinces, clergy). C.H. Beale, ed. *Reminiscences of a Gentlewoman of the last Century* (Birmingham, 1891), 15, 18.

1779–81: at 3 (provinces, clergy and gentry), or at 4 (provinces, aristocracy). Beresford, ed. *The Diary of a Country Parson* (1924–31), vol. 1, 102 and passim.

1780s: between 2 and 3 (Edinburgh, gentry). H. Cockburn, *Memorials of his Time* (Edinburgh, 1856), 33.
1780s: at 1 (London, tradesmen); at 3 (London, middle-class); at 4 or later (London, aristocracy). J.W. von Archenholz, *England und Italien* (Karlsruhe, 1791), vol. 3, 7.
1782: at 3 (London, middle-class); at 4 or 5 (London, aristocracy/gentry). Moritz, *Reisen eines Deutschen* (1783), 85.
1783: between 4 and 5 (Edinburgh, gentry). Lettice, *Letters* (1794), 527.
1784: at 5 (London, aristocracy/gentry). Scarfe (ed. & trans.), 'A Frenchman's Year in Suffolk' (1988), 14.
1784: at 4 (provinces, aristocracy/gentry). Scarfe (ed. & trans.), 'A Frenchman's Year in Suffolk' (1988), 22.
1785: at 4 (Wales, clergy). R. Twining, ed. *Selections from Papers of the Twining Family* (London, 1887), 123.
1786: after 4 (provinces, aristocracy). Beresford, ed. *The Diary of a Country Parson* (1924–31), vol. 2, 283.
1786: at 4 (provinces, aristocracy). Adeane, ed. *The Girlhood of Maria Josepha Holroyd* (1896), 14.
1786: at 4 (London, gentry). S. von La Roche, *Tagebuch einer Reise durch Holland und England* (Offenbach am Main, 1791), 391.
1789: at 2 (provinces, aristocracy). C. Bruyn Andrews, ed. *The Torrington Diaries* (London, 1934–38), vol. 4, 100.
1790s: at 5 (London, Royal Society). Faujas, *Voyages* (1797), vol. 1, 55.
1790s: at 4.30 (Scotland, aristocracy), or at 4 (Scotland, gentry). Faujas, *Voyages* (1797), vol. 1, p. 290; vol. 2, 82.
1791: at 6 (London, aristocracy/gentry). Adeane, ed. *The Girlhood of Maria Josepha Holroyd* (1896), 30.
1795: between 5 and 6 (provinces, royalty/aristocracy). M. Meade-Fetherstonhaugh & Warner, *Uppark and its people* (1964), 58–59.
1798: at 3.30 (provinces, clergy). R.W. Chapman, ed. *Jane Austen's Letters* (London, 1952), 39.
1802: at 5 (provinces, gentry). A. Henstock, ed. 'The Diary of Abigail Gawthern' (*Thornton Society Record Series* 33, 1980), 97.

Tea

(Tea was normally taken 3 hours after the beginning of dinner; thus the hours here often supply further evidence for the dinner-hour as well.)
1751: at 6 (provinces, gentry). V.M. Macdonald, ed. *The Letters of Eliza Pierce* (London, 1927), 77.
1770s: at 6 (Scotland, aristocracy). Godber, 'The Marchioness Grey of Wrest Park' (1968), 90–91.
1770s: at 5 or 6 (provinces, middle-class). Gray, *Papers and Diaries of a York Family* (1927), 43.
1770: at 6 (provinces, clergy). Beresford, ed. *The Diary of a Country Parson* (1924–31), vol. 1, 102.
1779: at 6 (provinces, clergy). Beale, ed. *Reminiscences of a Gentlewoman of the last Century* (1891), 15–16.
1784: at 8 or 9 (provinces, aristocracy/gentry). Scarfe (ed. & trans.), 'A Frenchman's Year in Suffolk' (1988), 22.
1786: at 7 (London, gentry). La Roche, *Tagebuch* (1791), 391.
1792: at 7 (Bath, aristocracy/gentry). Adeane, ed. *The Girlhood of Maria Josepha Holroyd* (1896), 127.
1798: at 6.30 (provinces, clergy). Chapman, ed. *Jane Austen's Letters* (1952), 195.

Supper

1469: at 5 in summer, 4 in winter (princely household). Regulations for household of George, Duke of Clarence, in *HO* (1790), 89.

1470s: at 4 for officers and carvers, 5 for princess and household (princely household). Regulations…Cecily, in *HO* (1790), 38.

1474: at 4 (princely household). Regulations…Prince Edward, in *HO* (1790), 29.

1478: at 4 (royal household). Ordinance of 1478, in Myers, ed. *The Household of Edward IV* (1959), 214.

1512: at 4 (aristocracy). Percy, ed. *The Regulations and Establishment[…]* (1770), passim.

1550s: at 6 (London, gentry). Source D.N. Durant, *Bess of Hardwick* (London, 1999), 21.

1570s–80s: at 5 or later (aristocracy and gentry), or 6 (merchants), or 7 or 8 (farmers). Harrison, *The Description of England* (ed. Edelen, 1994), 144.

1595: after 5, probably around 5.30 (aristocracy). Viscount Montagu's household book, in Hope, *Cowdray and Easebourne Priory* (1919), 125.

1599: between 6 and 7 (provinces, gentry). Meads, ed. *The Diary of Lady Margaret Hoby* (1930), 67, 86–7.

1610: after 6, probably at 6.30 (princely household). Regulations…Henry, in *HO* (1790), 338.

1705: at 6 (Edinburgh, aristocracy/gentry). Scott-Moncrieff, ed. *The Household Book of Lady Grisell Baillie* (1911), xlvii.

1715: at 8, but this was a ball-supper (Bath, gentry). Matthews, ed. *The Diary of Dudley Ryder* (1939), 246.

1743: at 9 (Scotland, aristocracy/gentry). Scott-Moncrieff, ed. *The Household Book of Lady Grisell Baillie* (1911), 273.

1752: at 12, but this was a ball-supper (Windsor, royalty). Mrs A. Rathborne, ed. *Letters from Lady Jane Coke* (London, 1899), 104.

1756: at 12, but this was a ball-supper (provinces, gentry). Grant, ed. *The Receipt Book of Elizabeth Raper* (1924), 10.

1757: at 10.30 (provinces, aristocracy/gentry). Cust, ed. *Records of the Cust Family*, series 2 (1909), 283.

1758: at 10.20 (provinces, yeoman). D. Vaisey, ed. *The Diary of Thomas Turner* (Oxford, 1985), 137.

1765: at 10 (London, middle-class). Grosley, *Londres* (1770), vol. 3, 191.

1766: at 9 (Bath, clergy). Mitchell & Penrose (eds), *Letters from Bath* (1983), 75.

1770s: around 9 (provinces, middle-class). Gray, *Papers and Diaries of a York Family* (1927), 43.

1770: at 10, noted as late (provinces, clergy). Beresford, ed. *The Diary of a Country Parson* (1924–31), vol. 1, 102.

1770: at 9 (London, gentry); or at 10 (provinces, gentry, more festive). Abdy, 'Journal', in Houblon, *The Houblon Family* (1907), vol. 2, 118, 119, 131.

1771: at 11 (provinces, upper gentry). Climenson, ed. *Passages from the Diaries of Mrs. Philip Lybbe Powys* (1899), 137.

1777: at 12.30, but this was a ball-supper (provinces, upper gentry). Climenson, ed. *Passages from the Diaries of Mrs. Philip Lybbe Powys* (1899), 186–87.

1784: at 12 (provinces, aristocracy/gentry). Scarfe (ed. & trans.), 'A Frenchman's Year in Suffolk' (1988), 22.

1786: at 10 (provinces, aristocracy). Adeane, ed. *The Girlhood of Maria Josepha Holroyd* (1896), 14.

1790s: at 10 (Scotland, aristocracy and gentry). Faujas, *Voyages* (1797), vol. 1, p. 296; vol. 2, 86.

1791–2: at 11 or 12 (provinces or London, aristocracy). Adeane, ed. *The Girlhood of Maria Josepha Holroyd* (1896),. 32, 119.

1799: at 1, but this was a ball-supper (provinces, aristocracy). Climenson, ed. *Passages from the Diaries of Mrs. Philip Lybbe Powys* (1899), 322.

Being American: an Arab American Thanksgiving

William G. Lockwood and Yvonne R. Lockwood

The Thanksgiving feast is regarded as the most important meal in America. The menu is considered more or less fixed – roast turkey and dressing, mashed potatoes and gravy, cranberry sauce, and pumpkin pie – but there are infinite variations according to family, region, class, and ethnic group. It is, in the Hobsbawmian sense (Hobsbawm 1983), an invented tradition, a celebration of the American origin myth. In the minds of most Americans (e.g. Arnott 1975:15), this national holiday commemorates the settlement of Plimouth Colony, Massachusetts in 1621 and the pilgrims' first harvest, but there is no direct continuity between this feast and our present-day Thanksgiving feast.[1] Thanksgiving took on its present form only in the late nineteenth century, gradually evolving from a Day of Thanksgiving proclaimed by Abraham Lincoln during the Civil War, calling for divine guidance and support of the nation, and given shape by the writings and public urgings of Sarah Hale, publisher of a popular women's magazine (Pleck 2000). Over time the holiday has taken on many changes of function and meaning. It is today the major travel holiday in America and is celebrated by parades and endless football games, as well as the shared feast.

Today, scholars and Native Americans[2] question every aspect of what has become the origin myth of Thanksgiving: the date, place, participants, food, etc. Regardless, this well-known legend with its powerful historical memories is reinforced by federal authority, schools, and the media, and despite variants is the most uniformly celebrated of all of our national holidays (Humphrey 1996:706). Thanksgiving is promoted as a time of national unity (Anderson 1975:11; Long 2000:144) commemorated by family reunions centring on a feast of abundant traditional foods associated with the harvest season. On the fourth Thursday of November, every American shares in the ritual of America's origin myth, family ties, and national unity.

For a number of years, we have been working with American ethnic groups on culinary aspects of what folklorists have come to call 'creolization'. We think of the concept as a critique of and a response to the old, somewhat simple-minded notion of straight-line assimilation, where the culture of an immigrant community becomes more and more like the culture of the majority population. Creolization implies a somewhat different process: the creation of a new culture, drawing on the cultures of both the homeland and the host country, fused, reshaped, and given new meanings and functions in the very special circumstances of emigration and ethnic community life (Mintz 1998:119).

For some time now, our research has focused on Arab American foodways in the Detroit metropolitan area to try to more sharply define the concept of creolization for an understanding of social and cultural processes in ethnic American communities. What we are presenting here is a small slice of this larger body of work, just that dealing with the Arab American celebration of the Thanksgiving feast

There are now some 300,000 people of Arab descent living in or around Detroit, making it the largest and densest Arabic-speaking community outside the Middle East and North Africa. Immigration has extended over a very long period, from the late nineteenth century to the present, with Arabs still constituting one of the largest groups of immigrants to the area each year. It is also a community that is very complex. No immigrant or ethnic group in America is homogeneous, of course, but we know of none other with this degree of heterogeneity. There are four major national components of the community: Lebanese, Muslim, Christian and Druze; Palestinian, both Muslim and Christian; Yemeni, many of whom arrived when that country was divided into north and south Yemen, and the Detroit Yemeni community still tends to be divided by sharp differences in political opinion; and Chaldeans, eastern-rite Catholics from northern Iraq and Bagdad who are traditionally Aramaic speakers but many of whom assimilated to Arabic prior to immigration. There are also somewhat smaller groups of Jordanians, Syrians, both Muslim and Coptic Egyptians, and other still smaller groups. The newest groups to arrive are Shiite Muslims from southern Iraq and Kurds.

The first to arrive in numbers were Christian Lebanese in the late nineteenth century from what was then called Syria. They settled in downtown Detroit but have since migrated – now much acculturated – to the eastern suburbs. A smaller number of Muslim Lebanese also came in this early period. They settled first in Highland Park near the original Ford automotive plant, then relocated adjacent to the new Ford plant when it was built in Dearborn during the interwar period.[3] There – in a neighbourhood called the South End – they established businesses and built a mosque among fellow automotive workers from eastern Europe and elsewhere. Later, there was a big influx during and after the civil war in Lebanon that has continued to the present day.

Yemenis began to come in numbers in the 1960s, also settling in the South End, with a smaller community around the Dodge automotive plant in nearby

Hamtramck. Until recently, this was mostly a male sojourner community. Now, more and more families are arriving. Yemenis now constitute the largest group in the South End, although Lebanese, Palestinians, and remnants of the Eastern European population who dominated the area prior to World War II are still present. But as the South End came to be dominated by the more conservative Yemenis, most Lebanese Muslims relocated several miles north in central Dearborn, and most new Lebanese immigrants now go directly there.

Chaldeans number about 60,000 in the Detroit area. They began to arrive in the early 1900s but the largest numbers came in the 1960s and 1970s. They own most of the grocery and liquor stores in the inner city and, increasingly, in the nearer suburbs. There is a Chaldean commercial district in northern Detroit considerably removed from the other Middle Eastern commercial districts. As Chaldeans moved up the economic and social scale, they relocated to the northern suburbs, but the Detroit community continues to serve as a reception centre for new Chaldean immigrants.

These three business districts constitute what has been called 'urban villages'. They include a full range of goods and services, including most any Middle Eastern foodstuff you might want.

In general, we have found abundant examples of culinary creolization, including the amalgamation of different social and regional traditions from the homeland; the substitution of American foodstuffs or some combination of them for ingredients unavailable here; and the adaptation of culinary traits from both mainstream America and from other ethnic groups encountered in America (Lockwood and Lockwood 2000). In our examination of this creolized cuisine, we've taken a special look at holiday foods, both the form which celebrations of the homeland have taken on in America and American holidays, as they are celebrated in food by Arab Americans.

During the first decades of the twentieth century, a period of great concern and consternation over mass migration, Thanksgiving was seen as an important tool in the process of making 'real Americans' out of immigrants (Pleck 2000: 27–30). Immigrants were encouraged to accept rituals commemorating the history of the nation. The Fourth of July (celebrating the Revolution and the founding fathers) and Thanksgiving (eulogizing the Protestant Anglo-Saxon tradition) were particularly important, but other national rituals, such as Columbus Day and the pledge of allegiance, were invented in this same period. For many Americans the Pilgrims provided the perfect model of the good immigrant 'imbued with religious conviction, a member of the Chosen People, striving to make a life in a new world' (Siskind 1992:183). Schools and their teaching of the Thanksgiving legend to immigrant children were a particularly important part of the process.

But not all immigrants immediately accepted this alien holiday. Many Jews and some Catholics at first rejected Thanksgiving as too Protestant Christian (Applebaum 1984: 225). Pennsylvania Germans, who had their own harvest festival, were reluctant to adopt a national celebration (Pleck 2000:26). We found remnants of this sentiment in the 1990s among a few Arab Americans. A Muslim congregation in Dearborn, for example, criticized its imam for accepting a family's invitation to celebrate Thanksgiving, because they regarded it as an overtly Christian observance. This minority view, however, has not hindered most Arab Americans, both Muslim and Christian, from participating in this national American holiday.

The date is Thanksgiving, November 23, 1995. We are in the home of a first-generation Yemeni Muslim family in Dearborn, Michigan. The room is filled with men only – family, relatives, and friends—who are seated around a tablecloth spread on the floor and laden with food. The host is a working-class Yemeni who came to the United States several decades earlier. Having been married before to an American, he had instructed his newly arrived wife on how to prepare a Thanksgiving meal. She roasted a turkey with packaged Stove-Top dressing and made potato salad, white rice, and a green salad dressed with bottled French dressing. The husband had purchased three Jell-O salads from a delicatessen. Served with this was Yemeni lamb and vegetable stew with Arab bread. The men each had been provided a plate and tableware, but these were quickly dispensed with and the 'American' meal was finished in the traditional Yemeni village manner, with bread and fingers. When the men had enough, the women moved the food to the table and completed the Thanksgiving feast.

Fatme Boomrad is Muslim Lebanese and came to America in the early 1950s. She is a matriarch of a three-generational family. Her Thanksgiving menu for her extended family reflects her idea of what an American feast should be. She herself said, 'I cook American; no Arab food,' but the menu demonstrates differently. In 1995, her Thanksgiving meal consisted of turkey without stuffing; *hashwa* (rice with ground meat – traditionally lamb but now sometimes mixed with or wholly beef – almonds, pinenuts, and sweet spices); yogurt; canned cranberry sauce; canned creamed corn; mashed potatoes; gravy; green salad; and canned peaches and cottage cheese on lettuce. Dessert included home-made apple pie and Sara Lee pumpkin pie and cheesecake. This is a woman who is recognized as one of the best Arab cooks in the community, and who usually cooks only Arab food (except for special American treats for her grandchildren), yet her Thanksgiving meal relied heavily on the mass-produced foods of the American supermarket.

A middle-class, third-generation, mixed Palestinian/Lebanese Christian family in Flint celebrate their Thanksgiving in a consciously ethnic manner. The grandmother had been introduced to Thanksgiving by an American friend soon after her arrival in the United States. This friend's turkey recipe is still the basis of the family's Thanksgiving meal, perpetuated by each successive generation in memory of this friendship. In 1995, the meal began with a variety of roasted seeds as family and guests waited for dinner. *Mezza*, the traditional Lebanese course of appetizers, followed: hummus, *baba ghannouj*, Arab bread, and American-style, sliced raw vegetables. Subsequently, roasted turkey with 'American' bread dressing, green salad, cranberry Jell-O mould, biscuits, and gravy were augmented with two Cornish hens stuffed with *hashwa*, an Arab salad of lettuce, tomatoes, cucumbers, and parsley, dressed with lemon juice, garlic, olive oil and mint. Next there was fresh fruit (considered obligatory at traditional Arab American meals) and dessert of *harissa* (baked semolina steeped in sugar syrup flavoured with rose-water and lemon juice) and, finally, tea and coffee. On holidays, families like this, several generations removed from the immigrants, often resurrect traditional ethnic foods.

These three families represent diverse experiences based on different religions, class and economic statuses, and educational levels.

Both scholars and journalists writing about Thanksgiving tend to generalize about the participation of ethnic groups. They usually describe an ethnic table as holding a turkey, cranberry sauce, and pumpkin pie surrounded by ethnic specialities (e.g. Arnott 1975:20). Although this is sometimes so, it is not the whole story, at least not in the case of Arab Americans. A turkey is not always just another turkey, nor does the presence of 'American' foods always have the same meaning. We need to look beyond what meets the eye.

Inquiries of Arab Americans about Thanksgiving meals usually got a response dispelling any notions that their feasts are anything but ordinary American. We have been told: 'our Thanksgiving is fairly standard and routine'; 'I make everything everyone makes'; 'I cook the American way. No Arab food'; and, 'We have a basic Thanksgiving meal.' Interviews, however, tell otherwise and disclose evidence of modification and substitution, creolization, and changes of meaning.

Many Arab cooks have familiar routines of cooking American foods for their children. Unlike the process by which they learned to cook – from mothers, aunts, and mothers-in-law – American dishes are often learned from package labels, non-Arab neighbours, and the process of trial and error. Fatme described it this way: 'Maybe the first time it's not good. The second time you know what's wrong, and the third time you correct it.' But what is 'correct' in the opinion of Arab women who cook predominantly Arab food everyday? When questioned, Fatme admitted that perhaps her American food did have an Arab flavour. And this is no doubt true of the 'American' food of many Arab American families. Even the hamburgers a grandmother cooks for her grandchildren often have parsley and onion mixed with the meat, which in some cases is lamb instead of beef. Similar attributes appear in Thanksgiving menus. Almost every Arab American menu includes turkey, the defining feature of a Thanksgiving feast. Even though many Arabs don't really like turkey, it is the symbol of Thanksgiving and abundance at each Arab American table just as at other American Thanksgiving feasts. But the Arab American cook often rubs the turkey prior to roasting with olive oil, lemon, and spices. A Yemeni American experimented with her turkey for years, arriving finally with a turkey rub of salt, cumin, Accent (a brand-name monosodium glutamate flavour enhancer), garlic, and lemon. This, then, is not everybody's Thanksgiving turkey. In most American households, the Thanksgiving turkey is presented whole on the table, to be admired by one and all, before it is publicly carved by the head of household.[4] In many Arab American homes, the turkey is carved in the kitchen before the dinner is served.

Equally important, but with different meaning, is the stuffing. Rarely is the stuffing at an Arab American feast anything other than *hashwa*, that combination of rice, meat, nuts, and sweet spices that is traditionally used to stuff smaller fowl and lamb. Seldom, however, is this stuffed into the turkey. Rather, it is the requisite side dish for a whole roasted turkey just as it is traditionally served with a whole roasted lamb at traditional Arab feasts. Chaldean cooks, on the other hand, provide *biryani*, the most popular Chaldean rice dish, as the necessary side. A few cooks do make 'American' bread stuffing, which they cook in the turkey. In a typical example, a first-generation Palestinian, who arrived in Michigan some 25 years ago, makes bread stuffing because the children prefer it. In her extended family only she will make it for them; however, she also serves the traditional *hashwa* at the same meal. The American menus for this American holiday are consciously chosen, but cooked in the only way an Arab cook knows. After all, what other way is there to cook green beans except with olive oil and lemon juice?

In Arab American culture a feast demands an auspicious and bountiful presentation of food. Although a turkey fills this requirement, many cooks augment it with other meats, which they are encouraged to do because so few like turkey. Many also include chicken or Cornish hens (which are stuffed with *hashwa*). Leg of lamb is a favourite addition to many Arab American tables. Others augment the table with ham or roast beef. Often three to four types of meat are served. Other Arab food items often included on the tables in greater Detroit are stuffed grape leaves, *tabbouli*, yogurt to eat with the rice side dish, and Arabic sweets alongside American pies. *Mezza* or appetizers are usually served. In a better restaurant in Lebanon, an elaborate *mezza* might consist of as many as 70 dishes. In American homes, however, *mezza* as a separate course appears only on special occasions and holidays, such as Thanksgiving, and even then in much fewer and simpler items. For every day, if *mezza* dishes are served, they accompany the main course. The most typical *mezza* dishes include hummus, *baba ghannouj, labneh* (drained yogurt), *tabbouli*, pickles, olives, *fatay'r* (meat or cheese pies), *lahmajoun* (pizza-like flat bread with meat and vegetable topping). Eating the appetizers should be a long, slow process, allowing people to mingle and talk. It is traditional to drink alcohol with *mezza* – usually anis-flavoured *arak*, but today in America almost any alcoholic beverage might be consumed. Many Muslim Lebanese as well as Christians will drink when having *mezza*.

Present at almost every Arab American Thanksgiving feast are some foods that few if any eat and yet they are believed to be essential to the Americanness of the meal. Cranberry sauce, usually from a can rather than home-made, adds colour to the table but not much pleasure to the diners. No one we talked with admitted eating it. Nor are pumpkin pies high on the list of favourites. Most get eaten by children. As mentioned earlier, turkey is not highly relished. Many stated that they have turkey (as well as mashed potatoes) only on this particular feast day. The items that are considered essential can vary. One Palestinian woman told us she would never forget her first Thanksgiving. Her third-generation Arab American husband was very upset because she hadn't known to make gravy. Now she always keeps a can of commercial gravy on hand in case hers turns out not to be as good as his mother's.

A few of the substitutions and modifications that are so important a part of the creolization process (Mintz, 1989:119) are specific to the Thanksgiving feast. One woman, for example, substitutes sweetened squash-filled turnovers (in the style of *fatay'r*) for pumpkin pie. But much more commonly, the same modifications that are made in everyday cooking extend to the Thanksgiving menu: some cooks add mayonnaise to hummus to make it creamier, roasted lamb might be basted with soy sauce to enhance colour, vegetable oil is substituted for clarified butter, beef replaces lamb.

There is even more variation in the Thanksgiving menu of Arab Americans than among non-Arab Americans. Some of these differences reflect differences of religion, class, length of stay in the United States, and personal attitudes with regard to acculturation. Those Lebanese families who came to America after lengthy stays in Brazil or Africa demonstrate this in their Thanksgiving feast just as they do in daily diet.

Differences between national groups remain pronounced. We have found considerable amalgamation in the cuisine presented by Lebanese, Yemeni, and

Chaldean restaurants and their menus continue to coalesce toward a pan-Arab American cuisine. But this is much less so of food prepared in the kitchens of private homes, and this is particularly true of festive food.

The Thanksgiving meal, within or outside the Arab American community, provides a reflection of family history (Santino 1994:176–177; Long 2000). Since Thanksgiving is a family holiday in America, rooted and observed according to traditions passed down the family line, we can expect such differences to continue even as these patterns continue to evolve. We certainly did find patterns in the Arab American celebration of Thanksgiving, but the differences between them and the standard American menu lie even more in the *meaning* of the event than it does in content.

The recently-arrived Yemeni family gathered for the first time around a Thanksgiving turkey doesn't invest it with the symbolic load of Pilgrims, cooperative Native Americans, and giving thanks, but, rather, with the meaning 'Now we are Americans.' Arab immigrants and their descendants have, indeed, become Americans, but not in the assimilated sense intended by those early twentieth-century reformers referred to earlier. The Arab American version of Thanksgiving feast is a demonstration of just what kind of American they are. It's an affirmation of their Arab American identity.

ACKNOWLEDGEMENTS

This work draws in part from informal contact with Metropolitan Detroit's Arab American community, particularly in public sector food and foodways, since our arrival in Michigan in 1969. More formal field research was conducted in 1988 and 1994–1996 with the support of the National Endowment for the Humanities, National Endowment for the Arts, Michigan Council for Arts and Cultural Affairs, the Arab Community Center for Economic and Social Services, and the Michigan Traditional Arts Program (Michigan State University Museum). We wish to acknowledge fieldworkers Barbara George Gallagher, Sally Howell, Haajar Mitchell, Rosina Hassoun, and Dawn Ramey, whose reports and discussions about food and celebration contributed to this paper. And last, but not least, we thank the many men and women who shared information and food with us.

BIBLIOGRAPHY

Abrahams, Roger 1982, 'The Language of Festivals: Celebrating the Economy', in *Celebration: Studies in Festivity and Ritual*, ed., Victor Turner, Washington, DC: Smithsonian Institution Press, pp. 161–77.

Anderson, Jay Allen 1975, 'Thanksgiving in the U.S.A. – The Meal as Medium and Message', *Reports from the Second International Symposium for Ethnological Food Research*, Helsinki, August 1973, pp. 9–14.

Applebaum, Diana Karter 1984, *Thanksgiving. An American Holiday, An American History,* New York: Facts on File Publications.

Arnott, Margaret Louise 1975, 'Thanksgiving Dinner. A Study in Cultural Heritage', *Reports from the Second International Symposium for Ethnological Food Research*, Helsinki, August 1973, pp. 15–28.

Baker, James W. 1984, 'What Was on the Menu for the First Thanksgiving Dinner', *Yankee* (November).

Hobsbawm, Eric 1983, 'Introduction: Inventing Traditions', in *The Invention of Tradition*, eds Eric Hobsbawm and Terence Ranger, Cambridge University Press, pp. 1–14.

Humphrey, Lin 1996, 'Thanksgiving Day', in *American Folklore: An Encyclopedia*, ed. Jan Brunvand, New York: Garland Publishing, Inc., pp. 705–706.

Koehler, Margaret H. 1974, 'Thanksgiving', *Early American Life* (October):28–31; 103; 84–85.

Linton, Ralph and Adelin 1949, *We Gather Together. The Story of Thanksgiving*, New York: Henry Schuman.

Lockwood, William G. and Yvonne R. Lockwood 2000, 'Continuity and Adaptation in Arab American Foodways', in *Arab Detroit: From Margin to Mainstream*, eds Nabeel Abraham and Andrew Shryock, Detroit: Wayne State University Press, pp. 515–49.

Long, Lucy 2000, 'Holiday Meals: Rituals of Family Tradition', in *Dimensions of the Meal. The Science, Culture, Business, and Art of Eating*, ed. Herbert L. Meiselman, Gaithersburg, MD: Aspen Publishers Inc., pp. 143–59.

Lowrance, Christie 1986, 'Thanksgiving Pilgrim-Style', *Americana* (Nov–Dec):44–7; 61.

Mintz, Sidney W. 1989, 'Food and Culture: An Anthropological View', in *Completing the Food Chain*, eds P.M. Hirschoff and N.G. Kotler, Washington, DC: Smithsonian Institution Press, pp. 114–120.

Mintz, Sidney W. 1998, 'The Localization of Anthropological Practice: From Area Studies to transnationalism', *Critique of Anthropology* 18 (2):117–133.

Pleck, Elizabeth 2000, 'Family, Feast, and Football', in *Celebrating the Family. Ethnicity, Consumer Culture, and Family Rituals*, Harvard University Press, pp. 21–42.

Santino, Jack 1994, *All Around the Year. Holidays & Celebrations in American Life*, Urbana: Illinois University Press.

Siskind, Janet 1992, 'The Invention of Thanksgiving: A Ritual of American Nationality', *Critique of Anthropology* 12 (2): 167–191.

NOTES

1. For typical examples of Pilgrim-oriented Thanksgiving as presented in popular media, see Lowrance 1986; Koehler 1974; Baker 1984. For the Plimouth Plantation Living History Museum's official story of Thanksgiving, see its website: http://www.plimoth.org . On the other hand, Siskind, among others, has pointed out the Pilgrims were neither the earliest nor the most typical of early settlers. But Plimouth carries mythic meanings 'precisely because it is unlike any other past or present American settlement. It was, and is, represented as a small homogeneous, egalitarian Christian community in which class differences were minimal, in which religion was central; a face-to-face community as a model of the national imagined community. It is a model which denies class domination, exploitation, racial and ethnic conflict, and covers imperialism with the Pilgrim's cloak' (Siskind 1992:184–185).

2. In September, 2000, the Wampanoag Indian Program at Plimouth Plantation offered a 'Thanks But No Thanks' day-long event to discuss misrepresentations and native ideas regarding Thanksgiving. Many local Native Americans in the Plimouth area hold a 'Day of Mourning' on Thanksgiving Day to protest what they believe to be the co-opting of a native concept of giving thanks for the gifts of the earth and making of it a stereotypical celebration of how well the Pilgrims and Indians got along. They make a point of eating fish that day. (Personal communication, Lynne Williamson, Connecticut Cultural Heritage Arts Program.)

3. Dearborn, a large suburb immediately to the west of Detroit, was founded by Henry Ford for his expanding industry. Similarly, the suburb of Hamtramck, completely enclosed by Detroit, developed around the first Dodge plant. Highland Park is a smaller suburb north of Detroit.

4. Some scholars with a psychological bent have made much of the Thanksgiving turkey being traditionally presented whole in mainstream American culture. Roger Abrahams (1982:176) describes the whole stuffed turkey as 'a symbolic object…presented whole and then cut to pieces, then shared and consumed by the family, each member of which must then become stuffed individually to induce a state of body and mind shared by all.'

The Fine Art of Eighteenth-Century Table Layouts

Fiona Lucraft

When Hannah Glasse declared in *The Art of Cookery Made Plain and Easy* that she thought it an impertinence 'to direct a Lady how to set out her Table' she chose to stand out from the crowd of eighteenth-century cookery writers who clearly believed it was pertinent.[1] This paper is concerned with the depiction of meals in the form of table layouts in eighteenth-century cookery books and will include a consideration of the underlying principles of elegance, proportion and variety in meals served *à la française*.

Table layouts: a definition

A table layout in an eighteenth-century cookery book is the depiction of a table with named dishes placed upon it. The style of dining in eighteenth-century Britain was referred to as service *à la française* and, in its simplest form consisted of one or more 'courses' successively laid out on the table. A course could include any number of dishes.

Table layouts appeared in early eighteenth-century English cookery books and may have developed from their seventeenth-century predecessors which included bills of fare in the form of lists of dishes but no table plans. It should be said, many eighteenth-century cookery books continued to include bills of fare, but the table layout became a useful addition as it enabled the reader to visualize an entire meal. A second influence in their appearance may be French seventeenth-century cookery books, such as François Massialot's *Cuisinier roial et bourgeois* (1st edition 1691) and Nicolas de Bonnefons' *Les Délices de la Campagne* (1st edition 1654) which included table layouts.[2]

Henry Howard's England's Newest Way *(1708)*

The first English cookery book to depict how a table should be laid *à la française* seems to be Henry Howard's *England's Newest Way* in 1708.[3] Henry Howard is described as 'Free-Cook of London, and late Cook to his Grace the Duke of Ormond, and since to the Earl of Salisbury, and Earl of Winchelsea'. Having stated Howard's credentials his publisher, Christopher Coningsby indicates that this book is aimed at 'Persons of the First Rank and Quality', or, perhaps more honestly, their cooks.

Howard's book includes bills of fare as well as several table layouts with strategically placed circles imitating dishes and the appropriate dish named within each circle. Immediately, several things are evident: that the table layout does not indicate how many are to be served. Unlike their French counterparts, English eighteenth-century publishers do not reveal the number of diners. That only two courses are indicated for each meal with no mention of the dessert course, a practice which continues in the majority of eighteenth-century table layouts. Occasionally, a separate dessert table layout is incorporated, such as can be found in John Nott's *Cook's Dictionary* (1726). Elizabeth Raffald in *The Experienced English Housekeeper* (1769) eschews a dessert layout, preferring to describe how to lay a dessert.[4] And finally, that symmetry in placing dishes on the table was essential. This is an unchanging rule of service *à la française*, although the engravers of table layouts vary their designs considerably.

There are three sizes of dish incorporated in the table layout and this practice continues in later cookery books, with surprisingly little variation. The size of the dish and where it is placed on the table appears to relate not only to the amount of food being served, but also to the quality or desirability of the item. Four of the largest dishes in Howard's second course contain varying quantities of game or poultry. The same size dish holds either 8 pheasants, 12 partridges, 2 geese or 1 turkey and 6 chicken. This may enable the cook to balance their appearance at table despite having very different quantities of food, but there may also be a link to sumptuary laws which dictated appropriate amounts of food for entertaining. The tradition may have continued even though the Tudor laws no longer applied. The quality or desirability of the dish is of great relevance to host and guest alike. Meat, game and fowl almost always occupied the largest dishes. Soups and some fish can also hold their own on the largest dishes or tureens, although they both can appear in medium sized dishes. There are some quirky dishes which may seem an unusual choice for the largest dishes, such as venison pasty. It was held in great esteem in the seventeenth and early eighteenth centuries and can often be found in the centre of the table, as in Howard's first course. A great pie or a sallamagundy would be equally esteemed. Medium-sized dishes were filled with smaller joints, stews and soups, with perhaps a hash, pudding or pie. Smaller dishes held small or less significant items, such as the mushrooms to be found in Henry Howard's layout or Elizabeth Raffald's scalloped potato where three scallop shells filled with mashed potato make a dish.

There are two practical problems, in that several of the dishes are written in what appears to be misspelt English or misunderstood French and recipes are not to be found in the book itself. In Howard's layout an unfortunately named 'Tourt demall' has no correlation in the text, as the recipe appears under its more recognizable name 'Tart de Moy'. Others which cannot be found are 'Butter'd Prasones' (Buttered Prawns) and 'Purpatoon of Pigeons'. This is a difficulty that is repeated in other cookery books and one imagines it must have been exasperating for a cook to plan a meal based on a layout, only to find that recipes were apparently not in the text. Amongst certain cookery writers there may have been a tacit understanding that simpler recipes were not required by a readership who were almost certainly experienced cooks. However, another possibility is that the table layouts were separately commissioned and therefore the writer was not able to rectify flaws. In later cookery books writers effectively exonerated themselves from blame by stating that equivalent dishes could be substituted.

A vast array and variety of food is evident in just one of Howard's courses which names fourteen different foods, to say nothing of the other ingredients required to cook them. Why was this variety and display necessary? Conspicuous consumption has long been a feature of hospitality, particularly amongst the wealthy, for whom Henry Howard was writing. The issue of symmetry was clearly significant for the Georgians, as can be seen in the elegance of the period's architecture which then influenced the table. However, from a practical point of view a varied and balanced arrangement of dishes is particularly important in distributing food around a table where each person would be expected to eat primarily (and sometimes exclusively) what was nearest to him.

Charles Carter (1730–49)

Charles Carter's *The Complete Practical Cook* (1730) is 'adorned with Sixty Curious Copper Plates' of table layouts and is almost certainly the largest and most varied eighteenth-century collection. They are also the most consistently elegant of eighteenth-century table layouts. In his preface Carter describes himself as cook to a host of nobility, including, 'Lord Whitworth in several of his splendid Ambassies, particularly to Berlin, the Hague, etc. as also Esquire Poley, formerly Envoy from the Crown of England to the Illustrious Court of Hanover; and to his excellency General Wade in Spain and Portugal, about the year 1710.' Then there is 'his Grace the Duke of Argyll…as well as my Noble Lords Pontefract, Lempster, Cornwallis, and other Truly Noble Peers'.

My concise *Dictionary of National Biography* has nothing to say about Lords Pontefract, Lempster and Cornwallis, nor Mr Poley, but is more forthcoming on his earlier employers. General George Wade (1673–1748), was an Irishman who served in Spain (1704–1710) and distinguished himself in the battles of Almanza and Saragossa. Presumably this was when Carter was with him.

Charles, Baron Whitworth (1675–1725), was a diplomat who rose to the giddy heights of envoy extraordinary and plenipotentiary at two diplomatic hot spots, the Court of Prussia (1716–1717 and again in 1719) and the Hague (1717–1719). Carter indicates that this is when he worked for him. Carter's claim that his travels had given him 'opportunities to get an insight into the Customs and Modes of different Nations' was no exaggeration.

Carter's most illustrious employer was John Campbell, 2nd Duke of Argyll (1678–1743), a friend of George II and a distinguished soldier who indubitably moved in the highest circles. He is notoriously remembered for refusing to allow his daughters to learn French; 'One language was enough for a woman to talk in'![5] Incidentally, one of those five daughters became Lady Mary Coke with an infamous husband and a marriage portion of £20,000 which she lost when they separated, but regained some £2,000 a year after her husband's death.[6] The Duke's homes were Inveraray House, Scotland and Sudbrook Park, Surrey. The latter is now the home of Richmond Golf Club, but perhaps it was Carter's home for a while.[7]

Carter's book was, not surprisingly, aimed at those who could afford 'Grand and Sumptuous Entertainments', though I can't help wondering if it also provided daydream material for lesser mortals. He does not disappoint! Carter's imaginary meals begin with two-course layouts for every month of the year. Each course has eleven dishes with two on a sideboard in case anyone at table should dislike what they see before them. He goes on to depict a 40-dish Lenten dinner which incorporates no less than 17 different fish. Further on there is a five-course dinner of seven dishes to each course. He also depicts twelve patterns for laying dishes on the table, from 17 to 25 dishes. The kaleidoscopic permutations of pattern are striking.

Even more eye-catching, however, are the 38 layouts which are set firmly in the real, élite world of nobility and royalty. Carter includes a triple-page layout of George II's coronation dinner and a further eight layouts for the King or Queen. Carter dates these meals but unfortunately does not give the year. A two-course dinner for the King on September 10th consists of 23 dishes for the first course and 25 for the second. A huge range of foods and cooking techniques is evident but notable in the centre of the second course is a great Sallad Mogundy surrounded by such delicacies as 'Bambooe, Mangoes, Olives, Guirkins, Cavear, Wallnuts, Capers, Oysters, Porargoe and Mushrooms'. There is no shortage of abundance and extravagance in other dated layouts. Carter includes a meal on shipboard, a couple of wedding dinners and 'an Instalment dressed at Windsor April 15th for His Grace the Duke of Newcastle'. This last is not the same as Patrick Lamb's table layout for the instalment feast for the Duke of Newcastle in 1698, so beautifully recreated by Ivan Day for a recent exhibition and visible in the catalogue for anyone to feast their eyes on.[8] It does seem extraordinary that two Dukes of Newcastle should have so much attention lavished upon them in cookery books!

Then there is the sumptuous and wonderfully named ambigue, or ambogue, of which Carter depicts a mere ten! A later edition of Dr Johnson's *Dictionary* defines the English ambigu as 'a medley of dishes set on together'.[9] Carter defines it as 'a Service both Hot and Cold, for a Wedding, hall, Masquerade, or any great Entertainment.' In France it continued well into the nineteenth century and a layout for a lunch ambigu complete with seating and cutlery is depicted in Mlle. Madeleine's *La Parfaite Cuisinière Bourgeoise et Economique* (n.d. [late nineteenth century], 27th edition).

Virginia Maclean points out that Carter's later books *The Compleat City and Country Cook* (1736) and *The London and Country Cook* (1749) include the same table layouts.[10] However, these are different from his first book and, with one or two exceptions, are more modest. Two of the layouts introduce an interesting adaptation of the service *à la française* by gradually increasing the number of dishes for each course. So the first course has one dish placed on the table. The dish is soup which is then removed and replaced with a fish dish. The 'remove' is a regular feature of meals *à la française* and is clearly indicated in table layouts. The second course consists of two dishes, the third has three and the fourth has four. This style of dining is unusual and does not appear to have been adopted in other cookery books. Perhaps it was influenced by Carter's extensive travels with his employers in Europe? Certainly *The Complete Practical Cook* reflects Carter's extensive travels, with recipes influenced by or named after France, Spain, Switzerland, Holland, Prussia and even Turkey. His 'Explanation of Terms of Art' clarify some of the language problems encountered in the layouts. Carter was exceptional in introducing such a range of innovative layouts to the English. They preserve the principles of symmetry, proportion and elegance in service *à la française* but also celebrate the abundance and variety of grand design.

Arabella Atkyns's The Family Magazine *(1741)*

It becomes increasingly noticeable when viewing a range of table layouts that variety is as much an issue as elegance even in humbler cookery books directed at the middle of society. In *The Family Magazine*, the pseudonymous 'Arabella Atkyns' includes some of the simplest and clearest table layouts, from two dishes to nine and so helpfully enables us to assess the combination of dishes.

In the simplest possible two dish layout Atkyns suggests boiled beef, pork or mutton and 'a Pudden of any kind' for the first course. The second course is roasted fowls and tarts. We may question the variety here as we cannot help but see food in terms of nutrition, but for eighteenth-century diners without such preoccupations the variety is evident in cooking techniques and foodstuffs. Atkyns instructs that 'boiled meats should be brought in first, baked next and roast last', implying a hierarchy of cooking techniques.[11]

In the nine-dish layout the largest and grandest dish is placed in the centre of a rectangular table: a chine of mutton, or veal, or roast beef or venison. At the top and bottom of the table are medium-sized oval dishes: a soup and a dish of tongue and cauliflower. In the middle of each of the longest sides are smaller, round dishes of marrow pudding and bacon and beans. At the four corners, between the larger dishes, are also small, round dishes of jugged hare, fried soles, stewed eels and roasted pig. Although the latter sounds like a grand dish it is likely to have been a smaller dish as it would need to balance the other three corners. Not only are there no repetitions of food, but the clear placement indicates that the two fish dishes are placed diagonally opposite each other, so catering for guests at both ends and sides of the table.

The second course has a dish of lobsters in the centre, with partridges or quails at the top and almond cheesecakes or custards at the bottom. In the middle of the longest sides are two vegetable dishes: artichokes and green peas. The four smaller 'corners' consist of lamb-stones, stewed carp, sturgeon and potted pigeons or collared eel. So frequent was the placement of smaller dishes in the corners of the table that it becomes common parlance for cookery writers to describe such dishes as a 'corner'. A further important feature of dining *à la française* is evident in this second course; the provision of sweet and savoury dishes at the same time.

Martha Bradley's The British Housewife *(1756)*

Martha Bradley's book is a salutary reminder that the greatest books are not always the most successful. If it were not for Prospect Books we might not have this wonderful book and, for my purposes, the unique table layout she includes for a dinner in July. I say it is unique as, unlike its predecessors, Bradley's is artistically drawn and considerable detail about the dishes is added in beautiful copperplate. It is the only one of its kind in the book. All of the other layouts either employ the older tradition of written dishes within circles or they are artistically depicted but without the extensive detail. Perhaps the cost was prohibitive.

The meal consists of seven dishes for the first course and eleven dishes for the second. The four extra dishes are placed in the corners. At the top of the first-course table is a boiled turbot surrounded by fried smelts. Balance and variety are evident immediately as the huge boiled fish is balanced by its tiny, crisp garnish. This is not a new combination but Bradley's engraver conveys great charm in the elegant drawing and the copperplate notes. It is further garnished with lemon, parsley and barberries and is served with lobster and shrimp sauce, providing a riot of colour and flavour. Bradley goes further than any other writer by conveying vital details about the dishes. At the other end of the table is the wonderful sight of 'a Neck of Venison in a Forrest of Watercresses'. Then there is a 'Green Goose' with its visually stunning garnish of sorrel leaves and 'lemon peal cut like narrow tape and ty'd in knots one upon each leaf of sorrel'. My favourite second course dish is simply 'Green Pease spread on mint for garnish'. Imagine the heat of the peas hitting the mint and then wafting its way to the dining room! The cook's skill and art is evident in this table layout as it appeals to all our senses. There are sometimes food combinations which surprise, such as 'Potted Lobsters with fresh greens round the dish', but the colour combination would be spectacular.

One final feature of Martha Bradley's layout is the decorative edging on the page which adds to the attractive design and seems very feminine in comparison to the strict linear arrangement of previous layouts.

Elizabeth Raffald's The Experienced English Housekeeper *(1769)*

Raffald includes only two layouts or 'covers' for one 'Grand' meal, depicting prettily-shaped dishes laid in generous profusion on the table. The term cover, from the French *couvert* is a late reminder of the influence of France on England's dining habits, though Raffald may not have intended such an admission. Indeed, her meaning may be the same as Hannah Glasse who talks of 'a great Variety of Dishes and a large Table to cover' (p. ii). The second course is a showcase for some exceptional confectionary items, including, 'Snowballs', 'Moonshine' '5 Globes of Gold Web with Mottoes in them', 'Rocky Island' and a 'Fish Pond'. Recipes for these can be found in her book and no doubt also at her confectionery shop.

Table layouts of the tavern cooks of the late eighteenth century

How did the table layout develop in cookery books of the late eighteenth century? In short, very little. Those in John Farley's *The London Art of Cookery*, and Collingwood and Woollams' *The Universal Cook and City and Country Housekeeper* echo previous ones. The only variation is in Collingwood and Woollams' book, where soups are indicated by soup tureens, an idea that goes all the way back to Massialot.

John Mollard's *The Art of Cookery Made Easy and Refined* appears to follow in his predecessors' footsteps and continues the table layout tradition virtually unchanged. However, by the turn of the century one interesting development occurs as separate dishes of vegetables, such as broccoli, mashed turnips and stewed spinach increasingly appear in their own right, often as the smaller dishes between the large roasts and boiled meats. I can't help speculating if this is a step in the direction of meat and two veg. Another, more endearing feature of the later table layouts is the unreliable but humorous English spelling. 'Slises Crimp'd Cod' and 'Triffle' are understandable variants, but there are also indications that the engraver may not have been as literate as the author. So, we read 'Harricott of Begetables', 'Mirangles' for meringues and potted beef is 'Moddled' rather than moulded! Mollard's engraver is, of course, not the only one to have a spelling problem. Richard Briggs' engraver in *The English Art of Cookery* gives us 'Asparagus a la Pittet Poi' and 'Nick Venison', not to mention 'Stew'd Indiff'!

This paper must end with a word of credit for the anonymous engravers who, for at least a century produced some fine works to enable the reader to visualize how to lay out an elegant table in the eighteenth century.

Henry Howard and Charles Carter's elegant and innovative layouts reveal the multicultural influence of the courts of Europe and the preoccupations of the mighty and wealthy. In contrast, Arabella Atkyns, Martha Bradley, Elizabeth Raffald and to a lesser extent the tavern cooks were concerned with a burgeoning middle class that required explanation and elucidation and, as such, their detailed descriptions enable the food historian to visualize how to serve a meal *à la française*.

BIBLIOGRAPHY

The Concise Dictionary of National Biography, Vol 1 To 1900. 1969. Oxford University Press, London.
'Atkyns, Arabella', 1741, *The Family Magazine*, J. Osborn, London.
Bradley, Martha, 1756, *The British Housewife*, Prospect Books, 1996.
Brears, Peter, 1994, 'A la Française: the Waning of a Long Dining Tradition', *Luncheon, Nuncheon and other Meals: Eating with the Victorians*, ed, C. Anne Wilson, Alan Sutton, pp. 91–116.
Briggs, Richard, 1794, *The English Art of Cookery*, 3rd ed. G.G. and J. Robinson, London.
Carter, Charles, 1730, *The Complete Practical Cook*, Prospect Books 1984.
Carter, Charles, 1736, *The Compleat City and Country Cook*, 2nd ed. A. Bettesworth, C. Hitch and C. Davis, London.
Carter, Charles, 1749, *The London and Country Cook*, 3rd ed. C. Hitch, S. Austen and J. Hinton, London.
Christie, Christopher, 2000, *The British Country House in the Eighteenth Century*, Manchester University Press.
Collingwood,F and Woollams, J, 1792, *The Universal Cook and City and Country Housekeeper*, J. Scatcherd and J. Whitaker, London.
Day, Ivan ed., 2000, *Eat, Drink and Be Merry: The British at Table 1600–2000*. Philip Wilson Publishers, London.

Farley, John, 1783, *The London Art of Cookery*, ed. Ann Haly, Southover Press 1988.
Glasse, Hannah, 1747, *The Art of Cookery Made Plain and Easy*, Prospect Books 1983.
Hibbert, C. 1983, *The London Encyclopaedia*, ed. Ben Weinreb and C. Hibbert, Macmillan, London.
Howard, Henry, 1710, *England's Newest Way*, 3rd ed. C. Coningsby, London.
Lamb, Patrick, 1726, *Royal Cookery: or, the Compleat Court-Cook*, 3rd ed. E. and R. Nutt and A. Roper, London.
Johnson, Dr Samuel, 1843, *Samuel Johnson's Dictionary of the English Language*, ed. Alexander Chalmers, Studio Editions, London 1994.
Maclean, Virginia, 1981, *A Short-Title of Cookery Books published in the English Tongue 1701–1800*, Prospect Books.
Madeleine, Mlle, n.d., *La Parfaite Cuisinière Bourgeoise et Économique*, 27th ed., Bernardin-Bechet et Fils, Paris.
Mollard, John, 1802, *The Art of Cookery made Easy and Refined*, 2nd ed., printed for the Author, London.
Moore, Lucy, 2000, *Amphibious Thing: The Life of Lord Hervey*, Penguin.
Nott, John, 1726, *Cooks and Confectioners Dictionary*, 3rd ed., Lawrence Rivington, London 1980.
Raffald, Elizabeth, 1776, *The Experienced English Housekeeper*, 5th ed., printed for the author, London.
Thorold, Peter, 1999, *The London Rich: The Creation of a Great City, from 1666 to the Present*, Penguin.
Todd, Janet et al., 1987, *A Dictionary of British and American Women Writers 1660–1800*, ed. Janet Todd, Methuen, London.
Wheaton, Barbara Ketcham, 1983, *Savoring the Past*, Touchstone, New York.
Wilson, C. Anne, 1991, 'Ideal Meals and their Menus from the Middle Ages to the Georgian Era', *The Appetite and the Eye*, pp. 98–122 ed. C. Anne Wilson, Edinburgh University Press.

NOTES

[1] Glasse 1747 p. ii.
[2] See Wheaton 1983 on the French table layouts, pp. 138ff.
[3] Wilson, 1991 p. 109 Wilson draws attention to the 2nd edition of 1708 which I have not seen. Howard's book preceded by just two years Patrick Lamb's *Royal Cookery* (1710) which also included layouts. Further research by the editor reveals that Patrick Lamb's 1726 edition of *Royal Cookery* includes 40 plates of layouts, some of which interestingly indicate the number of diners. See Day 2000 for a recreation of a meal *à la française*.
[4] Raffald 1776 p. 382.
[5] Moore 2000 p. 219.
[6] Todd 1987 p. 88.
[7] Hibbert 1983 p. 845.
[8] Day 2000 pp. 38–42.
[9] Johnson 1843.
[10] Maclean 1981 p. 23.
[11] Atkyns 1741 p. 27.

The Medieval Arab Meal, East and West

Charles Perry

In the Middle Ages, the eastern and western Arabs already had distinct eating habits, and one striking difference was the notion of what constituted the meal and how it was to be served. In Spain and North Africa, a meal was served in courses, as at a Moroccan *diffa* today. The thirteenth-century *Manuscrito Anónimo* gives a specific, rigid order of eight courses for a banquet:

> How the service of dishes is ordered, and which is fitting to be first, and which last. The first dish to be presented is a feminine one, such as *baqliyya mukarrara* and the various kinds of *tafâyâ*. After this the dish *jamli*, then *muthallath*, then the dish of *murri*, then *mukhallal*, then *mu'assal*, then *fartûn*, then another *mu'assal*. This is the succession of the seven dishes and the order in which they are eaten.
>
> Many of the great and their companions have ordained that the dishes be placed on each table before the diners separately, one after another in order. By my life, this is better than putting many platters all on the table, and more beautiful, cultured and elegant. This has been the practice of the people of Andalusia and North Africa, of their rulers, great figures and men of merit, from the days of 'Umar b. 'Abd al-'Aziz and the Banû Umayya to the present.[1]

Historians generally credit this difference between east and west to Ziryab (d. 854), a Persian-born musician, driven from Baghdad by a jealous rival, who became the *arbiter elegantiarum* of the Andalusian court. He was certainly an innovator – he added the fifth string to the oud, among other things. This passage claims that the practice is even older, dating to the Umayyad caliphs of Damascus ('Umar died in 720), which seems unlikely, since the cult of gastronomy is a feature of the later Abbasid dynasty of Baghdad. In any case, *fartûn* seems to have a Spanish name, *fardón* ('large bundle').

Manuscrito Anónimo gives recipes for all the dishes in this passage, but nowhere does it explain the term 'feminine dish' *(mu'annatha)*. Since the rest of the seven dishes are grammatically masculine, this might simply have meant a dish with a feminine name — perhaps it referred to a specific repertoire of dishes, perhaps to all stews with feminine names, which would seem an arbitrary way of making up the meal. At any rate, it is clear that the first course was the only one in which the cook or host had any choice or scope for originality.

To an extent, 'feminine' may mean dishes from the eastern Arab world. Although the examples of 'feminine dishes' given are North African or Andalusian, most dishes with a feminine ending in *Manuscrito Anónimo* come from the repertoire of Baghdad, which retained a gastronomic glamour despite the fact that the eastern and western Arab world had been politically divorced for half a millennium. Andalusian cookbooks give many Baghdad recipes, including those named for the Abbasid caliphs Andalusia did not recognize – even recipes for *ibrâhîmiyya,* named for the rival who had driven Ziryâb from Baghdad. It is a curious fact that in Baghdad newly-invented dishes were usually given a grammatically feminine name (agreeing with the word *sifa,* 'recipe'), while those in the west tended to have masculine names (agreeing with *laun,* 'dish, course').

As for the feminine dishes mentioned, *tafâyâ* was basically a mild stew of lamb with onions, pepper, coriander and almonds[2] and *baqliyya mukarrara* was much the same with greens (spinach, saltwort, Swiss chard, lettuce or chicory) in place of almonds, with the addition of caraway as a carminative.[3]

Another definition of a feminine dish might simply be that it is not flavoured with vinegar or *murri,* a sort of soy sauce made from barley, as the next four dishes are (cf. *tharîd mudhakkar,* 'masculine *tharîd,*' which was based on beef stewed with whole onions, pepper, coriander, cumin and vinegar).[4] The four are *jamli* (or perhaps *iumli*), which was meat stewed with oil, vinegar, spices and soy sauce, usually finished in the oven with a topping of eggs beaten with bread crumbs;[5] *muthallah* ('threefold'), meat stewed with a vegetable and the three flavourings vinegar, soy sauce and saffron;[6] *laun al-murri,* meat stewed with soy sauce and optionally a lesser amount of vinegar;[7] and *mukhallal* ('vinegared'), meat stewed in vinegar.[8]

Mu'assal was a sweetmeat of honey thickened with starch and optionally egg whites as well, flavoured with almonds and spices and stirred with oil.[9] It was supposed to ooze oil – there was a utensil called a *mu'assal* dish, which was also used for draining the cooking oil from fritters (*zulâbiya*); it sounds like a bowl that incorporated a strainer. *Fartûn* was a savoury custard, flavoured with vinegar, saffron, cinnamon and almonds, baked in a large cup and overturned on the serving plate.[10] *Manuscrito Anónimo* gives a specific recipe for the second *mu'assal* 'used among us as the last dish.' It is much like the first, but with optional camphor and sesame seed.

By contrast to Andalusia, in Egypt, Syria or Iraq, any and every dish was served at once. The tenth-century Caliph al-Mustakfi once asked his boon companions to recite poems about food, and they responded with a miscellany on relishes, stews, pies, puddings, crêpes, canapés and asparagus. The caliph then ordered every one of the dishes served, and the description in al-Mas'ûdi's *Murûj al-Dhahab* suggests that this was an extraordinary meal because of the literary inspiration, but not a bizarre one.[11]

The cuisine of the pre-Islamic Persian court influenced medieval Arab cooking profoundly, particularly in Baghdad. It seems to have had some notion of serving courses, to judge from the existence of a sort of canapé called *bazmâward*, which would seem to have been an appetizer (the name means 'that which brings the banquet' in Persian). Though the Abbasid court borrowed Persian customs wholesale, this did not survive in Baghdad. In Arab cookery writings, *bazmâward* is strictly a snack, eaten apart from a formal meal.

But there did seem to be a certain organization precisely in such informal eating. The sixth chapter of the thirteenth-century cookbook of al-Baghdadi (and of the fourteenth-century 'expanded edition', *Kitâb Wasf al-At'ima al-Mu'tâda*) looks like a curious miscellany – fried dishes *(mutajjanât)*, cold dishes *(bawârid)*, samosas *(sanbûsak)* – but the cold dishes and samosas, at least, appeared in the 'tray of cold dishes' *(sallat bawârid)*, which seems to have been an informal meal or perhaps picnic. In *K. Wasf* we find, 'As for *al-muba'tharât* (scrambled eggs), there are several varieties you need. That is, when you arrange the *sallat bawârid*, there need to be several kinds of *muba'tharât* made from hens' eggs, which I shall mention, God the Most High willing.'[12] They prove to be hardboiled eggs rubbed with saffron and then fried; plain scrambled eggs; scrambled yolks coloured with saffron; scrambled whites; eggs scrambled with boiled onions; eggs scrambled with meat; the same with a sour flavouring; samosa with meat filling; samosa with a sweet nut filling; and frittata-like egg cakes *('ujja)*, sweet or sour.

There are poems on a 'tray of rarities' and a tray of dairy dishes, but these seem to describe gifts of food, rather than collections of things to be eaten at one time.[13] And when the poet Kushâjam describes the *bawârid* he has assembled, they have an improvised air, like the humble potluck to which Horace famously invited a friend:

Hasten to our one pot – I have a congealed *tabâhaja* (sauté).
I think our cook has the remnants of a cold *'udaisiyya* (little lentil stew);
Scented with saffron, lightly sweet-sour, it strengthens the putrid stomach.
Dirhams (silver coins) of eggs are arranged on it, not left by a shopping

woman who pays in cash.
Then fried small birds presented at the beginning of the table;
When you are present, sir, they will press to us additional pullets.
And a *ma'qûda* (thickened sweetmeat) the colour of carnelian, it wearied
   and exhausted the hand of the cook who made it thick.[14]

Another Baghdad organized hors d'oeuvre platter seems to be the basket of relishes *(sallat kawâmikh)* to be enjoyed with bread, most of them varieties of *kâmakh ahmar,* a sort of liquid blue cheese with various flavourings. The Caliph Ibn al-Mu'tazz described it in one of the poems recited before the Caliph al-Mustakfi mentioned above:

Accept a wicker basket brought to you, enclosing rows of bowls.
In it are arranged plates of varieties, red and yellow, which there is no
   refusing.
Among them are *kâmakh* of tarragon with its blossom. *Kâmakh ahmar*
   is in it, and capers
With whose fragrance souls are pleased, as if a perfumer had crumbled
   musk into it.
Among them is marjoram *kâmakh,* opposite a favourite variety of cloves,
And cinnamon *kâmakh,* unrivalled in taste, flawless in its colour,
Like musk in aroma as it diffuses: sharp in taste, the aroma highly
   perfumed.
A *kâmakh* of fresh wild thyme, a variety which suggests musk and tar to
   us.
Garlic *kâmakh:* when you see it, you discern a perfume which incites to
   eat.
The olives are like the gloom of dusk beside soused fish like books.
When you contemplate the onions in it, they seem silver stuffed with
   fire.
[Sliced] round turnips with which a taste of vinegar is mingled face
   [the onions, also sliced] in rows.
It's as if the white and the reddish-brown of them were (golden) *dirhams*
   arranged in which there are (silver) *dinars.*
In every corner of the tray rises a keen-eyed star like the light of dawn.
[The tray] is like garden flower set against a full moon, a sun, darkness
   and lights.[15]

It's hard to think such an appetizing array of appetizers would not have been sampled at once.

NOTES

[1] Arabic text edited by Ambrosio Huici Miranda, *Revista del Instituto de Estudios Islámicos en Madrid*, v. IX, 1961; p. 109.
[2] Op. cit., pp. 82–83, 118–119.
[3] p. 159.
[4] p. 182.
[5] p. 26.
[6] p. 209.
[7] p. 120.
[8] p. 26.
[9] p. 201.
[10] p. 27.
[11] *Murûj al-Dhabab (Les Prairies d'Or)*, edited by Barbier de Meynard et Pavet de Courteille, revised by Charles Pellat (Université Libanaise, Beirut, 1974; vol. v, pp. 250–8). A.J. Arberry's translation of the passage appears in *Medieval Arab Cookery* (Prospect Books, 2001), pp. 25–35.
[12] *Medieval Arab Cookery*, pp. 384–387.
[13] See Ibn Sayyâr al-Warrâq, *Kitâb al-Tabîkh*, ed. Kaj Öhrnberg and Sahban Mroueh (Helsinki, 1987), pp. 96 and 355.
[14] Op. cit., p. 108.
[15] *Murûj al-Dhabab*, vol. v, p. 250.

African American Meals from Slavery to Soul Food

Tracy N. Poe

Soul Food has become commonplace in American cities. Street corners in African American neighbourhoods are crowded with rib joints, chicken takeout stands, and fish markets. There are take-offs on Soul Food kitchens in white neighbourhoods, replete with old licence plates hanging on the walls and hot sauce on the red-and-white chequered tablecloths. Until very recently, however, there was no such thing as 'Soul Food'. Of course, there was an oral tradition of using the word 'soul' as a signifier of African American culture. The term did not expand beyond colloquial usage, however, until the Black Power movement began to gain momentum.

Before Black Pride and Soul Food became watchwords of the Civil Rights Movement vocabulary, everyday eating in African homes simply happened within the context of a culinary tradition that had been created over the years out of many different regional cultures, both in Africa and in the American South. The traditions that survived the selection process became important symbols that dramatized solutions to African Americans' dilemma of being barred from full membership in American society. This paper will focus on the role of the Southern, and later 'Soul Food', meal in the development of social, cultural and political consciousness in Chicago's African American community since 1920.

In that year, Chicago was a city of approximately 2.7 million people. 109,000, or 4.1 per cent, of these were African American. A little under half were migrants who had come from the Deep South to join the workforce,[1] primarily in the meat-packing, domestic and personal service, and steel industries.[2] By 1944, African Americans made up 9.3 per cent of Chicago's 3.6 million residents. This 'Great Migration', as it has become known, brought hope for new opportunities to millions of African Americans suffering the political, social, and economical impoverishment of the South. But it was not without its problems. When the first trickle of migrants began arriving in Chicago in 1905, the prominent middle-class black reformer Fannie Barrier Williams predicted that migrants' presence of would result in increased segregation and economic woes for the established black middle class.[3]

In truth, most newcomers did not conform to Chicagoans' carefully cultivated standards of behaviour, especially in regard to outward signs of respectability, like attitudes towards leisure and consumption. For this reason, food became prominent in urban African American consciousness. In the earliest days of the Great Migration, disapproval of migrants' eating habits was most clearly demonstrated in the pages of the Chicago *Defender*, a nationally circulated and highly respected African American newspaper. In advertisements, feature articles, and restaurant reviews, the *Defender*'s middle-class prejudices were often demonstrated in discussions of food.[4] Regular columns such as 'The Housekeeper' by Mrs F. Fletcher demonstrated a clear bias against food practices that smacked of Southernness. Mrs Fletcher advised against eating vegetables, for example, recommending them 'for their laxative effect' only and claiming they 'have little nutriment value',[5] a notion that went against the Southern emphasis on greens, legumes, sweet potatoes, and corn. Dr A. Wilberforce Williams' health column regularly criticized eating habits associated with Southern food, remarking that heavy meats, excessive carbohydrates, and especially hot sauces and condiments were deleterious to the liver and would cripple the digestive system of anyone over forty. 'The normal stomach needs little or no condiments when food is properly cooked,' he wrote. These kinds of statements in the publication that was acknowledged as the voice of 'The Race' in Chicago contributed to a stereotype of migrants as backward, unclean, and sorely in need of modernization.

With their sidewalk barbecue pits, 'chicken shacks', and public consumption of meals on front porch stoops, an ugly stereotype of Southern migrants soon developed, no less among the black middle class than among white Chicagoans. All the negative attention actually seemed to have strengthened migrants' desire to preserve their traditions. Faced with seemingly inexplicable opposition from members of their own race, they began thinking of 'down-home cooking' as something unique and special. Migrants' symbolic identification with Southern foodways was reinforced as communal meals continued at family dinners, holidays, and community gatherings.

In order to understand the significance of foodways in Southern consciousness, it helps to consider the circumstances under which they were established. Southern cuisine was largely created by African American cooks, as an amalgamation of African, European, and early American resources and preparations. For the first slaves, meals served an important symbolic function. Knowledge of foods and preparations was an aspect of African village life that could be reproduced in the plantation setting. Significant evidence indicates that many dishes and food rituals persisted more or less intact for several generations after the Diaspora. Food sharing, communal eating, and familiar dishes all helped recapture some aspects of African culture, while transmitting that culture to children born in the New World.

Using foods indigenous to North America but resembling African plants, as the American sweet potato resembles the African yam, and foods imported from Africa and cultivated on American soil like peanuts (known as 'guba' on the West Coast of Africa and 'goobers' even today in the United States), watermelon, and okra, slave cooks created a new cuisine with the cornmeal and cured pork that were their daily staples on the plantation. Slaves also supplemented this diet when they could by growing some of their own vegetables, such as American leafy greens that resembled African ones, turnips, cabbage, eggplant, cucumbers, tomatoes, onion, garlic, and hot peppers, all of which had been cultivated in West Africa since they were introduced by traders in the sixteenth century. These fruits and vegetables had been important sources of nutrients in the African diet; fortunately, they also grew well in the Southern climate. Hunting small game and fishing provided additional resources. In some cases slaves were allowed to raise their own pigs and chickens. As a centrepiece of Sunday dinners with the family or guests, chickens had significant symbolic meaning in rural African American life, since they were precious sources of eggs and could only be spared for meat on special occasions.[6] On these occasions, the sacrifice of a chicken demonstrated a prodigious hospitality, a cultural trait that had often been remarked upon by traders and explorers in Africa in the sixteenth and seventeenth centuries, and for which American black families were well known.[7]

Slaves' meal structure varied from plantation to plantation, or from farm to farm. As a rule, breakfasts were large, in order to fortify workers for a day in the field. Lunch was made of breakfast leftovers carried to the worksite in buckets, and suppers were one-pot meals or 'boiled dinners', put on to cook in the morning and served up when people returned to quarters at the end of the workday. On the larger plantations, cooking was usually done by a staff of slaves who prepared meals for the whole group. In other places, slave women were expected to cook for their own families in their cabins during their 'time off'. In either case, on Sundays and holidays they typically ate large celebratory meals with extended kinship groups, sometimes with all the slaves on the plantation or from the surrounding area. This practice had a precedent in the communal style of eating which was, and still is, central to life in African villages. Communal meals persisted in the agricultural setting in the form of picnics and Sunday dinners after slavery was abolished, becoming one of the most important features of Southern African American culture.

African Americans also invented new rituals that combined African harvest celebrations and American agricultural procedures. Hogkilling in particular, became a time of year for large group meals. Between Christmas and New Year's Day hogs would be slaughtered and preserved. Fresh organ meats like the jowl and chitlins were prepared with special side dishes such as black-eyed peas, an indigenous African legume believed to bring good luck for the New Year. In early July, when the corn was 'laid by' and the cotton and hay had been harvested, slaves traditionally indulged in religious meetings at which they thanked God for a good season and consumed a great quantity of fresh chicken, fish, vegetables, and that summer favourite, ripe watermelon. This festival was enhanced in the years after Emancipation by its connection to American Independence Day.[8]

Emancipation from slavery, with all its new-found freedoms, also brought with it harder times on the nutrition front for many black families. Former slaves, resourceful as they had always been, made the best of the situation by continuing to live 'low on the hog', growing as much of their own small food crops as they could manage, preserving perishables during the harvest season, and relying heavily on small game, foraging and fishing for their sustenance. Communal eating became increasingly important to freemen. Eating traditional foods together forged a spiritual connection between those present and the ancestors of the past, as each family cobbled together what little they had into the great feasts described by Southern black authors like Zora Neale Hurston.[9]

For all these reasons – economic hardship, personal pride, and the need for community – food came to represent the resilience of the African American people in the South. Furthermore, traditional cooking was seen as nutritious. Despite bouts with starvation and disease, when black people had enough food, they felt they could work harder and longer than anybody else. This belief was ratified by a 1939 US Department of Agriculture study, which showed that at least during summer months when fresh fruits and vegetables were available the vitamin, mineral, and protein content of poor, Southern African American families' diets was higher than that of whites who spent the same amount of money on food.

The economic, social, and nutritional roles that Southern foodways had historically played in the lives of African Americans were not going to be easily cast aside after migration. Black families' justified faith in the food traditions learned from generations of mothers and grandmothers were not likely to be displaced by the nutritional warnings of *Defender* critics like Mrs Fletcher and Dr Williams. Quite the contrary; migrants managed to retain their foodways despite opposing forces much more pressing than their new neighbours' disapproval. Overcrowded housing with scant-to-inoperable kitchens[10] and work schedules that kept many people away from home at meal-times both could have prevented migrants from continuing time-consuming food preparation and elaborate extended family dinners.

But nutritional anthropologist Norge Jerome, in her work on African American migrant diets, noted that while the industrial work schedule did cause some changes in the structure of daily meals, it did so slowly and without a great deal of impact on the *content* of the meal. As a result, migrants' eating habits remained remarkably consistent with their rural Southern roots.[11] Furthermore, Jerome's work indicates that migration enhanced African Americans' awareness of the role of food in their heritage, since the practice of Southern cooking and ritual of the Sunday dinner or church picnic consciously reinforced the cultural connection between the rural South and the urban industrial setting.

Jerome noted two major changes in migrants' daily meal patterns over the course of a two-year period: one, meals became lighter, often excluding some of the high-calorie, high-protein foods that had been necessary to the performance of heavy manual labour in the South; two, the order in which meals were eaten changed to accommodate urban work and school schedules. Both of these changes, however, occurred within the context Southern food traditions, and the Sunday meal remained unchanged from its Southern model in either content or context.[12]

Specifically, migrants maintained the Southern 'heavy breakfast' tradition for about two years into their urban residency, when it gradually began to get smaller. The heavy breakfast consisted of an egg dish, a fried meat dish (pork chops, ham, or bacon), a hot cereal (rice or grits, and sometimes oatmeal or farina), fried potatoes, biscuits or toast, gravy, butter, assorted sweet condiments (preserves, cane syrup, molasses, or jelly), and hot drinks (coffee, tea, and hot chocolate). The traditional lunch consisted of breakfast leftovers. When the structure of the meal began to change in a migrant household, it usually meant dropping the fried meat dish, the potatoes, and/or the eggs, and switching to sandwiches for lunch. Biscuits or toast and hot cereal, with condiments and a hot drink, remained essential to the breakfast meal in the urban setting. On weekends and holidays, the heavy breakfast was resumed, with the addition of pancakes to the menu.

Dinner or supper, the traditional names for the weekend heavy meal and the daily evening meal, also changed for migrants. In the traditional household, food preparation fell into two general categories: boiling, constituting the five daily evening suppers, and frying, occurring on the weekends as a midday dinner. 'Boiled dinners' consisted of a piece of meat simmered with vegetables or legumes. The lighter type of boiled dinner, made with fresh seasonal ingredients, was eaten mostly in warmer months, while heavier dinners made from dried legumes such as black-eyed peas were eaten mostly in cooler months. The 'fried dinner' was the template for the elaborate Sunday meal, which usually consisted of a roasted or fried meat such as chicken or pork, with vegetables and legumes as side dishes. Both boiled and fried meals required cornbread, butter, and an iced drink to be complete. Sunday dinners consisted of a variety of vegetable dishes; two or more starches such as sweet potatoes, white potatoes, rice, and/or corn; and desserts. Wheat rolls or biscuits were a special addition to the Sunday dinner, a hangover from slavery times when white flour was handed down from the 'big house' kitchen as a special treat.[13] As migrants became more accustomed to the urban setting, boiled dinners were prepared only 2 to 3 days a week, and the fried dinner became much less common *except* on Sundays or holidays. In the urban pattern, dining out or eating more 'American' foods such as hot dogs or spaghetti made up one or two meals a week.[14]

A few factors in this dietary pattern emerged as significant indicators of the persistence of Southern foodways in Jerome's study. One was the subjects' valuation of the time spent, cost, and variety of dishes in their urban meals, especially Sunday dinners, in order to maintain the quality of the food they had been accustomed to in the South. They did not, for the most part, use canned or convenience foods so readily available in the city to prepare traditional meals, although they had no objection to eating them as 'American' food.[15] One exception to this was in the preparation of sweet desserts, which were sometimes prepared from processed ingredients.[16] Another is the persistence of seasonal eating. Migrants continued to eat lighter, vegetable-based boiled dinners in warm seasons and heavy, dried-legume-based dinners in cold seasons, despite the year-round availability of fresh vegetables and dried legumes. Also, Jerome's subjects considered the accessibility of favourite Southern foods, rather than exposure to new foods or more dietary variety, to be one of the chief advantages of moving to the city. This was particularly true of sweets and desserts, once served primarily at special dinners, which became more common in the urban setting with the year-round availability of cake mixes, commercial jellies and preserves, processed sugar, and fresh milk.[17]

The combination of the cash wage, the variety of businesses at which consumers could choose to eat, and a visceral attachment to traditional Southern black culture made a potent broth in which urban African American culture as we know it today is steeped. At the centre of this new-found consumer power was the idea of freedom. Ralph Ellison's nameless migrant in *Invisible Man* describes the excitement one could feel over its simplest expression, after purchasing a baked sweet potato from a sidewalk vendor:

I took a bite, finding it as sweet and hot as any I'd ever had, and was overcome with such a surge of homesickness that I turned away to keep my control. I was walking along, munching the (sweet potato), just as suddenly overcome by an intense feeling of freedom – simply because I was eating while walking along the street. It was exhilarating. I no longer had to worry about who saw me or about what was proper. To hell with all that, and as sweet as (it) actually was, it became like nectar with the thought.[18]

The pursuit of pleasure in the form of traditional meals was an integral part of migrants' sense of freedom. A colourful example from St. Clair Drake and Horace Cayton's ground-breaking 1945 study of life in the *Black Metropolis* may serve as an illustration:

Baby Chile called us to the kitchen for supper – a platter of neckbones and cabbage, a saucer with five sausage cakes, a plate of six slices of bread, and a punchbowl of stewed prunes (very cold and delicious). Baby Chile placed some corn fritters on the table, remarking, 'This bread ain't got no milk in it. I did put some aig (sic) in it, but I had to make it widout any milk'…

Though this household represented extreme poverty and social disorganization, its members attempted to maintain a few family rituals … Everyone always said a Scripture verse before meals. Sometimes, Mr. Ben would playfully give as his verse, 'rise, Peter, slay and eat,' or Slick would quote the shortest verse in the Bible – 'Jesus wept.'… Christmas, Thanksgiving, Easter, birthdays, or a Joe Louis victory usually called for a special party of some sort.[19]

Along 'the Stroll', the section of State Street between 29th and 36th Avenues, leisure activities of all kinds awaited anyone with money in his or her pockets. Music clubs, dance halls, theatres, and movie houses owned by both blacks and whites offered an after-hours escape from the grey world of the factory, as did restaurants that catered to both the refined tastes of the middle class and the more down-home desires of migrants. Even as the middle class emulated urban white culinary trends, enterprising newcomers and their wiser native counterparts were beginning to exploit migrants' spending power.

Business owners began marketing themselves to these new consumers. 'When you are walking out stop at the Blue Bird Inn' advertised Mrs Eva C. Bird in the 1921 edition of *Black's Blue Book,* a directory of African American businesses. Owners appealed to the round-the-clock schedules of their customers with signs such as 'Open All Night' or 'Open from 4:30 a.m. to 1 a.m.' Some business owners appealed directly to their Southern clientele's tastes. 'Home cooking our specialty', became *de rigueur* in *Defender* advertisements, even as Mrs Fletcher's column reviled the Southern definition of 'home cooking'. 'Freshest fish Received Daily, Live Shrimp and Crabs', announced S.L. Williams' ad, designed to attract clients from the coastal regions of Georgia, Louisiana, and the Carolinas. 'Hot Biscuits', 'Barbecued Chicken—Barbecued fish', and 'Watermelon' said others.[20]

But having fun was not migrants' only motivation for patronizing black-owned businesses. Migrant entrepreneurs also played a social role in the African American community. New migrants commonly sought out businesses owned by people from their hometowns and congregated with old friends and acquaintances there, just as they had done in the South. Produce and meat markets served as neighbourhood meeting places. Since communal eating was characteristic of Southern black foodways, lunch counters, 'chicken shacks', and barbecue wagons took their place alongside urban fixtures such as ice-cream shops, hot-dog stands, and chili parlours as sites where people ate and socialized together.

In a study of the social world of elderly black men in Chicago's Near South Side neighbourhood, University of Chicago sociologist Mitchell Duneier emphasized the role restaurants played in sustaining a sense of a living past being practised in the context of a modern community:

> If it is impossible to transplant to (the café) the particular sounds, smells, and sights of the old neighbourhood, at least here black regulars can enjoy the kind of solid food in good company that brings back images of a world that once existed for them…just the fact that an inexpensive meal is prepared the old-fashioned way, with natural ingredients on a stove or in an oven satisfies their longings… Comments such as 'Mamma cooked from the basics' or 'Mamma never used packaged stuff' are typical of a generation of black men who feel very much at home in a cafeteria that offers its patrons a kind of food that is symbolic of the integrity of their older way of life.[21]

By the 1930s the influence migrant business owners wielded in the Black Metropolis began to be felt in the reduction of public clashes between natives and migrants over respectability issues. The prejudice against migrant foodways faded as they became more normalized within the African American community. As early as 1925 even the *Defender* began urging tolerance for Southern food rituals, noting their underlying common sense if not their modernity.²² In addition, the children's page began running a cooking column for girls. Although most of the recipes were for the kind of European dishes Mrs Fletcher favoured, occasionally something with a decidedly Southern name turned up. Amid the recipes for Cucumber Sauce, Angel Lemon Pie, and Spanish Potatoes were those for 'Mammy's Sweet Potato Pudding', 'Southern Fried Chicken', and 'Creole Stew'. That the latter, unfortunately, was a blend of shellfish, parsley, flour, and salt that no Louisianan would recognize is less significant than the fact that this seems to demonstrate an effort to grant some Southern dishes a bit of respectability, and to acknowledge their role in African American traditions worth passing on to a younger generation.²³

The gradual adaptation of migrant meal practices by the mainstream African American community demonstrates the integration of rural Southern culture into urban African American consciousness and the acceptance of migrants not as backward, unclean, and in need of modernization, but as brothers and sisters with common traditions and heritage. Food was just one of those symbols, but it was a natural vehicle for the expression of migrants' sense of individual freedom.

*****

The period between the end of World War II and the spread of the Civil Rights Movement welcomed a new wave of Southern migrants to Chicago's African American community. By 1970, African Americans made up nearly one-third of Chicago's total population. New migrants entered into a much more socially and politically cohesive community than had their predecessors, one that was much more accepting of their Southern culture. Symbols of that culture – like food – had an important role to play in the evolving social ethos of the Civil Rights movement. Being black was special. Black was Beautiful. Blacks had a right to Pride and Power. The core of this awareness was the concept of 'soul'.²⁴ Soul unified African Americans of all social classes, regions, educational and occupational backgrounds, and genders into an ethnic group with a unique identity.

Soul also conferred authenticity on entrepreneurs' efforts to boost the economic vitality of the African American community. The word was used to modify any project which claimed to support the notion of a unique African American ethnicity: Soul brothers and Soul sisters were encouraged to internalize the values of Soul Music and Soul Food – values which were inherently connected to the heritage of slavery – literally by consuming them. Southern migrants were the natural ambassadors of this heritage, carrying its symbolic forms from their rural homeland to the urban North. The everyday, transparent aspects of blacks' cultural life in the South now came to be seen in as deeply imbued with the essence of African Americans' historic struggle for their human rights.

In this sense, the 'discovery' of Soul Food was not particularly original, but rather a continuation of an ongoing cultural practice under a new, Black Power nickname. A more self-conscious application of Southern cuisine in the lives of urban migrants and their children took hold as home and restaurant cooks emphasized an attitude towards food, especially in regards to 'old-fashioned' approaches to seasoning and preparation time. In other words, the diner who sits down in the Soul Food restaurant or the children who look forward to their mothers' Sunday dinners expect that by definition, their meals will be prepared using traditional methods and served according to traditional expectations of hospitality.

Soul Food restaurants in particular have had an undeniable power in the political, social, and economic life of the industrial city. In their social role, they have provided a gathering place for African Americans where communal eating and traditional standards of hospitality are maintained. In their economic role, they have allowed African American consumers and producers to operate in a closed system of economic participation which gives legitimacy and some degree of financial autonomy to the neighbourhoods in which they are located.

It is in its political role, however, that Soul Food demonstrates most clearly its part as a fixture of urban black consciousness. Soul Food business owners, many of them women, have kept African American heritage alive in a material way, but they also contribute to the community as activists, with the clout to bring city-wide attention to the community's political agenda. The idea that food had a political role to play in African American life as well as an economic and social one was certainly something that gained credence as the Civil Rights Movement evolved from a purely political struggle into the Black is Beautiful ideology. The values of home, family, and hospitality symbolized by Soul Food served as a counterpoint to the militancy of the Black Power side of African American identity-building. Its emphasis on the more feminine aspects of African American heritage made the Black Pride political agenda more palatable to the average African American community member, who may have been nervous about the anarchistic, aggressive rhetoric espoused by the movement's younger leaders.

In fact, the city's Soul Food restaurants have become a virtual 'Washington slept here' of Chicago and Civil Rights Movement politics. Any owner of an institution that has been around since the 1950s can tell tales about Martin Luther King, Jr.'s strategy meetings over platters of fried chicken or Jesse Jackson's cravings for sweet potato pie during Operation Push staff meetings.

Edna's, for example, opened by a Tennessee farm family that came North in the wake of the civil rights struggles of the 1950s, has had a special place in the community. It was apparently a particular favourite of Martin Luther King, Jr. when he came to town in 1965 for his Chicago campaign. 'I was a little bit too young to remember it,' said Melvin Mitchell, current manager of Edna's and grandson of its founder, 'But I know that Dr King used to sleep at one of the churches nearby when he was in town. They didn't have anything to eat or anyplace to meet. So they came here.'[25] Edna's was one of the only buildings left untouched during the riots that rocked the neighbourhood following Dr King's assassination in 1968.

It is clear that Soul Food restaurants have served as a conduit between the symbolic ethnicity of African American people and the political motives of community members and politicians who claim to serve them. Food easily serves as a rather benign form of identification with the community, as participating in its consumption does not require a commitment to any particular ideology, but it does allow for a dramatization of a politician's acceptance of black culture. In the wake of the Civil Rights movement, Illinois governors, Chicago mayors, and legions of local aldermen, judges, and candidates have made a tradition of meeting with black voters over plates of chicken and dumplings and pitchers of sweetened iced tea. Coming together around plates of Soul Food has come to be an important point of identification for the city's leaders, who have leveraged eating into a way of demonstrating their purported affinity for black voters.

Ultimately, in the 'discovery' of Soul Food, African Americans have created a powerful symbol for the heritage of slavery and reconstruction, the adaptability and innovation of rural African American culture, and the awakening consciousness of African Americans' unique ethnic identity. The degree to which politically, economically, and socially Soul Food now represents that community as a whole, especially when one considers the disdain with which it was evaluated by urban blacks during the Great Migration, is a powerful testament to the importance of the meal in the development of ethnic identity.

NOTES

[1] Drake, St. Clair and Horace R. Cayton, *Black Metropolis: A Study of Negro Life in a Northern City,* University of Chicago Press, 1945, pp. 8.
[2] Burgess, Ernest W. and Charles Newcomb, *Data of the City of Chicago, 1920,* University of Chicago Press, 1931, pp. 59–63.
[3] Williams, Fannie Barrier, 'Social Bonds in the "Black Belt" of Chicago' in *Charities and the Commons,* Vol. XV, No. 1, pp. 9.
[4] *Defender,* January 10, 1920, editorial page.
[5] *Defender,* March 15, 1915, women's page.
[6] There are many excellent sources on slave diets, notably in Eugene Genovese's *Roll Jordan*

Roll: The World the Slaves Made, New York: Pantheon, 1974; Lawrence Levine's *Black Culture and Black Consciousness: Afro-American Folk Thought from Slavery to Freedom.*, New York: Holt, 1977; and Ira Berlin's *Many Thousands Gone: The first Two Centuries of Slavery in North America*, Harvard University Press, 1998. See also the cookbooks of Jessica B. Harris and Kathy Starr, which provide histories of African American food, often handed down orally through these women's families.

[7] Harris, Jessica, 'Same Boat, Different Stops: An African-Atlantic Culinary Journey', lecture presented at Northwestern University, November 10, 1997.

[8] Cookbook author Kathy Starr remembers her grandmother telling her that the Fourth of July 'is our most important holiday. It means freedom to black people, freedom from slavery', pp. 42.

[9] For a particularly vivid account of a Southern black community's food sharing, read Hurston's *Their Eyes Were Watching God*, especially Chapter 5, in which villagers throw a huge picnic to commemorate the lighting of the town's first street lamp.

[10] Spear, Allan H., *Black Chicago: The Making of a Negro Ghetto, 1890–1920*, University of Chicago Press, 1967, p. 148.

[11] Jerome's study was conducted in 1965–66, but there is no question that the food patterns she describes are contiguous with those of the earlier twentieth century. She compares the dietary patterns of her migrant subjects to those collected by Vance in 1932, Cussler and Debive in 1941, and the USDA food consumption report of 1935–36. Jerome, Norge, Randy F. Kandel and Gretel H. Pelto eds, *Nutritional Anthropology: Contemporary Approaches to Diet and Culture*, Redgrave Publishing, 1980.

[12] Jerome, Norge, 'Northern Urbanization and Food Consumption Patterns of Southern Born Negroes', in *American Jnl of Clinical Nutrition*, vol. 22, no. 12. December 1969, pp. 1667–9.

[13] Genovese, pp. 567.

[14] Jerome, *NACADC*, pp. 286.

[15] Jerome, *NACADC*, pp. 287. Folklorist Anne Sharman, in interviews with urban African American women, discovered that her subjects did make a distinction between 'Southern' or 'soul' foods and 'American food'. American food was defined in various ways, but generally referred to 'food that white people eat' or 'foods they might eat if they had unlimited financial resources' – things like steak, fast food, and processed food. Curiously, some respondents also included Chinese and Italian food in this category. 'From Generation to Generation: Resources, Experience, and Orientation in the Dietary Practices of Selected Urban American Households', in *Diet and Domestic Life in Society*, Anne Sharman Janet Theophano, Karen Curtis, and Ellen Messer eds, Philadelphia: Temple University Press, 1991, pp. 174–203.

[16] Interestingly enough, processed American sweets were also popular among Italian immigrants, also accustomed to a vegetable-, offal-, and legume-based diet, to a degree that appalled social workers. See Elizabeth Ewen, *Immigrant Women in the Land of Dollars: Life and Culture on the Lower East Side, 1890–1925*, New York: Monthly Review Press, 1985.

[17] Jerome, *NACADC*, pp. 293–300.

[18] Ellison, Ralph, *Invisible Man*, Random House, 1952, p. 258 (originally published 1947).

[19] Drake and Cayton, pp. 608–609.

[20] All advertising is listed in Black's *Blue Books* of 1917 and 1921 and issues of the *Chicago Defender*, 1915–1935.

[21] Duneier, M., *Slim's Table: Race, Respectability, and Masculinity*, Univ. of Chicago Press, 1992.

[22] *Defender*, June 21, 1925, editorial page.

[23] *Defender*, February 14, 1925, 'Defender Junior' page.

[24] Jones, LeRoi, *Blues People: The Negro Experience in White America and the Music that Developed From It*, New York: William Morrow and Company, 1963.

[25] Interview with Melvin Mitchell, December 16, 1997.

A Sumptuous Meal: Navigating the Laws Restricting Wedding Banquets of Fourteenth-century Florence

Eden Rain

Along with many other Italian cities of the fourteenth century, Florence sought to legislate a simpler code of behaviour for its citizens. Enacting sumptuary laws primarily for the regulation of ostentatious dress, they also regulated the pomp and circumstance allowed at weddings and funerals. In the Pragmatica of 1356, the meal one could serve for a wedding was curtailed to only three *vivande* (a dish, course or viand), and the foods comprising these *vivande* were fairly strictly defined. Obviously, there were those who preferred to pay the fines and work outside these rules, but there would also have been many who chose to work within the letter of the law while still attempting to create as ostentatious a meal as possible. Using the framework of these sumptuary laws, along with contemporary recipe collections, one can conjecturally build a lavish nuptial meal of fourteenth-century Tuscany.

The relevant text in the 1356 Pragmatica is inserted among rules about how many guests, musicians and other attendants were allowed at weddings. It spells out strict limitations on what foods could be served at even noble weddings of the time. To help promulgate this law the Signoria of Florence commissioned a translation of the original Latin text into the vernacular.

Italian Text of 1356:[1]
Ordinamenta circa sponsalitias
E che il dì delle nozze solamente si possa dare confetti, e non si possa dare alsuno confetto prima overo poscia a cinque die, a la pena di lire venticinque; ed intendasi due manere confetti, contandosi la traggea tutta per una maniera. E che alle dette nozze non possa avere più di tre vivande tra le quali possa essere uno rosto con torta chi vuole. E quello arrosto e torta s' intenda sola una vivanda, non intendendosi per vivanda frutti e confetti. E che non possa apparecchiare nè avere per tutto el

corredo de le nozze più che venticinque taglieri de ciascuna vivanda, intendendosi per vivanda raviuoli overo bragiere o tortelletti; salvo ch a le nozze di cavalieri possano avere quelle donne e uomini che a loro piacerà, e dare di quatro vivande, e confetti e iocolari quanti e quanto tempo a loropiacerà, pena lire cinquanta al marito che contra facesse, e per quante volte; e pena di lire venticinque de ciscuna donna e ciascuno trombatore, naccarino o altro qualunque iocolare che che facesse contra. E che lo coco che farle tali nozze, sia tenuto e debbia denunziare a l' officiale, almeno uno dì dinanziquelle cotali nozze, e quante e quali vivande dee fare, e chi è lo marito, e di quali quar.[2] e popolo, a la pena de lire vinticinque: e se più vivande facesse ch' è ordinato, caggia nella detta pena. E se darà vitella, non possa dare alcuna altra carne con essa, e non passi la possa più di lire sette; nè più d' una possa dare per taglieri, a la pena di lire venticinque per ciascunacosa e volta; dichiarando che in su lo taglieri de lo arrosto non possa dare nè avere altro che uno cappone colla torta, e uno paio di pollastri con uno pippione, o due pippioni con uno pollastro, overo uno anitrottolo e non più, a la detta pena per qualunque cosa fosse contra fatta.

Translation:

And that the days of the wedding only can you give *confetti*,[3] and you cannot give any confetto before or after for five days, at the penalty of twenty-five lire; and this means two types of confetti, including all the *traggea*[4] for one type. And that at the said wedding you cannot have more than three vivande among the which can be a roast with [whatever] tart you wish. And this roast and tart mean only one vivanda, not meaning for vivande fruit and confetti. And that you cannot prepare nor have for all the furnishings of the wedding more than twenty-five platters of each vivanda, meaning for vivande ravioli or blancmanges,[5] or *tortellini*; saving that at the weddings of knights they can have such women and men that to them are pleasing, and give of four vivande, and confetti and jugglers as many and at what time shall please them, [at] penalty [of] fifty lire to the husband who goes counter, and for each time, and penalty of twenty-five lire for each woman and each trumpeter, drummer or other whatever juggler that goes against. And that the cook that makes for them such a wedding, should be obliged and have to denounce to the officials, at least one day prior to these such weddings, and how much and which vivande he has to make, and who is the husband, and of which neighbourhood and people, at the penalty of twenty-five lire: and if he makes more vivande than were ordered, he falls in the said penalty. And if you give veal, you cannot give any other meat with this, and cannot exceed the cost[6] of seven lire; nor can you give more than one per platter at the penalty of twenty-five lire for each thing and time; declaring that on the platter of the roast you cannot give or have other than one capon with the tart, and one pair of pullets with one pigeon, or two pigeons with one pullet, or else one duckling and not more, at the said penalty for whatever thing is done counter.

Interestingly, this law makes clear that the intent was only to limit the meat and pasta courses, not courses of fruits or other foods. Contemporary laws of Prato specified that cheeses were exempt as well.[7]

Looking through the *Libro della cucina*, a collection of recipes from late fourteenth-century Tuscany, certain dishes almost seem to have been designed with the purpose of working around these restrictions, combining multiple meats into one dish or meats and pastas together.

While it is fairly certain that these recipes were not originally created for the purpose of circumventing such laws (similar dishes exist in regions that did not regulate their banquets), it does seem likely that these, or similar, recipes would have been used as a tool for enriching a meal otherwise restricted to a simplicity somewhat in contrast with the flamboyant mindset of the era.

The most obvious example of these is the Torta Parmesana, a dish with layers of different raviolis, sausages, prosciutto and stuffed eggs, all in the same tart:[8]

> De la torta parmesana.
> togli pulli smembrati e tagliati, e friggili con le cipolle ben trite, con lardo in bona quantità: e, cotti i polli abbastanza, mettivi su spezie e sale abbastanza. Poi togli erbe odorifere, mettivi su zaffarano in bona quantità, e trita forte e ex coriatam[9] in bona quantità, e poni la medolla sopra 'l grasso di quello, e batti col coltello fortemente, e spessa e mesta colle dette erbe con alquanto di cascio grattato. Poi togli di queste un' altra quantità, e fànne ravioli; e togli anche cascio fresco, e fanne ravioli bianchi. Togli anche petrosello e altre erbe odorifere e cascio fresco, e fanne ravioli verdi, e tutte cose sopradette distempera con ova, togli anche amandole monde; pestale forte e dividile in due parti; nell' una mettivi de le spezie in bona quantità, nell' altra mettivi zuccaro; e de l' una e de l' altra quantità fanne ravioli spartitamente: poi togli ova e fàlli pieni. Togli anche budelli di porco bene grassie lavati, empili di bone erbe e cascio, e lessali bene. Togli presciutto crudo e tagliato sottile, e fa similmente salsuccie: poi togli ova dibattute, e mesta con li dette polli

in uno vaso, e pòllosu la bragia, e mescola, mescola con la mescola fine che sia spesso; poi levalo dal fuoco, e assaporato di sale. Poi togli farina bene monda, e fanne pasta salda, e forma al modo de la tegghia o la padella. Poi collo cocchiaio togli del brodo dei detti polli, e ungi la datta pasta: poi nella detta pasta fà un solaio di carne d' essi polli; nel secondo solaio poni ravioli bianchi col savore di sopra; nel terzo solaioponi presciuto e salsuccie, tagliate come detto è. Nel quarto solaio poni de la detta carne. Nel quinto poni dei cervellati, cioè budelli pieni di sopradetti. Nel sesto de' ravioli d' amandole; e in ciascuno solaio vi si ponano dei dattari; e anche metti sopra la detta carne, il savore, e in ciascuno solaio poni spezie abbastanza: poi metti spezie di sopra che basti: e abbi la braggia, a poni il testo sopra; e di sopra e di sotta sia la bragia. Scopri spesso la detta torta, e ungila con lardo; e se la si rompesse, togli la pasta sottile, e sottilmente menata, e bagnala coll' acqua, a poni su la rottura, e metti il testo caldo di sopra.

Translation:

Of the Parma Tart

Take dismembered and cut up pullets, and fry them with well-minced onions with lard in good quantity: and cook the pullets enough putting on enough spices and salt. Then take fragrant herbs, put on saffron in good quantity and mince well and excoriate[10] in good quantity. And put the marrow over the fat of this and beat with the knife strongly, and thicken and stir with the said herbs with some grated cheese. Then take of these another quantity, and make of them ravioli and take also fresh cheese and make of them white ravioli. Take also parsley and other fragrant herbs and fresh cheese and make of them green ravioli, and all the things said above distemper with eggs, take also peeled almonds, pound them well and divide them in two parts: in the one put of spices in good quantity, in the other put sugar, and of the one and of the other quantity make raviolis separately: then take eggs and make them stuffed. Take also clean intestines of fat pork, stuff them of good herbs and cheese, and boil them well. Take raw prosciutto and cut it thin, and do similarly sausage: then take beaten eggs, and mix with the said pullets in a vessel, and put this on the embers and mix constantly with the spoon so that it becomes thick: then take it from the fire, and flavour [it] of salt. Then take good pure flour, and make firm pasta and form it in the shape of the pot or frying pan. Then with the spoon take of the broth of the said pullets, and anoint the said pasta: then in the said pasta make a layer of meat of these pullets: in the second layer put white ravioli with sauce over them; in the third layer put prosciutto and sausages cut as it was said. In the fourth layer put of the said meat. In the fifth put of the cervelatti,[11] that is of the stuffed intestines above said. In the sixth of the ravioli of almonds, and in each layer put some dates; and also put over the said meat, the sauce, and in each layer put enough spices: Then put enough spices on top: and have the embers to put over the pot lid: and above and below will be the embers. Frequently, uncover the said tart and anoint with lard, and if it breaks take the soft pasta and gently bring it, and wet it with water to put on the rupture and put the hot lid over it.

Another way to work around the restrictions of the Pragmatica can be found in several recipes for large roasts which are stuffed with poultry, thereby presenting two or more meats to the table within what is technically only one dish. Thus, we have a roast of veal stuffed with goslings, capons and other birds:

A empiere uno vitello.
Togli el vitello giovene scorticato, ovvero pelato; arrostilo e empilo, come tu vuoli: puoi ponervi papari, galline e capponi e l' empitura che sopra e detta, e qualunque altra bona: mettivi però molto lardo battuto, nel ventre; poi togli il grasso che ne cade quando s' arrostisce, e poni en peverata col pane abbrusticato, e zaffarano; e bolla un poca da per sè la detta peverata: e dà a mangiare.

Translation:
To Stuff a Calf
Take a young calf, flayed, that is to say skinned; roast it and stuff it, as you like; you can put in it goslings, chickens and capons and the stuffing that above is said, and whatever else [is] good: put to it however much beaten lard, in the paunch; then take the fat that falls from it when you roast it, and put [this] in Pepper Sauce with toasted bread, and saffron; and boil it a little by itself the said Pepper Sauce: and give [it] to eat.

The traditional medieval peacock redressed in its feathers has an interesting variation in this cookbook. Peacock meat is mixed with pork and formed into gilded meatballs, both stuffed inside and served as garnishing around the body of the roasted peacock:

de la salsa cercha tra l'altre [this note appears above the text in the original manuscript]

A empiere uno pavone.

Scortica il pavone, rimanendo il capo colle penne: poi togli carne di porco non troppo grassa, e anche pesta de la carne del ditto pavone o altro, e tritale e pestale insieme. Anche pesta spezie, canella e noci moscate, quelle che tu vuoi: le quali, bene trite e peste colli albumi d' ova, mestale insieme, e disbatti colle dette spezie e carne fortemente, e riserva le tuorla da per sè. Poi empi il ditto pavone de la detta carne trita e pesta, e spezie predette: e invogli il detto pavone in una rete di porco e fermalo con broche de legno: e così il metti nella caldaia in acqua tepida, a bolla soavemente. E quando serà ristretto bollendo, arrostilo in spiedo o in graticola, e coloralo con le tuorla d'ova dibattute, le quali tu servasti; e non le torre tutte, ma del resto faraine pome, come seguita, cioè. Togli lumbo di porco crudo, e tritalo minutissimamente col coltello, e battilo forte; poi mesta la detta carne con le dette tuorla d'ova riservate, e spezie predette, a fàlle si spesso, che intra la palme de le mani facci pome piccioli; e involgili in tuorla d'ova, colorali, e mettili a bollire in acque bollente. Poi così bolliti puoi arrostire e coloralli con tuorla d' ova sottilmente con penne. Di queste pome ne puoi mettere dentro nel pavone, e di fuore, sotto la detta rete. E, fatto questo, rivasti il detto pavone del suo cuoio, pelle e penne riservate, e portalo a taola: e, levato su il cuoio, dà a mangiare.

Translation:

For the sauce search among the others.[12]

To stuff a peacock

Flay the peacock, keeping behind the head with the feathers: then take pork meat, not too fat, and also pound the meat of the said peacock or another, and mince and pound them together. Also pound spices, cinnamon and nutmeg, those which you like: the which, well minced and pounded with egg whites, mix them together, and stir briskly with the said spices and meat, and keep the yolks by themselves. Then stuff the said peacock with the said minced and pounded meat, and spices aforesaid: and wrap the said peacock in a caul of pork and fasten it with skewers[13] of wood: and thus put it in a cauldron in tepid water, to boil softly. And when it is barely boiling, roast it on the spit or gridiron, and colour it with the beaten egg yolks, the which you saved; and don't take it all, but of the rest make of it apples, as follows, that is to say: Take raw loin of pork, and mince it minutely with a knife, and beat it well; then mix the said meat withthe said reserved egg yolks, and spices aforesaid, to make it be thick, that in the palms of the hand you make little apples;

and coat them in egg yolk, colour them, and put them to boil in boiling water. Then thus boiled, you can roast and colour them with egg yolks softly with feathers. Of these apples you can put them inside the peacock and outside, under the said caul. And this made, dress the said peacock in its reserved hide, skin and feathers, and take it to the table: and lifting up its skin, give it to eat.

In addition to the roasts, there are also dishes of boiled meats which could be used to work around the law such as this recipe for whole partridges, which are supplemented with pieces of chicken:

De le starne.
Togli starne bullite e polli smembrati con erbe odorifere, sale, e bone spezie trite nel mortaio: e soffritta la detta carne con lardo, pòlla a cocere in un poco d' acqua nella pentola, e mettivi su latte d' amandole: e a la fine de la cocitura, mettivi cuoriandoro: distemperalo col loro brodo, e fà brodo granato, se vuoli. Simile modo si pò fare de pavoni, fagiani, pollastri giovini, e uccelli piccioli.

Translation:
Of the Partridges
Take boiled partridges and dismembered pullets with fragrant herbs, salt, and good spices stamped in a mortar and sautèe the said meat with lard, put it to cook in a little water in the pot, and put over it almond milk: and at the end of the cooking, put coriander: distemper it with it's broth, and make Brodo Granato,[14] if you want. [In a] similar mode you can make of peacocks, pheasants, young pullets, and small birds.

Similar recipes that could have been used to work around the sumptuary laws can be found in contemporary cooking manuscripts from other regions of Italy. The recipe for Torta di Lasagna from the *Liber de coquina*, a fourteenth-century Neapolitan manuscript, combines both lasagna and ravioli in one dish. In the Venetian manuscript *Libro per cuoco* the recipe for Limonaia, a dish popular in both Spain and Italy at this time, of poultry in lemon sauce, calls for both chickens and capons.

These meat and pasta courses would also have been supplemented with various vegetables, as at the Milanese wedding of Violante Visconti and the Duke of Clarence in 1368 where the peacocks were served 'with green vegetables and beans'.[15]

Thus, structuring our meal upon the few contemporary menus available[16], and including several of the vegetable and fruit dishes found in the Tuscan *Libro della cucina*, a sumptuous wedding banquet within the letter of law might have run something like this:

Proposed Menu
Confetti #1:
Traggea[17] – candied nuts or simple sugar candies
Soup:
Piselli – pea soup with sautéed onions
Vivanda #1:
De le Starne – stewed partridges and chickens with fresh herbs
Served with:
    Dei Cauli – cabbage fried with onions, apples and fennel
Vivanda #2:
Torta Parmesana – a tart with layers of ravioli, sausage, prosciutto and stuffed eggs etc.
A empiere una pavone – roasted peacock redressed in its own skin, both served and stuffed with meatballs made of pork and peacock meat
Served with:
    Savore per l'arrosto – a sauce of basil and vinegar
    Salsa di finocchio – fennel sauce
    De fasoli – beans cooked with cheese onions and spices
    De le foglie minute – spinach and orach sautéed with herbs and spices
    De la suppa – bread dipped in egg and fried.[18]
Vivanda #3:
A empiere un vitello – a roast of veal stuffed with capons and other birds
Served with:
    Peverata – pepper sauce[19]
    De gli fungi – mushrooms cooked with leeks and spices
Cheese:
Cascio arrostito – melted cheese, served on toast
    Pecorino: Parmigiano: Olives[20]
Fruit:
De le pere – pears cooked in almond milk with saffron, spices and sugar
    Apples: Grapes: Almonds: Walnuts
Confetti #2:
Nucato – a candy of honey and nuts
Traggea – candied nuts or simple sugar candies

This 'simple' meal of eight courses technically contains only the three meat courses allowed, but as you can see, each of the main recipes actually incorporates at least two items within one dish, thus affording a more extravagant repast.

While the Pragmatica of 1356 severely limited the foods that one could serve at a wedding banquet, given the ostentatious mentality of early Renaissance Florence, many people would have attempted to serve as bountiful a feast as possible without incurring the stiff penalties levied for disobeying the law. Looking at the many recipes of the time that provide the possibility of hiding multiple foods under the auspices of one dish, one can create a speculative menu that might have allowed a rich merchant of fourteenth-century Florence to avoid directly violating the sumptuary regulations while still presenting a sumptuous meal.

BIBLIOGRAPHY

& Coquatur Ponendo...: cultura della cucina e della tavola in europa tra medioevo ed età moderna, Prato: Istituto Internazionale di Storia Economica 'Francesco Datini', 1996.
Benporat, Claudio, *Cucina Italiana del Quattrocento*, Florence: Leo S. Olschiki, 1996.
Emiliani-Giudici, P., *Storia Politica Dei Municipi Italiani*, Florence, 1851.
Corio, Bernardino, *Storia di Milano*, Turin: Unione Tipografico Editrice, 1978.
Faccioli, Emilio, *L'arte della cucina in Italia*, Turin: Einaudi Tascabili, 1992.
Florio, John, *A Worlde of Wordes*, London: Arnold Hatfield for Edward Blount, 1598 (facsimile, Hildesheim: Georg Olms, 1972); also the 1611 edition: *Queen Anna's New World of Words*, facsimile, Menston: Scolar Press, 1968.
Grieco, Allen J., 'From the cookbook to the table. A Florentine table and Italian recipes of the fourteenth and fifteenth centuries', in Lambert, C., ed., *Du manuscrit à la table*, University of Montreal Press, 1992.
Libro della Cucina, ed. Francesco Zambrini, Bologna: Gaetano Romagnoli, 1863 (repr. 1968).
Muir, Dorothy, *A History of Milan Under the Visconti*, London: Methuen, 1924.
Origo, Iris, *The Merchant of Prato: Francesco di Marco Datini 1335–1410*, New York: Alfred A Knopf, 1957.
Redon, Odile, Sabban, Francoise, and Serventi, Silvano, *The Medieval Kitchen: Recipes from France and Italy*. trans. Edward Schneider, University of Chicago Press, 1998.
Rainey, Ronald E., *Sumptuary Legislation in Renaissance Florence*, dissertation Columbia University, 1985

NOTES

[1] See Emiliani-Giudici, Vol. 2, p. 431 App. This is a transcription of the 1356 Tuscan translation.
[2] *quar.* seems to be an abbreviation for *quartiere*.
[3] *Confetti*: comfets, confections, candies etc.
[4] *Traggea*: candied nuts or simple sugar candies, these were traditional candies served at medieval Italian weddings.
[5] *Bragiere*: this is how it is written in the Italian text, but in the Latin text the word is

bramangeria.

[6] *Possa*: wealth – Florio 1598.

[7] See *& Coquatur Ponendo* p. 392.

[8] This and all other recipe translations are from Zambrini's edition of *Libro della Cucina*.

[9] Apparently this word is somewhat unclear in the original Tuscan manuscript, however it is written as *excoria* in the Parma Tart from the *Liber de Coquina*, a fourteenth-century Neapolitan manuscript, which confirms Zambrini's transcription.

[10] Presumably meaning to remove the marrow from the bones.

[11] *Cervelatti*: a kind of dry sausage – Florio 1598.

[12] There is no sauce which specifies it is for peacock in the manuscript, so this may intend you to simply choose among the sauces available.

[13] *Broche*: twigs or nails

[14] *Brodo Granato* is a recipe given earlier in the manuscript for a chicken soup with fresh herbs and spices.

[15] See Muir.

[16] See Redon et al., Muir, and Corio.

[17] Unfortunately, I have found no recipes for *traggea* in either the *Libro della Cucina* or other contemporary manuscripts, although they are called for as an ingredient in the Venetian *Libro per Cuoco*. In *The Merchant of Prato* however, the primary ingredients are given from a contemporary *tregea* recipe which included cinnamon, nutmeg, mace, ginger, anise, sugar and galingale.

[18] This recipe specifies that it is to be served with peacock.

[19] As called for in the veal recipe.

[20] According to the poem *Il Saporetto* by Prudenzani, there would also have been olives, and nuts served at this stage in the meal.

Lust, Fear and Loathing on the Village Green

Gillian Riley

Much ink and a certain amount of good fresh blood has been spilled in the analysis of genre scenes depicting the village fête or kermis, often incorporating a church festival or peasant wedding. Early generations of art historians were content to see these as affectionate celebrations of everyday life the way it was lived, with all the warmth, charm and pathos of picturesque but essentially happy countryfolk.[1] This mind-cast produced the charming genre scenes of nineteenth-century England, where rosy-cheeked barefoot children romped with boisterous high spirits around the Sunday roast, in the picturesque thatched cottage where a mellow autumn sunshine dappled the clean-swept brick floor and quaint old-fashioned crockery. Content with their enviably simple life, these honest humble folk were no threat to the anxious, insecure middle classes who hung these mendacious images on their cluttered walls. Agricultural and industrial unrest threatened to unleash disruptive forces, scary social and political changes loomed. But these images of happy barefoot peasants in their humble cots offered a comfortable if fraudulent reassurance. Was this also the case in the sixteenth and seventeenth centuries?

We shall be looking at village festivities depicted by various engravers and painters in Germany and the Low Countries and examining some of the different interpretations of them by art historians today. The benign idea that they were a serene presentation of everyday life has been overtaken by more sombre views, many of them in violent conflict with each other.

It is hard to be certain, without more documentary evidence than is at present available, just who bought these paintings and why. The peasants themselves did not. But many versions of the wedding feast were produced and appear frequently on the art market today. The well-known 'Peasant Feast' by Pieter Bruegel the Elder at the Kunsthistorisches Museum in Vienna was produced in at least nine versions by various members of the family, and 'A Peasant Wedding in a Village' in nine more. Many consisted of a series of four or five scenes showing different stages in the Peasant Wedding – from the procession of bride and groom to the church to the nitty gritty of dowries, marriage settlements and presents. These are just a fraction of the rustic scenes for which there seems to have been an almost insatiable demand.

One aspect of these village fêtes is the wedding feast. The rituals of the wedding have been touched upon, but the nature of the feast might help us to understand the meaning and purpose of the paintings. Although gluttony, drunkenness and their inevitable consequences – excessive merriment, libidinous behaviour, incontinence and belligerence – are all portrayed in considerable detail, the food gets less attention. Was it just a matter of quantity rather than quality? 'Enough is as good as a feast and more than enough is even better than a feast,' as Oscar Wilde put it? Jugs of beer, bowls of some anonymous soup or stew, hunks of bread and lumps of cheese abound. Sometimes a bride cake is offered to the bride, who sits in the centre of a long table, her hair loose, topped with a crown, with more crowns and garlands suspended from the curtain hanging behind her. In most versions she sits in demure silence, hands folded in her lap, rarely eating or drinking, hardly speaking, as custom demanded. It was her day – a rare moment of passivity and calm amidst the bustle and mayhem of life. But this is not a sentimental rendering of a bashful bride, very often the lass is grotesquely ugly, sometimes already pregnant or suckling an infant, occasionally breaking with convention and reaching greedily for a tankard or bowl. Some versions of the feast show the point at which gifts are brought by friends and neighbours and matters of dowry are discussed. At this point the bride becomes more animated. The dish before her contains money, not sweetmeats. These are serious matters, property, inheritance and worldly goods. There might be something comic about the stools, frying pans, chamber pots and wooden spoons that are offered, but they reflect wider concerns, those of the painter and his patrons as well as of the peasants.

The Vienna Bruegel shows a peasant feast set indoors, perhaps at harvest time, with crossed sheaves of corn, symbol of fertility and fecundity, suspended on the wall to the bride's left. Merriment continues out of doors in the top left-hand corner; in the bottom right, two men carry between them a dozen bowls of food on a stretcher. More bowls are being passed down the long trestle table, and a small child in the foreground is busy licking one clean. The angle at which a bowl is being handed across the bride seems to imply that the food in it is solid, but it is impossible to tell more than that about it. Maybe some fairly solid porridge or stew? Perhaps pancakes or crêpes? Eaten with fingers, not spoons certainly.

A painting by a follower of Marten van Cleve of a wedding feast might help here: the white-aproned cook or servant hands from the tray of food items which are clearly tarts or, as we would say, quiches, with the delectable puffy golden-brown surface and the friable, crinkly edges of the pastry. The pensive bride sits calmly by whilst her guests are already red-nosed and boisterous, clamouring for more. On a pewter dish in front of her is a different kind of tart or cake, darker in colour and with a reddish centre. Can this be the Bride Cake? In a version of this scene by Peter Bruegel the Younger we have a similar scene; musicians on the right, stretcher of food on the left, this time unequivocally bowls of something or other, but with quite an ornate thing, maybe a tart decorated with fruit, on a large pewter plate in front of the bride. This was one of seven known variants of this composition, one of a series of pictures of five stages in a village wedding. This indicates something of a busy production line, churning out these scenes to meet a healthy demand. Perhaps the Bruegel family machine was reproducing a best-selling line in a fairly routine way, without too much attention to detail. This satisfied clients but leaves the food historian frustrated and uninformed.

A painting by Joris Hoefnagel, 'A Wedding Scene in Bermondsey', is more helpful. It has been analysed meticulously by Ivan Day in his exhibition catalogue *Eat Drink & be Merry*.[2] Topographical details place it in a village on the south side of the Thames, with identifiable buildings, including the Tower of London, in the background. Some fairly decorous dancing and merrymaking is happening in the foreground, peasants roistering in the farthest distance, on the right a procession wends its way from the church, mainly gentlefolk, some in sombre black, a number of them carrying enormous bride cakes, suspended in stout linen slings round their necks, while another waves a ceremonial posy, decorated with ribbons with mottoes on them. In the background is a table laid for the wedding feast, and nearby we can see into a kitchen in full blast, with prepared dishes ready to be served and meat and fowl turning on spits. In spite of doubts about which of the women in the painting is the bride, there are no doubts about the massive cakes. Following a recipe in Robert May's book, Ivan recreated one of these, weighing in at a good two stones, a robust pastry dough of a crust enclosing a softer filling full of spiced dried fruit and perfumed with musk and ambergris. A highly erotic brew, which must have mingled with the incense in the church, and perfumed gloves of the revellers to intensify the convivial warmth of the subsequent revelry.

Ivan Day's researches came up with a genteel mid-eighteenth-century wedding in the Home Counties, with the procession to the church and the formal cutting of the bride cake, followed by the very explicit ritual of passing small finger-sized pieces of cake several times through the wedding ring.

It might seem that both rustic and genteel weddings had a certain amount in common. Processions to and from the church, dancing and merrymaking, posies, garlands and ritual objects, much drinking, and a feast. The food varied according to social class, but it is possible to surmise, although more work has been done to clarify the situation, that there were foods, like certain kinds of tarts and cakes, associated with weddings and fertility offerings, which were common to all social classes.

Was it the picturesque 'otherness' of peasants that made them so compelling? The frissons of pity and terror that a contemplation of their grotesque appearance, uncouth ways, and unbridled emotions, aroused in the troubled breasts of the insecure middle classes? Or are we applying facile anthropology-and-water to a situation more complex than trendy sociology would allow? Scenes of aristocratic banquets are certainly more decorous and elegant, but not without their own fairly explicit depictions of lust, lechery and over-indulgence. Symbolism and double meanings pervade most genre, kitchen and market scenes, and to unravel this tangled web is a perilous though beguiling task. Perhaps food is a sort of mitigating element in all this, a corrective to both excessive pedantry and naive credulity. Some peasants must have eaten with restraint and dignity, and many aristocrats habitually wallowed in swinish luxury.

Many paintings of village feasts contain, usually on the fringes of the composition, gentlefolk looking on but not participating in the scene. This and the bird's-eye view certainly reinforces the sense of 'otherness'. A contemporary of Bruegel, Karel van Mander, told how the painter often dressed in peasant costume and infiltrated himself into rustic wedding parties, bringing gifts and claiming to be a distant relative. His sketchbooks show studies of peasants from life (naer het leven) annotated (in handwriting that it is now claimed to be that of a contemporary) with details of fabric and colour. Perhaps the most haunting of his sketches is 'The Beekeepers', whose protective head-covering gives the impression of mindless automata stumbling through arcane ritual movements.

Karel van Mander also said: 'There are few works by his hand which the observer can contemplate solemnly and with a straight face; however stiff, morose or surly he might be, he cannot help chuckling or at any rate smiling.' Svetlana Alpers puts this remark in the context of contemporary views of the comic mode in theatre and literature and concludes that although there was a moralizing element in Bruegel's work, the depiction of fun and the enjoyment of earthly pleasures was more important.[3] After all, we all go to weddings and eat and drink too much, become lecherous or poorly, romp around, throw up, are rude to the bride's mother. A universal human condition, linked to the cycles of procreation, birth, maturity and death – surely these festive scenes proclaim our common humanity, linking peasantry with other social classes, promoting social cohesion rather than divisiveness.

Other commentators take a bleaker view of what was then funny. Laughing at cripples, the deformed and the unfortunate is not our idea of fun. How can we really know what Bruegel's clients enjoyed or loathed?[4]

'Laet die boeren haer kermis houuen' said the playwright G.A. Bredero; a less mellifluous translation is 'Let the peasants have their kermis'. Or, as van Mander commented, describing fun and games in the woods south of Haarlem 'Just like a kermis; people, like clothing, must be aired.'[5]

There was an interest in peasant costumes, manners and dialects at this period, but historians dispute whether this expressed a sense of solidarity or feelings of fear and loathing. One point of view, with specific reference to the woodcut representations of peasant weddings by the German artist Sebald Beham, is that, shattered by the peasant revolt of 1525, the German middle classes, encouraged by Luther, whose views on equality before God did not include any hint of equality on this earth, saw them as dangerous vermin rather than fellow revellers.[6] His massive woodcut 'Large Peasant Holiday' in the British Museum, is over 1 foot tall and nearly 4 feet long, printed in sections and probably destined to be a decorative frieze in the homes of those who would be unlikely to buy oil paintings. Moxey quotes Bruno Weber's calculations: the print sold at 3 Pfennigs per sheet, 12 for the lot, which in Nurnberg at that time would have bought 6 sausages, or 18 herrings or 2 gallons of cider; an average daily wage of 22 Pfennigs indicates prosperous artisans or middle class clients. This bleak and hostile view of rustic celebration reinforces Luther's disapproval of their licentious and socially threatening behaviour. He had already written in 1520 'Since feast days are abused by drinking, gambling, loafing and all manner of sin, we anger God more on holidays than we do on other days. Things are so topsy-turvy that holidays are not holy, but working days are.' The inevitable solution being to abolish holidays.

The woodcut certainly does not cast a warm glow over the peasant wedding. Standard examples of squalid behaviour abound. It remains a mystery why good folk would decorate their homes with it, if fear and loathing were their only response to vulgar enjoyment. Looking ahead to the dissolute family gatherings painted by Jan Steen which graced the homes of sedate, prosperous Dutch burghers, we can speculate that society's response to the peasant wedding was complicated enough to incorporate many of the points of view disputed so passionately by historians today, while a closer look at the food on offer might help our understanding of the event.

NOTES
[1] Eugene Fromentin, *The Masters of Past Time*, London, 1913.
[2] Ivan Day, ed., *Eat Drink & be Merry*, London, 1999.
[3] Svetlana Alpers, 'Bruegel's Festive Peasants', *Simiolus* 6, pp. 165–71.
[4] Hessel Miedema, 'Realism & comic mode: the peasant', *Simiolus* 9, pp. 205–19.
[5] Svetlana Alpers, 'Realism as a comic mode: low-life painting seen through Bredero's eyes', *Simiolus* 8, pp. 115–44.
[6] Keith Moxey, 'Sebald Beham's church anniversary holidays', *Simiolus* 12, pp. 107–30.

Meals and Morality

Barbara Santich

Food, drink and morality

Food and drink have long been regarded with ambivalence in the Western world. The 'virtue' of eating to live has been opposed by the 'vice' of living to eat. While it was recognized that some food and drink were necessary, too much was considered dangerous, from both a health and a moral perspective. Hippocratic medicine was based on an ideal of harmony and balance, internal balance in the individual and harmony between the individual and his environment. Upsetting this balance – too much of a particular food, for example, as well as too much food in general – could lead to ill health and disease.

Philosophers, too, praised the qualities of simplicity and frugality and denigrated excesses in eating and drinking. In the fourth century BC Plato recommended, for the citizens of his ideal state, a simple diet which would satisfy the essential need of sustaining the body. He envisaged that they would 'feed on barley-meal and flour of wheat, baking the one and kneading the other, making noble cakes and loaves; these they will serve up on a mat of reeds or on clean leaves, themselves reclining the while upon beds strewn with yew or myrtle. And they and their children will feast, drinking of the wine which they have made, …and they will take care that their families do not exceed their means.' They would also have 'salt, and olives, and cheese; and they will boil roots and herbs such as country people prepare, for a dessert we shall give them figs, and peas, and beans; and they will roast myrtle-berries and acorns at the fire, sipping their wine in moderation. And with such a diet they will be expected to live in peace and health to a good old age.'[1] On the other hand, a diametrically opposed fate – illness and war – could be expected of a state whose inhabitants desired luxuries, such as 'sofas, and tables, and other furniture; also dainties, and perfumes, and incense, and courtezans, and cakes, all these not of one sort only, but in every variety.'[2]

In Plato's philosophy, eating and drinking served primarily to sustain and nourish the body; while he did not explicitly deny that simple foods could also be pleasurable, he condemned the desire for luxuries and eating for pleasure. He viewed cookery as a form of flattery which cares 'nothing for men's higher interests' but 'angles for folly with the bait of present pleasure,' it 'aims at pleasure without any thought of the best.'[3]

Similarly, the Stoic school founded in the late fourth century BC, the ideal of which was to lead a life in harmony with nature, advocated a simple, frugal diet of principally plant foods. A Roman Stoic of the first century AD, Musonius Rutus, proposed that the most useful foods were those that could be eaten without cooking.[4] He also dismissed the idea of eating and drinking being pleasurable. 'No reasonable being,' he argued, 'will think it desirable ... to spend his life in the chase after pleasure derived from food.'[5]

The basic premise underlying such beliefs was that food and drink are, or can be, sources of pleasure and, as such, dangerous. Among the ancient philosophers, only Epicurus (3rd–4th century BC), it seems, allowed and approved the pleasures of the senses: 'I know not how I can conceive the good, if I withdraw the pleasures of taste, and withdraw the pleasures of love, and withdraw the pleasures of hearing, and withdraw the pleasurable emotions caused by sight to beautiful form.'[6] Further reasoning postulated that if eating and drinking are enjoyable, and precisely because they are enjoyable, then people will be tempted to eat and drink to excess, exceeding the limits of self-control. Another first-century philosopher, Philo of Alexandria, wrote that the pleasures of the table 'produce drunkenness, effeminacy and greediness [and] ...make the man a glutton, while they also stimulate and stir up the stings of sexual lusts.'[7]

In the Christianized medieval world, this same logic was the basis of the sin of Gluttony.

The sin of Gluttony in the medieval era
Gluttony, once the original and the first of the Seven Deadly Sins, had been relegated to sixth on the list by the fourteenth century. What constituted Gluttony was solemnly spelled out. It included excess in eating – specifically itemized as eating too early in the morning, before prayers; eating too often (which meant more than two main meals a day); eating too quickly, swallowing foods without bothering to chew them; and eating too luxuriously.[8] These, however, were only superficial slips compared with the real sin of disrespect towards God and the established order. For overeating or, more particularly, over-drinking led to loss of self-control, and this could have dangerous consequences. It could lead to supplementary sins such as blasphemy and ribaldry (considered particularly shameful in a woman), or absence from work or prayers because of a hangover, or other sins of which discretion usually forbade mention.

Francesc Eixeminis, a fourteenth-century Catalan cleric, condemned the drunkenness which usually accompanies eating to excess but in addition denounced the desire for foods that were too refined and, in particular, not appropriate to one's social status, as well as the desire to distinguish oneself by the lavishness of the meal.[9] A century later an anonymous Genoese poet described Gluttony as one of the vanities of this world, diverting man from the path to heaven and leading him to damnation; further, he added, overeating and over-drinking were not only wrong in themselves but also they predisposed individuals to Lust and provoked illnesses.

Gluttony, then, was situated beyond the bounds of what was considered fit and proper (according to the standards of society in general, or a particular social class); it represented deviant behaviour, outside the limits of normality. As such it threatened the equilibrium of society at the same time as it compromised the physical harmony of the body.

In sum, medieval authorities viewed Gluttony as a contravention of both written and unwritten rules; it was disrespectful of church principles and supremacy. Nevertheless, the measure of respect for religious ideals seems to have diminished when these were at variance with courtly values. It is significant that Gluttony and Lust are omitted from the allegorical figures which adorn the Garden of the Rose (in the *Romance of the Rose*) and which represent most of the better-known sins plus three other images more properly considered as misfortunes (Sadness, Old Age, and Poverty). In a courtly society, Poverty and Jealousy might exclude one from the garden, but not Gluttony.[10]

Fifteenth-century developments

In the fifteenth century – coincidentally, about the same time as the spiritual authority of the Church began to be questioned – a few individuals began to speak out in favour of pleasure and of '*honesta voluptas*'. 'What evil can there be in well-considered indulgence?' asked Bartolomeo Sacchi – biographer of the popes, librarian to the Vatican, and better known as Platina, author of *De Honesta Voluptate et Valitudine*, recognized as the first printed cookbook. In his doctrine of '*honesta voluptas*', which can be roughly translated as 'measured pleasures', Platina argued that there is pleasure to be had in eating and drinking (in moderation), that there is nothing shameful in the enjoyment of good food and wine, and that pleasurable eating is not incompatible with good health. (In her edition of the work, Mary Ella Milham translates the title as 'On Right Pleasure and Good Health'.)[11] He realized, however, that he had to justify this ethic and defend himself against criticism.

> I know well enough that the spiteful will speak out vehemently that I ought not to have written about pleasure for the best and most continent of men, but let those voluptuaries who pretend to be Stoics (who make judgments with upraised eyebrows, not about human experience but only about the sounds of words) say what evil well-considered pleasure

> has in it, for the term is neutral, neither good nor bad, as is health. Far be it from Platina to write to the holiest of men about the pleasure which the intemperate and libidinous derive from self-indulgence and a variety of foods and from the titillations of sexual interests. I speak about that pleasure which derives from continence in food and those things which human nature seeks, for up to this time I have seen no one so libidinous and incontinent that he was not touched by some pleasure if he had ever drawn back from coveted pursuits which were more than sufficient.[12]

This philosophy expressed the essence of the humanistic revival of the fifteenth century, 'the cult of the individual whose happiness derives from intellectual and sensual enjoyment'.[13] Platina's advice – which covered the choice of site for the house as well as how and when to eat, sleep, exercise and indulge in sexual intercourse – was formulated on the basis of the individual, and legitimized pleasure within limits which varied with the individual. In this way it differed from the universality of church precepts.

Platina's book was the equivalent of a medieval best-seller. At least eight manuscripts still exist; it was published in eighteen Latin editions between 1470 and 1541 and in numerous Italian translations from 1487. (Milham believes the first manuscript was penned before 1468, and cautiously dates the first edition to 1470.)[14] It was first published in French in 1505, and another thirteen French editions were published up to 1586; a German translation was published in 1542.[15] The success of the book was probably more a function of its culinary detail than its philosophy, but it seems likely that wide circulation of the book helped spread the doctrine of 'well-considered indulgence'.

Also around the fifteenth century, a new form of festivity began to flourish: the banquet. As a lavish, ceremonial meal in honour of an individual or exceptional occasion, such as a wedding, the banquet celebrated conspicuous consumption with blatant demonstrations of wealth and power. It was distinguished not only by its extravagance and ostentatious scale but also by its theatricality and use of symbolism.

Initially, it appears, the banquet was a lavish meal presented in a different style, with various dishes set out on a long table, as would be a buffet today. Both the term and the event had their origins in fourteenth-century Italy, the Italian word 'banchetto' deriving from 'banco', a long bench or table. By the early sixteenth century, the form of the banquet had evolved considerably, according to the accounts of Cristoforo di Messisbugo, and included theatrical and musical performances. In his capacity of steward at the court of the dukes of Este, Messisbugo orchestrated many banquets and in his book, *Banchetti:*

Compositioni di vivande et apparecchio generale, he describes, in unparalleled detail, the management and staging of these lavish, formal, ceremonial feasts, from the setting of the tables with several tablecloths and ornamental figures of sugar or marzipan to the accompanying music and the dances performed during the course of the meal.[16]

It is in this context – the dissemination of a philosophy legitimizing pleasure, and the spread of a new form of festivity which promoted sensual enjoyment – that the morality play, *La Condamnacion de Bancquet*, first appeared.

La Condamnacion de Bancquet

The morality play, *La Condamnacion de Bancquet*, was first published in 1507, presumably not long after the play was written – and performed.[17] In his introductory notes, Edouard Fournier remarked that the details and staging instructions recorded – such as 'Notez que Soupper et Bancquet les espient par quelque fenestre haulte'; 'Ce premier repas se fera sur une table ronde ou carré'; and 'Experience, dame honnestement habillée, sera assise en siege magnifique' – indicate the likelihood of the play having been previously performed. Further, he added, it seems to have been a popular success, since a series of tapestries illustrating the principal scenes from the play was woven in the sixteenth century. (These are now on display in the Musée Lorrain, Nancy.)

In its published form, the play formed a kind of entertaining appendix to a more serious work, *La Nef de Santé, avec le gouvernail du corps humain, et la condamnation des Banquets à la louenge de la diepte et Sobrieté, et traicté des passions de l'âme*. As if this did not provide a clue to the play's message, the author made clear in his written prologue that his intention was to 'denounce and eradicate the vice of gluttony, drunkenness and greediness, and in contrast, to praise, exalt and magnify the virtue of sobriety, frugality, abstinence, temperance and good diet, in accordance with the book entitled *La Nef de santé et gouvernail du corps humain*'.[18] Further, the Docteur Prolocuteur introducing the play would have left the audience in no doubt as to the message they should take home:

Pour vous plus a plain informer	To explain in simple terms
De ce qui sera recité:	The performance you will watch:
Nous desirons de reformer	We want to reform
Excès et superfluité,	Excess and luxury,
En detestant gulosité,	Detesting greediness,
Qui consume vin, chair et pain,	To those who consume wine, meat and bread,

Recommandant Sobrieté,	We recommend temperance,
Qui rend l'homme legier et sain.	Which keeps people healthy and nimble.
Medecine consent assez	Doctors agree that
Qu'on doit disnmer competemment;	One should eat just enough;
Car l'estomac point ne casse	For the stomach will not burst
Pour disner raisonnablement.	If one eats within reason.
Or faut-il soupper sobrement,	And one should sup moderately,
Tant les druz que les indigens,	Both the well-off and the needy,
Sans banqueter aucunement,	Without any banquets,
Car bancquet fait tuer les gens.	For banquets are deadly.

Despite this blunt announcement, the play would have been delightfully amusing and entertaining, almost in the style of a pantomime. Its originality lies in its personification of the three meals, Disner, Soupper and Bancquet, and also of the maladies and misfortunes which eventually befall the guests.

At the start of the play, Disner, Soupper and Bancquet are talking among themselves (possibly to one side of the stage) when the guests enter, led by Bonne Compaignie. Bonne Compaignie epitomizes the predispositions of the group, saying that all she desires is happy laughter and an abundance of pleasure. Gourmandise adds that she likes fattened beef, rice, capons and well-fed chickens; Friandise admits that she could do with a little pie while waiting. Passetemps avows his aim is to have a good time; Je-boy-a-vous and Je-pleige-d'autant discuss the merits of various wines; and Acoustumance explains that people can become accustomed to a way of doing something if they do it long enough. Bonne Compaignie then announces that the day should begin with a toast – wine, bread, pies and damson plums – after which Passetemps leads them into a dance.

Observing all this, Disner, Soupper and Bancquet express a wish to take part and, remarking that the happy band of revellers willingly follow Bonne Compaignie, salute her and introduce themselves. Bonne Compaignie invites them to join in and Disner, Soupper and Bancquet take a glass of wine with them. Approving of the group ('Ce sont gens de rejouyssance,' says Soupper), they each agree to reciprocate the hospitality – politely accepted, on behalf of all the guests, by Bonne Compaignie.

There is no indication, prior to the enjoyment of Disner's hospitality, that any double-crossing is intended, although the staging notes make clear that Soupper and Bancquet are not present at this meal. At its conclusion, Soupper and Bancquet, as observers, comment that the diners do not know how to restrain their appetites and, as the various maladies appear in the background,

Bancquet adds that 'Nous en aurons brief la vengeance.'

The maladies waiting in the wings are Appoplexie (Apoplexy), Paralisie (Paralysis), Epilencie (Epilepsy), Pleuresie (Pleurisy), Colique (Colic), Esquinancie (Quinsy), Ydropsie (Dropsy), Jaunisse (Jaundice), Gravelle (Kidney stones) and Goutte (Gout). Modern medicine would hesitate to suggest a link between diet and paralysis, for example; but it must be remembered that the intention of this morality play's author was to leave the audience in no doubt as to his message: greedy eaters and drinkers come to a sorry end.

The maladies all announce themselves before they are consulted by Soupper and Bancquet, who each confide their plans. Soupper explains that he and Banquet will invite Bonne Compaignie and her friends to enjoy themselves, recognizing that in doing so the guests will be negligent of their health and will need to be reminded of the fact. Soupper suggests that they hide in his house and attack at a given signal in order to show that spending too long at supper is dangerous.

At the end of their meal *chez* Disner, Soupper and Bancquet approach the diners and invite them to two more meals; Soupper takes the arm of Bonne Compaignie and the other revellers follow. Soupper's meal is considerably more elaborate and varied than was Disner's ('Nous sentirons bien les espices,' remarks Friandise). While the guests are eating and drinking, however, Soupper sneaks off to consult with the maladies, an absence that is noticed by Bonne Compaignie. Nevertheless, when the maladies do attack, the guests are able to beat them off, though not without suffering some wounds. They regroup and discuss events, agreeing with Bonne Compaignie that 'Long Soupper nuyt' (Extended suppers are harmful). When Bancquet offers welcome to his table, they are happy to forget their interrupted supper (though some suspicion remains) and to resume their pleasurable activities at another meal.

At Bancquet, the dishes are all laid out on the table for the guests to help themselves, and they hardly hesitate. Meanwhile, Bancquet talks to the maladies, urging them to be armed and ready. As the guests tuck into the feast, the Docteur Prolocuteur appears at a higher level of the set and, in a long speech, explains why eating and drinking to excess have for long been condemned. At Bancquet's call the maladies attack and, among the guests, only Bonne Compaignie, Passetemps and Accoustumance survive unscathed.

The response of Bonne Compaignie is to lodge a complaint with Dame Experience. We have been tricked, ill-treated, insulted and attacked, explains Bonne Compaignie, and the culprits are Soupper and Bancquet. Dame Experience listens sympathetically, then calls her assistants, all of whom might have been part of a sixteenth-century doctor's treatment: Secours (Relief),

Sobriété (Sobriety), Clistere (Enema), Pillule (Pill), Saignie (Blood-letting), Diette (diet) and Remede (Medicine). She also calls, as experts, the doctors Hippocrates, Galen, Avicenna and Averroes.

Bonne Compaignie outlines her case before a submissive Soupper and reluctant Bancquet who, she accuses, are guilty of the deaths of her comrades. Soupper denies the charges, saying that it is Bancquet who is guilty of homicide, Banquet, astonished at this about-face, pleads that, in effect, the guests should have known the risks. After these statements are recorded, Dame Experience agrees to judge the case, with recourse to expert advice – and proceeds to do so, overruling Soupper's and Bancquet's last-minute objection that women should never occupy the seat of judgment.

The four doctors enter into earnest discourse, with many references to medical authorities and the lessons of history, until Hippocrates summarizes their conclusion: overindulgence is a danger for everyone.

Faced with the decision, Soupper pleads that the culprit is Bancquet, not him. Banquet confesses his guilt and Soupper eventually accepts blame for the lesser crime of grievous bodily harm. As punishment, the doctors decree that Bancquet should be executed and Soupper ordered to stay away from Disner by a good six hours. Bancquet makes his confession before the priest and then bids final farewell to all the delectable sweetmeats of his domain: friandises, sugar, sweet confits and spices. He also asks that each of the doctors he has made wealthy, through treating the illnesses he has permitted, promise to have a mass said.

The execution of Bancquet means that gourmands will no longer have that pleasure, decrees Dame Experience, from now on Disner and Soupper will satisfy all needs for food and drink. Chastened by their ordeal, Bonne Compaignie and Passetemps agree and the Docteur Prelocuteur spells out the moral of the play. Gluttony is shameful and detestable; two meals a day are enough for anyone, Bancquet corrupts and harms; and finally, to give oneself over to such sensual pleasure is sinful, reprehensible, injurious and perverse.

The message and the medium

Clearly, *La Condamnacion de Bancquet* subscribes to a long established moral tradition which approves eating and drinking to the extent that they sustain the body and condemns not only overindulgence but the desire to eat and drink beyond the limits of necessity for the pleasure and enjoyment this affords. It shows that the ambivalence surrounding the meal – the need to sustain the body balanced against the risk of succumbing to pleasure – persisted to the sixteenth century (and, incidentally, continues to inform present-day attitudes). Equally clearly, the play is an attack on banqueting; Bancquet is portrayed as promoting a pleasure-seeking lifestyle which contravenes church teachings and leads to the sin of Gluttony. The consequences of overindulgence are explicitly expressed – a series of diseases and afflictions – but rather than insisting on the path to virtue the play presents two alternatives (while leaving no doubt as to which the audience should choose).

The message may be familiar, but the medium is different. In dramatizing the moral in this way, the author – a professor of law, according to the researches of Edouard Fournier – may well have been attempting to spread the message to the general community. There is no evidence, to my knowledge, that the play was performed in public to a popular audience but it should have had this kind of appeal. It has suspense and drama, action and humour; its language is witty, full of verve and vivacity, alliterations and puns; it entertains while delivering its moral. At times it reads more like a farce or pantomime than a morality play, with the personification of the meals and the misfortunes that stalk the diners. Further, while there was nothing novel in the moral of the play, the use of the meals to illustrate the message is exceedingly original (and predates the writings of Rabelais). The personalities of the three meals are as different as the style and contents of the meals themselves. With these qualities it should surely have been able to reach more people than a philosophy or medical treatise, and be more meaningful and personally relevant than a thundering Sunday sermon.

Whether the play did in fact reach and influence a wider audience is debatable; there does not seem to have been a general abandonment of banquets in the sixteenth century. Onthe contrary, the popularity of the banquet as a celebratory meal featuring the most exquisite dishes, the most extravagant displays, probably increased in this period. Nor is there any indication that diet-related disorders were less prevalent, nor doctors less busy treating them.

I suspect that sixteenth-century audiences simply enjoyed the play, finding it amusing and diverting in a light-hearted way. *La Condamnacion de Bancquet* is so entertaining to read that one suspects the author had so much fun writing it that he could never be as fully committed to delivering the moral as he pretended to be. And indeed, the last words (before the closing song) belong to the Fool, who says: 'Mais je crois que finablement Bancquet ne soit longtemps en place,' which can be interpreted to mean, 'I don't think Bancquet will accept this fate for very long.'

NOTES

[1] The *Dialogues of Plato: The Republic*, Book II, trans. Benjamin Jowett, fourth edition, Oxford: Clarendon, 1953, Vol. 2, 214–215.
[2] Idem., Vol. 2, 215.
[3] *The Dialogues of Plato: Georgias*, trans. Benjamin Jowett, fourth edition, Oxford: Clarendon, 1953, Vol. 2, 553.
[4] Grimm, Veronika, 'Keeping Body and Soul Apart: The Nature and Legacy of the Ancient "Philosophic Diet"', paper presented at the Second International Conference of the Research Centre for the History of Food and Drink, Adelaide University, 2–4 July 2001.
[5] Musonius, xviiia, cited by Grimm.
[6] Gaskin, John, ed. *The Epicurean Philosophers*, London: J.M. Dent, 1995, 55.
[7] Philo of Alexandria, Cont. IX, 74, cited by Grimm.
[8] Brereton, Georgine E., and Janet M. Ferrier, eds., *Le Menagier de Paris*, Oxford: Clarendon, 1981, 35–37.
[9] Eiximenis, Francesc, *Com Usar Be de Beure e Menjar. Normes morales contingades en el 'Terc de Crestia'*, intro. and ed. Jorge E.J. Gracia, Barcelona: Curial, 1977, 66–68.
[10] Lorris, Guillaume de, and Jean de Meun, *Le Roman de la Rose*, ed. Félix Lecoy, Paris: Honoré Champion, 1968, Vol. 1, 5–15.
[11] Milham, Mary Ella. *Platina's On Right Pleasure and Good Health: A Critical Abridgment and Translation of De honesta voluptate et valetudine*, Asheville: Pegasus, 1999.
[12] Idem., 3.
[13] Renouard, Yves. 'Affaires et culture à Florence au XIVe et au XVe siecle', in *Il Quattrocento: Libera Cattedra di Storia della Civilta Fiorentina*, Florence: Sansoni, 1954, 159–176.
[14] Milham, 1999, xv.
[15] Milham, M.E., 'The manuscripts of Platina "De Honesta Voluptate..." and its source, Martino', *Scriptorium* 26 (1972): 127–129; 'The Latin editions of Platina's "De Honesta Voluptate"', *Gutenberg-Jahrbuch* 52 (1977): 57–63; 'The vernacular translations of Platina's "De Honesta Voluptate"', *Gutenberg-Jahrbuch* 54 (1979): 87–95.
[16] Messisbugo, Cristoforo di, *Banchetti: Compositioni di vivande et apparecchio generale*, Ferrara, 1549.
[17] de la Chesnaye, Nicolas, 'La Condamnacion de Bancquet', in *Le Théâtre Français avec La Renaissance 1450–1550: Mystères, Moralités et Farces*, ed. Edouard Fournier, Paris: 1872 (facsimile edition, New York: Burt Franklin, 1963), 216–271.
[18] Fournier, op. cit., 217.

Manners Maketh the Meal: Table Etiquette in England and Iran

Margaret Shaida

It is difficult to discuss 'a meal' without looking at the rituals and formalities that surround eating and drinking. Indeed, I would suggest that manners – the presentation of the food and the behaviour of the diners – actually define the meal. These, in turn, reflect the social behaviour of the nation, so that in discussing the rituals of the individual meal one touches upon national attitudes. In this paper, I look at the differences in the dining etiquette in England and Iran, from presentation and service, to manners and prayers, principally in the one-hundred-year period from the late nineteenth century to the late twentieth century.

Presentation of food

Most formal meals in the West consist of at least two courses, sometimes three or even more, served one after the other. In England, this results in a variety of cutlery and crockery being laid out on the table, as well as a number of wine glasses for different wines to accompany each course. By the time the starched napkins are folded into elegant shapes, the name cards and condiments placed before each setting, and the table decoration of candles, flowers and silver ornaments arranged down the centre of the table, there is little room, if any, for food. This hardly matters, since the food is brought course by course to the table. In wealthy establishments and formal settings, waiters will proffer the dishes to the seated diners, while in less affluent homes, the hostess will serve her guests, individually, also course by course.

Such arrangements were totally alien to the Iranians. Even though modern Iranians – and Iranian restaurants – in the West today may offer several courses as part of a meal at tables laid with cutlery, crockery and glasses, no such practices traditionally existed in Iran.

In the first place, the Iranians did not eat at a table, but sat on the floor. The *sofreh* (or 'table' cloth) would be laid on top of the Persian carpets, and everyone would sit around it. The idea that the *sofreh* should be filled with pretty decorations, cutlery, plates, glasses, flowers and other items not for consumption would have seemed very strange. The food was decoration enough. Indeed, even the 'plates' often consisted of a flap of bread.

As Dr. C.J Wills explained in his book,[1] 'Each guest was supplied with a loaf of flat bread as a plate, and another for eating.' He continued:

> We sat on the ground, some twenty in all, round a huge tablecloth of red leather, if I may use that expression for a large sheet of leather laid on the ground. Huge china bowls of sherbet were placed down the centre of the sufrah (tablecloth), and in each bowl was an elaborately carved wooden spoon, which were used indiscriminately, these spoons held a gill, and were drunk from, no glasses being used.
>
> A great variety of food (rice, stews, barbecued meats and fish, vegetables and salads) would all be placed upon the *sofreh* at one time, and individuals encouraged to make their own selection.

It seems that the dinner described by C.J. Wills consisted of more than 100 dishes, a prodigious amount for just twenty people. Of course, once the host and his guests had dined, all the other members of the household would also eat. Nevertheless, the selection was vast, including:

> ...*pillaws* of mutton or fowls, boiled and smothered in rice, in rice and orange-peel, in rice and lentils, in rice and haricots, in rice and *schewed,* a herb somewhat resembling fennel [actually dill]; the *fezanjans* of fowls and boiled meats; also partridges boiled and served with the concentrated juice of the pomegranate and pounded walnuts; kabobs of lamb and antelope; a lamb roasted whole, stuffed with dates, pistachios, chestnuts and raisins; salt fish from the Caspian; *dolmas,* or dumplings made of minced meat and rice, highly flavoured and wrapped in vine leaves and fried; rissoles; wild asparagus, boiled; new potatoes, handed round cold, and eaten with salt; while roast quails, partridges and doves were served with lettuces, drenched with honey and vinegar.

And these were just the dishes that C.J. Wills thought 'may be favourably mentioned.' If one tried a little of everything, it would be a staggering quantity.

Even today, the amount and variety of food presented at an Iranian meal is bounteous. With the introduction of tables (and the subsequent greater mobility of the diners), 'self service' is preferred as it allows each diner to make his or her own choice. Even the most formal of banquets will often be served as a buffet, with everything arrayed on the table (which is still called the *sofreh*) for the delectation of the diners.

If everyone sits around the table, a complete range of dishes is set before every two or three people, so that they may serve themselves and their neighbours without reaching across the *sofreh*. This is not to say that Iranian hostesses do not serve you, they do. But your plate is laid in front of you, and because the food is also there in front of you, you can simply help yourself to more whenever you wish. And the *moment* you have cleared your plate, you will be pressed to eat more. Your hosts will not wait for everyone's plate to be empty – with only the 'greedy' few being given a second helping!

Manners at table

But do not be deceived into thinking that such an Iranian meal, eaten with the hands and on the floor, is a casual free-for-all, like some sort of a big family picnic. Not at all. The manners expected at a meal in Iran are quite as strictly defined as those adhered to in England. First of all, when you eat directly with your hands, the washing of hands before and after the meal is absolutely vital. In former times, a team of waiters would formally present bowls of fresh water for washing, followed by ewers of rose-scented water for rinsing, and hand towels for drying.

The act of eating with the hands is also done with delicacy, elegance and great skill. No one would dream of plunging their hands into the dishes. Only two fingers and the thumb of the right hand should be used to carry the food from dish to mouth. (The left hand is never used at the meal.) It is an act of great dexterity and beauty, and the use of metal implements would have seemed quite abhorrent to many Iranians.

There is no 'head' of the table – it would be shocking for an Iranian to sit at the head of the table, and to allow his guests to sit in places perceived to be lower in status – with the exception of royal and court circles. The expression 'below the salt' would appear strange and objectionable in Iran. Often, the host does not even sit with his guests, but spends his time making sure the wishes of his visitors are met. He will ensure that his guests, even the most humble, eat before he does. The best morsels will be found and urged upon his guests. When pressing his most senior guests to eat, he will say '*Bismillah*' (in the name of God) so that they may feel free to eat. Indeed, each diner will try to ensure that his immediate companions eat before he does, so there is much deferential politeness, and great reluctance to be the first one to start eating. There is nothing new in this habit. An eighth-century Persian poet, Ibn Moqaffa' advised his son as follows:[2]

> My son, when you are invited to a dinner party, do not glance too often towards the kitchen, nor pay too close attention to the direction from which the food will appear; keep the reins of restraint in hand, be master of yourself. Never be the first to reach for the food, nor consider it proper to begin before others. Likewise, never be the last to withdraw your hand from the platter, lest the guests judge your soul to be gluttonous, or consider greed your master and appetite the measure of your personality. On such occasions, then, avoid these faults which I have mentioned, and consider abstention the prerequisite of patience, firmness and deliberation.

It wasn't necessary for the poet to mention that his son's feet and legs must always be tucked beneath him and never allowed to stray near the *sofreh*, because he would have learned this at home at a very early age, just as he would have been taught to sit quietly without wriggling. He would also have known that he should never eat with his mouth open nor blow his nose at the *sofreh*. Indeed, he would also have been taught to remain silent throughout the meal. The food is the important factor at an Iranian meal, and talkative diners are deemed unappreciative and boorish. Time enough for spirited conversation and witty discourse after the meal, traditionally while smoking the *qalyân* (water pipe), which is passed companionably from one to the other, much as port is passed from one gentleman to another in England.

C.J. Wills noted this absence of conversation over the meal with some disapproval: 'During the time dinner was progressing, little conversation took place, everybody being engaged in eating as much of as many dishes as possible.' The most important lesson of all is that your guests are served before you are. Neither the host nor any of his family members will *ever* start to eat before the guests.

In fact, Iranians think it's very odd in England, when as guests of honour, they are served first but are then are expected to sit and wait – watching their food congeal – until everyone else is served and the host is ready to eat. Indeed, they wonder why they are not served last, so that their food will at least be hot!

There is, of course, one more gesture of good manners in earlier centuries in Iran, one that has received much attention in the West, and that is the matter of belching at the end of the meal to show one's appreciation. C.J. Wills found this habit so displeasing that he could not even bring himself to use the word: 'As soon as every one had (literally) eaten his fill, in lieu of grace, each man said, *'Alhamdillah!'* (Thank God!) and from politeness most of the guests eructated, showing that they were thoroughly satisfied. This ceremony is common through the East, and it is considered the height of rudeness to the host to abstain from it.' There is considerable debate in Iran as to the origins of this habit. It is not thought to be an ancient Iranian custom, but is popularly believed to have come with the Arabs in the seventh century. Certainly, it is not practised at all today.

Formal grace before the meal has no place in Iran. Indeed, there is a saying: '*Nakhordeh shokre nakon*' or 'Don't give thanks until you've eaten.' A simple '*Bismillah*' (in the name of God) is said before the first mouthful – but this is said before the commencement of any activity. Only at the end of the meal will each diner thank the Lord by saying '*Alhamdolillah*' (praise be to God). Finally, when the *sofreh* has been cleared, the folded cloth is kissed as a sign of respect and gratitude before being put away.

Women were absent from all these formal banquets and, even within the home, women frequently did not eat with their menfolk. Only after they had served the men would they eat in their own apartments with the children.

At this point, I should like to quote from a book written in 1828, about the experience of the first Iranian ambassador to the Court of St James, as observed by one of his companions, Hajji Baba. They are attending their first formal dinner in London. Hajji Baba said:

> Without even thinking of washing our hands before we began to eat, both men and women proceeded to the scene of action… We entered a large room, in the centre of which was spread a table more curiously ornamented than any we had yet seen. Around this we placed ourselves… Much more noise was heard than during one of our entertainments; for the unceasing activity of the servants with creaking shoes, the clash of plates, the ringing of glasses, the slashing and cutting with sharp instruments, and, above all, the universal talking of the assembly, created a din to which we were little accustomed, and which in Persia would be esteemed as highly indecorous.

He continued by noting that his ambassador managed the spoons, knives, claws and pincers with surprising dexterity.

> I must own that I was not so fortunate, for I made one or two mistakes merely from the force of previous habit, which evidently had an unfavourable effect upon those around me. I shared my neighbour's bread, which is here looked upon as offensive as it is otherwise in Persia. I drank out of his glass; and once I presented a bit with my fingers from a dish before me, at which he made a start as if I had ordered poison.[3]

Modern Iran

So far I have mostly looked at meals and traditions in nineteenth-century Iran and earlier. With the shrinking of the world, the differences between Eastern and Western table manners have also been much reduced. I have eaten many meals at a *sofreh* in Iranian homes, but I have always been given my own plate, glass and cutlery. My family and close friends dine at a table, much as we do in the West.

However, hospitality still plays a dominant role in the Iranian way of life, and many dining traditions reflect this. For instance, one can never quite know how many people will sit down for a meal. All casual visitors and friends in the house at mealtimes will be pressed to stay and eat together. And when Iranians are invited for a meal, it is not unusual for them to bring along their house-guests and visiting friends. Indeed, it would be inexcusable to leave them behind.

Such practices can cause considerable consternation among foreign hosts, unused to Iranian ways. I have seen many a foreign hostess flustered by having to arrange extra chairs and table-settings at an exquisitely arranged table for unexpected visitors. Even foreign ambassadors' wives quickly learn that it is simply not possible to organize a sit-down meal – with a full table-setting and name cards (and portions) for a specific number of people.

The buffet meal overcomes such problems, and ensures a warm welcome for all who may come along. A wide choice of dishes will also be presented, so that there are always at least one or two dishes to please everyone. In being given the chance to help oneself to the food of one's choice, one can take as little or as much of whatever one wants. It also means that the meal can be eaten fresh and warm.

A personal experience

But perhaps I can best illustrate the differences that still exist, even in an informal setting, when entertaining guests at a meal, by relating a personal experience. When we lived in Iran, my husband and I entertained a number of our Iranian and English friends for dinner one evening. I arranged a buffet-style meal, with several dishes of rice, a choice of stews, as well as a number of salads, yoghurt dishes, bread, cheese and herbs.

The English all arrived for dinner within fifteen minutes of the appointed time, bringing a bottle of wine or possibly some flowers. The Iranians (though quite Westernized) drifted in at least half an hour or so late, sometimes bringing an extra guest or two. (Gifts are brought only on the first visit to someone's home.) When invited to come to the buffet table, the English would step forward promptly, while the Iranians would stand back, insisting that others go before them. 'After you,' they would say, 'no, no, after you.'

When they reached the table, the English would take just a little of each dish, murmuring modest praise, and trying a little of everything. They would have dispersed by the time the Iranians arrived at the table. The Iranians would help themselves generously and, amid many compliments and much fulsome approbation, they would pile their plates with their favourite foods. While the English had gone over to a far corner with their plates, the Iranians would stand around the table, eating, socializing and recommending the best dishes, taking more whenever they wanted. (The gregarious nature of Iranians has led to the happy adoption of the habit of conversation over dinner.)

When it was time to leave, the English would get up, thank their hosts and leave quietly, so as not to break up the party. The Iranians would take an hour or two to leave, speaking to everyone in the room, exuberantly thanking and praising and after-you-ing!

The English thought they behaved better than the Iranians. The Iranians, of course, thought they behaved better than the English.

A footnote

Briefly, the main differences that still remain between the manners at meals in England and Iran in the shrinking world of today are that at a formal dinner, the Iranians expect a choice of service *and* self-service, while the English expect to be served. The Iranians have adopted many habits from the West in the last hundred years or so, and I wonder if now the West will adopt the habit of giving their guests this choice. If the experience of self-service in shopping in the West is anything to go by – well, who knows?

NOTES

[1] Wills, C.J., *The Land of the Lion and the Sun,* London: Ward, Lock & Co., 1891, pp. 90–1.
[2] Beny, Roloff, *Bridge of Turquoise,* Thames & Hudson, 1975, p. 308.
[3] Morier, James, *Hajji Baba of Isfahan in London,* London, 1824.

A Northern Gourmet: Benjamin Newton on the Move, 1816–1818

Layinka M. Swinburne

Benjamin Newton was a good trencherman, as he noted in his diary.[1] He entertained frequently and ate at friends' houses in return. Visitors often stayed the night and, when numerous, the overflow was boarded out in neighbouring houses. In fact, eighteen months after moving to his living in Wath, he commented that he and his wife were dining tête à tête for the first time. He had been tutor to Lord Ailesbury of Jervaulx Abbey in his youth and was later presented to the living of Wath and Kirklington as rector. He had a pleasant life, recycling his father's old sermons, visiting the local gentry and admiring the statuary and garden innovations at Newby Hall. The rectory sits adjacent to Norton Conyers Hall, which is one of the houses supposed to have given Charlotte Bronte ideas for Rochester's house in *Jane Eyre,* including the madwoman in the attic. The Newton family ate well, as he was the true country clergymen and regularly hunted, kept greyhounds and horses, shot on Catterick moors and fished up and down the river Ure on which his rectory and the neighbouring Norton Conyers estate both lay. He exchanged gifts of game with his friends. When swapping grouse with a friend at the Wath Feast, the cats ran off with one brace. He grew many vegetables for the table and was mindful of the best time for harvesting and sowing. He recorded his successes with pride, 'today I cut the first melon'; 'gathered Jargonelles and ate the first medlar which was v. good.' He bemoaned the failures like 'my poor beans'. He bought wine in quantity and spent time bottling it up with some satisfaction.

Social occasions were important. Sadly, although he carefully noted in his diary the company, and the squabbles over precedence at table, unless there was something not up to standard he did not record the daily menus. (After a visit to friends he noted 'We dined on a very bad haunch of Lord Darlington's venison'.) There were nineteen people at the Norton Conyers christening feast – 'we had plenty of turtle'. But at the Ripon Ball there were only three single men present. He had three daughters and a niece all unmarried.

He attended sittings of the local magistrates courts and meetings of the turnpike committees in local inns – 'The Oak Tree', 'The New Inn', and 'York Gate', all on the Great North Road (the old A1) – who would meet once a year to eat venison. Only one now survives, as 'New Inn Farm', a short way north of Wetherby. His notes on the court proceedings end with 'there being no other business except the eating of a good dinner'. The type of meal would be similar to that enjoyed by members of the court leet who also met in the same hostelries, ending the session with a huge joint of roast beef, accompanied by pease pudding, new potatoes and raw brandy to toast the King's health.[2]

On July 20th 1818 he followed the fashion set by the romantic poets, who popularized the Lake District by extolling its beauties. Such travellers called themselves 'Lakers'. He set out with his family on a Lakeland tour and set down many of the meals he had on the journey. The party consisted of Newton, his wife, and two of his daughters. The support team consisted of John the coachman, and two horses. He purchased an old barouche from Lord Ashton for £140, which included a new boot and repainting the crest. They followed the River Ure upstream through the Yorkshire Dales to Middleham and Wensley and then up to Sedburgh where they dined. They breakfasted at Kendal and drove on to 'The White Lion' at Bowness close to Windermere. 'The Royal Oak' at Keswick being full, they put up at 'The Queen's Head'. With some local diversions and sightseeing they continued over to Cockermouth and Maryport, exploring the coast south of the Solway Firth. They returned via Whitehaven and the risky crossing over the sands at Ulverston to call in at Lancaster, finally following a similar line to the outward journey. The first mishap was leaving the road-book behind. These precursors of modern road maps indicated the main features of the routes and occasionally named an important inn. Another mishap occurred on the first day when they had to get out and walk when the coach got stuck in the mud and rain. Needless to say, the ladies had packed their walking shoes in their bags and were wearing new bonnets 'projected on a certainty of fine weather'. When possible they stayed with friends, but most of the trip involved staying overnight at coaching inns, or at a nearby cottage when the inn ran out of rooms.

The first day they had a very mundane picnic of an egg, bread and cheese and water by the wayside, for which they paid the exorbitant sum of 5/-. After that they dined off the fat of the land. The usual arrangement was for gentry travellers to eat in a common dining-room or hire rooms for their own use. On one stop he noted that they were 17 women and 5 men at table. (Some attempt at recreating this atmosphere was made by a landlady at 'The Punchbowl', Lanreath in Devon, in the 1970s.) The servants and less wealthy travellers ate in the kitchen. Several writers have described the simple fare to be expected –

bread, cheeses, milk, or ale by the fireside.[3] Cobbett traversed the same territory on his rural rides, living very simply. The impecunious Charles Fothergill (1806) pursued his amorous adventures with milkmaids and servants a little earlier. As a solitary foot-traveller he knocked on cottage doors to get a night's lodging or might have to share a bed. Foot-travellers were sometimes assumed by innkeepers to be vagabonds and were treated with suspicion. On the regular coaching routes class-distinction was strictly maintained. The gentry sat inside the coach and were offered the private rooms and coffee room while those who endured the hardships of the roof made do with the kitchen. Thomas de Quincey wrote:

> What words could express the horror and sense of treason in that case…where all three outsiders, the trinity of pariahs, made a vain attempt to sit down at the same breakfast table as the consecrated four? The course taken with the infatuated outsiders was that the waiter… sang out: 'This way, my good men,' and then enticed these good men away to the kitchen.

The Newton family expected all the privileges. It was a summer journey and the main dishes set before them were at least one kind of fish, and several meat dishes varying with the number at table. They ate only the finer local fish – salmon, trout, sole, pike, eels, and perch, with shrimps and oysters when they were near the coast. While travellers in the past sometimes complained about the staleness of the salmon or poor quality trout, Newton, a fisherman, made only commendatory comments and sometimes caught the fish for dinner himself. On one occasion in Lancaster, he was served crimped salmon, which can be properly prepared only when the fish is very fresh. He heard salmon being cried 'about the town of Lancaster for sale in the New Inn yard'. He had again 'an excellent dinner, trout top and bottom only excelled by Lord Ailesbury's trout before the cutting of the Kennet and Avon canal.' Or later we had 'some fine pike' and 'dined a fine salmon and some fine pike'. Other ways were used to maintain supplies of perishable fish to feed an erratic clientele. Keats' friend described rowing out to an island to collect trout, which were kept in porous boxes in the lake. An enterprising innkeeper dammed the stream behind his inn to make a pool in which he kept trout, pike and perch.[4] Newton did not mention the well-known Lakeland delicacy of potted char, which many other travellers enjoyed; it was to be savoured later in the year between Michaelmas and Christmas.

The puddings and desserts were mainly apple, currant, and gooseberry pies and tarts, fresh fruit, and occasionally raspberry cream. Elizabeth Raffald described the latter as 'suitable for a middle at supper or a corner at dinner'. Of the 22 meals recorded, the majority included tarts and it was evidently the height of the gooseberry season. Things had changed little since the days of Celia Fiennes and John Byng 'who met with gooseberry pies at some of his inns'.[5] A typical meal was: pike, beef steaks, Westmoreland ham, and apple pyes, or pike, leg of mutton, pies, jelly, peas.

The number of meat dishes of course varied with the size of the company. At supper at 'The Ship Inn' in Allonby they had 'trout top and bottom, boiled leg of mutton, quarter of lamb, ducks, apple pyes, and puddings.' They consistently ate well, although the inn had been called nothing better than a common alehouse a few years before. Allonby enjoyed a brief vogue as a tourist resort and Newton would probably have classified it as a superior inn, since by an inferior inn he meant 'the best inns in places of little resort'. He selected his inns not only on the food, but on the availability of a sitting room and the quality of the mattresses.

They generally had three meals a day. The timing was flexible. They sometimes set off before breakfast, and sometimes afterwards. They ate dinner at any time between late afternoon and early evening, generally about 4 p.m. They took tea about 6 p.m. and supper at 11 o'clock, but did not necessarily expect the whole range of meals each day.

Rum pudding and rolled pudding of prunes were noted and several meals included raspberry cream, for which there are various recipes. The best was made by raising raspberry juice and cream to a froth with a chocolate mill, which was skimmed off and piled on the remaining material in a deep china dish. Mrs Raffald advised, 'stick a light flower in the middle and send it up'.[6] Bread and butter pudding, apple dumplings and savoury puddings such as veal pudding were also offered.

Vegetables were not often mentioned but may have been abbreviated to 'etc.' in his notes. C. Anne Wilson states that travellers had few comments to make on the fruits and vegetables of the northern parts other than to note how late they ripened. However Newton complained that 'green devils have haunted us all the way being none other than green peas a month too old to be eaten by me who am very fond of them when young...should be brought to anything but pigs after the pods are full.' Cabbages, lettuce, and cucumber and potatoes were also noted.

The food was generous but they also took long walks or rides to see the local beauty spots and no doubt had hearty appetites. Some dishes were often on the menu. Scotch collops (slices of veal dipped in egg, fried and served with a cream sauce) recur, and the still fashionable crimped salmon was offered at Lancaster. Crimping was introduced in the late seventeenth century. It involved gashing the fish as soon as possible after being caught so that the juices seeped out and the flesh became firm. It should be gently boiled and 'sent up in a napkin.' It was still fashionable in Mrs Beeton's time. Elizabeth Raffald gave recipes for crimped skate as well as salmon.

The food was similar to good home-cooking of the period, of the sort they would be used to. Peter Brears describes the wealth of traditional foods to be found in the region, and the limitations of cooking with peat-fired ovens. However, Newton gave little hint of any regional flavour, apart from mentioning Westmoreland ham. He did not inspect kitchens nor describe breakfast or tea, the meals at which local oatcakes, clap-bread and the like might have been encountered, apart from one mention of 'the best cakes ("pains" we should call them),' which took his fancy at breakfast at 'The Globe' in Cockermouth. He did not comment on the cheeses they were offered.

The party soon met the sort of health problems which concern travellers to this day – constipation and gastro-intestinal upsets. Within two days of setting out he was calling at a druggist for tincture of rhubarb, and when his daughters were unwell a couple of days later, topped them up with six doses of calomel, a powerful aperient. On one occasion the family sat down with the general company at a long table in 'The Ship Inn', Allonby (near Cockermouth) to:

> A dish of trout at top and a fine piece of salmon and a pair of soles 'next me at bottom'. A fillet of veal, a ham, a couple of boiled fowls, a round of beef, a loin of mutton with plenty of pyes and puddings, a dessert followed of gooseberries, currants, cherries; Shrimps, roast rabbits, roast apples, cold ham pyes, cold round of beef, potatoes etc. for supper.

'My wife and daughter eat ravenously'.

At breakfast they were 'plentifully served with meat, eggs, etc. as we had been yesterday at dinner and supper.' Thirty-six hours later, 'it appears that the liberties in eating and drinking my wife had taken did pretty well as long as she was moving but the salmon, gooseberry, currant and apple pyes now she is stationary seem to tell. My wife is not able to dine at the ordinary. ...I was affected in much the same way and cannot account for it except by eating trout which gave me a violent lax which I have experienced by eating salmon.'

When Mr Pickwick and his friends returned from an evening at 'The Blue Lion' rather the worse for wear, Mr Snodgrass murmured in a broken voice 'it wasn't the wine, it was the salmon.' Dickens observed 'somehow or other it never *is* the wine in these cases.'[7] Stale salmon was sometimes a problem in large inns away from a good source. Food storage in remote parts might have been a problem, but Newton recorded only the instance quoted of what may have been food poisoning. Following it there was three days' silence on matters of eating in his diary!

Tourists at the height of the coaching era ate perhaps more lavishly but in essence little differently from their predecessors. A few years later the railways began to crisscross the country, and while the Lakes and North Yorkshire remained untouched for a time, the coaching inns lost their trade almost overnight. 'The Angel' at Wetherby had stables and fodder for a hundred horses. By 1863 it had been purchased by an entrepreneur. The old courthouse, which it held, was pulled down and converted into printing offices. 'The Unicorn' (still in the market square in Ripon), tried to survive by providing coaches to meet the train at the new stations. However the new class of travellers did not need to eat or stay the night at the coaching inns, and the provision of food for rail travellers is another fascinating story. Refreshment rooms and train meals perpetuated the class distinction to be found in the old inns (now to be found in airport lounges). The Furness Abbey Hotel, opened in 1847, was one of the earliest of the new railway hotels. It sought to tempt 'the lakers' by advertising itself as 'lying in the heart of the Lake District', hardly complying with modern ideas of trade descriptions, as one can see from a map![8] The Keswick Hotel was built by the rail company and communicated directly with the platform. For a short time they ran the station refreshment rooms but closed them because of the rowdiness of the tourists a few years later. The annual accounts of an early refreshment room show that tourists washed down their Banbury cakes, queen cakes, and sandwiches with hefty sales of alcoholic drinks:

Tea	1,277 lb	Ale	25,692 bottles
Coffee	2,920 lb	Ginger beer	5,208 bottles
Cream	16,425 qts	Port	547 bottles
Milk	1,095 qts	Sherry	2,096 bottles
Lemonade	8,088 bottles	Gin	666 bottles
Soda water	10,416 bottles	Rum	464 bottles
Stout	45,012 bottles	Brandy	2,392 bottles

For thirty years before the first cyclist appeared, the roads of England had been empty of virtually any but farm traffic.[9] The bicycle brought a resurgence of tourism and the concept of cheap bed & breakfast. A monotonous menu of ham and eggs, tea and toast of varying quality punctuates the diaries of later travellers. Four American ladies made a summer tour of English inns early in the twentieth century, mainly by rail.[10] Although they got no further north than Derbyshire, their experiences were probably typical. Their lunch was a pared-down version of Newton's fare:

> [Lunch] consisted of chops, new potatoes and gooseberry tart, an excellent specimen of many of the same kind which we are destined to consume before our trip comes to an end.

They commented on the sweet simplicity of English cooking. 'Hot luncheon "price two and six", was just like any other hot luncheon. It consisted of the usual joint, potatoes, cabbage and a tart.'

At the Dukeries, 'We need no menu – we know what we shall have to eat.' Her companion described it as a simple cuisine, innocent of flavour with as little salt as possible. In fact even at the historic Star Inn, Yarmouth, 'with eyes closed, we could imagine eating it in any part of England through which we had passed, but, looking over the well-known menu, we forgot its monotony because of the noble room in which it was served.'

Worse was to come. At Bolsover they became desperate. 'Inns there are in plenty. We have been to them all but they only sell drink, not a morsel of food and we are very hungry.' In the end they appealed to the village policeman, who marched at the head of the party and thundered on the door of 'The Devonshire Arms', where, after his intervention, they were unwillingly served with ham, eggs and a little tea in an uninviting room.

This nadir led to changes in licensing laws. There was a distinction between alehouses, victualling houses, and inns, and by law the latter had to served *bona fide* travellers on demand with food as well as drink. About the turn of the century, members of the Temperance Association took delight in challenging such establishments and raising a prosecution if they were refused nourishment. Josephine Tozier commented, 'I can hardly believe that such inhospitality exists in England.' Her journey took place when the old coaching inns were at their lowest ebb. Happily the situation has improved, at least in the Lake District. One can again find good food at some of the spots which Newton and his family visited nearly two hundred years ago. Newton's Lowood Inn is now a much-enlarged Lowwood Hotel.

NOTES

[1] Fendall, C.P. and Crutchley, E. A., *The Diary of Benjamin Newton 1816–1818*, 1933.
[2] Brears, Peter, 'Food in the Lake Counties', in *Traditional Food East and West of the Pennines*, 1991, ed. C. Anne Wilson.
[3] Wilson, C. Anne, 'Travellers' Fare: Food encountered by some earlier visitors to the Pennine Region', in *Traditional Food East and West of the Pennines* ut sup.
[4] Lindop, Grevel, A *Literary Guide to the Lake District,* quoting Joseph Budworth (1792), *A fortnight's ramble to the Lakes.*
[5] Wilson, 'Travellers' fare'.
[6] Raffald, Elizabeth, *The Experienced English Housekeeper*, New edn. 1800.
[7] Dickens, Charles, *The Pickwick Papers*, 1826.
[8] Wooler, Neil, *Dinner in the Diner*, 1987.
[9] Bruning, Ted and Paulin, Keith, *The David and Charles Book of Historic English Inns*, 1982.
[10] Tozier, Josephine *Among English Inns*, 1904.

From Menu, to Recipe, to Meal: a Renaissance Wedding Banquet

David S. Walddon

Births, deaths, and marriages are now, and have always been, marked by two things: the people gathered for the events and the food eaten at the events. There is, however, a major difference between the food served at births and deaths and the food served at weddings. Food consumed at the first two is most often forgotten after the day is over. Not so with wedding food, it remains afterwards in many different ways. It is visually recorded in paintings. It is recorded with words in diaries, letters, and stories. It can be accounted for with figures and costs in ledger books, and is evidenced in court cases and sumptuary laws.[1] Menus, written at the time of the nuptials, or later commemorating the event, also keep wedding meals alive. But most significantly, and almost invisibly, wedding food is recorded in the recipe collections of the Renaissance. The wedding feast of Giovanni Giacomo Trivulitio and Beatrice di Avolos d'Aquino is an excellent illustration of a recorded menu, that can be paired with extant recipes, to recreate a meal.

The Menu

The Trivulitio were an important Milanese family with ties to the church and the military infrastructure, the two powers behind the growing cities and states of Renaissance Italy. Giovanni worked in the Milanese army of Ludovico Sforza, Duke of Milan, then for Ferdinand of Aragon, King of Naples and, finally, he commanded the French army of Louis XII,[2] King of France. His bride was from a prestigious family as well, with blood ties to Giovanni's second eminent employer. Like most noble weddings this one was a significant social and, more importantly, political event.

The account of the wedding feast in *Historia dell'Antichita di Milano* by Paolo Morigia[3] is a vivid depiction of the power of the Trivulitio family and the wealth and importance of the house of Aragon. Held on April 22nd, 1487,[4] the meal was extravagant, consisting of fifteen courses with over thirty recorded dishes. Delicate sweets opened and, along with a myriad of tarts, closed the feast. A virtual menagerie of roasted birds, sheep and suckling pigs were strewn throughout the menu, and of course the ubiquitous peacock, re-dressed in all its finery and shooting fire from its mouth,[5] was the centrepiece in the eleventh course. Dainty meat rolls and sausages were served as one course, contrasted by whole heads of beef and veal as another. This juxtaposition of sizes was echoed in the flavours of the food as well. Sweet, sour, salty, and bland were all represented in this sumptuous meal.

Some dishes are conspicuous by their absence. There is no mention of fish and a decided lack of fruit and vegetables. Since the wedding feast occurred on the first Sunday after Easter and the long Lenten period without meat, the lack of fish is somewhat understandable. The only fruits mentioned in the menu are 'olives as a condiment'. Other fruits, such as sour cherries, prunes and grapes, are essential ingredients used in extant recipes that could be paired with the dishes included in the menu. This would add some fruit to the menu, but not in any quantity. This early in the year, fruit, and especially fresh fruit, was not plentiful. Only one vegetable is noted in the text: 'very beautiful and admirable asparagus'. It was probably mentioned because of the size, or the quality, or because it was unusual at this time of year so far north. However, the lack of vegetables is not so easily explained as that of the fish or the fruit. At this time of the year, spring vegetables, especially greens, would be plentiful. Perhaps they were assumed to be included, much the same way as they are in modern menus. The extant recipe collections also have only a small percentage of vegetable dishes in them.

Were vegetables something left to the apprentice cooks or court physicians or were they left out of the meal entirely? We know vegetables were an important part of the Italian meal. In the first five books of *De Honesta Voluptate et Valetudine,* Platina describes the preparation of a cornucopia of vegetables. The medical treatises of the time also include, as well as advice on the humoral nature of many different vegetables, specific instructions on how to prepare them.

The Italian description of this meal, and the following recipes from the Martino manuscript, are transcribed as closely as possible to the original documents. All line breaks, scribal markings, archaic spellings, contractions, word spacing, etc. are retained. The symbol ſ denotes the long s.

Deſcrittion fatta del conuito del magno Giouan Gia-
como Triuultio, quando egli preſe moglie.

Volendo deſcriuere il sontuoſo banchetto, che fece Gio. Giacomo
Triuultio detto il Magno, quando egli prese per moglie Beatrice di A-

ualos d'Aquino, di sangue regale d'Aragon, & descritto nel libro 12. dell' Epistole d'Angelo Pollitiano. Prima fu data l' acqua alle mani con l' aqua Rosa, poscia furono portati certi pasticci di granelli di Pino, et zuccaro, & certe fugacie fatte di mandole & zuccaro à sembianza di marzapani, con certi ritorti, & altre cose delicate. Appresso furono portati sparesi molti belli, et d' ammiratione. Terzo furono arreccate picciole polpe, cibi delicatssimi, et fegatelli acconci con grand' arte. Quarto si portò carne di starne arostita con saporetti. Quinto arreccarono teste di Manzetti, & di Vitelli intieri, con le sue pelli. Sesto portarono Caponi, e Piccioni, accompagnati con duoi salati, & persuti, & altre cose di Porco, aggiontoui potaggi delicati. Appresso fu portato un Castrato intiero arrosto per ogni piattio con brodo fatto de cerase brusche. Ottauo portarono in tauola Tortore, Pernici, faggiani, quaglie, tordi, Beccafichi, et d'ogni altra sorte d'Vcelli a rosto con gran diligenza acconci, agiontoui oliue per condimêto. Nono arreccarono Polastri cotti col zuccaro, bagnati con l'acqua rosa. Decimo vn Porcellettto intiero a rosto, Cõ certo brodetto aspretto per ogni piatto. Vndecimo fu messo per ogni piatto vn Pauone a rosto, con diuersissimi condimenti, & varietà di cose delicate. Duodecimo vna mistione fatta d'voui, Late, Saluia, fior di farina, e zuccaro. Decimoterzo fu arrecato alla tauola pomi cottogni con zuccaro, carelli,[6] pini, & arcichiochi; Decimoquartro varij cibi fatti di zuccaro, e mele, & altre cose prouocatiue alla gola. Quintodecimo s'an recarono diuerse sorti di torte delicatamente acconcie. Et tutte queste uiuande furono portate alla tavola con piatti d'argento, & oro.

Description made of the feast[7] of the noble[8] Giovanni Giacomo Trivulitio, when he took a wife.

Desiring to describe the sumptuous banquet, Giovanni Giacomo Trivulitio, called the noble, had made when he took for a wife Beatrice di Avolos d'Aquino, of regal blood of Aragon, and described in book twelve of the Epistle of Angelo Pollitiano. First was given the water for the hands with rose-water. After they were brought certain little pies with grains of pine and sugar and certain cakes[9] made of almonds and sugar similar to marzipan with certain *ritorti*[10] and other delicate things. After they were brought very beautiful and admirable asparagus. Third they were delivered little meat rolls, very delicate food, and liver sausages dressed with great art. Fourth they were brought roasted meat of partridge with sauce. Delivered fifth, whole head of young beef and of veal with their skin. Sixth they were brought capon and pigeon,[11] accompanied with two salted meats and *prosciutto*[12] and other things of pork added to these a delicate pottage. After they were brought a whole roasted sheep for every platter with broth made of sour cherries. Eighth they were brought to the table roasted turtledoves, partridges, pheasants, quail, thrush, figpecker, and every other sort of birds dressed with great diligence, adding olives as a condiment. Ninth they were delivered pullet cooked in sugar, bathed in rose-water. Tenth a whole roasted suckling pig with certain tart broth for every platter. Eleventh they placed, for every platter, a roasted peacock with diverse condiments and a variety of delicate things. Twelfth, one mixture made of eggs, milk, sage, the best flour and sugar. Thirteenth they delivered to the table quince with sugar, cinnamon, pine nuts and artichokes. Fourteenth various made foods of sugar and honey and other things to challenge the throat. Fifteenth they were delivered diverse sorts of tarts dressed delicately. And all the meats were brought to the table on platters of silver and gold.[13]

The meal

The above description gives us a glimpse of a Renaissance wedding meal, but it is not until the descriptions are paired with recipes that we can truly taste the banquet. The Martino collection of recipes is the most appropriate of the existing manuscripts to use when matching the recipes to the menu description. Recipes for almost all the food items listed in the menu can be found within it. Also the introduction to the Riva del Garda manuscript, one of the seven related manuscripts,[14] tells us that Martino was the cook for 'Jo. Iacobo Trivultio'.

Unfortunately not all the dishes in the menu could be explored within the space of this paper. The five recipes chosen give an overview of the menu. They start with a sweet dish, move on to a flavourful appetizer, give a choice between a roasted poultry dish or a pork dish and finish with a torte. Each recipe is introduced with the line from the menu describing the dish, then is followed by the original Italian, the English translation, and finally a modern redaction.

Recipe One

'First was given…certain cakes made of almonds and sugar similar to marzipan'

LCMartino #149[15]

Per far caliscioni.
Renderai simil pieno ó compositione, quale
E, la pr sopraditta del marzapane, & ap
parichiarai la sua pasta[16] *laquale im*
pastarrai cō zuccharro, & acqua rosata, &

di stendi la ditta pasta amodo ch si uole
sse far ravioli gli metterai di questo pieno
facendoli grandi, ó mezani, o, piccioli cō
mo tipari Et hauendo qualch forma de
ligno ben lavorata cō qualch gentile
za í formando li & premendoli di sopra
pariranno piu belli avedér, Poi li farai
cocér í lapadella como il marzapane
hauendo bona diligentia ch nó fardino.

To make *caliscioni*[17]

Render them similarly filled or composed of the above said marzipan[18] and prepare your pasta, which is kneaded with sugar and rose-water. And spread the said pasta in the manner like raviolis are made. Then place these filled made-things, big or medium or little, as they seem to you. And having some form of well worked line with some dainties, form and press them from above so they appear more beautifully made. Then have them cooked in the pan like marzipan. Having good diligence that they do not become open.

Marzipan Dainties

1 cup flour ♦ 2 teaspoons rose-water
1 large egg ♦ 8 oz pre-made marzipan
2 teaspoons oil ♦ 1 beaten egg (optional)
a pinch of salt ♦ 2 tablespoons sugar (optional)
2 tablespoons sugar

Pre-heat oven to 325°F (163°C). In a large bowl make a well in the flour. In the middle place the egg, oil, salt, sugar and flavouring. Beat the liquid ingredients with a fork until well combined. Slowly incorporate the flour into the liquid. Once all are combined turn the dough out onto a floured surface and knead until the dough becomes smooth and elastic. Roll a quarter of the dough fairly thin with a pin or in a pasta mill.

Place a layer of dough in a ravioli form. Place a small piece of marzipan in each ravioli space. Cover with more dough and press the two pieces together with a rolling pin. Repeat until all the dough and marzipan are used up.

Although not specified in the original recipe these dainties are best brushed with egg and sprinkled with sugar before baking them.

Bake for 20 to 25 minutes, or until they are golden brown. Serve warm or at room temperature. Makes approximately 24.

Note: rose-water will vary greatly in strength from brand to brand. Start out with a few drops and add until the fragrance and flavour are enough. If rose-water is unavailable or undesirable replace it with orange, lemon or vanilla flavouring.

Recipe Two
'Third they were delivered little meat rolls'

LCMartino #18[19]
Er fare polpette dicarne de vitello, o de altra bona carne, In prima togli de la carne magra delacoṣsa & tagliala ì fette longhe & sottili & battile bene sopra Vn tagliero, o tauola cō la-coṣta del coltello, & togli ṣale, & finocchio pesto & ponilo sopra la ditta fetta dicarne, Dapoi togli de pretroṣimolo, maiorana & de bon lar-do & batti queste cose inseme cō vn poche di bone ṣpetio, & diṣtendile bene queste cose ì la dicta fetta Dapoi ì uoltela ì ṣeme & polla nel ṣpeto accocer, Ma nō la laṣsara[20] troppo ṣec-car al focho.

To make meat rolls, of the meat of veal or of other good meat. First take of the lean meat of the haunch and cut in slices, long and thin, and beat well on a trencher or table with the side of a knife. And take salt and fennel pounded and put on the said slice of meat. Then take parsley, marjoram, and of good lard and beat these things altogether with a little of good spice and spread well these things on the said slices then roll-up[21] together and put them on the spit to cook. But do not leave them to dry too much at the fire.

Savoury Meat Roll-ups

4 pounds beef or veal roast • ½ cup fresh marjoram, chopped
3 teaspoons salt • ⅓ pound lard
3 teaspoons fennel seed
¾ cup fresh parsley chopped (approx. ½ a bunch)
pepper, cinnamon, nutmeg to taste

Slice the roast into strips approximately ¼ inch thick, 2 inches wide and 4 inches long. With the side of a cleaver or a meat tenderizer, pound the strips until they are thin and tender.

In a mortar or spice grinder combine the salt and fennel seed and process until completely combined. Season the meat strips with the fennel salt. Beat parsley and marjoram into the lard. Spread a teaspoon of the herb mixture onto the strips. Season the strips a second time with a pinch each of pepper, cinnamon and nutmeg. Roll up the meat strips and secure with butcher twine, toothpicks or wooden skewers.

Grill over a medium flame for approximately 10 minutes turning occasionally. Serve hot. Makes approximately 24 meat rolls.

Note: these meat rolls are best grilled. If a grill is not available they could be roasted or broiled in a hot oven for 10 to 15 minutes.

Recipe Three
'Sixth they brought capon and pigeon'

LCMartino #4[22]

per fare ogni bello arrosto:
Per[23] fare bello arrosto de pollastri, de capponi,
de Capretti, ó de qualunche altra carne ch
merti essere arrosta : prima se fosse carne
grossa, fagli trare un boglio, excepto se fosse
de vitello giouine, et poi lardala, come se
fáno li arrosti : se fosse Cappone, Fasano, pol-
lastro, capretto, ó qualunchaltra carne, ch
meriti arrosto, fa ch sia ben netta, et polita,
poi mettila in aqua bollente, et subito caula
fore, et ponila in aqua freda, et questo se
fa, aZio ch sia piu bella, & meglio se possa
conciare : poi lardala, Zio, e, con lardo baituto
& altre chose conuementi odorifere onta bn,
secondo el gusto del tuo signore : et drento se
te piace gli pond de bone herbe con prune secche,
marasche, et viscioli, ó in temp, del agresto.
et altre chose simile : poi mittila ordinata-
mente nel speto, et ponila al foco, et daglilo
nel principio ad ascio ad ascio, perche sia bello
& bono arrosto se deue cocere pian piano : Et
qn tipare, ch sia presso ch cotto, piglia vn pane
bianca, et grattugialo menuto, et con esso pane
mescola tanto sale, quanto te pare necessario

*p*²⁴ *lo arrosto : poi gitta qsta*²⁵ *mescolanZa de pane,*
& de sale sopra lo arrosto in modo ch ne uadi
in ogni loro : poi dalli vna bona calda de
foro, facendolo uoltar presto : et in questo
modo hauerai el tuo arrosto bello, et colorito:
*De poi mandalo á Tabula, qto*²⁶ *piu psto,*²⁷ *e, meglio: ~*

To make every good roast
To make good roast of pullet, of capon, of kid, and of whichever other meat that merits being roasted. First if it was coarse meat bring them to a boil except if it was of young veal and then lard it like you make the roasts. If it is Capon, Pheasant, Pullet, Kid, or whichever other meat that merits roasting, make it well cleaned and trimmed up then put it in boiling water and at once extract it out and put it in cold water. And this is done so that it will be very good and better when you dress it. Then lard it, that is to say with beaten lard and other convenient, fragrant, good anointments, according to the taste of your lord. And within it you put, if you like, good herbs with dried prunes, sour cherries and entrails, or sometimes unripe grapes and similar things. Then set it, arranged on the spit, and put it to the fire and give it from the beginning very soft, because it is beautiful and well roasted if you have cooked it very gently. And when it seems to you that it is almost cooked, take a white bread and grate it very small and with this bread mix enough salt, as much as you think necessary for the roast. Then cast the mixture of the bread and of the salt over the roast in the manner that it goes in every place. Then give it a good heat at the fire having it turned quickly: And in this manner you will have a beautiful and colourful roast. And to be best, hand it to the table quickly.

Roasted Capon with a Fruit Stuffing

1 medium capon or chicken ♦ ¼ cup lard
1 16oz can sour cherries ♦ ½ cup fresh herbs, chopped
1 cup dried prunes, chopped ♦ ½ cup bread crumbs
½ cup fresh herbs ♦ 1 teaspoon salt ♦ ½ cup chicken livers

Pre-heat oven to 375°F (190°C). Wash the capon and set aside. Drain the sour cherries. In a bowl combine the cherries, prunes and fresh herbs. Briefly sauté the chicken livers in a few tablespoons of the cherry juice. Chop the livers into medium size pieces and add to the cherry mixture. Stuff the mixture into the cavity of the capon.

Combine lard and second amount of fresh herbs. Spread the lard and herb mixture onto the bird.

Roast for 1 hour or until internal temperature reaches 190°F (88°C).

Combine the breadcrumbs and salt. Just before the capon reaches temperature, sprinkle it with the seasoned breadcrumbs. Turn the oven temperature up to 450°F (232°C) for the last five to ten minutes until the breadcrumbs have browned.

Note: use whatever fresh herbs you have at hand. Oregano, marjoram, parsley, and rosemary are all appropriate.

Recipe Four
'Tenth a whole roasted suckling pig with certain tart broth'

LCMartino #15[28]

> Er aconciár bene vna porchetta, Fa in prima
> ch sia ben pelata in modo ch sia biancha & net-
> ta Et poi fendila per lo deritto, de la schina, &
> caccia[29] fore le interiori & lauala molto bene,
> Et da poi togli ifigatelli de la ditta porchetta,
> & battili bene col coltello i séme con bone
> herbe, & togli aglio tagliato menuto, & vn
> pocho di bon lardo, & vn pocho dicaso grattu-
> giato, & qualch ouo, & pepero pesto, & vn
> pocho, zafiano, & mescola tutte queste cose
> & mettele í la ditta porchetta, reuersandola
> a modo che sI sanno le tenche, cio, e, ponendo
> quello di dentro difor, Et dapoi cusila í seme
> & ligala bene & pomla accocer nel speto, ó
> uero su lagraticula, Ma falla cocér adafcio
> ch sia ben cotta cosi lacarne como etiam dio
> il pieno Et fa vn pocha di salamora có aceto
> pepero & zafrano, & tolli doi ó tre ramicel-
> le de lauoro, ó salvia, o rosmarino, & gietta
> spesse uolte di tal salamora í su la porchetta,
> Et simile sí po fare de oche, Anatre, Gruue,
> Capponi, Pollastri, & altri Simili.

To cook well one suckling pig. See first that it is well skinned in the manner that it is white and clean. And then cleave it straight down the backbone and take out the internals and wash them very well. And then take the liver of the said suckling pig and beat well with a knife together with good herbs, and take garlic, cut small, and a little grated cheese, and some eggs, and ground pepper, and a little saffron and mix all these things. And place them in the said suckling pig, returning them in the manner that is known for a Tench that is to say putting this within. And then sew the whole and fasten well. And put to cook on a spit, or properly on the grate. But fail not to cook leisurely, that it is well cooked, the meat, as well as the stuffing. And make a little brine with vinegar, pepper and saffron and take two or three twigs of laurel or sage or rosemary and cast many times this brine upon the suckling pig. And similarly one can made Geese, Ducks, Crane, Capon and other similar things.

Roasted Pork with Cheese Stuffing

1 lb pork loin • 2 teaspoons fresh rosemary, crushed
3 cloves garlic, crushed • ¼ cup fresh herbs, chopped
2 cups Asiago Cheese, grated • saffron
1 teaspoon pepper • ¼ cup red wine
2 eggs, slightly beaten • ¼ cup red wine vinegar
2 tablespoons olive oil

Pre-heat oven to 400°F (204°C). Create a hollow inside the pork loin by inserting a knife down the centre, then enlarge by inserting a wooden spoon into the hole and rotating it until there is a sizable hole. Alternately butterfly the loin, stuff then tie shut.

Combine garlic, cheese, pepper, eggs, and saffron. Stuff this mixture into the pork. Close each end of the loin with skewers.

In a very hot oven-proof pan, sear all sides of the loin.

Mix rosemary, herbs, saffron, wine, and vinegar together. Baste the meat with one-third of this liquid. Roast the loin in the oven for approximately 30 minutes, basting twice with the remaining liquid during this time.

Remove the meat from the oven and let sit for 5 minutes before slicing into rounds. Serve hot. Makes enough for 4 small servings or 2 large servings.

Note: the liver has been left out of the modern redaction of this recipe. This stuffing is also very good in a pork shoulder roast or thick-cut pork chops.

Recipe Five
'Fifteenth they were delivered diverse sorts of tarts dressed delicately'

LC Martino #139[30]

A bi le Cerase de la piu negre ch tu troui, &
cauatene fora le ossa macinarale molto
bene nel mortale, & habi de le rose roscie
batture molto bene colcoltello, cō vn pocho
di cascio fresco, & vn pocho di bon cascio uec
chio, A gigendoli dele spetie, cioie Canella
Zenzeuero, & pocho pepe, & del Zuccharo
& mescolarai molto bene tutte queste cose
Agiangendoui etiam tre o quattro ova
secundo laquantita ch vorrai fare & cō
crosta di sotto la metterai acocer abello
agio í la padella, Et quando sia cotta gli
metterai di sopra del Zucchero, & dellac
qua Rosata

Have the blackest cherries you find, and take out from the stones. Grind very well in a mortar and have the red roses beaten very well with a knife, and with a little fresh cheese and a little old cheese. Add spice, that is cinnamon, ginger, and a little pepper with some sugar and mix these things together very well. Also add three or four eggs according to the quantity you want to make. And with crust underneath put it to cook a good while in a pan. And when it is cooked put on top some sugar and water of roses.

Cherry Cheese Tart
1 16oz can sour cherries ♦ ¼ cup white sugar
¾ cup rose petals (reserve 10 petals for garnish)
1 teaspoon ground ginger ♦ ¼ teaspoon ground pepper
½ pound fresh goat cheese ♦ ½ teaspoon cinnamon
½ pound cream cheese ♦ pre-baked 9-inch shortbread crust
½ cup grated Parmesan
3 tablespoons flavoured water (rose, orange, etc.)
3 beaten eggs ♦ ¼ cup extra fine sugar

Pre-heat oven. Purée cherries in a food-processor until they are smooth, place in a large non-reactive bowl. Coarsely chop rose petals and fold into cherries.

Beat until smooth the goat cheese, cream cheese and Parmesan cheese. Add to this mixture the eggs and white sugar. Continue to beat until smooth. Add spices and mix until combined.

Fold the cheese and egg mixture into the cherries. Pour into a pre-baked pie shell and bake at 350° F (177°C) for 45 minutes or until pie is set and slightly golden.

Cool slightly. Then drizzle with rose-water and sugar, then garnish with reserved petals. Serve at room temperature. Makes approximately ten slices.

Note: please use only organically grown roses or flowers from your own garden that you know have not been sprayed or fertilized with anything toxic. If you can not find edible roses omit from the recipe. Rose-water can be found in Indian grocery stores.

Conclusion

All of the above recipes have been tested, tasted and served with great success. Through the description of the wedding feast of Giovanni and Beatrice we are able to reach back into the past and peek at the social rituals of the time. Pairing the description with extant recipes from the Martino collection extends our knowledge of the wedding meal beyond description and into the kitchen of the time period. Recreating the recipes and sharing them with guests brings the wedding meal into the present and allows us a taste of the Renaissance.

BIBLIOGRAPHY

Arn, Mary-Jo, ed. *ACTA Vol. XXI, Medieval Food and Drink,* Binghamton, New York: Center for Medieval and Early Renaissance Studies, 1995.

Arano, Luisa Cogliati, ed., *The Medieval Health Handbook: Tacuinum Sanitatis,* trans. O. Ratti and A. Westbrook, New York: George Braziller, Inc. 1976.

Benporat, Claudio, *Cucina Italiana del Quattrocento,* Florence: Leo S. Olschki, 1996.

Bendiscioli, Mario, *Documenti di Storia Medioevale 400–1492,* Milan: U. Mursia & Co. 1970.

Brucker, Gene, *Giovanni and Lusanna, Love and Marriage in Renaissance Florence,* Berkeley, CA., 1986.

Epulario. London: A.I. for William Barley, 1598 [Microfilm copy].

Faccioli, Emilio, ed. *L'arte della Cucina in Italia,* Torino, 1987.

Florio, John, *A world of Words,* London, 1598; reprint, Hildesheim: Georg Olms Verlag, 1972.

Martino, MS, *Libre de Arte Coquinaria.* 1460(?) [Microfilm copy]. Special Collections: Library of Congress, Washington, DC.

——, MS, *Libre de Arte Coquinaria.* 1460(?), Urb. 1203, [Microfilm copy]. Biblioteca Apostolica Vaticana.

Morigia, Paolo, *Historia dell'Antichita di Milano* Venice, 1592 reprinted in *Historiae Urbium et Regionum Italiae Rariores,* Bologna: Forni Editore, 1948.

Origo, Iris, *The Merchant of Prato – Francesco di Marco Datini,* London: Cape 1957.
Platina: On Right Pleasure and Good Health, tr. Mary Ella Milham, Tempe, Arizona: Medieval and Renaissance Texts and Studies, 1998.
Rachum, Ilan, *The Renaissance: an illustrated encyclopedia,* London: Octopus Books, 1979.
Rainey, Ronald Eug, *Sumptuary Legislation in Renaissance Florence (Italy),* Ann Arbor, Michigan: UMI Dissertation Services, 1985.
Rebora, Piero, *Cassell's Italian Dictionary,* New York: Macmillan Publishing, 1958.
Rosselli, Giovanni de, *Opera Nova Chimata Epulario,* 1518; reprint, Rome: Bimo, 1973.
Santich, Barbara, *The Original Mediterranean Cuisine: Medieval Recipes for Today,* Totnes, Devon: Prospect Books, 1995.
Scully, Terence trans., *The Neapolitan Recipe Collection: (New York, Pierpont Morgan Library, MS Buhler, 199): A Critical Edition and English Translation, Cuoco Napoletano*, University of Michigan, 2000.
Vehling, Joseph Dommers, *Platina and the Rebirth of Man,* Chicago: Walter M. Hill, 1941.
Westbury, Lord, *Handlist of Italian Cookery Books,* Florence: Leo S. Olschki, 1963.

NOTES

[1] There are many examples of these records. For a few see: 'The Merchant of Prato', 'Sumptuary Legislation in Renaissance Florence', and 'Giovanni and Lusanna'.

[2] Louis XII awarded Giovanni many noble titles. He is often referred to as 'the great' or 'the noble' in historical as well as modern historical texts.

[3] Paolo Morigia, page 688, originally from book twelve of the Epistle of Angelo Pollitiano. Santich, page 37, describes the meal in English and Benporat, page 69, describes the meal in modern Italian. Yet another description appears in Bendiscioli, page 267, which is transcribed from a different edition of Morigia than the one used here.

[4] Benporat, page 68.

[5] LCMartino, recipe #14 'Per fare pavoni' records just such a recipe complete with iron apparatus to hold it upright, the aqua vita for the fire and a gilded and re-feathered body.

[6] Carelli is the only typographical error in this text. This word should read canelli.

[7] Florio – 'Conuito, Conuiuio, a banquet, a feast, a guest-meale or eating together.'

[8] Florio – 'Magno, great, high, mightie, large, big, notable, noble.'

[9] Florio – 'Fuggaccia, Fugazza, a cake a tarte, a cheese cake.'

[10] Florio – 'Ritortelli, a kinde of wrethed or crooked meat made of paste used in Italy. Also a kinde of cake, simnell, or ginger bread.'

[11] Florio – 'Piccioni, a pigeon, a dove. Also a chicken.'

[12] Florio – 'Persutto, Persuto, dride bakon. Also a gammon of bakon.'

[13] The account of the banquet continues for a few more sentences with a description of the stage players, musicians and other entertainers who were brought into the room after the feast.

[14] There are seven manuscript sources. In brief, with the abbreviations used throughout the rest of the paper, they are 1) Martino, MS Library of Congress (LCMartino); 2) Martino, MS Vatican (VatMartino); 3) Martino, Riva del Garda (Riva); 4) Platina, De Honesta Voluptate (PlatinatrMilham); 5) Martino Bühler 19 (Bühler); 6) Rosselli, Epulario (Rosselli); 7)Epulario (EP1598). The Riva and Bühler manuscripts are included in Benporat. The reference numbers provided before each recipe for these manuscripts are from the Benporat transcription.

[15] VatMartino #146 'Per fare chaliscioni', Riva #164 'Per fare calisoni', PlatinatrMilham Bk. VIII #49 'Rolls which they call Canisiones', Bühler 19 #161 'Calisoni boni', Rosselli #188 'Per fare caliscioni', EP1598 #194 'To make an Italian meat called Caliscioni'.

[16] The scribe has written over top of the original middle letters with a long 's' and a 't'.

[17] Florio – 'Calisoni, a kinde of comfets so called.'

[18] In LCMartino the recipe immediately before this recipe is for marzipan.

[19] VatMartino #18 'Per fare polpette di came de vitello, o de altra bona carne', Riva #18 'Per fare polpite de carne de vitelo o de altra bona carne', PlatinatrMilham Bk.VI #18 'On Veal', Rosselli #25 'Per fare polpette di carne di vittella', EP1598 #25 'To make Olives of Veale or other flesh'. This recipe does not occur in Bühler.

[20] A scribal marking resembling a capital 'H' is present over the 'r' in this word.

[21] Florio – 'Voltolare, to roule up and downe, to tumble, to tosse, to overturne, to rumble, to wallowe, topsi-turvie.'

[22] VatMartino #4 'Per fare ogni bello arosto', Riva#3 'Per fare bello Rosto de pollastri de caponi…', PlatinatrMilham Bk VI #4 'Roasts', Bühler # 52 'Per fare bello Rosto', Rosselli #4 'Per fare ogni bello arrosto', EP1598 #4 'To make all kind of meat to roast faire & white'.

[23] The 'p' of this word sits outside the body of the recipe in the margin and is in a large roman capital that stretches from the top of the first line to the bottom of the second line.

[24] The descender of the 'p' is clearly struck through.

[25] The scribe has placed a joining mark above the 'q' in this word.

[26] The scribe has placed a joining mark above the 'q' in this word.

[27] The scribe has placed a joining mark above the 'p' in this word.

[28] VatMartino # 15 'Per conciare bene una porchetta', Riva #29 'Per cocere et teen coconare una porcheta', PlatinatrMilham Bk VI #15 'On Roast Piglet', Bühler #63 'La…porcheta a Rosto reversata', Rosselli #20. 'Per cuocere bene una porchetta', EP1598 #20 'To Rost a Pig'.

[29] The scribe has clearly indicated an insertion mark and another 'c' in this word.

[30] VatMartino #137 'Per fare torte di cerase rosse rosse', Bühler #138 'Torte de Cerase', Rosselli #202 'Per fare torte di cerase rosse', PlatinatrMilham Bk Viii #40 'Sour Cherry Pie', EP1598 #208 'To make Tartes of red Cherries'. This recipe is not included in Riva. It is mentioned in the index but is missing from the body of manuscript.

Colonel Hawker Tells How to Get a Decent Meal with a Bad Cook and Poor Ingredients

Harlan Walker

If even a nobleman ... were to enter an alehouse, the most that could be procured for him would be mutton or beef, both perhaps as tough, and with as little fat, as the boots or gaiters on his legs. A chop or steak is provided. If he does not eat it, he may starve; if he does, his pleasure for the next day is possibly destroyed by his unpleasant sufferings from indigestion. He gets some sour beer, which gives him the heartburn, and probably calls for brandy or gin; the one execrably bad and unwholesome; the other of the worst quality; and, *of course*, mixed with water, by which adulteration is derived the greatest of the publican's profit. ... Our young sportsman, at last, retires to a miserable chamber and a worse bed; where, for want of ordering it to be properly aired, he gets the rheumatism; and, from the draughts of air that penetrate the room, he is attacked with the toothache. He rises to a breakfast of bad tea, without milk; ... and, in the evening, returns to his second edition of misery.

On the other hand, an old campaigner would, under such circumstances, do tolerably well, and have his complete revenge on the fish or fowl of the place.[1]

This is from Lt.-Col. P. Hawker's book *Instructions to Young Sportsmen in all that relates to Guns and Shooting*. Peter Hawker (1786–1853) is best known for this book which was first published in 1814. Although obviously concerned mainly with other matters, the book has a chapter entitled 'General advice for the Health and Comfort of a young Sportsman' which contains information on how the 'old campaigner' can avoid the worst of such hardships and get a satisfactory meal under difficult circumstances.

If we are not 'Sportsmen', experts with gun and rod, we will probably be unaware of Colonel Hawker so, before describing his recommendations, I will give some details of his life. He was born in London in 1786 in a military

family. He was gazetted cornet in the 1st Royal Dragoons in 1801 at the age of fifteen, for which he, or his family, paid £735.[2] In 1803 he exchanged into the 14th Light Dragoons and a year later was promoted captain. In 1809 he led his squadron at the battle of Oporto. In that same summer he took part in the battle of Talavera, where he was badly wounded in the thigh.[3] He was brought back to England and operated on (of course without anaesthetic) several times. His leg was saved, but he never fully recovered. Although he talked his way back to the Peninsular to rejoin his regiment, it soon became clear though that he was quite unable to take any useful part in the campaign and he was ordered back to England. He had been keeping a diary from his teens and the following entries describe an incident during his second voyage home from Lisbon to Spithead on the transport *Sally*.

April 19th 1811
Passed a turtle sleeping on the water. A boat was immediately sent after him, and when, with great caution, the crew had rowed close to him, he was taken up and brought on board.
April 21st
Having neither aldermen's cooks nor London recipes on board, we were so hard run for dressing our turtle, that I was the man honoured with that appointment; and, as my recipe was most highly approved, I have

made a memorandum of the way precisely in which I dressed it, viz: Having the turtle killed, boned and well cleaned with scalding water over night, it was put in the saucepan about half-past nine in the morning, with more than twice as much water as would cover it, and then left to keep boiling. At eleven I put in two onions (cut in quarters), a piece of butter half the size of an orange mixed with flour (and a teaspoonful of fine sugar), and a crust of burnt bread. At twelve I added half a pint of Madeira, and a small teaspoonful of cayenne, a tablespoonful of anchovy essence, two tablespoonful of Coratch sauce, some allspice, cloves, cinnamon and peppercorns; some pickled samphire and capsicorn, with all the juice and half the rind of a large lemon. At two I added another squeeze of lemon, with two glasses more Madeira, and (after it had boiled with these a few minutes) it was served up.[4]

After more operations on his thigh, to his fury he was invalided out of the army. I 'was driven out of the Service for no other reason than what ought to have been a recommendation – namely, the very severe wounds with which I had till lately been deprived from doing my duty.'[5] He was however active in the North Hampshire Militia in which he served as major from 1815 and lieutenant-colonel from 1821. He married twice and several of his descendants continued in the military tradition. He died in 1853.

It is not as a soldier though that he is best known, but for his skill with a shotgun and to a lesser extent as an angler. Less known today was his skill as a musician. He had piano lessons from the best teachers in London and Paris. He wrote a book on piano playing and even invented and patented a mechanical device to aid learning scales involving 'very ingenious handmoulds for use on the pianoforte.' I have never heard that this was very successful though. His varied interests and indeed passions are well exemplified in this passage in the *Diary* about a visit to Ullswater in the Lake District.

October 30th 1812
The view creates the sort of sensation which we feel on hearing Mozart's music, seeing Shakespeare's tragedies, hearing Braham sing, or seeing ourselves surrounded by a good evening flight of wild-fowl.[6]

He was perhaps the most skilful shot with various types of shotgun that has ever lived. He excelled in the early autumn in his pursuit of partridges and even more so in his punt in January in the Solent between the Isle of White and the south coast. In spite of his poor health he would spend whole nights in his boat, preferably when it was freezing, coming in in the morning and then perhaps going out during the day and again the following night. It was on these occasions that he needed to make special arrangements for his comfort whether on the Solent or in East Anglia. Here he is on the former.

> *January 14th 1817*
> …I had only time to scramble up (near the quay) some infamously bad bread, a few red herrings, and a little paper of salt butter. Even this was well worth exportation, as the family who occupied the only hovel I could be sheltered in at Southhaven almost entirely subsist on bad potatoes and sour beer.
> … an incessant pour of rain, which with a foul gale of wind, kept me (cut off from Poole) a close prisoner all the 15th and nearly all the 16th with the worst of campaigner's fare … Attempted to get out in the evening, but was again driven in by rain, when I had just killed a heron, which I voted well worth my charge, in order to make me a substitute for giblet soup.
>
> *January 20th*
> A tremendous hurricane all day. … I was obliged to stand in water boots, and cook my dinner, where there was water enough to float a boat. … A scarcity of provision, except red herrings and the few wild fowl we had shot. … My pilot poorly with the rheumatism, and my servant put to bed with a cold, where he could only be approached by means of water boots or a bridge of chairs.[7]

We will now look at his advice to young sportsmen to assist them on such occasions, given in the *Instructions*.[8]

> I may possibly be the means of saving them from unnecessarily hard fare when quartered in a small public-house, on some shooting or fishing excursion, as many of the little publicans live chiefly on fat pork and tea; or, if on the coast, red herrings; the experienced traveller well knows, that, when in a retired place of this sort, where, from the very circumstance of the misery attending it, there are fewer sportsmen, and consequently, there is to be had the best diversion, we have often to depend a little on our wits for procuring the necessaries of life.
> ………
> His [the Young Sportsman's] plan, knowing the improbability of getting anything to eat, would be to provide himself with a hand-basket at the last country town which he had to pass through, before he reached his

exile; and there stock it with whatever good things presented themselves. He then arrives at the pothouse, which the distance, or the badness of the roads, might oblige him to do the previous day. ... He then, supposing he would not be at the trouble of carrying meat, sends for his beef or mutton. Having secured this for the *next* day's dinner, he takes out of his basket something ready dressed, or some eggs, or a string of sausages, or a few kidneys; or a fowl to broil, a cake or two of portable soup, or a little mock turtle, ready to warm, or, in short, any other things that the town may have afforded; and with this, he makes up his dinner on the day of his arrival. If the beer is sour, and he does not choose to be troubled with carrying bottles of other beverage, he is provided with a

Little *carbonate of soda*, which will correct the acid; a little nutmeg or powdered ginger, to take off the unpleasant taste; and, with a spoonful of brown sugar and a toast, he will make tolerably palatable that which, before, was scarcely good enough to quench the thirst.[9]

There follow several pages, and recipes, on the subject of punch, hot and cold, Sedlitz powders and tobacco. He is against the latter except, when in danger of catching the ague, 'smoking becomes not only justifiable, but sometimes necessary.' He continues:

The old sportsman then retires to his well-aired bed ... after passing a good night, he rises to breakfast. If he has brought no tea with him, he makes palatable that of the place by beating up the yoke of an egg (first with a little cold water to prevent its curdling) as a good substitute for milk or cream, a little powdered ginger, and a teaspoonful of rum. He then, previously to taking the field ... deputes a person to the cooking of that [meat] intended for himself; which if bad in quality, as will most likely be the case, there is but one good and easy way of dressing. This I shall now translate from my French recipe: *viz*. – Let your servant take

Three pounds of meat, a large carrot, two onions, and two turnips. [The Frenchman adds also a cabbage: here John Bull may please himself.] Put them into two quarts of water, to simmer away till reduced to three pints. Let him season the soup to the taste, with pepper, salt, herbs, &c. &c. He must then cut off square about a pound of the fattest part of the meat, and put it aside, letting the rest boil completely to pieces. After he has well skimmed off the fat, and strained the soup, let him put it by till wanted.

On your return, while seeing your dogs fed, which every sportsman ought to do,

Let the soup be put on the fire for twenty minutes, with some fresh vegetables (if you like to have them), and, for the last ten minutes, boil again the square piece of meat which was reserved. ...

You will then have a good wholesome gravy soup to begin with; and afterwards, some tender meat, which if

Eat with mustard, a little raw parsley chopped fine, and a few anchovies,

you will, it is presumed, find an excellent dish. A pot of anchovies might easily be carried in a portmanteau, being, of all the luxuries from an oil shop, one of the most portable and the most useful. But nothing is worse than a mock anchovy, which is merely a salted bleak, or other inferior small fish, flavoured with a little anchovy liquor. ...

Be careful to keep anchovies in a small *stone* jar; as an earthen one might break with them, and spoil your clothes.

Let me now add the simple receipt for as wholesome a mess as anyone who can 'rough it' would wish for—the dinner, of all others, for an invalid—and an alternative against starvation, where there is not even a piece of meat to be got.

Have a fowl skinned and quartered;

Put it over the fire in a quart of cold water;

Boil it *full two hours*;

Then add two ounces (or a handful) of pearl barley;

Three blades of mace; about two dozen peppercorns; and

Salt to your taste;

Then let *all* boil *together* for *one more* hour;

And it may be eat immediately; or put by, to warm again whenever you want it.

The convenience of this camp cooking is, that it will serve for any kind of fowl. For instance, if you have an old barn-door hen; old game that is shot all to pieces; two or three couple of gulls; coots; or even curlews, – by consigning them in this manner, to constant boiling and steam, you make those birds eatable and digestible, which, in roasting, or common cooking, would prove offensive in taste, and hard in substance.

N.B. – The pearl barley (or *rice*, by the way, if you prefer it) does well with all poultry, and with birds of white flesh. But with coarse birds (here we cease to have a dish for *invalids*), such as curlews, herons, gulls, or coots, it becomes necessary to omit the pearl barley; because you there require onion; fish sauce; lemon, and even a glass of Madeira, if you can get it; similar to dressing a turtle, or making giblet soup. This you would, of course, make stronger, and boil, perhaps, an hour more than chicken soup. All such messes may be eat with anchovy, curry powder, or what you may fancy, to give them an additional *goût*.

He then lists various medical preparations that should be taken, with recommendations for their use, and a final few articles desirable for comfort:

Cayenne pepper.
A pot of anchovies.
A phial of lemon acid.
A bottle of the best olive oil.

 With these ingredients, and half as much knowledge as usually belongs to all our old campaigners, he may perfectly enjoy his dinner on fish, flesh, and fowl, in those wild places where they are most abundant, but where we are the least able to have them dressed in perfection. For example; –

There is no better sauce for a wild-fowl, plover, or snipe, than *equal quantities of olive oil and lemon juice*. Cayenne pepper, when mixed with a little vinegar, gives a fine relish to a pheasant, or any other game. With good oil you can, in most places, during the fishing season, have a French salad made with the young leaves of the wild dandelion; or, in the shooting season, a German salad, called in some parts of Germany, I believe, 'kartofel salat,' with *slices of cold boiled waxy potatoes*. Either of these, with a few onions, an anchovy, and two spoonsful of oil to every one of vinegar (or *equal quantities* of each to the *German* one), make a very good salad; or, at all events, a good substitute for one, where perhaps the lettuce, cress, or endive, are scarcely known to the inhabitants. *Tarragon* vinegar, for salads, is generally preferred to the other vinegar. (Let me observe, by the way, that the chief art of dressing a salad consists in *wiping perfectly dry* whatever it is made with, and cutting off the flabby parts from the leaves of the herbs.) If you have no good butter, for your fish, you will find, that with a little cayenne, a spoonful of the liquor from your anchovies, and some lemon, or vinegar, *olive oil*, and mustard, it will be perfectly good. Nothing is better than a dish of small birds *fried*, and eat with oil and lemon juice; and if you have no good butter to fry them with, here again some *oil* must be your substitute.

If you have no biscuits to eat with your wine, or, what you may drink for want of it, cut some slices of raw potato very thin; have them broiled, or fried, brown and crisp with your oil, and sprinkled with a little cayenne pepper; but, in dressing them, let the *slices lie independent of each other*, or they will become soft by fermentation. If you wish for a hash, or anything dressed by way of variety from plain cooking, you can always give it a flavour, if you have cayenne, lemon, and anchovy.

In short, the ingredients here named, as general acquisitions to your eating in comfort, will be found, I trust, some of the most useful; and I therefore need add no more, as I neither profess, nor wish, to gratify the palate of an epicure; but have merely attempted to show, how one man could make himself comfortable, where another would starve, by the foregoing hints to young caterers and young sportsmen.[10]

These are Hawker's suggestions for making oneself comfortable in difficult conditions, but his book also includes a recipe for use in more controlled and civilized circumstances which was very well known in his day. We should not miss the opportunity of giving it here as it is now quite forgotten.

> With regard to *dressing* birds, there are so many various methods, for which every cook or epicure has his favourite receipt, that it would be absurd to enter on the subject; but as so many fail in adapting their sauces to *wild-fowl*, I shall take the liberty of giving one that has been preferred to about fifty others; and was, at one time, not to be got without the fee of a guinea.

> RECIPE FOR SAUCE TO WILDFOWL.

Port wine, or claret	1 glass.
Sauce à la Russe* (the older it is the better)	1 tablespoon.
Catsup	1 ditto.
Lemon juice	1 ditto.
Lemon peel	1 slice.
Shalot (large)	1, cut in slices.
Cayenne pepper (the darkest, not that like brickdust)	4 grains.
Mace	1 or 2 blades.

> To be scalded, strained, and added to the mere gravy, which comes from the bird in roasting.
> To *complete* this, the fowl should be cut up in a silver dish, that has a lamp under, while the sauce is simmering with it.
> Let a goose, or any strong or fat wild-fowl, be roasted with the addition of a small onion, and a *pared* lemon, in the inside; as this will draw out the strong fat, and give the bird a milder taste.

> Water-birds, in order to be less susceptible of cold, are, by nature, of a warmer temperament than land-birds. This may be proved by cookery: – for instance, a common fowl to be roasted, or boiled, will require three-quarters of an hour; whereas a tame duck, of equal size, will be done in half an hour.† This is an observation worthy of notice for the naturalist, the sportsman, and the cook.
> * Introduced by the late Mr. Aveling, in Albemarle Street, and now sold there by his successors.
> † Vide an admirable little book on plain cookery, with valuable receipts and good

advice on other things, written by Mrs. Childe, in America, and called the 'Frugal Housewife,' and which every campaigner, or sportsman, should have in his possession.

We have been studying Colonel Hawker in the environment where he is most famous and to which he was perhaps the most passionately attached, and where his gastronomic taste may seem very modern and indeed often almost in line with today's fashions. However he was equally at home in the great world of English society and we will close this paper with a glimpse of his opinions about French cuisine of the period. He is comparing aspects of life in Paris with his experiences ten years earlier.

August 17th 1828
The cooking is much the same – most exquisite for those who like made dishes, and prefer messes of butter, sugar, and Lord knows what to plain, wholesome food. Our English sauces – cayenne &c. – may now be had, if called for, at most of the *restaurateurs*'. The wines are decidedly not so good as in former times, and you have still the same difficulty in getting a good-sized glass to drink out of at your dinner. There are, however, some English people who have set up soda and ginger-beer shops, so that, by going to them, you have now the means of quenching that insufferable thirst which is produced by the greasy, sugary, salt, and acid mixtures, that the French dishes abound with, not to say a word of the tricks that are now played as to meat, wines, and spirits.

… Tortoni's still the best ice shop, and Véry's (in the Palais Royal) now become the best *restaurateur's* in Paris. Formally I thought it about the third best.[11]

BIBLIOGRAPHY

Hawker, Peter, *Journal of a regimental officer during the recent campaign in Portugal and Spain under Lord Viscount Wellington; with a correct plan of the battle of Talavera*, 1810, J. Johnson, St. Paul's Churchyard. Facsimile, 1981, Ken Trotman.

—— *Instructions to Young Sportsmen in all that relates to Guns and Shooting*. Many editions from 1814 to 1922. The quotations are from the 9th edition, 'corrected, enlarged, and improved', Longman, Brown, Green, and Longmans, 1844. This is the last one worked on by Hawker. The relevant parts are unaltered in a 1922 edition, ed. Eric Parker, pub. Herbert Jenkins Ltd.

—— *The Diary of Colonel Peter Hawker, 1802–1853*, 2 volumes, Longmans, Greene, and Co.,

1893. This is not the complete diary, but a very substantial part of it. The shooting aspect is stressed, and fascinating it is, but it would be interesting to know what the rest covers. I don't know if the original manuscript exists. A facsimile of the above was published by Greenhill Books in 1988.

—— *Instructions for the best Position on the Pianoforte*. I have not seen a copy of this work.

NOTES

[1] *Instructions*, 524.
[2] *Diary*, I–72.
[3] He describes his experiences in Portugal and Spain in *Journal*.
[4] *Diary*, I–28.
[5] *Diary*, I–71.
[6] *Diary*, I–49.
[7] *Diary*, I–149/50.
[8] All the quotations from here until the bottom of page 5 are from *Instructions*, 524 et seq.
[9] The varying sizes of print in the quotations from *Instructions* are as in the original.
[10] This is the end of the quotations from the chapter of 'General Advice' in *Instructions*.
[11] *Diary*, I–337.

Charles Fourier (1772–1837) and the Phalansterian Banquet

Bee Wilson

There are many things that you might associate with the idea of a 'socialist meal', but probably not this.

It is dinner time. You arrive on foot, walking through the comfort of a covered gallery, keeping you warm and dry in case of rain. You are seated among an assortment of convivial companions. Everyone seems interested in everyone else: some professionally, some in a familial way, some amorously. Conversation flows merrily and easily. No one feels obliged to make smalltalk. There are no bores and no marital squabblers. You are surrounded by architecture of elegant simplicity. Even if the food were terrible, the meal would be a success. But in fact, there is an astonishing variety of dishes and all of them delicious: not just one but twelve different soups, so that if you are someone who happens to love consommé but hate minestrone, you will be provided for. Even if you are very poor, you will be able to choose from a selection of three dozen dishes; if you are rich, there will be many hundreds of magnificent things to choose from. All the meat comes from well-husbanded animals, and every last scrap of flesh is exquisitely prepared, yet no one has to eat it up out of duty. There are dishes tailored to exactly your temperament and the wines have been modified exactly to the dishes. No one expects you to eat anything which gives you displeasure. Your love of plums and your dislike of leeks have already been anticipated and catered for. What's more, everything seems easily digestible. You eat pastry after delicate pastry for dessert, each one lighter and more buttery than anything you could find in the finest *pâtisseries* of Paris, and bowlful after bowlful of fragrant compotes, yet miraculously your stomach feels none the worse for it. You retire, happily, to see the best theatrical show ever staged, and, if you like, to be paired up with the lover of your dreams.

This is the sort of meal you would enjoy every day of your life, five times a day, if only it were possible to live in the future state of Harmony, as envisaged by the early French socialist François Marie Charles Fourier (1772–1837), who saw meals as an essential – if not the essential – component of human happiness. Harmony was the future state in which humans were destined to live, where every passion, however trifling – a love of bergamot pears or a penchant for having your heels tickled – would be encouraged and fulfilled. In Fourier's theory, passions would achieve fulfilment not in families (too small) or nation states (too big) but in modestly-sized social units known as 'phalansteries'. 'Civilization' was the current era, merely a passing phase, in which the majority of human passions were thwarted, and people lived in a contradictory state of commerce, waste, repression, hypocrisy, war and lies.

Charles Fourier has been described as 'the nineteenth-century's complete utopian'.[2] He is usually bracketed with Robert Owen and Henri, comte de Saint-Simon as one of the three founding fathers of modern socialism (though Fourier himself frequently denounced Owen and Saint-Simon as charlatans).[3] Marx damned him with faint praise as a 'critical utopian socialist' stuck in an unscientific mindset; Engels praised him as 'one of the greatest satirists of all time'; Dostoevsky saw him as a visionary.[4] Modern critics often try to fillet Fourier's theory for the saner and more prophetic bits: for example, his advocacy of the right to work, his satires on the hypocrisy of modern life, his belief that the state of women was an index of all social progress, or his prediction that the globe would one day warm up. But to read these bits in isolation is to miss the point of Fourier. For his was a total theory of everything, a complete theodicy, in which all that was bad or superfluous would one day be put to use: lions would turn into friendly anti-lions, the sea would become a drinkable lemonade-like substance and cooking, instead of being an occupation which consumed the lives of miserable housewives in the pointless and laborious skimming of mediocre stocks, would be recognized as the most important science of all, and the first thing taught to children in schools. (The French literary critic, Ernest Seillière, once argued that there has never existed a man of such fame and influence who was more clearly or more obviously mad than Fourier.)[5]

Fourier was related by marriage to Brillat-Savarin, author of *La Physiologie du goût*, with whom he had travelled to Paris on his first visit as a young man.[6] So far from admiring Brillat-Savarin, however, Fourier attacked him as a 'simplist', who never learned the 'art of combining the refinements of consumption and preparation with rivalries and hygienic methods'.[7] Fourier did much of his thinking and writing during the Napoleonic period, when former chefs of the aristocracy were finding work in the newly proliferating restaurants of Paris, when Grimod de la Reynière was publishing his *Almanach des gourmands*, and gastronomic writing was crystallizing into a kind of science – from gastromania to gastronomy as Rebecca Spang has recently put it.[8] But, to Fourier, all previous gastronomes were nothing but 'gastro-idiots', who had neglected the essential components of their own subject. Grimod de la Reynière and Joseph

Berchoux, the latter the author of a famous poem entitled *La Gastronomie* published in 1801,[9] were like all the other Apiciuses of the day, in that their entire knowledge consisted of 'working the jaws' or seeking out 'the secret of Vitellus, the art of eating a lot'.[10] They knew nothing of the complexity of the science of taste. For this reason, Fourier disdained even the name 'gastronomy' – a superficial science – and instead invented his own science of 'gastrosophy' or the art of refined gluttony, which would show up the simplistic understanding of earlier so-called 'gastronomes'.

Gastrosophy consisted of five components: 1) agriculture 2) preservation 3) cooking 4) gastronomy and a fifth element entitled, in the kind of jargon that was typical for Fourier, 'hygiene in equilibrium'.[11] Gastrosophy entailed the understanding, in combination, of all five components. The practice of gastrosophy depended in turn on Fourier's conception of human personality. Having witnessed the destructive and bloody consequences of 'liberty, equality and fraternity' during the French Revolution, Fourier was violently opposed to all theories of equality, especially those which tried to fashion any sort of universal human nature. For Fourier, equality was both a nonsense and a poison, because advocates of equality tried to damp down the huge variety of human temperament, resulting in damaging forms of repression. According to Fourier's new science of 'passionate attraction', there were not one but 810 basic human temperaments. He attacked the current state of 'Civilization' for failing to realize this. Only in the future state of 'Harmony' would human passions achieve their full expression. The ideal social unit would be one of approximately 1620 individuals (one of each temperament of each sex), organized in a non-coercive social system known as a 'phalanstery'. Therefore, the science of 'gastrosophy', rather than pronouncing on the finest culinary achievements in an abstract way, depended on the art of adapting the act of feeding to these 810 different temperaments.

Fourier, with his own mania for classification, also divided the science of gastrosophy into three branches, each of which affected the organization of meals in the phalanstery.[12] First there was practical gastrosophy or cooking according to temperament. The preparation of food in Harmony involved the linking up of production and consumption. Work, such as fruit-growing, would take place in organizations known as 'series' in which tasks would be precisely coordinated with passions. His most famous example was the pear-grower's series, which consisted of seven unequal groups, ranging from quince-growers at the hard end to medlar-growers at the soft end, with juicy pears, the most popular choice, in the middle.[13] If you were passionate about crisp pears, you would both grow them and eat them; and no one would ever force you to try russets or floury pears. Fourier believed that the universe was founded on the principle of analogy, and that there was a natural correspondence between human tastes and the raw materials of the globe.[14] Fourier admired those with particularly striking food passions, such as a nine-year-old girl he had met who enjoyed eating whole bulbs of garlic, or a little boy who adored green pippins but couldn't abide yellow. Such people were vivid proof that people needed to be fed in varied and immoderate ways. And in Harmony, Fourier argued, because passions corresponded with the raw materials of the universe, it 'would cost less to serve 30 sorts of bread, 30 sorts of soup, 30 sorts of ragout, of roasts and of wine, than to serve a single sort; because in work done by a series of 30 graduated and contrasted groups, the result will be graduated and contrasted products, like the 30 sorts of bread or soup, which will need to be eaten in the same order'.[15]

Next there was theoretical gastrosophy, including the fact of 'accelerated digestion' which meant that people in Harmony would be able to eat five – or even nine[16] – ample meals a day without any ill-effects. Fourier lived through an era of upheaval in mealtimes in France, when the standard time for eating main meals got ever later and when restaurants enabled people to flout standard mealtimes altogether if they liked and eat as often as they could afford. Fourier's timetables for meals in Harmony reflected both these facts. His schedule for a typical poor person in Harmony included 'déjeuner' at 7, 'dîner' at 1 and 'souper' at 8.30.[17] For a rich person, there would also be 'délité' at 4.30 in the morning (another side-effect of living in Harmony would be a huge reduction in the amount of sleep one needed) and 'goûter' at 6, with 'souper' half an hour later than for the poor, at 9.[18] There would also be a great number of snacks eaten on the move while at work in Harmony's many, constantly shifting activities. Fourier's conception of happiness – having a lot of passions, and the means to satisfy them – depended on the constant reignition of appetite.[19] In Harmony, 'even after a big meal, easily enough to satisfy us, we will rediscover an appetite at dessert for sweetmeats and so on.'[20] Fourier's theory of accelerated digestion was linked to his certainty of the superiority of sugar over bread. Like Marinetti, Fourier was an implacable opponent of pasta and stodge. (Though Fourier would have recoiled from Marinetti's supermasculine agenda; he was a staunch advocate of the liberation of women, especially lesbians, whose cause he saw it as his mission to promote.) He was convinced that the fact that nature had given children a taste for sugary things such as 'jam, sweetened cream, lemonade etc.' showed that it must be our destiny to eat these foods in abundance in the future.[21] Once the 'torrid zone' had been brought under cultivation in accordance with Fourier's agricultural predictions, the finest sugar would cost no more than wheat flour.[22] 'Consequently, the poorest children everywhere will find their tables loaded with the sugared dairy-products and candied fruits they are so fond of, and which seem to be harmful to their temperament because we cannot provide them with the acidic drinks which would counteract the vermicular influence of these substances. But as soon as the torrid zone is cultivated, lemonade and other costly drinks will be as plentiful as small beer and cider are now. Lemons in the torrid zone, and pippins in the temperate zone, will be so abundant that their only cost will be transport.'[23] Moreover, meals founded on sugar would be much more digestible, Fourier believed, than those founded on bread: the fact that people ate dessert at the end of big meals proved that sweet things acted as digestifs.[24] Therefore, the staple food of Europe would no longer be bread but a mixture of fruit and sugar called Harmony bread.[25] (What about tooth decay? Fourier naturally had an answer: teeth would become replaceable, once people were living in Harmony.)

The final branch of gastrosophy was 'mixed gastrosophy' or the direction of the first two branches and, therefore, the knowledge of the 810 temperaments and the proportions of every product cooked. The true 'gastrosophe' would understand that the excellence of a meal did not depend on the excellence of dishes in themselves, but on matching them correctly to the passions of those eating them. At its most accessible level, gastrosophy ordained that a successful meal was not just a question of 'working the jaws' (although even on this level, most civilized meals fell short). In his first book, *La Théorie des Quatre Mouvements,* Fourier expressed this in particularly dramatic terms:

> The material pleasures that I describe are insufficient in themselves; it is not enough for the poorest among you to have a table better provisioned with food and drink than the richest of kings. The well-being that this provides, however real, will only ensure half the pleasures of the table. For although good food provides the basis, there is another no less essential condition, the judicious mix of fellow-diners, the art of varying and matching the parties, making them more interesting each day by creating delightful and unexpected encounters, assuring even the poorest people of spiritual pleasures which are never to be had in your normal household gloom. On this point, your Civilization is completely absurd. Your costly gatherings and your most celebrated banquets are generally so badly arranged and the guests so ill-matched that everyone would die of boredom if it were not for the food. But food alone is a boorish pleasure, and perhaps not even that; for peasants are jovial and lively enough in their taverns, enjoying the pleasures of the senses and the spirit together, whereas people have to yawn away a solid hour waiting in a fashionable drawing room for their dinner. And

oh! how dearly you have to pay for the dinner with the boredom of keeping up faltering discussions about rain and good weather, the health of friends and relations, the progress of the worthy children of virtuous fathers, the good behaviour of daughters, the kind nature of aunts, and the tender sentiments of tender dispositions. What a deluge of insipid nonsense you get at these civilized gatherings, even though no expense has been spared in their preparation and in the outlay on good food! The whole occasion is as tedious for the guests as it is for the mistress of the house, who has all the trouble of arranging and preparing it. How on earth can civilized people dare to lay claim to gastronomic excellence when they know nothing of the art of organizing the stimulating and varied parties which constitute half the pleasure of the table! It seems that on this point kings are even worse off then their subjects, as isolated as hermits and as solemn as owls throughout their meals, thus demonstrating that at table, as elsewhere, the pleasures of the most powerful kings are inferior to those the poorest of his subjects will enjoy in the combined order. Added to which, the sovereign must think himself lucky if, amidst the isolation and gloom of his meals, he can forget the ever-present threat of being poisoned. Oh, how vain are the pleasures of Civilization![26]

Fourier was admiring, like many others in the early nineteenth century, of the 'economical soup' invented by Benjamin Count Rumford (1735–1814), the inspiration behind many subsequent soup kitchens.[27] But while he admired Rumford's concern with efficiency in cooking, and with the problem of feeding many people all at once, Fourier did not share his solution to communal dining. Fourier was a socialist but not a communist. Perhaps scarred by his years of eating *table d'hôte* as a *commis voyageur*, Fourier shunned any sort of eating arrangement where everyone had to eat the same thing. 'Listen at table to some civilized men expressing different tastes about an unimportant matter, an omelette: a sage will believe that he is pronouncing philosophically, in saying that all omelettes are equal in rights, and that one should eat without discrimination all that are presented to us.'[28] Such obtuse belief in uniformity had no place at Fourier's ideal table. Omelettes were not all born equal. He was fond of quoting the popular German dramatist, August von Kotzebue, who said that the *traiteurs* of Paris knew how to cook eggs in 42 different ways.[29] But Fourier himself went much much further. For the purposes of the 'harmonization' of the passion for omelettes, it was necessary to open them up to 810 paths of development, by 'a classification of 810 varieties applied to the same number of temperaments, and adopted by a Sanhedrin, who would theoretically transmit to all the empires of the globe the rules for making the 810 omelettes'.³⁰ The omelettes would then be made by special omelette-legionnaires.

When problems arose, they would be decided by peaceful battles. For example, if ever a soufflé-omelette should disagree with those of a certain temperament, people would stage a 'battle of soufflé-omelettes' between armies of different empires, to decide the correct new formula.³¹ Fourier's gastrosophic battles were like a grandiose version of Grimod's *jurys des dégustateurs*. There would be international battles of pastries and of sweet creams, with armies of chefs gathered on great concourses in giant cook-offs to decide the finest recipes in the world. To those who thought that such battles were puerile, Fourier replied that they were no more 'ridiculous than our wars of Religion, on Transubstantation and other quarrels of the same value, which are hardly worth the torrents of blood which they cause to be spilled.'³²

Equally serious was the problem of repugnance certain people felt for certain foods. Fourier gave himself as an example:

> In a series of 30 different kinds of soup, 27 of them will often excite repugnance in a single man. Just speaking for myself I can cite 27 kinds of soup which disgust me. Barley makes me vomit, the pastas and vermicellis of Italy make me feel as sick as if they were wallpaper paste, soup made from root vegetables sets me against beautiful moral antiquity;³³ I loathe soup with cheese, and soups with cabbage, carrots and parsnips, and even onions, if you don't separate out the onions, which I can't swallow. I hate all soups containing dairy products, which make me ill; I fear all the insipid potages of Germany, whose name I have never asked for, because I am disgusted by them all; I even fear acidulated bouillons with celery and with saffron; and as for garlic soups, the *bourrides* and *bouillabaisses* of the Midi, I send them to the Devil with an easy heart. However, I am a great eater of soup. Eh! of what kind, then? Of soups of bread and of rice, so long as this is neither rice with water nor rice with milk, nor soups of softened bread.³⁴

Fourier's ideal banquets were communal without being at all communist. This is best illustrated by his descriptions of an ideal *pot-au-feu*. In the state of Civilization, the *pot-au-feu* was Fourier's favourite image of the oppression of women in the 'egoistical' patriarchal household. The *pot-au-feu* chained women to a stockpot which required constant skimming, but which most of them had no interest or talent in skimming anyway, thus producing very inferior bouillons for their virtuous republican husbands.³⁵ Women got no rewards for their labours nor yet did the men benefit from keeping their wives chained inefficiently in 'incoherent little households'. The only social purpose of the *pot-au-feu* was a negative one, in that it acted as a bar against adultery because women were so busy skimming they had no time for extramarital liaisons.

In Harmony, however, the *pot-au-feu* could become a truly great meal, serving the interests of rich and poor, men and women, though in a carefully nuanced rather than an equal fashion. If 800 people were living together harmoniously, instead of going individually to butchers to buy their meat, a very wasteful and expensive process, they could band together and buy and butcher an entire cow.[36] All three classes of society (100 of the first class, 200 of the second and 400 of the third, plus 100 children) had an interest in the beef being good. The bouillon produced would be better than anything even the most gifted individual cook could produce in Civilization. The third class would not eat the choicest fillets of the beef 'but the portions allotted to the tables of the 3rd class will be good, if the beast is good; and if it is of poor quality, the fine morsels allotted to the tables of the 1st class will be dry, stringy, etc. It is therefore in the interests of the rich as much as the poor that the animals purchased…should be of good quality; there will be on this point a coincidence of interests between the 3 classes, a REAL fraternity, not a DREAMED one, like those of our moral and political treatises.'[37] Fourier's ideal *pot-au-feu* was a vision of a society in which no one would eat well unless everyone ate well.

Not only would the Harmonian *pot-au-feu* provide a delicious meal, it was also a possible route to glory, for women as well as men. Great stew-makers and soup-makers would be recognized in Harmony and given large amounts of money, titles of sovereignty and, in exceptional cases, even sainthood. Fourier gives the imaginary example of Dorimène, a great 'potagist' whose talents might win her the title of 'culinary magnate of the globe' and a prize, pooled from all the phalansteries, of 1,500,000 francs, as well as a jewel-encrusted decoration depicting the vessel for making *pot-au-feu*. 'In this way the *pot*, by itself, can open up to housewives the route to immortality: the name and the triumph of Dorimène will ring out in the whole universe, and the *pot*, in her hands, will glitter with all the brilliance of a daystar.'[38] No one would begrudge Dorimène her prize, moreover, because Harmonians fully realized what a complex science soup-making was, comprising nine different branches of knowledge: '1. Fires tailored to each bouillon. 2. Ditto the various things to be cooked in the bouillon. 3. The choice of vegetables and purées. 4. Ditto the quality of bread. 5. Ditto the quality of serving vessels. 6. Additions, *coulis*, liquids. 7. Flavourings. 8. Rice and cereals. 9. Doughs for disguising bad bouillons.'[39] Most civilized housewives had not mastered a quarter of these branches of knowledge, because the civilized did not see what an opportunity mealtimes provided for harmless rivalry and competition.

Fourier's ideal meal is ultimately both a deeply serious and an entirely playful affair. It might look as if he were turning the world upside-down with his carnivalesque dreams, but Fourier would reply that, to the contrary, it was the existing world of Civilization which was the wrong way round.[40] It was our destiny, he thought, never to go hungry, never to dine monotonously and alone on heavy bread and badly-made soups, but to enjoy intensely varied, sugar-laden and sociable banquets every day of our lives. If only he were right.

NOTES

[1] Good general secondary works on Fourier and food include: Rolande Bonnain Moerdyck, 'Fourier gastrosophe', in Henri Lefebvre et al., *Actualité de Fourier,* Paris, 1975; Michel Onfray, 'Fourier' in *Le ventre des philosophes,* Paris: Bernard Grasset, 1989.

[2] Jonathan Beecher, *Charles Fourier: The Visionary and His World,* Berkeley: University of California Press, 1986, p. 1.

[3] See, e.g., *Pièges et charlatanismes des deux sectes Saint-Simon et Owen...,* Paris: Bossange, 1831.

[4] Karl Marx, *Selected Writings,* edited David McLellan, Oxford University Press, 1977, pp. 243–4; Frederick Engels, *Socialism Utopian and Scientific,* Peking: Foreign Languages Press, 1975, p. 55; Dostoevsky, *The Diary of Writer,* translated by Boris Brasol, 2 vols, New York, I, p. 7.

[5] Ernest Seillière, *La philosophie de l'imperialisme,* vol IV, *Le mal romantique,* Paris: Librarie Plon, 1908, p. 3.

[6] Charles Pellarin, *The Life of Charles Fourier,* translated from the French, New York, 1848 p. 120; Beecher, op. cit., p. 33.

[7] Charles Fourier, *Oeuvres complètes* (Paris, anthropos, 1967), VIII p. 283 [henceforth cited as *OC*]. Fourier did not allow for the complexity of 'gastronomy' as defined by Brillat-Savarin, which takes in physics, natural history, commerce, chemistry and political economy as well as cooking (Brillat-Savarin, *La Physiologie du goût,* Paris, 1825, chapter 3) though he was right that Brillat-Savarin laid much less weight than he, Fourier, on hygiene and temperament.

[8] Rebecca Spang, *The Invention of the Restaurant: Paris and Modern Gastronomic Culture,* Cambridge MA: Harvard University Press, 2000, chapter 6; Grimod de la Reynière, *Almanach des gourmands* (1803–1810); Jean-Paul Aron, *Le Mangeur du XIXe siècle,* Paris, 1973; Stephen Mennell, *All Manners of Food: Eating and Taste in England and France from the Middle Ages to the Present,* Oxford: Blackwell, 1985, especially chapter 6.

[9] Joseph Berchoux, *La Gastronomie, ou l'Homme des champs à table,* Paris, 1801.

[10] *OC* VI pp. 155, 259; *OC* VII p. 127.

[11] *OC* V p. 104. Elsewhere (*OC* VI p. 258), Fourier omitted this fifth element.

[12] *OC* VII p. 126.

[13] Charles Fourier, *The Theory of the Four Movements,* translated by Ian Paterson with introduction by Gareth Stedman Jones, Cambridge University Press, 1996, pp. 290–2.

[14] *OC* VII p. 128.

[15] *OC* X (PM 2) p. 161. It has been remarked, for example by Seillière that Fourier fell into the fallacy of believing that what people enjoy eating they must also enjoy consuming.
[16] *OC* VII p. 134.
[17] *OC* VI p. 67.
[18] Ibid. p. 68.
[19] This is a theme in Roland Barthes's essay on Fourier, 'Fourier', in *A Roland Barthes Reader*, edited by Susan Sontag, London, Vintage, 1993.
[20] *OC* VII p. 134.
[21] Charles Fourier, *Theory*, p. 166.
[22] Ibid., p. 165.
[23] Idem.
[24] *OC* VII p. 134.
[25] Beecher, op. cit. p. 252.
[26] Fourier, *Theory*, pp. 168–169.
[27] See, e.g. Fourier, *Theory*, p. 315. On Rumford as a source for Fourier, see also Hubert Bourgin, *Fourier. Contribution à l'étude du socialisme français,* Paris: Société Nouvelle de Librairie et d'Edition, 1905, p. 122.
[28] *OC* V p. 360.
[29] *OC* VI p. 138; *OC* X (PM2), 'L'opéra et la cuisine'.
[30] *OC* V pp. 360–361.
[31] Idem.
[32] *OC* VII p. 346.
[33] One of Fourier's recurring themes, which he gnawed at like a dog with a bone, was the attachment of ancient republicans and their modern champions to the idea that bad food was morally purifying; that Spartan black broth, dry bread and the radishes of Cincinnattus were somehow good for you. Fourier believed that both republicanism and black broth were very unhealthy things.
[34] *OC* X (PM2) p. 166.
[35] See, e.g., *OC* IX pp. 572–573.
[36] Archives Nationales, Paris, Fonds Fourier, 10 AS 17 (Microfilm 681 MI 27), last dossier.
[37] Idem.
[38] *OC* IX p. 573. Cf. *OC* V pp. 358–359.
[39] *OC* IX p. 574.
[40] The phrase he used was 'le monde à rebours'.

Drink in the Structure of the Meal: Middle Eastern Patterns

Sami Zubaida

Alcoholic drink features in the structure of the meal in many parts of Europe. Wine, for instance, plays a central part in the structure of the 'classic' meal of the prosperous classes in Latin Europe (France, Italy and the Iberian countries), and indeed as an accompaniment to the meals of the common people in certain periods. Beer plays a lesser part in meals of northern Europe, being drunk often outside mealtimes. The Middle East presents a contrast to this pattern, with alcoholic drink largely absent from accounts of meals, high and low. The prohibition of alcohol in Islam may be cited as a reason for this absence. Yet alcohol was, and remains, prevalent in the region. Anyone familiar with the poesy of the region, for instance, will know the extensive literature on the pleasures of wine, and the *belles-lettres* are equally eloquent on tales of drink. Drink, however, does not feature systematically in accounts of meals. In this paper, I shall explore patterns of eating and drinking on the two sides of the Mediterranean, and their consequences for modes of sociability.

Mubadele: *the exchange of ambassadors*
The history of the exchange of ambassadors between the Ottoman and the French courts in the eighteenth century provides an interesting illustration of contrast in modes of formal eating. Fatma Muge Gocek, *East Encounters West: France and the Ottoman Empire in the Eighteenth Century* (OUP 1987), narrates this history. The French ambassador reported that as part of the formalities of presentation at court, he was invited to take a meal with the courtiers:

> The Ottoman officials all sat on the sofas around the room with the Grand Vezir at the center. The Grand Vezir usually had two translators on either side and the ambassador in front of him. The ambassador and his small retinue, all across from the sofa, were seated on small stools around the small low tables. This style of eating in small groups around tables emphasized the privacy the Ottomans attached to eating. The meal consisted of numerous courses rapidly served. (p. 37)

The whole affair was over within the hour. Fast-food has a long historical ancestry!

The story from the Ottoman ambassador, one Yermisekiz Celebi Mehmed Effendi (a notable figure of wit and intrigue), was quite different. He took to French courtly and aristocratic life with curiosity and pleasure. He marvelled at the leisurely dinners, well irrigated with wine and animated by conversation, wit and flirtation. It was the presence and the leading role of women on these occasions which most intrigued Mehmed Effendi, and his gallantry was much favoured by the ladies. He did not drink wine in public, but had taken to champagne (coming into fashion at that point in the early eighteenth century) in private gatherings.

Patterns and sequences of food and drink

These are clearly totally different conceptions of a meal. I must hasten to add that the French ambassador's experience of the sullen meal was not the general norm of the Ottoman court. We also have accounts of leisurely banquets with wit and conversation, but usually between intimates, and the ambassador did not count as such. Most of this conviviality, however, was likely to have centred around the wine table, and the wine table was often distinct from the meal, though timed with reference to it. We may note parallels between this pattern and the ancient Greek symposium in which the symposium, centred around wine and conversation, always followed the meal. Middle Eastern cultures, however, did not feature any of the formality and organization of the symposium. Many narratives and accounts, including the tales of *The Thousand and One Nights*, seem to indicate that the wine table was set up after the meal was cleared away. There are other accounts, however, which suggest drink before or with the meal, as advised by doctors. There doesn't seem to have been a systematic connection between the two in terms of aesthetics or manners. Accounts of banquets rarely feature wine and accounts of drinking are centred around music and song, and the beauty and charm of the maids and boys who served the wine and entertained the company: food doesn't get a mention. Exceptions are to be found in the medical literature which connected wine to food in terms of humours and digestion. David Waines ('Abu Zayd al-Balkhi on the Nature of Forbidden Drink: A Medieval Islamic Controversy', in Manuela Marin and David Waines eds, *La Alimentación en las Culturas Islamicas*, Madrid 1994) quotes a medieval medical treatise on the virtues of wine, one of which is facilitating conviviality:

> Speaking from personal experience, he [Al-Balkhi] notes that on the occasion of small or large invitations where food is served but there is

no *sharab* [wine] available, the guests quickly depart once the food is finished excusing themselves to attend to other matters. The presence of drink, however, has the opposite effect. It acts as a bond among the guests preventing their departure until the real pleasures of such gatherings, discussion and listening, occur and an atmosphere of sociability and pleasure prevails. (p. 116)

Plus ça change …!
The vast literature, especially poetry, on wine in Arabic (known as *khamriyat*), Persian and Turkish, ranges over themes of intoxication, song, love and eroticism – mostly the charms of the *saqi*, the server of wine. It also features religious themes of sufi mysticism, playing on divine and earthly love, and intoxication as religious ecstasy. There is also an occasional sufi theme of addressing God as a friend and companion, and in the poetry of Omar Khayam this extends to reproaching the Lord for making the world a place of sin! Food, if mentioned at all in this literature, is only a metaphor. There is also in Arabic a considerable literature on food and banquets and recipes, one that equally excludes mention of wine. There is the famous banquet of the Caliph Mustakfi (d. 946), narrated in Mas'udi's *Muruj al-Dhahab* (Meadows of Gold) and quoted at length by Arberry (included in *Medieval Arab Cookery*, Prospect Books 2001). At this banquet, the Caliph asked each participant to recite a poem on the virtues of a particular dish or item of food, at the conclusion of which recitation the item in question was brought to table. Many flowery and ornamental verses were proclaimed, among which there is hardly any mention of wine, except rarely as a metaphor for some excellent quality of the food item.

We find accounts of drinking cultures at the lower level of society. Typically, we have anecdotes and amusing stories of low-life characters in the *Maqamat* genre of *belles-lettres*. Charles Perry introduced and translated 'The Wine Maqama by Badi' al-Zaman al-Hamadhani' (in *Medieval Arab Cookery*, as above). Amusement is procured from the theme of hypocrisy of rogues who pretend religion but partake of the pleasures of wine to excess. And there are many more such stories, at all levels of society, including many drinking tales featuring judges or religious scholars. There are also stories in this kind of literature about food, banquets, gatecrashers, parasites and misers. These, however, are separate from stories of wine. The savants of the Middle East clearly thought of food and wine in two separate registers.

Drink and the Table in the Modern Period
E. W. Lane (*Manners and Customs of the Modern Egyptians*, first published 1836, The Hague and London 1978) writing in the early nineteenth century, devotes

a mere paragraph to the drinking habits of prosperous Egyptians. Himself a teetotaller, he was never invited to drinking occasions, but learnt about them from reports. He noted that in the tales of *The Thousand and One Nights* the table of viands is removed, to be followed by the table of wine (p. 153). Contemporary Egyptians, though generally abstemious, included many who 'habitually indulge in drinking wine with select parties of their acquaintance' (which did not include Lane). He continued that drinking wine 'was indulged in by such persons before and after supper, and during the meal; but it is most approved *before* supper, as they say that it quickens the appetite.' (p. 153) He went on to describe the wine-table, set with cut-glass jugs of wine, water and perfumes, with a vase of flowers, with saucers of dried fruit and pickles. This latter suggests the *mezze* genre, which was to predominate in modern times.

Mezze, *Drink and the Meal*

The concept of *mezze* (Greek *mezedes*) seems to be a general Mediterranean phenomenon of offering a range of small dishes, mostly savoury but also sweet, to accompany drink. In North Africa it is *kemya* and in Spain *tapas* (though tapas seems to differ in that it is often a small portion of a cooked dish, but that overlaps with mezze). The word 'mezze' is the Persian for 'taste', though not normally used in Iran in the sense of accompaniment of drink. The common translation of 'mezze' as 'hors d'oeuvre' is not accurate: while 'hors d'oeuvre' relates to a particular concept of the meal with a number of courses or services, 'mezze' does not refer to a meal, but is intrinsically linked to drink, at any time.

It is difficult to trace the origin and development of the concept and practice of mezze. Of course, serving little tastes with drink is not remarkable or peculiar and must have been common practice in many drinking cultures, as illustrated by Lane's account, above. What is specific, however, is the institution of mezze as a genre of dishes, with particular repertoires and sequences, and especially in public drinking-places. This practice appears to have been established primarily in Mediterranean cities with prominent Christian populations, notably Istanbul and the Aegean cities, as well as the main cities of Lebanon, Palestine and Syria. It is in these cities that venues of public drinking were established in the modern period (i.e. from the later nineteenth century) which were 'civilized' centres of sociability and leisure, as against the rough taverns prevalent throughout the region.

Throughout Islamic history, and especially in the later centuries, it was Christians and Jews who were primarily involved in the making, distribution and serving of alcoholic drink. (Jews were also prominent practitioners of the musical arts and entertainment, which often went with drink.) Historically, the prosperous strata did not drink in wine-shops and taverns, but in private spaces behind closed doors. The taverns were frequented by poorer people, including rough elements such as soldiers, *ashqiya* and *lutis* (genres of popular 'tough guys'). What emerges in the modern period is public drinking venues for the middle classes (primarily the male of the species). These were known by various designations: *maykhana/meyhana*, the old word for a tavern, *qahwa* or *maqha*, café, and with entertainment, *casino/gasino*, or the Arabic *malha*. In Istanbul and other Turkish cities during the earlier parts of the twentieth century these were primarily owned and run by Armenians and Greeks, and a few remain so to the present day. In Syria/Lebanon it was primarily the Arab Christians. It was primarily in these establishments that the conventions and repertoires of mezze and drink were established, drawing on different food traditions, some popular/domestic (foul, falafel, hummus, etc. in the Arab lands; dolma, fava, barbounya, pasturma in Istanbul). Add specific ethnic foods (bearing in mind that Greek and Armenian cultures in Istanbul were often distinct from mainland Greece and Armenia proper) such as the Armenian *topig* and numerous Greek fish preparations, as well as adaptations from European food such as 'Russian salad'.

This pattern of food and drink had a 'civilizing' effect on both activities. Typically in Middle Eastern cultures, people eat quickly. You have the original fast-foods in markets and food shops of kebabs, kebbes and pastries. But even elaborate dishes prepared with much labour for special occasions are devoured in minutes, much like the experience of the French ambassador in the Ottoman court noted above. The drink/mezze pattern represents an important departure, in that food is consumed at a leisurely pace, with conversation and entertainment. However, mezze was not the meal: how did it relate to the meal?

As already noted, the mezze concept is intrinsically coupled with drink. In practice, a long evening of drink and mezze was concluded with a quick supper. When drinking out, the supper could be provided in the same establishment, ordered from a nearby food stall to consume in the café/bar, or taken somewhere else altogether. There was, for instance, the tradition in many cities of concluding an evening of extensive drinking at a tripe-joint in the early hours. The drink/mezze pattern also penetrated the home entertainments of the more prosperous and 'modern' urban classes (in this respect it may be seen as a continuity with the wine-table pattern). Many of us experienced this home entertainment in which the guests arrive at eight, to be seated in the drawing-room with little tables set with varieties of nuts, fruit, cucumber and lettuce, and drinks are served (often soft drinks for the ladies and children and heavily diluted whisky/soda, Black Label for preference, to the men). Conversation, card-games and television coexist, and the drinking and increasingly urgent munching of the hungry continue until about eleven o'clock, at which point an elaborate meal of many sumptuous and labour-intensive dishes is served. The hungry guests crowd around the table, mostly standing, and eat at a fair pace, to conclude in half an hour or so, after which everyone goes home.

The emerging pattern in more recent times is for the mezze in public establishments to become the meal. This kind of meal becomes more 'civilized', with leisurely eating and drinking, which becomes a night-out in its own right, much like the restaurant meal of Latin Europe (and which probably also had its origins in the tavern), now generalized world-wide. The mezze meal pattern is also now 'globalized' by the prevalence of Arab, Greek and Turkish eateries in European and American cities, as well as by many adaptations in 'fusion' restaurants.

Other Papers Given at the Symposium

As in previous years, it has not been possible to include all the papers presented in this volume. This in no way implies that the papers excluded are of inferior quality; several of them will be or have been published elsewhere.

Chitrita Banerji
The Propitiatory Meal
An exploration of the Bengali Hindu customs of preparing and serving propitiatory meals in order to appease or placate those powers – gods, ghosts, or human beings – that rule one's life.

John Carafoli
The Meal: how to Create a sense of Style
The paper examines the role of the food stylist, illustrates the stylist's work, and analyses misconceptions which have developed about food styling.

Helen Day
Reel Meals
The author considers the work of TV chefs Delia Smith, Nigella Lawson and Jamie Oliver and concludes that, rather than wanting either instruction or entertainment, what we want is a framework to measure taste and images we can desire.

James G. Ferguson
Repast as Prologue: Déjeuner à Dijon
Consideration of the replacement of the traditional convivial family meal by fast-food – even in France.

Sri & Roger Owen
Stirring Continuously: Factors Influencing Changes in SE Asian Meals and Eating Habits during the Nineteenth and Twentieth Centuries
A preliminary look at changes in food eaten, presentation, customs and manners at various social levels and their possible causes.

June di Schino
The Pope, the Queen and the Mystery Banquets
The author describes the background to and details of an astonishing banquet given by Pope Clement IX in honour of Queen Christina of Sweden on 21 November 1668. The banquet itself is described in detail in a contemporary manuscript that she discovered in the Vatican Secret Archives.

Colin Spencer
The Anglo-Saxon Gastronomic Meal
The fleeting glimpses we have of Anglo-Saxon food suggests a type of feasting not conducive to the palate of a gourmet; but there is one interchange in Aelfric's oft-quoted *Colloquy* which suggests that gastronomy around AD 900 might not have been such an alien concept.

Mary Wondrausch prepared a satirical table layout for the twentieth century where everything was not quite right.

Caroline Yeldham
Table Manners at the Late-Medieval Dinner in England: a Social and Religious Nexus
An investigation of elements such as manners, courtesy, education, household and guild discipline, and the links between them, in the context of a religiously aware society.

Russell Zanca
Take! Take! Take! Host-Guest Relations and All That Food: Uzbek Hospitality Past and Present
The paper addresses both historical and ethnic roots of contemporary Uzbek cuisine in the context of the culture of hospitality and feasting. Whereas long-established practices of hospitality, with an emphasis on meals, show remarkable continuity throughout centuries, this may not be the case when it comes to the meals' contents.